Apache®, MySQL®, and PHP
Weekend Crash Course®

Apache®, MySQL®, and PHP Weekend Crash Course®

Steven M. Schafer

WILEY

Wiley Publishing, Inc.

Apache®, MySQL®, and PHP Weekend Crash Course®

Published by
Wiley Publishing, Inc.
10475 Crosspoint Boulevard
Indianapolis, IN 46256
www.wiley.com

About the Author

Steven M. Schafer is a veteran of technology and publishing. He programs in several languages and works with a variety of technologies. He has been published in several technical publications and written online articles. He is currently the COO/CFO for Progeny, an open-source-based service and support company. Steve can be reached by e-mail at sschafer@synergy-tech.com.

Credits

Acquisitions Editor
Jim Minatel

Development Editor
Marcia Ellett

Technical Editor
William Patterson

Production Editor
William A. Barton

Copy Editor
Luann Rouff

Project Coordinator
Maridee Ennis

Graphics and Production Specialists
Beth Brooks
Sean Decker

Quality Control Technician
Carl William Pierce

Permissions Editor
Laura Moss

Media Development Specialist
Angela Denny

Proofreading and Indexing
Publication Services

To Steve Hunger, for being a hard worker, a great friend, and a constant source of inspiration.

Preface

In the early 1990s, a revolution was begun. Pioneers such as Richard Stallman, Linus Torvalds, Eric Raymond, and others created a program called Linux, a concept called *open source,* and a governing document called the *General Public License (GPL).* Although the revolution was sparked by the advent of Linux, it was not limited to the operating system — the concept of open source software spread to all manner of programs, generating innovation across the boundaries of computing.

Innovations in open source software spawned servers such as the Apache HTTP server, the MySQL relational database, and scripting languages such as PHP.

However, open source software is not confined to running on open source operating systems — Apache, MySQL, and PHP run as well on Microsoft Windows (and other operating systems) as they do on Linux.

Thankfully, the open source world is both close-knit and prolific. Not only do these technologies work well on their own, they work even better together. Combining Apache, MySQL, and PHP, you can easily create and deploy dynamic content on your Web sites.

If you are reading this, you have already decided that knowing these technologies can be useful, and you want to learn how to use them. In that case, you have obtained the right book — this structured approach to Apache, MySQL, and PHP teaches you about all three technologies and how to integrate them in one short weekend.

Who Should Read This Book

This crash course was designed to provide you with short lessons to get you up to speed on Apache, MySQL, and PHP over one weekend. This book is for the following individuals:

- Someone who is new to running Web servers, using relational databases, and/or programming using scripting languages. This book covers many of the basic concepts and techniques necessary to get going with these three technologies. If you are new to them, you receive a serviceable background to get up and running quickly.

- Someone who has experience with similar technologies — administering servers, working with Web technologies, using relational databases, or programming. This book covers how the technologies interact, bolsters the knowledge you might already have, and shows you how to apply it to the technologies discussed in this book.

What You Need

To perform the tasks in this book, you need the following:

- **A machine running a recent copy of Linux or Windows.** This book uses Red Hat Linux 8.0 and Windows 2000 Professional. (Almost any version of Windows will do, from Windows 95 to Windows XP. However, I strongly recommended that you use Windows NT, Windows 2000, or Windows XP. These platforms provide better performance and more stability for server applications.)

- **Apache version 2.x, MySQL version 4.x, and PHP version 4.x.** The first three sessions of this book tell you where to get them and explain how to install each. This book was written based on the aforementioned versions. If you use other versions, the instructions and examples in this book may vary. However, subsequent versions of each program should vary only slightly.

- **A fairly quick Internet connection.** You need to download various applications and utilities to follow along with the sessions in this book. It is highly advisable that you download current copies of Apache, MySQL, and PHP from the Internet. The sessions provide several Web sites, which you should visit while reading this book.

- **A local area network and a separate machine with a Web browser.** These are handy to test your server's configuration.

- **A text editor.** Those readers using Linux can use any one of the many text editors provided with their distribution — vi, vim, Emacs, GNUmacs, and so on. Several other tools can help make your work easier; these tools are covered where appropriate in the text.

- **Ample time and patience.** This book is designed to occupy most of a weekend — set aside enough time to complete each section. In addition, although the concepts are fairly easy to understand, mastering them and getting everything to work as desired can take practice and patience.

What You Can Expect from This Book

This book, believe it or not, contains everything you need to use Apache to deliver dynamic content via PHP and MySQL. Although three technologies are covered in this book, they are all remarkably well-behaved and easy to integrate. In three short days and 30 sessions, you learn how to utilize all three technologies.

Of course, to accommodate such a broad spectrum of technologies, the coverage isn't as deep as that found in a book dedicated to each one individually — Apache, MySQL, or PHP. Although you learn the basics of each technology, including how to use each for various purposes and how they integrate, you will not learn *everything* about each. After getting acquainted with the technology, you need to continue learning about each on your own.

Weekend Crash Course Features and Layout

This book follows the standard Weekend Crash Course format and layout. It is designed to be fast-paced, with each session taking 30 minutes to complete. However, a lot of information is covered in each session, and you should take some time to relax after each session to let the information sink in and to prepare for the next session.

The format of each session is set up to provide the information in a structured fashion that reinforces the information through several levels. At the beginning of each session is a summary of the information covered within that session. At the end of the session, a short review section covers what you should have learned; and a Quiz Yourself section provides a few questions about the material you just covered. At the end of each part is a Part Review that provides questions on the content covered in that part of the book — answers to the Part Review questions can be found in Appendix A, "Answers to Part Review Questions."

Layout

The Weekend Crash Course is divided into 30 individual, half-hour sessions. The sessions are divided into six parts, each of which corresponds to a particular time period of a weekend, from Friday evening through Sunday afternoon.

Part I: Friday Evening

Your weekend starts with installing the three technologies and getting acquainted with the basics of the Apache Web server.

Part II: Saturday Morning

Saturday begins with more details about the Apache Web server's configuration and moves on to the configuration and operation of the MySQL database server. Coverage of MySQL proceeds through coverage of SQL queries.

Part III: Saturday Afternoon

The afternoon wraps up basic MySQL coverage and begins the basic coverage of PHP. You learn how to write basic scripts and progress to more advanced techniques.

Part IV: Saturday Evening

Saturday evening covers more advanced scripting techniques, including how to work with standard HTML and forms, and how to write scripts that work with multiple users.

Part V: Sunday Morning

Sunday morning wraps up the PHP coverage with more advanced scripting techniques, and then describes how to integrate PHP with MySQL. Finally, this section begins the hands-on projects covered in this book by showing how to create a simple calendar using PHP's date-handling functionality.

Part VI: Sunday Afternoon

Sunday afternoon's sessions kick into high gear by extending the calendar example and providing two projects for deploying dynamic content via PHP and MySQL. The last session and project show how dynamic content can be multipurposed by exporting it in various formats.

Features

As mentioned in the previous section, each session is designed to take 30 minutes. To aid with the pacing for each session, the following icons appear:

30 Min. To Go

The 30-minute icon appears at the beginning of each session to remind you of the time frame.

20 Min. To Go

A 20-minute icon appears when you have progressed through a third of the session and have roughly 20 more minutes to go.

10 Min. To Go

The 10-minute icon appears at the two-thirds mark, when you have roughly 10 more minutes to go in the session.

Done!

The Done icon indicates that the current session's tutorial is complete and you can move on to the Quiz Yourself questions.

The following icons indicate special information throughout each session:

This icon indicates special information relating to the current section that you may find useful.

This icon indicates information that explains the best way to do something or alerts you to special considerations you should be aware of when performing a routine task.

This icon indicates a reference to related information in another session.

This icon indicates cautionary information, alerting you to potential hazards encountered within the tasks at hand.

Other Conventions

Additional conventions are used for special purposes throughout this book:

Code in Text

This is a special font used to indicate code within normal text. It appears as follows: `<?php print "hello world"; ?>`.

Syntax Listings

For most commands, functions, and the like, a syntax listing is given. This listing shows you the command's basic syntax. The following conventions are used for these listings:

- Required items are shown in a normal, monospaced font.
- Variable items — such as parameters — are shown in angle brackets or italics with mnemonic names.
- Optional items — such as optional parameters — are shown enclosed in square brackets ([and]).

For example, the following line shows the syntax for a MySQL query:

```
SELECT * FROM <database_name> [WHERE <conditions>];
```

In this example, `<database_name>` would be replaced by the name of the database, the WHERE section is optional, and `<conditions>` would be replaced by conditions for the WHERE (if the WHERE were used).

Notice that the angle-bracketed text appears in italic text to avoid causing confusion in the syntax. For example, the following HTML syntax replaces the angle brackets with italic because the HTML code uses angle brackets:

```
<input type=text name=field_name value=field_value>
```

Code Listings

```
Code listings appear in specially formatted fonts
and paragraphs like these lines.
```

User Input

Two methods are used to indicate user input:

```
Bold text
Within listings, it represents commands you should type.
```

Variable text in commands is indicated by an italic keyword or phrase enclosed in angle brackets:

```
mysql -p <user_name>
```

For example, *<user_name>* would indicate that you should replace the text within the brackets with a specific username (which varies depending on the situation or use). As with syntax listings, italic text is used in place of the angle bracket text if the angle-bracketed text would cause confusion.

Feedback

Wiley Publishing and I value your feedback. We welcome suggestions for making the books better — including hearing about errors and omissions in this book. You can visit www.wiley.com for information on additional books and ways to provide feedback to the publisher. I can be reached at sschafer@synergy-tech.com.

Acknowledgments

A book such as this is not a singular effort. Many people came together and worked hard to produce this work. As such, I'd like to thank each one, especially those who interacted with me during this process:

The management team at Wiley Publishing, for recognizing this as a publishable topic.

Jim Minatel, for giving me the chance to put more of my knowledge into print.

Marcia Ellett, for keeping me on track and organized, despite my best efforts to the contrary.

William Patterson, for checking my technical words and examples to ensure their accuracy and for adding numerous bits of value throughout. (Note that any deficiencies in this area remain my sole responsibility.)

Bill Barton, for coordinating the final steps of editing, and Luann Rouff for making me look like English is indeed my first language.

The Composition Services crew, who packaged the raw material into this nice, tidy product you now hold.

Last, but definitely not least, I would like to thank Angie and Ashley, for believing in me, letting me know when it was truly time for sleep, and supporting me in everything I do.

Contents at a Glance

Preface ix
Acknowledgments xv

FRIDAY 2

Part I—Friday Evening 4
Session 1–Installing Apache 5
Session 2–Installing PHP 21
Session 3–Installing MySQL 33
Session 4–Apache Basics 47

SATURDAY 56

Part II—Saturday Morning 58
Session 5–Configuring Apache 59
Session 6–Apache Security Concerns 69
Session 7–The Basics of MySQL 79
Session 8–MySQL Security 89
Session 9–Working with Data 97
Session 10–Queries 111

Part III—Saturday Afternoon 130
Session 11–Troubleshooting MySQL Commands and Queries 131
Session 12–Advanced MySQL Concepts 139
Session 13–Getting Ready to Use PHP 151
Session 14–PHP Basics 159
Session 15–Program Flow 175
Session 16–PHP Functions 185

Part IV—Saturday Evening 196
Session 17–Working with Files 197
Session 18–HTML Constructs 213
Session 19–Working with Forms 219
Session 20–Multiple-User Considerations in PHP 233

SUNDAY 246

Part V—Sunday Morning 248
Session 21–Good Coding Practices 249
Session 22–Debugging and Troubleshooting PHP 257
Session 23–MySQL Through PHP 273
Session 24–Debugging and Troubleshooting MySQL in PHP 287
Session 25–Odds and Ends 293
Session 26–Project: Calendar I 303

Part VI—Sunday Afternoon **320**
Session 27–Project: Calendar II 321
Session 28–Project: Content Publishing I 341
Session 29–Project: Content Publishing II 381
Session 30–Project: Building an RSS Feed 405

Appendix A–Answers to Part Review Questions **415**
Appendix B–What's on the Companion Web Site **425**
Index **427**

Contents

Preface ix

Acknowledgments xv

FRIDAY 2

Part I—Friday Evening 4

Session 1–Installing Apache 5

   Why Use Apache? 5

      Apache Is Free 6

      Apache Is Open Source 6

      Apache Is Cross-Platform 6

      Apache Is Continually Undergoing Rapid Development 6

      Apache Capabilities 7

   Gathering Required Materials 7

      Windows Downloads 9

      Linux Downloads 9

   Installing Apache 10

      Installing Apache on Windows 10

      Building and Installing Apache for Linux (from Source) 13

      Installing Apache on Linux from Packages 16

   Testing the Installation 18

Session 2–Installing PHP 21

   Understanding Preprocessed HTML 21

   Gathering the Required Materials 22

      Compiling PHP for Linux 22

      Installing PHP on Linux from a Package 24

      Installing PHP on Windows 26

   Getting PHP to Work with Apache 26

      Updating httpd.conf on Linux 27

      Updating http.conf on Windows 28

   Testing PHP 30

Session 3–Installing MySQL 33

   Introducing MySQL 33

   Gathering the Required Materials 34

      Compiling MySQL for Linux 35

      Installing a Linux Binary Version of MySQL 35

      Installing MySQL on Linux from a Package 36

      Installing MySQL on Windows 37

   Testing Your MySQL Installation 42

Session 4–Apache Basics 47

   Understanding HTTP Servers 47

      The Evolution of Feature-Rich Web Content 47

      HTTP Services over TCP 48

   Apache: Status, Starting, and Stopping 48

      Apache Status 48

      Starting and Stopping the Server 50

      Automatically Starting Apache 51

   Locating Apache Files 52

   Apache Log Files 54

SATURDAY **56**

Part II—Saturday Morning **58**

Session 5–Configuring Apache 59

   Understanding the httpd.conf File 59

   Apache Directives 60

      Scope Sections 64

      Conditional Directives 65

      Access Directives 66

   MIME Types 67

Session 6–Apache Security Concerns 69

   The Web — A Great Security Hole 69

   A Review of Apache Security 70

   Securing the Entire Site 71

   Securing Individual Directories 72

      Securing Directories with <Directory> 72

      Securing Directories with .htaccess 72

      Securing Directories with Authentication Control 73

   Securing Script Access 76

   Performing a Security Audit 77

Session 7–The Basics of MySQL 79

   Understanding MySQL 79

   What's New in MySQL 4.0? 80

   Configuring MySQL 80

      MySQL Linux Configuration 80

      Windows MySQL Configuration 81

   Building Blocks of Databases 83

      Tables 83

      Records (Row) 84

      Fields 84

      Putting It All Back Together 84

   Running the MySQL Server 85

   Using the MySQL Monitor 86

Session 8–MySQL Security 89

   Setting the Root Password 89

An Overview of the MySQL Privileges System 90
The MySQL Privileges Database 91
Setting and Changing User Privileges 91
    The GRANT Command 92
    The REVOKE Command 94
    Column Privileges 94
Updating Privileges 94

Session 9–Working with Data 97
Creating Databases 97
Dropping Databases 98
Creating Tables 98
    Column Attributes 99
    Column Data Types 100
        Text Column Types 100
        Numeric Column Types 102
        Date Column Types 103
    Column Indexes and Primary Keys 104
Altering Tables 105
    Changing a Table's Name 106
    Adding Columns 106
    Changing Column Definitions 107
    Dropping Columns 107
    Changing Primary Keys and Indexes 107
Dropping Tables 108
Informational Commands 108

Session 10–Queries 111
Sample Data 111
Understanding Queries 113
Adding Data with INSERT 113
Selecting Data with SELECT 116
    The Basics of SELECT 116
    Choosing Specific Rows with WHERE 117
    Using LIKE to Find Data 119
    Using Complex Expressions with WHERE 120
    Ordering Results with ORDER BY 120
    Limiting Results with LIMIT 121
    Selecting from More Than One Table 122
Deleting Records with DELETE 124
Updating Records with UPDATE 124

Part III—Saturday Afternoon 130
Session 11–Troubleshooting MySQL Commands and Queries 131
The MySQL Monitor 131
    Running the Monitor 132
    MySQL Monitor Basics 132

Logging the Monitor Session 133
Piping Files to the Monitor 133
Troubleshooting Queries **134**
Format Your Queries with Line Breaks 134
Try SELECT 135
Simplify Your Query 135
Session 12—Advanced MySQL Concepts **139**
Counting Result Sets **139**
Using SELECT with More Than One Table **140**
Specifying Columns from Multiple Tables 140
The Equi-Join 141
The Outer Join 142
Database Normalization **144**
First Normal Form 144
Second Normal Form 145
Third Normal Form 147
Backing Up and Restoring MySQL Databases **147**
Session 13—Getting Ready to Use PHP **151**
Reviewing Apache and PHP Configuration **151**
Reviewing Windows PHP Setup 151
Reviewing Linux PHP Setup 152
Understanding How PHP Works with Apache **153**
Command-Line PHP **153**
PHP as a Command-Line Scripting Language **155**
Session 14—PHP Basics **159**
Basic Script Syntax **159**
PHP Beginning and Ending Tags 159
Command Termination Character 160
PHP's Use of White Space 160
Commenting Code 161
PHP Variables **162**
print and echo **164**
Quoting Output 164
Escape Characters 165
Here Document Output 166
PHP Data Types **167**
The Different Data Types 167
PHP Arrays 168
Changing Data Types 168
Testing Data Types *169*
Converting Types *169*
Operators and Expressions **169**
Assignment Operator 170
Arithmetic Operators 170
Concatenation Operator 171

Comparison Operators 171
Logical Operators 172
Operator Precedence 173

Session 15–Program Flow **175**
  Programming Blocks **175**
  Conditional Statements **176**
    General if Structure 176
    else and elseif 177
    Multiple Choice with switch 178
  Understanding Loops **180**
    while Loop 180
    do while Loop 181
    for Loop 181
    Breaking and Continuing Code 182

Session 16–PHP Functions **185**
  Understanding Functions **185**
  Built-in PHP Functions **186**
  User-Defined Functions **187**
    Function Definition 187
    Returning a Value from a Function 188
    Function Arguments 189
      Default Argument Definition and Use *189*
      Optional Arguments *189*
      Call by Reference *190*
    Variable Scope 191

Part IV—Saturday Evening **196**
Session 17–Working with Files **197**
  File Operations with PHP: The Good and the Bad **197**
  Accessing Files with PHP **198**
    Opening a File 198
    Closing a File 200
    Reading from or Writing to a File 200
      Writing to a File *200*
      Reading from a File *201*
  Additional Reading and Writing Techniques **204**
    Positioning the File Pointer 204
    Reading a File One Character at a Time 205
    Locking Files 205
    Deleting Files 206
  Working with Directories **206**
    Making Directories 206
    Removing Directories 207
    Reading the Contents of a Directory 207
  File Information **208**

Session 18—HTML Constructs 213
   The Automatic HTML Header 213
   Other Content Headers 214
   Outputting HTML 215
      Large HTML Blocks 215
      HTML Formatting Conventions 217
Session 19—Working with Forms 219
   Understanding How HTML Forms Work 219
      Standard HTML Form Elements 219
      Form Actions 222
      How Form Data Is Returned 223
   PHP Form Data Handling 224
      Parsing $_POST 224
      Auto-Register Globals: Easier, But Less Secure 226
   Working with File Uploads 227
Session 20—Multiple-User Considerations in PHP 233
   The Old Counter Example 233
      The Problem 233
      The "So What if a Simple Counter Fails?" Argument 235
      Letting the Technology Sort It Out 235
   Data Locking Schemes 235
      Using flock() 236
      Using a Lock File 236
      Clearing Stale Locks 237
   Keeping User State with Sessions 237
      Session Mechanics 237
      Key Session Configuration Options 237
      Using Sessions 238
         Starting or Resuming a Session 239
         Registering Variables with a Session 239
         Unregistering Variables with the Session 240
         Destroying a Session 240
         Manually Dealing with Session IDs 240
         Encoding and Saving Session Data 241

SUNDAY...246

Part V—Sunday Morning 248
Session 21—Good Coding Practices 249
   Building Solid Code 249
      The Value of the Right Tools 250
      Coding It Right the First Time Around 251
      The Value of Consistency 251
      Using Functions 252
      Revisiting Old Code 252
   Code Libraries 252

Commenting and Creating Documentation 253

Comment Placement 253

"Look Here!" Comments 253

"War and Peace" or "Reader's Digest"? 253

Documentation 254

Applying Good Coding Habits Universally 254

Session 22–Debugging and Troubleshooting PHP 257

Modular Code for Easy Debugging 257

A Nonmodular Coding Example 258

Modular Coding Techniques 260

Use Functions *260*

Using Global Variables *260*

Group Global Variable Declarations *261*

A Modular Code Example 261

Dividing and Conquering 263

Error Control and Processing 264

Controlling the Error Level 264

Sending Errors to a File or E-mail Address 265

Custom Error Handling 266

Print Everything 267

Command-Line PHP 269

Session 23–MySQL Through PHP 273

Connecting to and Disconnecting from the MySQL Server 273

Connecting to the MySQL Server 273

Disconnecting from the MySQL Server 274

Selecting a Database 275

Querying the Database 275

Returning the Result Set Row by Row 276

Resetting the Result Set Pointer 277

Returning the Result Set in an Associative Array 277

Working with Result Sets 278

Determining Affected Rows 283

Letting MySQL Do Some Work 283

Other MySQL Functions 283

Session 24–Debugging and Troubleshooting MySQL in PHP 287

Turning Off Verbose Error Reporting 287

Avoiding Common Errors 288

Error Testing, Trapping, and Reporting 289

Error Testing and Trapping 290

Error Reporting 290

Testing Queries and Functions 291

Session 25–Odds and Ends 293

PHP Libraries 293

What Is PEAR? 294

PHPBuilder.com 294

PHP Classes Repository 295
New York PHP Components 295
Object-Oriented PHP **295**
Monitoring Apache Traffic **295**
Analog 296
Webalizer 297
AWStats 297
Finding the Right Log Analyzer 298
Virtual Hosting with Apache **299**
Monitoring Several IP Addresses 299
Monitoring One IP Address 300
Setting Up Virtual Hosts 300
Putting It All Together 301
Three Domains, Three IP Addresses *301*
Three Domains, One IP Address *301*

Session 26–Project: Calendar I **303**
Project Description **303**
Taking Stock of Assets in PHP **304**
Robust Date Handling 304
Integration with Forms 305
Pseudocoding Our Calendar **305**
Pseudo-Table 305
Pseudo-Form 307
Data and State 308
Pseudo-PHP **308**
Calendar Code **309**
Calendar.php 309
Explaining the Code 315

Part VI—Sunday Afternoon **320**
Session 27–Project: Calendar II **321**
Defining the Project **321**
Database Definition **322**
Web and Flow Design **322**
Web Design 323
Application Flow 324
Coding the Application **325**
Calendar.php 325
Appt.php (Day View) 326
Editappt.php (Edit Appointment) 330
The Scripts in Action **337**
Room for More **340**
Session 28–Project: Content Publishing I **341**
The Scope of the Project **341**
The Publishing System 341
Necessary Tools 342

The Publishing System Database 342
  The Authors Table 342
  The Categories Table 343
  The Articles Table 343
Designing the Editing Tools 344
  Understanding Monolithic Scripts 344
  Controlling State with Submit 345
  A Basic Monolithic Editor 347
  States for the Article Editor 348
Coding the Article Editing Script 349
  The Start State 349
  The Find State 349
  The Edit State 352
  The Add/Update State 352
  The Delete State 353
The printform() Function 354
The Finished Article Editing Script 359
Category and Author Editing Scripts 371
Putting It all Together 379
Session 29—Project: Content Publishing II 381
Methods of Publishing Dynamic Content 381
  Full Page from PHP 382
  Only Dynamic Content from PHP 383
    Turning PHP On and Off 383
    Server-Side Includes 384
Publishing Scripts 385
  Common Library 385
  Full Article 386
  Headlines Only 388
  Category Listings 390
  Teasers 392
Enabling Search Functionality for Users 394
  Simple Substring Searches 394
  Full-Text Index Searches 397
    Creating a FULLTEXT Index 397
    Searching a FULLTEXT Index 397
    Modifying the Find Script for Full-Text Searching 399
Adding Authentication to Your Scripts 400
Using Authentication with PHP and MySQL 401
Scalability 403
Session 30—Project: Building an RSS Feed 405
What Are RSS Feeds? 405
  RSS Syntax 406
  Publishing the Feed 406
Creating an RSS Feed for the Publishing System 407

    When to Run the RSS Generator 410
    Additional RSS References 411
Appendix A–Answers to Part Review Questions 415
Appendix B–What's on the Companion Web Site 425
Index 427

Apache®, MySQL®, and PHP
Weekend Crash Course®

☑ **Friday**

☐ Saturday

☐ Sunday

Part I — Friday Evening

Session 1
Installing Apache

Session 2
Installing PHP

Session 3
Installing MySQL

Session 4
Apache Basics

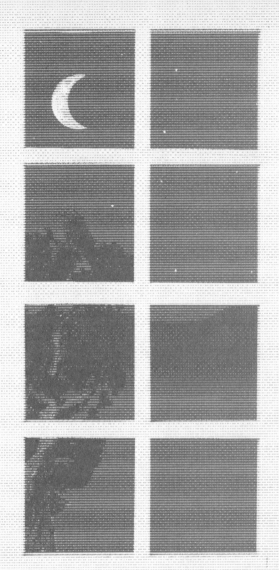

PART

I

Friday Evening

Session 1
Installing Apache

Session 2
Installing PHP

Session 3
Installing MySQL

Session 4
Apache Basics

SESSION

Installing Apache

**30 Min.
To Go**

This book shows you how to knit together Web server, database server, and scripting technologies. These three technologies enable you to deliver powerful and dynamic content via the Web. Before you can begin using the technologies, you need to install all three components, starting with the Apache Web server. These first three sessions walk you though the process of installing the technologies, testing each, and testing their interactions to ensure that you are ready to start working with each.

Why Use Apache?

Apache powers the Web. Although this seems a grandiose claim, there is a lot of truth to it. Recent surveys show that an overwhelming number of Web sites run Apache as their Web server. That being the case, why do all these Web sites use Apache?

- Apache is free.
- Apache is open source.
- Apache is cross-platform.
- Apache is continually undergoing rapid development.
- Apache is powerful, yet modular.

Apache Is Free

Apache is a full-featured, powerful Web server available absolutely free. Because the Apache Software Foundation is not deriving revenue from the Apache server, however, it cannot afford to offer robust technical support. Amenities such as phone or online support are not included with Apache. Abundant documentation is available, but support at the level you may be used to with commercial software is not.

Apache Is Open Source

You can get the source code for Apache and modify it to your heart's content. Most people don't use the source code to modify how Apache works; they use it to modify how Apache is built — that is, what options are compiled into the server. If you need a mean, lean server, you can recompile the source code to create a custom server with only the options you need. That said, if you ever find a problem or need to make a rudimentary change to the Apache source code, you can.

The concept of *open source* software is not new, but the idea can be rather intricate. For more information on Open Source software, visit GNU.org and read the various licenses: www.gnu.org/licenses/licenses.html.

Apache Is Cross-Platform

Apache is available for multiple platforms, including the following:

- Unix
- Linux
- Windows (9x through XP, although server versions — NT/2000 — are preferred)
- Novell NetWare
- Mac OS X (BSD under the GUI)

Besides a few minute details, such as the placement of its files in the file system, Apache operates the same on all of the aforementioned platforms.

Apache Is Continually Undergoing Rapid Development

Apache is maintained by the Apache Software Foundation and is under continual development and improvement. Bug and security fixes take only days to find and correct, making Apache the most stable and secure Web server available.

The relative stability and security of any Web server depends on the system administrator as much as, if not more than, the underlying software.

Another advantage of rapid development and releases is the robust feature set. New Internet technologies can be deployed in Apache much more quickly than in other Web servers.

Apache Capabilities

Apache gets its name from the way it was originally developed. Originally, the server was made of several components or "patches," making it "a patchy server."

Apache continues to implement its features with distinct pieces, or *modules*. Utilizing a modular approach to feature implementation enables Apache to be deployed with only the amount of overhead necessary for the features you want. It also facilitates third parties developing their own modules to support their own technologies.

Apache supports almost all Internet Web technologies, including proprietary solutions such as Microsoft's FrontPage Extensions. Apache supports all manner of HTTP protocols, scripting, authentication, and platform integration.

 Visit the Apache module Web site (`http://modules.apache.org`**) for information on the modules included with Apache and the registered third-party modules.**

For our purposes, we care about the following capabilities:

- Robust HTTP delivery
- Configurable, reliable security
- Integration with PHP
- CGI and other scripting integration

Gathering Required Materials

Everything that you need to install Apache can be found at the Apache Web site, at www.apache.org. You can download the source and/or binary files for Unix/Linux installations or a binary install package for Windows. The main Apache.org Web site is shown in Figure 1-1.

 Apache is also packaged for most Linux distributions. For example, Red Hat maintains an Apache Red Hat Package Manager (RPM), which can be used to install Apache on a Red Hat system. If you don't need the absolute latest version of Apache and don't need it configured a particular way, it is worth visiting the Web site for your distribution to download an appropriate Apache package.

The Apache Software Foundation maintains several different projects — the HTTP Server Project being the most prominent. The main page for the HTTP server can be found at `http://httpd.apache.org`. Various links from this page lead to source and binary code downloads, documentation, and other resources. The main HTTP Server Project page is shown in Figure 1-2.

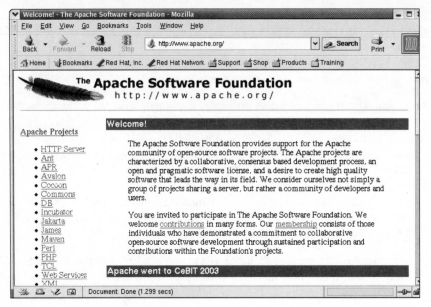

Figure 1-1   *The Apache.org Web site*

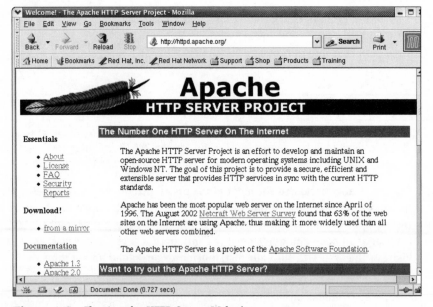

Figure 1-2   *The Apache HTTP Server Web site*

At the time of this writing, the current Apache server version is 2.0.47.

Documentation on Apache is also available from the Apache Web site. Downloading the PDF version of the documentation for later use is worth the time.

At the time of this writing, the PHP project is still issuing warnings about using PHP 4.*x* on Apache 2.0 in a production environment. Although I've not seen any issues combining the two, a warning from the project should not be taken lightly. If you are going to use PHP and Apache in a production environment, you might want to consider running Apache 1.3.*x* instead of Apache 2.0.*x*.

Windows Downloads

Windows users should follow the download links to the Windows binary install (currently available as an MSI Installer — a special program for installing packages on Windows). Download this file to a temporary folder on your local hard drive.

If you need a specially compiled version of Apache, the source files for the Windows version are also available. You need to have a suitable C++ compiler installed — Microsoft C++ version 5.0 or later is recommended. Other tools and special configuration options are also necessary to compile Apache. You can find additional information on compiling Apache for Windows at `http://httpd.apache.org/docs-2.0/platform/win_compiling.html`. **This session covers installation of the Windows binaries only.**

Linux Downloads

Many methods for installing Apache on Linux are available; the method that you choose depends on your answers to the following questions:

- What distribution of Linux are you running?
- Does your distribution have a package with a recent version of Apache?
- Do you need to compile your own version for compatibility or capability reasons?

If you are running one of the major Linux distributions (Red Hat, Mandrake, United Linux, Debian, and so on), chances are good that a recent copy of Apache is packaged for your distribution. A recent installation of Red Hat 8.0, for example, contains Apache version 2.0.40 release 8 on CD #2 in RPM form (`httpd-2.0.40-8.i386.rpm`). After installation, you can use the Red Hat Update Agent to update Apache to 2.0.40 release 11, the latest version of Apache packaged for Red Hat.

If your Linux version does not have a recent version of Apache packaged, you can download the generic binary version for installation on your system. An `Other files` link is available from the Download page on the Apache HTTP Server Web site. Follow the resulting links (starting with `_binaries_`) to identify and download the version that most closely matches your distribution and configuration. If you are using Red Hat version 7.3 on a Pentium III or IV processor, for example, you want to download the following file:

```
httpd-2.0.40-i686-pc-linux-gnu-rh73.tar.gz
```

Download and read the README file associated with the archive before you download and install the archive. The README file contains the options the binary was compiled with. (Notice that the term *archive*, as used here and throughout this book, evolves from the Unix world, where archives of collections of files were written to magnetic tape. The utility *tar* stands for *Tape ARrchive*. Today, it simply means a collection of files bundled together for a particular purpose.)

If you need a specially compiled version of Apache, you can download the source and compile Apache yourself.

Installing Apache

20 Min.
To Go

Despite the fact that Apache is a full-featured HTTP server, installing it is actually as simple as installing a regular application. Because it is a server, you face many implications on system security after Apache is installed. Security issues are covered in depth in Session 5.

Installing Apache on Windows

If you are installing Apache on Linux, you can skip this section and move on to the section "Installing Apache on Linux from Packages," later in this session.

To install Apache on Windows, you need to download the Windows binary installer, as covered in the section "Windows Downloads," earlier in this session. This file is usually named as follows:

```
apache_2.0.*-win32-x86-no_ssl.msi
```

The asterisk (*) indicates the minor version number. At the time of this writing, the minor version is 45.

Although you *can* run Apache on Windows 9x/Me, doing so is not advised. Windows NT/2000/XP provides a substantially more stable and secure base for any server application. The following instructions were performed on a copy of Windows 2000 Professional.

Place this file in a temporary directory and follow these steps to install Apache:

1. Log into Windows as an Administrator.
2. Use Windows Explorer to locate the file on your hard drive, as shown in Figure 1-3.
3. Double-click the installer to begin the installation.
4. The Apache installer performs like many other Windows installers, using a Wizard-like approach, as shown in Figure 1-4.

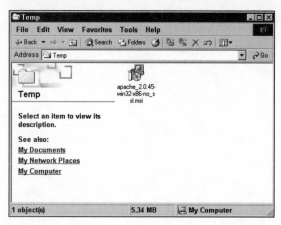

Figure 1-3   *Find the installer on your hard drive.*

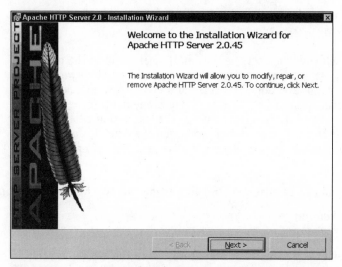

Figure 1-4   *The Apache installer runs like many Windows installers, presenting information and settings in Wizard-like form.*

5. Click the Next button, read and confirm your acceptance of the license agreement, and click Next again.

6. The next Wizard window displays useful information about running Apache on Windows for anyone new to the process. Read it before clicking Next.

7. The next window enables you to specify server information. This information should be populated from information already present in Windows, as shown in Figure 1-5. The information should be okay as is; review it before clicking Next. If necessary, modify the information to suit your needs.

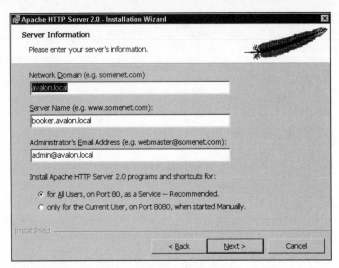

Figure 1-5　*The Server Information window enables you to specify the domain, server name, and how the server is to run.*

If you need to edit the dialog box, set the Network Domain field to the name of your domain. In this case, you are running Apache on an internal network, so you specify .local as your top-level domain instead of a .com, .org, or other top-level domain. The Server Name field should be the machine name (or www), complete with the fully qualified domain information. The last option enables you to control how the server is run. You're best off accepting the default, for All Users, on Port 80, as a Service—Recommended. Click Next after the settings are complete.

This information can be changed later by editing the Apache configuration files.

8. The next window enables you to select to install Apache in the typical location with the typical components, or specify a custom installation. The typical installation installs Apache in the directory C:\Program Files\Apache Group. (The drive letter may vary, depending on your individual installation.) The typical installation installs the Apache binary files and documentation but not the headers and libraries. You should select the typical installation unless you need to change any of these settings. Click Next to continue the installation.

9. You are given a chance to change the default directory where Apache is installed. Accept the default by clicking Next.

10. A confirmation window gives you one more chance to correct any installation options. Click Back to change any options or Install to begin the installation.

11. After the installation completes, a completion window is displayed. Click Finish to end the installation program.

After Apache is installed, the server starts automatically. You can verify that the server is running by checking the Apache Service Monitor icon in the system tray, as shown in Figure 1-6.

**The Apache Service
Monitor tray icon**

Figure 1-6   *The Apache Service Monitor tray icon displays the server's status.*

If the icon has a green arrow, the server is running. If the server is not running, a red dot replaces the arrow. You can double-click the icon to display the Apache Service Monitor. Using this monitor is covered in Session 4.

Unless you also need to install Apache for Linux, you can skip the next section and resume at the section "Testing the Installation," later in this session.

Building and Installing Apache for Linux (from Source)

If you need to compile Apache, you need an appropriate source archive. You can download one of the standard archives from Apache.org or obtain one from your distribution vendor. This session covers compiling from the source files on Apache.org. If you have a binary archive or package to install, you can skip this section.

The source files are available from the Apache HTTP server download page as a gzipped tarball or a compressed tarball. Download the appropriate file into a temporary directory or the typical location for source files on your system (usually /usr/src).

 Tarball is a common name for an archive packaged with the tar **utility and is a common means of distributing software, much like ZIP files are used for Windows. In their raw form, tarballs do not incorporate compression; they must be compressed by using special tools such as** gzip **or by using the compress options in the** tar **utility.**

You can use several methods to unpack the source files; the methods available depend on the utilities you have installed and the file you downloaded.

If you downloaded the gzipped tarball file (with a tar.gz extension), you should use the gzip utilities to unzip the file before it is unpacked with tar. The following command line, performed in the directory where the source archive is located, uncompresses and unpacks the gzipped archive:

```
tar -zxvf httpd-2.0.*.tar.gz
```

If you downloaded the compressed tar file (with a tar.Z extension), you can uncompress and unpack the archive with the following command line:

```
tar -zxvf httpd-2.0.*.tar.Z
```

Either of the preceding methods results in unpacking the Apache source code into an appropriately named directory — namely, httpd-2.0.*, where * is the minor revision number.

 Uncompress and unpack the archive in the directory reserved for source files (for example, /usr/src). This results in a httpd-2.0.* directory under the source directory (for example, /usr/src/ httpd-2.0.*) in which the Apache source files are stored.

The instructions for building and installing Apache are contained in the file named INSTALL within the source file directory. Essentially, the build and install consists of three commands, as follows (as taken from the INSTALL file):

```
./configure --prefix=<directory>

make

make install
```

These commands should be issued in the directory where the source files were expanded (httpd-2.0.*), and the commands should be run as root.

The first line configures Apache for compilation on your system. The <directory> should be replaced with the directory in which you want to install Apache. If you wanted to install Apache into the directory /usr/local/apache2, for example, you would use the following command line:

```
./configure -prefix=/usr/local/apache2
```

The output from the configure command resembles the following:

```
checking for chosen layout... Apache
checking for working mkdir -p... yes
checking build system type... i686-pc-linux-gnu
checking host system type... i686-pc-linux-gnu
checking target system type... i686-pc-linux-gnu

Configuring Apache Portable Runtime library ...

checking for APR... reconfig
configuring package in srclib/apr now
checking build system type... i686-pc-linux-gnu
checking host system type... i686-pc-linux-gnu
checking target system type... i686-pc-linux-gnu
Configuring APR library
Platform: i686-pc-linux-gnu
checking for working mkdir -p... yes
APR Version: 0.9.3
checking for chosen layout... apr
checking for gcc... gcc
...
```

If `configure` finds any errors or unmet dependencies on your machine, it informs you. Correct the problem and run the `configure` command again until it generates no errors.

The next command, `make`, compiles Apache following the directives in the make files created by the configure step. The output of the `make` command resembles the following code:

```
Making all in srclib
make[1]: Entering directory '/root/temp/httpd-2.0.45/srclib'
Making all in apr
make[2]: Entering directory '/root/temp/httpd-2.0.45/srclib/apr'
Making all in strings
make[3]: Entering directory '/root/temp/httpd-2.0.45/srclib/apr/strings'
make[4]: Entering directory '/root/temp/httpd-2.0.45/srclib/apr/strings'
/bin/sh /root/temp/httpd-2.0.45/srclib/apr/libtool --silent --mode=compile
gcc -g -O2 -pthread   -DHAVE_CONFIG_H -DLINUX=2 -D_REENTRANT -
D_XOPEN_SOURCE=500 -D_BSD_SOURCE -D_SVID_SOURCE -D_GNU_SOURCE    -
I../include -I../include/arch/unix  -c apr_cpystrn.c && touch
apr_cpystrn.lo
...
```

After several minutes, the compilation is complete and you are returned to a system prompt. If any errors are found during the process, they are reported. Fix the problems encountered and rerun the `make` command.

The last command, `make install`, installs Apache into the default location you specified with the `-prefix` parameter. The output of the `make install` command resembles the following:

```
Making install in srclib
make[1]: Entering directory '/root/temp/httpd-2.0.45/srclib'
Making install in apr
make[2]: Entering directory '/root/temp/httpd-2.0.45/srclib/apr'
Making all in strings
make[3]: Entering directory '/root/temp/httpd-2.0.45/srclib/apr/strings'
make[4]: Entering directory '/root/temp/httpd-2.0.45/srclib/apr/strings'
make[4]: Nothing to be done for 'local-all'.
make[4]: Leaving directory '/root/temp/httpd-2.0.45/srclib/apr/strings'
make[3]: Leaving directory '/root/temp/httpd-2.0.45/srclib/apr/strings'
Making all in passwd
make[3]: Entering directory '/root/temp/httpd-2.0.45/srclib/apr/passwd'
...
```

At this point, Apache should be installed into the directory you specified in the first step. To verify that Apache is installed, run the server with the `-v` parameter. This does not start the server but causes it to output its version information. The server executable is named `httpd` (HTTP Daemon) and is located in the `bin` subdirectory of the Apache install directory. Running `httpd` with the `-v` switch should output something similar to the following:

```
Server version: Apache/2.0.45
Server built:   Apr  8 2003 01:42:52
```

If you do not see this information the server possibly did not compile or install correctly. Verify that the httpd executable exists and try running it again, giving the complete path on the command line (for example, `/usr/local/apache2/bin/httpd -v`).

To start the server, use the Apache control script, `apachectl`, as follows:

```
/usr/local/apache2/bin/apachectl start
```

To verify that the server is running, you can use the process command, ps, as follows:

```
ps -A | grep "httpd"
 8094 ?           00:00:00 httpd
 8095 ?           00:00:00 httpd
 8096 ?           00:00:00 httpd
 8097 ?           00:00:00 httpd
 8098 ?           00:00:00 httpd
 8099 ?           00:00:00 httpd
```

You should see several instances of httpd running; the actual number depends on the server's configuration.

Installing Apache on Linux from Packages

Most Linux distributions have their own packaging scheme, a means of distributing programs so that they can be easily installed onto systems. Red Hat distributions, for example, have the *RPM* (*R*ed Hat *P*ackage *M*anager) format. The advantages to using packages are as follows:

- The programs can typically be located and installed very easily. For example, you can easily find packaged programs on the Red Hat network, and you can download and install them by using the Red Hat Update Agent.
- Packages typically handle dependency issues for you. That is, if you need other tools or programs to use a particular program, the package has those dependencies encoded in it and at least alerts you before you try to use the new program.
- The packages expand themselves, installing their components into the correct directories — typically with one command. Applications that are installed from packages also follow the base distribution's conventions for locations of binaries, configuration files, and so on.

As previously mentioned, in the section "Linux Downloads," Red Hat 8.0 ships with a version of Apache version 2. Using one of the built-in file browsers, such as Nautilus, as shown in Figure 1-7, you can install an RPM simply by double-clicking its name.

You can also use the console rpm command to install a package. The form of the command for RPM installation is as follows:

```
rpm -i <rpm file name>
```

To install the Apache RPM that ships with Red Hat 8.0, for example, you would use the following command:

```
rpm -i httpd-2.0.40-8.i386.rpm
```

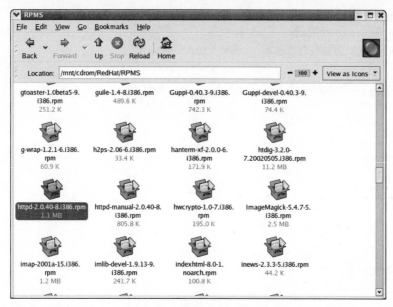

Figure 1-7   *You can install a package by finding it with a file manager (such as Nautilus, pictured) and double-clicking the file name.*

The rpm application inspects the package, tests the system for any dependencies, and installs the package. Notice that, if you use the RPM package to install Apache, the various pieces are installed according to Red Hat's file location scheme. The binary is placed in /usr/sbin, the configuration files in /etc/httpd, and so on. The rest of this book assumes that you installed Apache on a Red Hat system, using the Red Hat Apache RPM.

If you do not install the latest version of Apache from Apache.org, using your distribution's update service to see whether any critical updates have been made to Apache since the version you installed was released is a good idea. If you are using Red Hat, you can use the Red Hat Update Agent, as shown in Figure 1-8, to download and install any updates.

You can test whether the server was installed by running it with the -v parameter, as follows:

```
/usr/sbin/httpd -v
```

The server should respond with its version and build date.

Start the server by using the apachectl script with the following command:

```
/usr/sbin/apachectl start
```

Figure 1-8 *You can use the Red Hat Update Agent to update the packages on your system with the latest and greatest available from Red Hat.*

Testing the Installation

10 Min.
To Go

After Apache is installed and running, you can test it simply by pointing a browser at the machine running the server. On the server machine itself, you can point a browser to the following address:

```
http://localhost
```

A page similar to the one shown in Figure 1-9 should appear. If you are using another machine to connect to the server, replace localhost with the server's fully qualified name or its IP address.

An unmonitored Web server can present a security hazard to the system running it, as well as to any attached network(s). Immediately implementing security measures or stopping the server whenever you don't need it is wise. Rudimentary security measures are covered in Session 4. To stop the server, use the following command:

```
/usr/sbin/apachectl stop
```

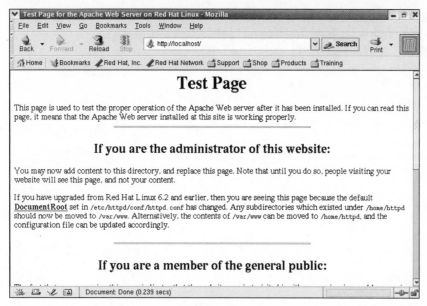

Figure 1-9 *The Apache test page confirms that the server is up and running.*

Done!

REVIEW

This session showed you how to determine what you need to install the Apache HTTP server. You learned where to find the components you need, how to compile the Linux-based server from source code, and how to install the server on both Windows and Linux. Finally, you learned how to start and stop the server, as well as how to verify that it is running.

QUIZ YOURSELF

1. What organization is responsible for the Apache HTTP Project? (See "Apache Is Continually Undergoing Rapid Development.")
2. Why would you want to compile Apache from source files? (See "Apache Is Open Source.")
3. What is the Windows application for controlling Apache called, and how do you access it? (See "Installing Apache on Windows.")
4. What is the Linux application for controlling Apache called, and how do you access it? (See "Building and Installing Apache for Linux (from Source)" or "Installing Apache on Linux from Packages.")

Installing PHP

Session Checklist

✔ Understanding the power of preprocessed HTML

✔ Gathering the required materials

✔ Installing PHP

✔ Testing the installation

**30 Min.
To Go**

Now that you have installed Apache (in Session 1), it is time to install PHP and test the server to ensure that it has been configured to serve up PHP scripts. The next session covers the installation of MySQL, the third of our trio of technologies. Subsequent sessions show you how to work with each technology separately and then integrated together.

Understanding Preprocessed HTML

HTTP is a static delivery system. A client requests a page and the server delivers it. With the advent of server-side scripting, which goes beyond HTTP, Web developers gained more control over the content, and the capability to tailor the delivery for the individual requesting the page or the activities leading up to the request.

Hypertext Preprocessor (PHP, for short) is essentially a general-purpose scripting language with the following features:

- Based on open source technologies
- The capability to run before the resulting page is displayed
- A Perl-like structure and syntax
- Robust HTTP handling capabilities

- The capability to coexist with raw HTML in the same file
- Modules for interacting with other technologies, such as MySQL

PHP's power results from the fact that the script is run prior to any data being delivered to the requesting client and from its heritage — PHP was devised to deliver HTTP content and does so via many built-in constructs.

Although the description of PHP may sound similar to how Perl or other CGI-based Web technologies can be used, once you start using PHP, you see exactly how revolutionary the language is.

PHP is another open source technology. Its use requires no heavy licensing fee, and it benefits from the open source community and related technologies. The PHP Web site (www.php.net) provides plenty of language and usage support. Like the Apache HTTP server, PHP is a project of the Apache Software Foundation.

Gathering the Required Materials

As with Apache, the materials you need to install PHP vary according to the platform you are using:

- If you are using a Linux distribution that provides PHP in a native package format (such as RPM), you can install the package provided by the distribution vendor — if it is a recent version.
- Windows users have it easy; installation requires uncompressing an archive and moving a few key files into position.
- If you are using a Linux distribution that does not offer a native PHP package, or you need a specially compiled version of PHP, you can download the source code and compile PHP yourself.

You can download all the required materials from the PHP Web site (www.php.net). Alternative installation methods, such as installing from a package included with your Linux distribution, may require a PHP package from the disks that came with your distribution or the distribution vendor's Web site.

The following sections cover each installation method in turn; follow the section that best suits your platform and needs.

The rest of this book assumes that you have installed PHP on a computer running Red Hat Linux, using the Red Hat-provided RPM package, and updated as needed from Red Hat's archives.

Compiling PHP for Linux

It's best to perform the actions in this section while logged in as root.

To compile PHP, you need to download the PHP source files from the PHP Web site, www.php.net. From the php.net home page, click the Downloads link at the top of the page and download the appropriate tarball (zipped with bzip2 [.tar.bz2] or gzip [.tar.gz]). Put the file in the usual place for source code on your system (that is, /usr/src).

Use the appropriate commands to uncompress the tarball. The resulting source code is uncompressed into a directory named php-*version*, where *version* is the particular version of PHP you downloaded. For example, at the time of this writing, the current version of PHP is 4.3.1, so the tarball would be named php-4.3.1.tar.* and the decompressed source directory would be php-4.3.1.

Before you can compile PHP, you must configure the make scripts for your particular platform. The PHP default options are adequate for most installations, save one: You must tell the compilation process that it needs to generate an appropriate Apache module for PHP. To configure the make scripts with this option, use the following command in the PHP source directory:

```
./configure --prefix=/usr/local/php \
--with-apxs2=/usr/local/apache2/bin/apxs
```

If you want PHP installed to another directory, substitute the path in which you want PHP installed (using the prefix **option, to something other than** /usr/local/php**). If you installed Apache to another directory, you will need to change the path to the** apxs **directory on your system (in the** with-apxs2 **option).**

You can use the help **option with the configure script to see what other options are available:**

```
./configure --help
```

Pipe the output through the more **command, or to a file to better review it.**

After running the configure script, run the following commands to compile PHP:

```
make
make install
```

After the make install process finishes, PHP is installed on your system. There is one more step to perform: moving the php.ini file to its expected location. Use the following command to move the default configuration file to the correct location:

```
cp php.ini-dist /usr/local/php/lib/php.ini
```

If you installed PHP somewhere other than the default path, be sure to change this destination path to coincide with the path in which PHP was installed.

A few more steps are necessary to get PHP working with Apache; continue this session from the section "Getting PHP to Work with Apache."

Installing PHP on Linux from a Package

At the time of this writing, Red Hat Linux 8.0 ships with PHP version 4.2.2 in RPM form, as shown in Figure 2-1.

Figure 2-1   *Red Hat Linux version 8.0 includes PHP version 4.2.2 in RPM format.*

There are many advantages to installing from a native package, including having the package install PHP to the default location for applications on your system.

You can install this package by using a file browser such as Nautilus, as shown in Figure 2-2; just double-click the file name. Alternatively, you can download the package to a local hard drive and use the RPM command to install it, as follows:

```
rpm -i php-4.2.2-8.0.5.i386.rpm
```

Replace the name of the RPM package with the appropriate name of the package included in your distribution.

When installing an RPM, the system verifies that all dependencies are met and that the package has not already been installed. If everything goes as planned, PHP is installed. If any errors appear, correct the source of the errors and try the installation again.

After installing PHP from a package, a good idea is to run your distribution's update service to make sure that you are using the latest version of PHP available. For example, using the Red Hat Update Agent, the 8.0.5 subversion of PHP 4.2.2 can be updated to subversion 8.0.7, as shown in Figure 2-3.

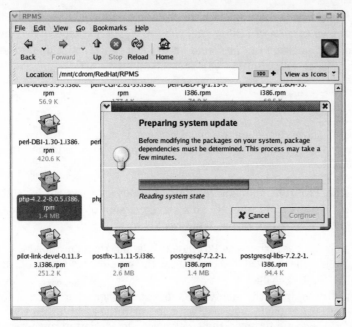

Figure 2-2 *In Nautilus, double-click an RPM, and the system attempts to install it.*

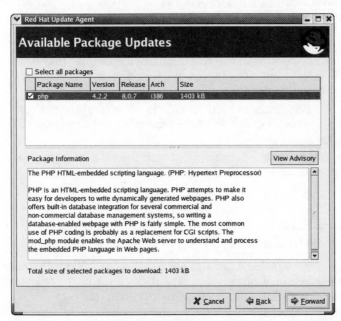

Figure 2-3 *The Red Hat Update Agent can update your installation of PHP.*

Red Hat PHP packages are known to have problems with MySQL connectivity. Compile your own version of PHP or find the PHPMySQL package that fixes the problem. This package can be found on the Red Hat FTP site under the RPM directory for the distribution you have installed.

Installing PHP on Windows

The installation of PHP on Windows, although a manual process, is very straightforward. Simply download the binary archive, expand it to a location of your choice, and move a handful of files to new locations.

As does Apache, PHP runs on many versions of Windows. However, for stability and security, you should run PHP on a server version of Windows, such as Windows NT, Windows 2000 Pro, or Windows XP Pro.

From the PHP Web site's home page, click the Downloads link and then download the Windows binary archive. An installer is available too, but at the time of this writing, it is specific to Web servers other than Apache.

Use your favorite ZIP utility to unzip the archive to a location on your hard drive where you want PHP to be installed. For example, you may want to unzip the archive into your system's root directory (C:\). Be sure to unzip the archive with folder definitions intact, ensuring that all the necessary subdirectories are created.

When you unzip the archive, a directory named php-*version*-Win32 is created, where *version* corresponds to the version of PHP you downloaded.

To finish the installation, you must perform the following steps:

1. Copy the php.ini-dist file (located in the PHP installation directory) to php.ini and locate the new file in your system's windows or winnt directory, depending on the version of Windows you are running.

2. Copy the php4ts.dll file (located in the PHP installation directory) to your system's windows/system or winnt/system directory, depending on the version of Windows you are running.

3. Edit the php.ini file and change the path specified with the extension_dir parameter to the directory of your PHP installation (for example, extension_dir = c:\php-*version*).

Getting PHP to Work with Apache

20 Min.
To Go

A few steps need to be performed to enable Apache to serve PHP pages. Essentially, Apache must know what pages are PHP and what processor to send them through. The following sections describe how to integrate PHP in Apache on Linux and Windows.

Updating httpd.conf on Linux

To get PHP to work with Apache, you must edit Apache's `httpd.conf` file. This file's location depends on your platform and the method you used to install Apache. On Red Hat Linux systems where Apache was installed from an RPM, this file is located in the `/etc/httpd/conf` directory. You can use the following command on your system to find the main Apache configuration file:

```
locate httpd.conf
```

The first addition to the configuration file enables the PHP Apache module. This module enables Apache to correctly process PHP files (by running them through the PHP processor).

Open the configuration file in your favorite text editor and find the location that resembles the following:

```
#
# Dynamic Shared Object (DSO) Support
#
# To be able to use the functionality of a module which was built as a DSO you
# have to place corresponding `LoadModule' lines at this location so the
# directives contained in it are actually available _before_ they are used.
# Statically compiled modules (those listed by `httpd -l') do not need
# to be loaded here.
#
# Example:
# LoadModule foo_module modules/mod_foo.so
#
LoadModule access_module modules/mod_access.so
. . .
```

Add the following line after the existing `LoadModule` lines:

```
LoadModule php4_module modules/libphp4.so
```

Ensure that the `libphp4.so` module is in the same directory as the other Apache modules. You may need to copy it to the correct location from your PHP source file's `lib` directory. In addition, if you compiled PHP support into Apache, you do not need to add the `LoadModule` line. (Check Apache's compiled modules by running `httpd` with the `-l` parameter to "list" the compiled modules.)

The second addition to the configuration file tells Apache what files to consider as PHP files — that is, what files to run through the PHP processor. Do so by adding the correct MIME type to the Apache configuration.

Find the location in the configuration file that resembles the following:

```
#
# AddType allows you to add to or override the MIME configuration
# file mime.types for specific file types.
#
AddType application/x-tar .tgz
. . .
```

Add the following lines after any existing AddType lines:

```
AddType application/x-httpd-php .php .phtml
AddType application/x-httpd-php-source .phps
```

The first line defines .php and .phtml files as PHP files. Any time the server encounters requests for such files, it passes them through the PHP processor and returns the processor's output to the requesting client. The second line defines .phps files as PHP source files. Any file with a .phps extension is treated as a PHP source file and is served to a client in raw text format, along with some minimal highlighting to help you debug your code. If you are using an editor with syntax highlighting, you probably never use the source highlighting through Apache, and you can omit the .phps line in the Apache configuration file.

After editing the configuration file, save it and restart Apache with the following command:

```
apachectl restart
```

Unless you also need to configure a Windows system, continue this session with the "Testing PHP" section.

Updating http.conf on Windows

To get PHP to work with Apache, you must edit the httpd.conf file. This file is commonly located in the \Program Files\Apache Group\Apache2\conf directory on the drive where you installed Apache.

The first addition to the configuration file enables the PHP Apache module. This module enables Apache to correctly process PHP files (by running them through the PHP processor).

Open the configuration file with your favorite text editor and find the section that resembles the following:

```
#
# Dynamic Shared Object (DSO) Support
#
# To be able to use the functionality of a module which was built as a DSO you
# have to place corresponding `LoadModule' lines at this location so the
# directives contained in it are actually available _before_ they are used.
# Statically compiled modules (those listed by `httpd -l') do not need
# to be loaded here.
#
# Example:
# LoadModule foo_module modules/mod_foo.so
#
LoadModule access_module modules/mod_access.so
. . .
```

After the existing LoadModule lines, add the following line:

```
LoadModule php_module c:\php-version\sapi\php4apache2.dll
```

Change the path of the `php4apache2.dll` **file to the correct path for your system. For example, if you installed PHP to the directory** `C:\PHP`, **you would specify** `C:\PHP\sapi\php4apache2.dll` **on the** `LoadModule` **line.**

The second addition to the configuration file tells Apache what files to consider as PHP files — that is, what files to run through the PHP processor. Do so by adding the correct MIME type to the Apache configuration.

Find the location in the configuration file that resembles the following:

```
#
# AddType allows you to add to or override the MIME configuration
# file mime.types for specific file types.
#
AddType application/x-tar .tgz
AddType image/x-icon .ico
. . .
```

Add the following lines after any existing `AddType` lines:

```
AddType application/x-httpd-php .php .phtml
AddType application/x-httpd-php-source .phps
```

The first line defines `.php` and `.phtml` files as PHP files. Any time the server encounters requests for such files, it will pass them through the PHP processor and return the processor's output to the requesting client. The second line defines `.phps` files as PHP source files. Any file with a `.phps` extension is treated as a PHP source file and is served to a client in raw text format, along with some minimal highlighting to help you debug your code.

After editing the configuration file, save it and restart Apache by double-clicking the Apache Service Monitor icon in the system tray and choosing Restart on the Apache Service Monitor window, as shown in Figure 2-4.

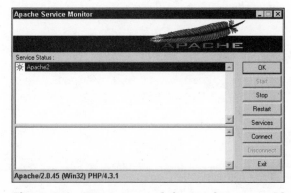

Figure 2-4   *You can control the Apache server with the Apache Service Monitor.*

If you don't see the Apache Service Monitor in your system tray, you can start and/or access it by choosing Start ➪ Programs ➪ Apache HTTP Server ➪ Control Apache Server ➪ Monitor Apache Servers. Other options are on the Windows Start menu for controlling the Apache server and editing the server's configuration file.

Testing PHP

**10 Min.
To Go**

To test the installation of PHP, create a simple script to be delivered by Apache. You need to create a text file in the main HTML directory for Apache:

- If you are running Apache on Linux, installed from an RPM package, the main Apache HTML directory (DocumentRoot) is usually /var/www/html.
- If you are running Apache on Linux, installed from source, the main Apache HTML directory (DocumentRoot) is usually /<whatever your prefix is>/htdocs.
- If you are running Apache on Windows, the main Apache HTML directory (DocumentRoot) is usually c:\Program Files\Apache Group\Apache2\htdocs.

If you don't know where your document root directory is, open the httpd.conf file and search for the DocumentRoot directive — the directory that appears after the directive should be the document root.

Create the following text in a plain text file and name it test.php:

```
<?php
  phpinfo();
?>
```

The syntax and format of PHP scripts is covered in Session 14. For now, enter the preceding text exactly as shown.

To test the file, open a browser on the machine running the server and point the browser to http://localhost/test.php. You should see a page similar to the page shown in Figure 2-5.

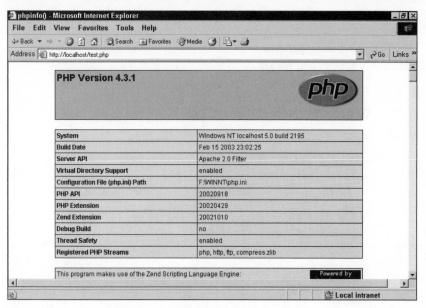

Figure 2-5 *The* `phpinfo()` *function displays a wealth of information about PHP's installation and running environment.*

Done!

REVIEW

This session showed you what is necessary to install PHP on your server. You learned what to download, how to use the download(s) to install PHP, how to integrate PHP with Apache, and, finally, how to test the installation. You were also introduced to several PHP and Apache configuration files.

QUIZ YOURSELF

1. What does PHP stand for? (See "Understanding Preprocessed HTML.")
2. Why would you want to compile PHP from source files? (See "Gathering the Required Materials.")
3. What version(s) of Windows are best for running server programs such as PHP? (See "Installing PHP on Windows.")
4. What is an Apache PHP module and why do you need it? (See "Updating httpd.conf on Linux" and "Updating http.conf on Windows.")
5. Where is the DocumentRoot for your Apache server installation? (See "Testing PHP.")

Installing MySQL

Session Checklist

✔ Introducing MySQL

✔ Gathering the required materials

✔ Installing MySQL

✔ Testing the installation

**30 Min.
To Go**

The last of our triad of technology is MySQL, the popular relational database server. As with Apache, MySQL installs as a server — several clients can then connect to the server and request data or operations on existing data. This session shows you how to install MySQL and how to integrate it with PHP so that you can write scripts that can access the database as clients.

Introducing MySQL

MySQL has an interesting past. The founders of MySQL started using mSQL to connect to tables using their own fast, low-level routines. After some testing, they determined that mSQL wasn't fast enough for their needs. They created a new SQL interface for their needs but maintained a very similar application program interface (API) to that of mSQL.

The base directory and several of the base libraries during early development had a my prefix. (One of the co-founder's daughters is also named "My." No one knows which co-founder contributed the "My" in MySQL.)

Today, MySQL has evolved into a powerful alternative to the commercial database products, including the king of databases, Oracle. In fact, recent benchmarks of MySQL version 4.*x* show it to be very capable; with new features, such as InnoDB (formally known as Innobase), which provides full ACID guarantee (Atomicity, Consistency, Isolation, and Durability), it rivals the performance and features of commercial databases.

MySQL is open source and license free. With its modular design and robust API, you can deploy a full-featured database very cheaply.

Gathering the Required Materials

MySQL is fairly easy to install and can be installed as a binary or built from source. The installation method you choose depends on the same criteria you used to decide how to install Apache and PHP in the previous two sessions:

- Are you installing on Linux or Windows?
- If you are installing on Linux, does your distribution have a recent copy of MySQL in packaged form?
- Do you need a specially compiled version of MySQL, or can the standard compiled version work for your purposes?

Most users find the version of MySQL they need from the MySQL Web site (`www.mysql.com`). Windows users want to download the binary installer, while Linux users can download a generic Linux version (specific to the hardware platform you are using), an RPM packaged version, or the source code.

Each of these options is available from the Download page of the MySQL Web site (`www.mysql.com/downloads/index.html`).

MySQL AB

MySQL AB maintains many distinct versions of MySQL. At the time of this writing, the production version, an alpha (in testing) version, a development version, and an older production release are all available. Sticking with the latest production version unless you have unique development needs is highly recommended.

In addition, several builds of each version are available — Standard, Max, and Debug. Most users prefer the Standard version. The Max build includes additional features such as the Berkeley DB (database) storage engine — features that haven't been extensively tested and are generally not required for general usage. The Debug build has been compiled with extra debug information and is not recommended for general usage. (The debug code may slow normal operation.)

MySQL AB does not recommend that users compile their own copy of MySQL. In fact, many warnings appear both on the Web site and in the software warning users of the potential problems associated with poorly compiled MySQL. Whenever possible, you should install a binary version of MySQL — to provide full coverage, this session explains how to compile MySQL, although doing so is *not* recommended.

Compiling MySQL for Linux

**20 Min.
To Go**

Compiling MySQL on Linux is straightforward and resembles the same process you followed when compiling Apache and PHP. However, as previously stated, compiling your own copy of MySQL, unless you literally have no choice, is not recommended.

To compile MySQL, download an appropriate source file from the MySQL Web site Download page. (At the time of this writing, the source downloads are at the very bottom of the Download page.) You can download a tarball or RPM. Download the version of your choice and expand and/or install it to where you normally store source files. At the time of this writing, the RPM MySQL source package simply places a copy of the source gzipped tarball in the `/usr/src/redhat/SOURCES` directory.

Read the documentation contained in the MySQL source file directory, especially the `README` **and** `INSTALL-SOURCE` **files. They are packed full of useful information on compiling and installing MySQL.**

Follow these steps (as root) to compile MySQL:

1. Change to the directory in which you unpacked the MySQL source files.
2. Execute the following commands to create a `mysql` group and user:
   ```
   groupadd mysql
   useradd -g mysql mysql
   ```
3. Run the configure script to build the make files by using the following command:
   ```
   ./configure --prefix=/usr/local/mysql
   ```
   Change the prefix argument's path if you want to install MySQL in another location.
4. Run the following two `make` commands to compile and install MySQL:
   ```
   make
   make install
   ```
5. Run the database install script with the following command:
   ```
   scripts/mysql_install_db
   ```
   This script creates the necessary tables for MySQL operation.
6. Run the following commands to set the correct permissions on the MySQL files:
   ```
   chown -R root /usr/local/mysql
   chown -R mysql /usr/local/mysql/var
   chgrp -R mysql /usr/local/mysql
   ```
   Be sure to change the path relative to your MySQL install directory.

At this point, MySQL should be installed. Continue this session with the section "Testing Your MySQL Installation."

Installing a Linux Binary Version of MySQL

Installing a binary distribution of MySQL is straightforward, but you must perform several steps to ensure that the installation is ready to run. If you need to install a generic MySQL binary, download the appropriate Linux binary archive from the MySQL Web site and follow these steps:

1. Place the archive in a temporary directory on a local drive.

2. Execute the following commands to create a `mysql` group and user:

   ```
   groupadd mysql
   useradd -g mysql mysql
   ```

3. Unpack the archive (using `tar`, `gunzip`, or a combination, depending on the archive you downloaded) to `/usr/local`. MySQL AB recommends that you run the following command line from the `/usr/local` directory:

   ```
   gunzip < /fullpath/mysql-build&version.architechture.tar.gz \
       | tar xvf -
   ```

At the time of this writing, one such binary archive is named as follows:

```
mysql-standard-4.0.12-pc-linux-i686.tar.gz
```

4. Create a symbolic `mysql` link to the longhand directory (where `*` is the rest of the directory name, including the version number — for example, `mysql-standard-4.0.12-pc-linux-i686`):

   ```
   ln -s mysql-* mysql
   ```

5. Change to the `mysql` directory and run the following script to create the initial databases:

   ```
   cd mysql
   scripts/mysql_install_db
   ```

6. Change the permissions as follows:

   ```
   chown -R root .
   chown -R mysql data
   chgrp -R mysql .
   ```

Be sure to read the `README` **and** `INSTALL-BINARY` **files in the** `mysql` **directory for other installation steps specific to your version.**

At this point, MySQL should be installed. Continue this session with the section "Testing Your MySQL Installation."

Installing MySQL on Linux from a Package

The easiest way to install MySQL on Linux is via a package for your specific distribution. For example, on a Red Hat system, use the MySQL RPM package downloaded from the MySQL Web site or an RPM from one of the Red Hat distribution CDs, if they contain a recent version.

Use an RPM available from the MySQL site whenever possible. The packages found there are the most current. However, keep in mind that you can install an earlier version and use services such as the Red Hat Network to update your version. The latter option (install and update) has the added bonus of installing a version specifically packaged for your Linux distribution, at the expense of possibly being a version or two behind the most current.

To install MySQL from a package, download the package to a local drive and use your distribution's package tools to install it. Be careful to install all the packages you need — usually the MySQL server and the MySQL client packages.

For example, to install MySQL on Red Hat from RPMs, follow these steps:

1. Download the RPM files (for example, `MySQL-server-version.i386.rpm` and `MySQL-client-version.i386.rpm`) to a local drive.

2. Execute the following command to install the RPMs:

```
rpm -i MySQL-server-<version>.i386.rpm \
    MySQL-client-<version>.i386.rpm
```

That's it. The RPMs ensure that the correct user and group (both `mysql`) are created, that the initial databases are set up, and that the MySQL database server is running.

The RPMs install the various MySQL executables in `/usr/bin`, and the database files in `/var/lib/mysql`.

The rest of this book assumes that you have downloaded and installed the latest version of MySQL from the MySQL Web site in RPM form.

Unless you need to install MySQL on Windows, continue this session with the section "Testing Your MySQL Installation."

Installing MySQL on Windows

Installing the binary version of MySQL on Windows is straightforward and is accomplished via an InstallShield-built installer. You can download the binary installer from the Download page of MySQL AB's Web site.

As with Apache and PHP, MySQL runs on many versions of Windows. However, for stability and security's sake, you should run MySQL on a server version of Windows, such as Windows NT, Windows 2000 Pro, or Windows XP Pro.

Download the ZIP file containing the installer, unzip its contents to a temporary folder, and run the `setup.exe` file. This starts the MySQL installer.

The following steps detail the typical installation process:

1. The first installation window, as shown in Figure 3-1, displays information about the version of MySQL that you are about to install. Click Next to move to the next step.

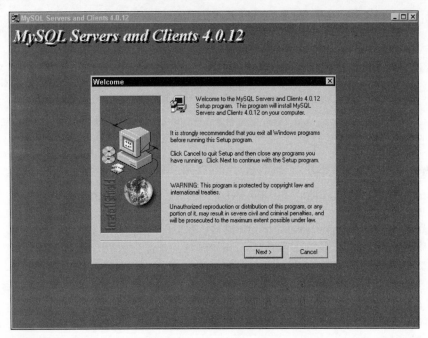

Figure 3-1   *The first installation window displays version and copyright information for MySQL.*

2. The information window shown in Figure 3-2 displays notes about installing MySQL, including information about creating a CNF or INI file for the server's use. (Both CNF and INI are common extensions for configuration files, stemming from the words *configuration* and *initialization*.) This information is especially important if you plan to install MySQL somewhere other than the default c:\mysql or if you plan to run MySQL as a service on a Windows NT computer. You may wish to highlight the text with your mouse and copy it to the Windows clipboard for later use. Click Next when you are finished reviewing this information.

3. The Choose Destination Location window, as shown in Figure 3-3, enables you to select the folder in which MySQL is installed. Unless you have a valid reason for not using the default (c:\mysql), accept the default by clicking Next. If you want to change the installation folder, click the Browse button and type the full path to the folder or use the file-browsing interface to find the folder. When you are finished selecting the installation folder, click Next to continue the installation process.

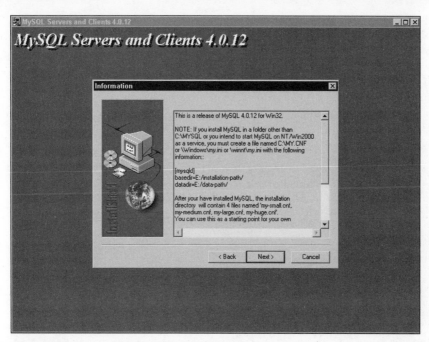

Figure 3-2 *The Information window displays important information about the install location for MySQL and running MySQL as a service.*

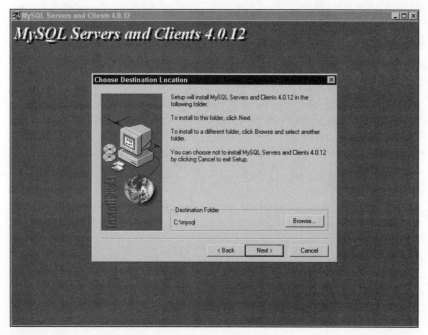

Figure 3-3 *The Choose Destination Location window enables you to select the folder in which you want MySQL installed.*

4. The Setup Type window, as shown in Figure 3-4, enables you to select the type of installation: Typical (installs the typical components), Compact (installs minimal components), or Custom (installs selected components). Unless you have specific needs and find it necessary to use the Custom option, select the Typical option and click Next to continue.

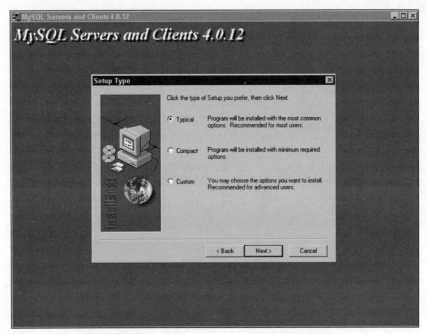

Figure 3-4   *The Setup Type window enables you to select the type of installation. Choose Typical unless you have a specific reason not to.*

5. The install program copies the necessary files to the location you specified and then displays the Setup Complete window, as shown in Figure 3-5. Click Finish to end the install process.

One of the programs installed with MySQL is WinMySQLAdmin, a graphical application that enables you to monitor the MySQL server. Use Windows Explorer to navigate to the bin folder in the MySQL installation directory and run the WinMySQLAdmin program.

A shortcut for WinMySQLAdmin is installed in your Windows Startup group and is accessible from the Start menu (choose Start ➪ (All) Programs ➪ Startup ➪ WinMySQLAdmin).

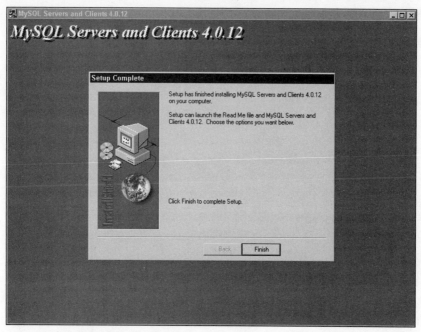

Figure 3-5 *The MySQL installation is complete.*

The first time you start WinMySQLAdmin, it prompts you for a username and password, as shown in Figure 3-6. This information is used to set up the initial MySQL user account. Type a username and password into their respective text boxes and click OK to create the user and display the main WinMySQLAdmin interface, as shown in Figure 3-7.

WinMySQLAdmin sets up an appropriate `my.cnf` **file for you the first time it is run.**

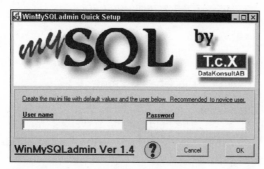

Figure 3-6 *WinMySQLAdmin prompts you for the initial username and password.*

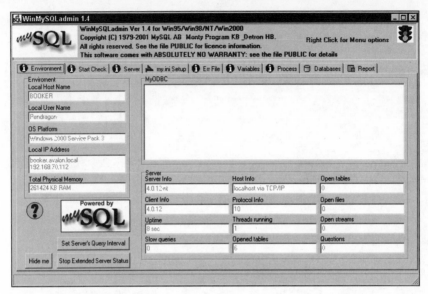

Figure 3-7 *The graphical interface enables you to view a multitude of information about your MySQL server.*

Browse through the tabs near the top of the window to preview the information available through the utility. When you are done reviewing the information in the graphical interface, right-click the window and choose Hide Me. The graphical interface window closes and a stoplight icon appears in the task bar, as shown in Figure 3.8.

Figure 3-8 *When hidden, WinMySQLAdmin displays a stoplight icon in the task bar. Click the icon and choose Show Me to redisplay the graphical interface.*

Testing Your MySQL Installation

**10 Min.
To Go**

Before you can test MySQL, you need to ensure that the server is running:

- **Windows users:** Click the WinMySQLAdmin icon and choose Show Me to open the graphical interface. If the stoplight is green and the fields in the Server section are populated, the server is running. If the stoplight is red and the fields are blank, as shown in Figure 3-9, the server isn't running.

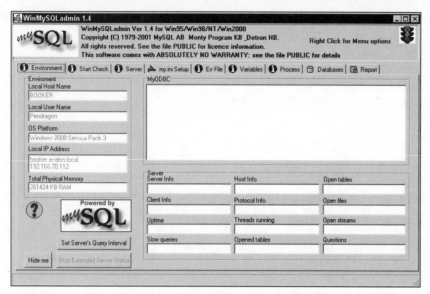

Figure 3-9 *The stoplight and Server fields show the current status of the server — if the stoplight is red and the fields are blank, the server is not running.*

If WinMySQLAdmin is not running, start it from the Start menu (by choosing Start ➪ (All) Programs ➪ Startup ➪ WinMySQLAdmin) or by double-clicking it in Windows Explorer.

If the MySQL server is not running, right-click anywhere on the WinMySQLAdmin interface and choose Win NT ➪ Start the Service. (This option varies between Windows 95, 98, and ME.)

- **Linux users:** Use ps to determine whether the server is running. Use the following command:

```
ps -A | grep "mysqld"
```

If the server is running, the ps command outputs lines similar to the following:

```
1114 tty1      00:00:00 mysqld_safe
1130 tty1      00:00:00 mysqld
```

If you need to start the server, use the following command:

```
mysql_safe &
```

Depending on your installation, you may need to specify the location of the mysql_safe script.

To test the installation, run the MySQL monitor and try a few commands. From a command prompt in the MySQL application directory (usually c:\mysql in Windows or /usr/bin or /usr/local/mysql in Linux), use the following command to start the monitor:

```
mysql
```

On Linux, you should prefix the mysql **command with** ./ **to specify the current directory or put the** *mysql/bin* **directory in your path.**

The MySQL monitor starts and displays something similar to the following:

```
Welcome to the MySQL monitor.  Commands end with ; or \g.
Your MySQL connection id is 1 to server version: 4.0.12

Type 'help;' or '\h' for help. Type '\c' to clear the buffer.

mysql>
```

Think of the MySQL monitor as a console window that you can use to talk directly to MySQL. You use this tool in other exercises in this book to perform maintenance, test queries, and so on.

At the mysql> prompt, type the following command:

```
use mysql;
```

The monitor should respond with the following:

```
Database changed
```

Now use the following command to display the tables in the mysql database:

```
show tables;
```

The monitor responds with something similar to the following:

```
+-----------------+
| Tables_in_mysql |
+-----------------+
| columns_priv    |
| db              |
| func            |
| host            |
| tables_priv     |
| user            |
+-----------------+
6 rows in set (0.00 sec)
```

At this point, MySQL is installed and configured enough to locate its data and respond to simple commands. Use the quit command to exit the monitor and return to a console prompt.

More information about troubleshooting MySQL is covered in Session 7.

Changing the Root Password for MySQL

It's best to immediately change the root password for MySQL, even if you are not on a network or connected to the Internet. Use the following command (in the MySQL binary directory) to change the root password:

```
mysqladmin -u root password new-password
```

Replace *new-password* with the password you want the root MySQL user to have. Thereafter, you need to use the -p parameter when starting the MySQL monitor, as follows:

```
mysql -p
```

The monitor prompts you to enter the root password. Notice that if you are not logged in as root or an Administrator, you also need to specify the root user when starting the monitor, as follows:

```
mysql -u root -p
```

Done!

REVIEW

This session showed you what is necessary to install MySQL on your server. You learned what to download and how to use the download(s) to install MySQL on Linux and Windows. You were also shown how to test MySQL to confirm the installation.

QUIZ YOURSELF

1. Where did the name MySQL come from? (See "Introducing MySQL.")
2. What is the name of the company behind the development of MySQL? (See "Introducing MySQL.")
3. How many versions of MySQL are available for download at any one time, and what is the purpose of each? (See "Gathering the Required Materials.")
4. What are the different builds of MySQL, and what is the purpose of each? (See "Gathering the Required Materials.")
5. Which is recommended, compiling MySQL, or installing MySQL binaries? (See "Gathering the Required Materials.")
6. What is the name of the GUI MySQL admin tool on Windows, where can it be found, and what are the two ways to start it? (See "Installing MySQL on Windows".)
7. What user and group are necessary for MySQL on Linux? (See "Compiling MySQL for Linux," "Installing a Linux Binary Version of MySQL," or "Installing MySQL on Linux from a Package.")
8. What command starts the MySQL monitor? (See "Testing Your MySQL Installation.")

Apache Basics

Session Checklist

✔ Understanding HTTP servers

✔ Running and testing Apache

✔ Understanding where Apache stores its files

✔ Learning the basic access and error logs

**30 Min.
To Go**

A pache is a complex application. However, it was designed to be easy to run, administer, and even extend. Before jumping into various Apache configuration options (covered in Session 5), it's important to know a bit more about Apache.

A full discussion of Apache, HTTP, and related technologies is beyond the scope of this book. If you want to learn more about Apache, pick up a copy of the *Apache Server 2 Bible, 2nd Edition*, by Mohammed J. Kabir (Wiley Publishing).

Understanding HTTP Servers

HyperText Transfer Protocol (*HTTP*) was conceived and put into practice as a specification in late 1995. Originally designed to replace the aging Gopher protocol, HTTP 1.0 provided a unique way of linking documents to other documents on the Internet. The result was the World Wide Web.

The Evolution of Feature-Rich Web Content

Early HTTP-delivered documents were text only. Shortly after the protocol was adopted, graphics became commonplace on the Web. Today, every conceivable kind of electronic content can be delivered via the Web — text, sound, movies, and so on.

HTTP is a fairly simple protocol. A client requests data from a server, the data is parsed against a list of content types, and the server sends the data to the client via the system required by the content type. Such content types are referred to as *Multipurpose Internet Mail Extensions* (*MIME*). These extensions enable non-ASCII data to be sent over the Internet. The HTTP server uses MIME types to figure out how to send specific files. You can find more information about MIME types in Session 5.

Today's HTTP specification is quite complex. Interested readers should visit the World Wide Web Consortium Web site (`www.w3.org`) for more information.

HTTP Services over TCP

Most Web traffic is conducted over TCP port 80. However, as the Web has matured, several other ports have begun to be utilized to serve up data to clients. Port 443, for example, provides secure Web connections via SSL. Other protocols have also been made available via a standard browser thanks to Netscape's innovative plug-ins. These plug-ins (now used by most browsers) enable other applications to send and receive data through the browser — not always via HTTP on TCP port 80.

You can configure Apache to operate on any port. Alternative port options include TCP ports 81, 85, and 8080. Most administrators choose to operate Apache on an alternative port only for the following reasons:

- The server needs to be hidden from casual hackers (who look for it on port 80).
- More than one server is running on a given machine.
- Some other port conflict or application needs the alternative port.

Some applications and services that piggyback on the browser interface (plug-ins are the most notable) do not use the configured port — 80 or otherwise — for their communication. When changing the default Apache port, you should generally pick a port above 1023 so as not to tread on a port used by another common Internet service.

Apache: Status, Starting, and Stopping

20 Min. To Go

Determining whether Apache is running is relatively easy. The following sections show you how to tell whether the server is running and how to start and stop the server, if necessary.

Apache Status

You can verify that the Apache server is running in several ways. The easiest is to point a browser at the machine running the server. On a fresh install, you should see the Apache test page. Figure 4-1 shows the results of using a browser on the server machine and viewing the URL `http://localhost`.

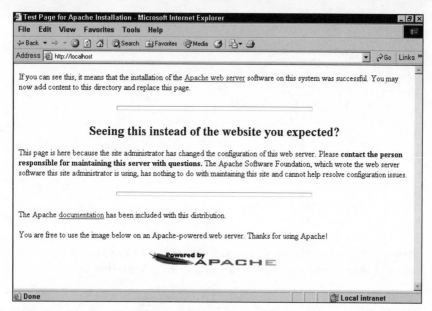

Figure 4-1 *You can check the server by viewing the root page. Fresh installs should display the Apache test page.*

On Windows machines, you can use the Apache Service Monitor to check server status. If the monitor is running, the server status is shown in the tray icon, as shown in Figure 4-2.

The Apache Service Monitor tray icon

Figure 4-2 *The Apache Service Monitor tray icon shows the status of the Apache server.*

If the icon contains a green triangle, the server is running. If the icon displays a red dot, the server has been stopped.

If the Apache Service Monitor is not running, you can start it from the Windows Start menu. (Choose Start ⇨ Programs ⇨ Apache HTTP Server ⇨ Control Apache Server ⇨ Monitor Apache Servers.)

On Linux machines, you can use the process status command, `ps`, to determine whether the server is running. Most Linux distributions report the Apache server processes as `httpd`, but some report it as `apache`. Using one of the two following commands should display the Apache processes currently running:

```
ps -A | grep "httpd"
```

```
ps -A | grep "apache"
```

On Red Hat Linux, the former command results in output similar to the following:

```
1109 ?        00:00:00 httpd
1110 ?        00:00:00 httpd
1111 ?        00:00:00 httpd
1112 ?        00:00:00 httpd
1113 ?        00:00:00 httpd
1114 ?        00:00:00 httpd
1115 ?        00:00:00 httpd
1116 ?        00:00:00 httpd
1117 ?        00:00:00 httpd
```

The exact number of server processes depends on the configuration and current load on the server. You can find more information in Session 5.

You can also use a `telnet` application to talk to the server directly on TCP port 80. For example, under Linux, you can use the command-line `telnet` program as follows (text in bold is typed by the user; the rest is the response from the server to the commands typed):

```
telnet localhost 80
Trying 127.0.0.1...
Connected to localhost.
Escape character is '^]'.
HEAD / HTTP/1.0
< Blank line>
HTTP/1.1 200 OK
Date: Sun, 20 Apr 2003 06:36:26 GMT
Server: Apache/2.0.40 (Red Hat Linux)
Accept-Ranges: bytes
Content-Length: 2890
Connection: close
Content-Type: text/html; charset=ISO-8859-1

Connection closed by foreign host.
```

Notice the blank line that you need to type after the HEAD request. This is necessary to end the command input to the server and ask for its response.

Starting and Stopping the Server

On Windows machines, you can use the Apache Service Monitor to start and stop the Apache server. If the monitor is running, double-click its tray icon to open the monitor window, as shown in Figure 4-3.

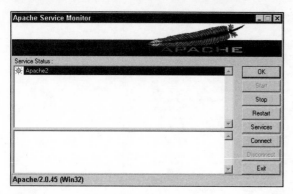

Figure 4-3   *The Apache Service Monitor has buttons for starting and stopping the server.*

To start or stop the server, select the server in the Service Status window and click the appropriate button (Start, Stop, or Restart).

On Linux machines, you can use the `apachectl` script to start and stop the server. The syntax for this script is as follows:

```
apachectl {start|stop|restart}
```

For example, to start the Apache server, you would use the following command:

```
apachectl start
```

To stop the server, you would use this command:

```
apachectl stop
```

    On most Linux machines, the `apachectl` script is installed in a binary direc-tory that is included in the command path — simply typing the script name at a shell prompt runs it. However, some systems might require that the script be moved, that a symlink be created to the script, or that the entire path be included in the script command (for example, `/usr/sbin/apachectl`).

Automatically Starting Apache

To automatically start the Apache server on Windows, Apache must be installed as a service. The Apache installation program automatically does this. You can use the Services Admin tool to verify that the Apache service is installed, as shown in Figure 4-4.

    You can start the Services tool from the Windows Control Panel — choose Admin Tools ➪ Services.

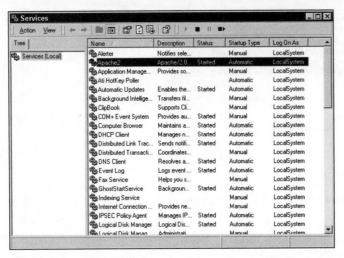

Figure 4-4   *You can use the Services tool to verify the Apache service's installation and status.*

If you need to install Apache as a service manually, use the following command from the Apache bin directory:

```
apache -k install
```

Optionally, you can give the service a name with the -n parameter:

```
apache -k install -n "Apache2"
```

On Linux, you need an init script to start Apache. Typically, an httpd script is installed in the default init directory. (On Red Hat, it is /etc/rc.d/init.d/httpd.) This script starts Apache when the computer boots. Although you can use several other methods to start the Apache server (placing an entry in inittab, creating scripts in appropriate rc.x directories, and so on), using the apachectl script to actually start the server is recommended.

Follow the methods for your particular version of Linux to create the appropriate init script(s), calling apachectl (with the start parameter) to start the server.

Locating Apache Files

10 Min.
To Go

Knowing the location of various Apache files is important. You need to edit the configuration files, write scripts to access the executables, view the log files, and so on.

Apache installs in a variety of directories, depending on the operating system you use. Table 4-1 summarizes the location of important Apache files on Windows and Red Hat Linux (installed via Red Hat-provided RPMs).

Table 4-1　*Location of Apache Files*

Files	General Windows Location	General RPM Location (Linux)	General Non-RPM Location (Linux)
Executables	\Program Files\ Apache Group\ Apache2\bin	/usr/sbin	/usr/local/apache2
Configuration Files	\Program Files\ Apache Group\ Apache2\conf	/etc/httpd/conf	/usr/local/apache2/conf
Modules	\Program Files\ Apache Group\ Apache2\modules	/etc/httpd/modules	/usr/local/apache2/ modules
Log Files	\Program Files\ Apache Group\ Apache2\logs	/var/log/httpd	/usr/local/apache2/logs
Document Root	\Program Files\ Apache Group\ Apache2\htdocs	/var/www/html	/usr/local/apache2/ htdocs

Some Linux distributions, including Red Hat, name the Apache executable httpd **instead of** apache.

If you have trouble locating the files in Table 4-1, try searching for the individual files listed in Table 4-2. On Windows, you can use the Search feature (by choosing Start ➪ Search); on Linux, you can use search applications such as locate, whereis, and find.

Table 4-2　*Individual Apache File Names*

Files	Windows	Linux
Executables	Search for the file Apache.exe	Search for the file apache or httpd
Configuration Files	Search for the file httpd.conf	Search for the file httpd.conf
Modules	Search for the file mod_access.so	Search for the file mod_access.so
Log Files	Search for the file access.log or error.log	Search for the file access.log or error.log
Document Root	Search for DocumentRoot in the httpd.conf file	Search for DocumentRoot in the httpd.conf file

Apache Log Files

By default, Apache maintains two log files, `access.log` and `error.log`. These logs record successful client accesses and errors reported by the Apache server, respectively. The `LogLevel` and `LogFormat` directives govern the amount of information stored in each log file.

A typical `access.log` entry resembles the following:

```
192.168.70.21 - - [26/Apr/2003:21:01:25 -0500] "GET / HTTP/1.1" 200 1494
192.168.70.21 - - [26/Apr/2003:21:01:25 -0500] "GET /apache_pb.gif HTTP/1.1" 200 2326
```

In the preceding case, a client from IP address 192.168.70.21 successfully made two requests on April 26 around 9:00 p.m. Both requests show status 200 (OK). The latter request was for a graphic, the Powered By Apache logo. (The request was for the Apache status page.)

A typical `error.log` entry resembles the following:

```
[Sat Apr 26 21:00:45 2003] [error] [client 192.168.70.21] client denied by server
configuration: C:/Program Files/Apache Group/Apache2/htdocs/
```

In the preceding case, a client was denied access from IP address 192.168.70.21 because of a server configuration.

Keeping an eye on the log files can help you spot system errors, misconfigurations, and hacker attempts to compromise your server. Because each log contains separate information, you should analyze both logs concurrently.

Done!

REVIEW

In this session, you learned a bit more about Apache: how it basically works, how to start and stop the server, and where it stores its files. This information is important to know to adequately administer an Apache server. The next few sessions delve deeper into Apache administration, how to correctly configure the server, and how to ensure that it is secure.

QUIZ YOURSELF

1. What does HTTP stand for? (See "Understanding HTTP Servers.")
2. Where can you go (on the Web) to learn more about HTTP and HTML? (See "The Evolution of Feature-Rich Web Content.")
3. What TCP port does Apache commonly use? (See "HTTP Services over TCP.")
4. What secure TCP port does Apache commonly use for SSL connections? (See "HTTP Services over TCP.")
5. Describe one method for determining whether the Apache server is running. (See "Apache Status.")
6. Where is the Apache configuration file (`httpd.conf`) on your system? (See "Locating Apache Files.")

PART

I

Friday Evening Part Review

1. What is HTTP?
2. Is PHP open source?
3. Where are Apache's log files kept on your system?
4. How many versions of MySQL are available for downloading for your platform?
5. What two databases are installed with MySQL?
6. Why shouldn't you compile your own copy of MySQL?
7. What TCP port does Apache commonly listen to?
8. Do you need to add any groups or users when you install MySQL?
9. Where is the Apache binary installed on your system?
10. Why are MIME types important for Apache?
11. What is the name of the MySQL admin script on Linux? On Windows?
12. How can you determine if the Apache server is running?
13. Why should you change the root password after installing MySQL?
14. How can you start and stop the Apache server on Linux? On Windows?
15. What is the name of the company that maintains MySQL?
16. Do Linux and Windows both ship with a version of PHP?
17. How many platforms is Apache available for?
18. How do you integrate PHP with Apache on Linux? On Windows?

☑ Friday

☑ Saturday

☐ Sunday

Part II — Saturday Morning

Session 5
Configuring Apache

Session 6
Apache Security Concerns

Session 7
The Basics of MySQL

Session 8
MySQL Security

Session 9
Working with Data

Session 10
Queries

Part III — Saturday Afternoon

Session 11
Troubleshooting MySQL Commands and Queries

Session 12
Advanced MySQL Concepts

Session 13
Getting Ready to Use PHP

Session 14
PHP Basics

Session 15
Program Flow

Session 16
PHP Functions

Part IV — Saturday Evening

Session 17
Working with Files

Session 18
HTML Constructs

Session 19
Working with Forms

Session 20
Multiple-User Considerations in PHP

Saturday
Morning

Session 5
Configuring Apache

Session 6
Apache Security Concerns

Session 7
The Basics of MySQL

Session 8
MySQL Security

Session 9
Working with Data

Session 10
Queries

Configuring Apache

Session Checklist

✔ Learning about the main Apache configuration file

✔ Understanding configuration directives and how to use them in the Apache configuration file

✔ Using MIME types

**30 Min.
To Go**

Apache is a powerful but flexible server — that's what makes it so popular. However, powerful and flexible can also equal complex. Knowing how to configure the server for your needs can be a daunting task unless you understand how Apache's configuration works. As you read through this session, you should begin to anticipate changes you may need to make to your Apache configuration. As you progress through the rest of this book, you find recommendations on how to best configure Apache for various tasks.

The default Apache configuration works fine for the purposes of this book. However, as you move from the learning stage to production, you are bound to run into unique configuration needs. Although you may not need this information immediately, you may find yourself returning to it for advice in the future.

Understanding the httpd.conf File

As installed, Apache is ready to serve content. However, you may need to change several configuration settings to suit your needs. You can find most of the configuration options for Apache in the httpd.conf file.

The following sections detail the various parts and parameters in the `httpd.conf` file. On Windows, you can find this file in the following default location:

```
\Program Files\Apache Group\Apache2\conf\httpd.conf
```

On Red Hat Linux, you can usually find this file in the following location:

```
/etc/httpd/conf/httpd.conf
```

However, you might also find the configuration file in these locations:

```
/usr/local/apache2/conf/httpd.conf
```

```
/etc/apache2/httpd.conf
```

If you have trouble finding the `httpd.conf` file, use your operating system's search feature to locate it.

While you are learning about the `httpd.conf` file, it is wise to take two precautions:

1. Back up the original file to a secure location.
2. When making changes to the file, comment out the old settings instead of removing them or typing over them.

You can change the default configuration file by starting Apache with the `-f` configuration option, followed by the full path to an alternative configuration file, as shown in the following example:

```
/usr/local/apache2/bin/apachectl start -f /usr/local/apache2/conf/
alt-httpd.conf
```

Open the file with your favorite text editor and follow along through the rest of this session.

Apache Directives

`httpd.conf` is a plaintext file filled with settings commonly known as *directives*. These directives are unique keywords followed by the setting for the directive. For example, one of the directives in the configuration file follows:

```
DocumentRoot "/var/www/html"
```

This directive tells Apache that the Document Root, the main directory for content, is `/var/www/html`. Note that all directives observe the following syntax:

```
Directive Setting1 Setting2 Setting3...
```

Directives and their options should be contained on one line. If you need to split a directive over two or more lines, use a backslash (\\) at the end of the incomplete lines to signal Apache that the directive is continued on the following line.

In addition, most directives are preceded by a comment line (or several) detailing the setting. For example, the DocumentRoot directive is preceded by the following comments:

```
#
# DocumentRoot: The directory out of which you will serve your
# documents. By default, all requests are taken from this directory, but
# symbolic links and aliases may be used to point to other locations.
#
```

Although Windows commonly uses the backslash (\\) to delimit directories in path names, the Apache configuration files typically use a normal slash (per Linux conventions). You can use either slash in Apache configuration files on Windows.

These comments are an important part of the configuration file and help administrators understand the configuration structure and settings. Whenever you add a directive to the configuration file, you should add similar comments to document your settings.

The Apache Web site, www.apache.org, has extensive documentation on configuration directives. At the time of this writing, the documentation can be found at http://httpd.apache.org/docs-2.0/mod/directives.html.

Table 5-1 outlines several common directives and their usage.

All directive directory name arguments should be full paths to the specified directory or a relative path off of the directory specified in the ServerRoot directive. Likewise, all file name arguments need to specify the full path to the file or a relative path off of the directory specified in the ServerRoot directive.

Table 5-1 *Common Apache Directives*

Directive	Use
ServerRoot	The root directory in which Apache files (binaries, modules, config files, and so on) are stored. (Argument: *directoryname*)
PidFile	The file where the server should store its process ID when it starts. (Argument: *filename*)

Continued

Table 5-1   *Continued*

Directive	Use
KeepAlive	Indicates whether the server should allow persistent connections (allow clients to send more than one request per connection). Setting this directive to On allows for better performance for connected clients. (Argument: On|Off)
Listen	The address and port on which the server should listen for connections. This directive enables you to specify the port and particular IP on which the server should listen. If you have only one server (physical or virtual) and you want it to listen to all incoming traffic, specify the port only. (Argument: *ipaddress:port*)
LoadModule	Loads the specified module. (Arguments: *status_module modulepath/modulename*)
ServerAdmin	The address for the Webmaster/administrator. This address is used on all server-generated pages. (Argument: *emailaddress*)
ServerName	The server's fully qualified host name. (Argument: *fullyqualified-domainname*)
UseCanonicalName	Indicates whether the server should use the name specified in the ServerName directive (On) or the name specified by the client (Off). (Argument: On|Off)
DocumentRoot	The root directory for server content. (Argument: *directoryname*)
UserDir	The directory to add to user directories when they are requested. For example, on Windows, the default My Documents/My Website is added to the user directory C:\Documents and Settings*username*\. (Argument: *directoryname*)
AccessFileName	The filename that the server should look for in each directory for additional access rules. (Argument: *filename*, usually .htaccess)
TypesConfig	The file the server should use to determine MIME types. (Argument: *filename*)
DefaultType	The default MIME type the server should use for a file if it is unable to determine otherwise. (Argument: *MIMEType*)
HostnameLookups	Indicates whether the server should look up the hostname of each client or only log its IP address. Note that turning this option on can significantly increase the server load. (Argument: On|Off)
ErrorLog	The location of the default error log. (Argument: *filename*)

Directive	Use
LogLevel	The amount of information the server should record to the log files. The default value, warn, provides the mid-range of information. (Argument: emerg|alert|crit|error|warn|notice|info|debug)
LogFormat	The format the server should use to record information in the log files. This directive's argument uses several placeholders and variables. See the documentation on the Apache Web site for explanations of each. (Argument: *logfileformat*)
CustomLog	The main log file and the information to be stored in the file. This directive takes two arguments: the first is the file in which to store the log information and the second is the type of information to store. If the second argument is *common*, all access info (including virtual host files) will be logged here. The second argument can also be a format string for the log file to follow. (Arguments: *filename common|logfileformat*)
Alias	Sets an alias for a particular directory. Clients can then use the alias as shorthand for the real directory. For example: Alias /icons/ "C:/Program Files/Apache Group/Apache2/icons" This enables clients to access the icons directory with http://*servername*/icons/. (Arguments: *fakename realname*)
ScriptAlias	Sets an alias for a particular directory and instructs the server to treat the contents of the real directory as scripts. (Arguments: *fakename realname*)
AddIcon	Adds icons to use next to file names when fancy directories are displayed. (Arguments: *iconfile filetypes*)
AddType	Adds or overrides a MIME type for the server. (Arguments: *MIMEType filetype(s)*)
Include	Allows additional configuration files to be included in the main configuration file and read at run time. (Argument: *filename*)

For more information on directives and their use, read the Apache manual online at http://httpd.apache.org/docs-2.0/mod/quickreference.html.

**20 Min.
To Go**

Scope Sections

Directives specified in the main section of the httpd.conf file apply to the entire server. If you need to specify options for particular files, directories, or virtual servers, you can use tags to delimit the directives.

For example, if you wanted to specify a handful of directives for a particular directory on the server, you would enclose the directives within <Directory> tags, as follows:

```
<Directory /var/www/html/specialdir>
   Directive Option(s)
   Directive Option(s)
   ...
</Directory>
```

Whenever the server accesses files in the /var/www/html/specialdir directory, the directives between the <Directory> tags apply.

You can use seven different tags to specify a scope for directives — limiting the effect of directives within certain constraints. Each tag set has an opening tag and a closing tag, much like tags in HTML. For example, the directory tags are <Directory> and </Directory> — any directory that matches the parameter in the opening tag will be affected by the directives between the tags. The tags are summarized in Table 5-2.

Table 5-2   *Apache Configuration Scoping Tags*

Tag	Use	Syntax
<Directory>	Specifies a directory for the directives to affect.	<Directory directory> </Directory>
<DirectoryMatch>	Specifies a regular expression to match against directories. The directives will affect matching directories.	<DirectoryMatch regex> </DirectoryMatch>
<Files>	Specifies a file name for the directives to affect.	<Files filename> </Files>
<FilesMatch>	Specifies a regular expression to match against files. The directives will affect matching files.	<FilesMatch regex> </FilesMatch>
<Location>	Specifies a URL for the directives to affect.	<Location scheme:url> </Location>
<LocationMatch>	Specifies a regular expression to match against URLs. The directives will affect matching URLs.	<LocationMatch regex> </LocationMatch>
<VirtualHost>	Specifies a specific virtual host for the directives to affect	<VirtualHost addr:port> </VirtualHost>

A *regular expression* (commonly abbreviated *regex*) consists of specially coded text to use in matching other text. The use of regular expressions varies from platform to platform, but Apache follows standard Linux regex format. A full explanation of regular expressions is beyond the scope of this book — for more information, a Linux programming reference is your best bet.

A few examples can help clarify the scoping tags.

If you wanted to add directives for any cgi-bin directory or its subdirectories, you could do so using the <LocationMatch> scope tag with the following:

```
<LocationMatch ".*/cgi-bin/.*">
```

The regular expression ".*/cgi-bin/.*" will match any location with /cgi-bin/ in it.

If you wanted special directives to apply to any file named special.file, the following <Files> scope tag would trap any access to any file named special.file:

```
<Files "special.file">
```

If you needed special directives to apply to a virtual server running on IP address 192.168.1.20, the following <VirtualHost> tag would be used:

```
<VirtualHost 192.168.1.20>
```

Conditional Directives

Apache's configuration file also supports the use of conditional statements for applying directives. Two tags are used for conditional directives: <IfDefine> and <IfModule>.

The <IfDefine> tag takes one argument, parameter-name. If the parameter was specified on the command line when Apache was started, the <IfDefine> evaluates as true and the directives within the <IfDefine> pair are processed. Suppose, for example, that you start Apache with the following command line:

```
apache -Dstrictsecurity
```

Then the directives in the following <IfDefine> would be processed:

```
<IfDefine strictsecurity>
```

The <IfModule> tag also takes one argument, module-name. If the module is currently compiled into Apache or loaded via a LoadModule directive, the directives within the <IfModule> tags are processed. For example, if you wanted some extra directives to be processed when the rewrite module (mod_rewrite) was loaded, you would use the following <IfModule> tag:

```
<IfModule mod_rewrite.c>
```

Notice that you must use the name of the module when it was compiled — for example, mod_rewrite.c instead of mod_rewrite.so.

Both `<IfDefine>` **and** `<IfModule>` **support the negation operator (!) in front of their arguments. If you use the operator, you can have the** `<IfDefine>` **directives processed if the parameter is not defined, and the** `<IfModule>` **directives processed if the specified module is not loaded. For example, to process directives if the** `mod_rewrite` **module is not loaded, you would use the following:**

```
<IfModule !mod_rewrite>
```

Access Directives

Apache has a very flexible access scheme, the details of which are covered in Session 6. However, it is important to cover the rudimentary Apache access scheme while reviewing the `httpd.conf` file.

**10 Min.
To Go**

Apache has two basic access schemes: *allow* and *deny*. The allow scheme provides access to anything specified. Deny denies access to anything specified.

Typically, you specify which rules you want to run first, allow or deny. In most cases, you want to allow everyone and make exceptions to deny or deny everyone and make exceptions to allow. The former, allow everyone, works well for a simple public server but doesn't create the most secure site, because you must think of every possible instance you want to deny. The latter, deny everyone, is a very restrictive security model, because you must think of every possible instance you want to allow.

The `Order` directive controls the basic model. The directive's syntax is as follows:

```
Order allow,deny   or   deny,allow
```

Individual `Allow` and `Deny` directives specify what to allow and what to deny. The syntax for the `Allow` and `Deny` directives is as follows, where `location` is one of those in the bulleted list:

```
Allow|Deny from location
```

- Fully Qualified Domain Name (FQDN)
For example, `apache.org`
- IP address
For example, `192.168.1.1`
- A partial IP address (the first few octets)
For example, `192.168`
- An IP address and subnet mask
For example, `192.168.1.0/255.255.255.0`
- The text `all`

As installed, the basic Apache security model is as follows:

```
Order allow,deny
Allow from all
```

Translated, this means process the Allow rules first (Allow from all), and then the Deny rules. Because Allow is specified as all, only those hosts that match subsequent Deny directives are actually denied access. For example, later in the httpd.conf file, you have the following directives:

```
<Files ~ "^\.ht">
    Order allow,deny
    Deny from all
</Files>
```

These directives prohibit anyone from viewing any files that begin with .ht (such files are typically Apache access or password files). In this case, the Order directive is not needed because of the earlier Order directive. However, it is good form to specify the order before every Deny or Allow directive to ensure that the Deny or Allow directive functions as you want it to.

Unless your Apache server is behind a firewall or is otherwise Internet-inaccessible, you probably want to lock it down with appropriate directives. If you access the server from only one subnet, specify that subnet as the only access point. An example of this scheme would be the following:

```
Order deny,allow
Deny from all
Allow from ip/netmask
```

Simply change the default permissions for the document root and any other areas you want open or restricted.

MIME Types

MIME (*M*ultipurpose *I*nternet *M*ail *E*xtensions) types provide a concise way of keeping track of files and the applications needed to view or edit them. Apache keeps track of most of its MIME types in the mime.types file, usually stored in the same directory as the httpd.conf file.

A few lines of this file resemble the following:

```
application/msword             doc
application/news-message-id
application/news-transmission
application/ocsp-request
application/ocsp-response
application/octet-stream       bin dms lha lzh exe class so dll
application/oda                oda
application/parityfec
application/pdf                pdf
```

The first column of this file defines the MIME type, and the second defines common file extensions for the type. For example, when a file is encountered with a .doc extension, it is identified as being an msword MIME type.

MIME is a somewhat antiquated acronym. The Apache documentation refers to this data by its common name today — Internet media types. This new name reflects the use of MIME for more than just mail.

Apache uses this data to indicate what should be done with specific files. For example, Session 2 covered the installation of PHP and added the following two lines to the Apache httpd.conf file:

```
AddType application/x-httpd-php .php .phtml
AddType application/x-httpd-php-source .phps
```

The first line tells Apache that files that have .php or .phtml extensions are PHP files and should be treated as such — namely, run through the PHP engine as per instructions in the PHP module. Likewise, when a nonbrowser-compliant MIME type is encountered (as in the earlier .doc example), Apache passes the MIME type definition on to the browser. If the browser knows how to handle the type, it does so (by loading MS Word, Adobe Acrobat, or another required helper).

You can use the AddType **directive to add additional types or change existing types. For example, you can add other extensions to the PHP MIME definition to cause the PHP engine to parse files with those extensions. However, each type you add is put through the PHP engine whether any PHP code is enclosed in the file or not. For that reason, you should add only those extensions you know will always contain at least some PHP code.**

Done!

REVIEW

In this session, you learned the basics about configuring Apache through its configuration file, httpd.conf. You learned about directives, what they are, how to use them, and the syntax for several key directives. You also learned how to apply directives conditionally, using scoped directive tags. You learned the basics of Apache security, more of which is covered in the next session. Lastly, you learned the basics of MIME types and how Apache handles them.

QUIZ YOURSELF

1. What is the main Apache configuration file and where is it stored? (See "Understanding the httpd.conf File.")
2. What does the ServerRoot directive specify? (See "Apache Directives.")
3. What does the Listen directive specify? (See "Apache Directives.")
4. How would you change the location of the default error log? (See "Apache Directives.")
5. What is the difference between the Directory and DirectoryMatch directive tags? (See "Scope Sections.")
6. How do you pass a parameter to Apache to trigger an <IfDefine> directive? (See "Conditional Directives.")
7. What does the directive "Order deny,allow" mean? (See "Access Directives.")
8. What is the common description of MIME? (See "MIME Types.")

Apache Security Concerns

Session Checklist

✔ Understanding how Web servers pose a security risk

✔ Reviewing basic Apache security

✔ Securing an entire Web site

✔ Securing individual directories on a Web site

✔ Securing scripts and performing a basic security audit

**30 Min.
To Go**

Apache can be a very secure Web server, because it is updated frequently and known security vulnerabilities are quickly fixed. However, much of the responsibility for running a secure site rests with the system administrator — the configuration of Apache and the machine it runs on play an integral part in determining how secure Apache is. This session outlines various security concerns and methods to ensure that Apache stays as secure as possible.

Security is less of a concern if your server is behind a robust firewall or not accessible outside of a local network. However, an unsecured server is asking for trouble on any network or machine. Read through this session carefully and make the changes required to secure your copy of Apache.

The Web — A Great Security Hole

In its infancy, the Web didn't pose much of a security threat because its use was very shallow. Only text and some trivial graphic content were available, and the browsers were quite simple. However, as the Web has matured, the security risks have multiplied — each additional type of content, server version, and browser presents new risks to servers and clients alike.

For example, recent viruses have attacked Microsoft's Web server (IIS) and, using advanced scripts, forced those servers to do the virus' bidding. Similarly, some CGI scripts can be used to exploit operating system vulnerabilities. Experienced hackers can treat your copy of Apache like an open door to your system and, perhaps, your network.

Don't be too dismayed by this news, just remain cautious. The major reason the Web poses such a security risk is the sheer complexity of content and the methods of delivering it. If you abide by the following rules, you can almost ensure that your site and network remain secure:

- **Keep your copies of the OS and Apache up-to-date**. Most operating systems have useful auto-update features — Windows has the Windows Update service, Red Hat Linux has the Red Hat Network. An operating system and Web server that are kept up-to-date are inherently more secure.

- **Add only one feature to your site at a time, securing each new feature before adding another**. New Web developers and system administrators are quick to add multiple features, lights, buzzers, and whistles to their site. However, each new feature has the potential of adding another security vulnerability. It serves you well to ensure that the features you have are nailed down before adding more.

- **Add only features you really need — and survey each carefully before adding**. Tons of scripts, programs, server add-ons, and so on are available for you to add features to your Web server. However, each has the potential of adding more security holes. Make sure the features or programs you add come from a reliable source that updates the software frequently. Read reviews and newsgroup messages about the software before implementing it. As they say, an ounce of prevention is worth a pound of cure.

The next few sections show you how to secure Apache from a variety of threats.

A Review of Apache Security

The base level of Apache's security structure was covered in the last session, "Configuring Apache." However, a short review is in order here:

- Apache security works on a system of allow and deny.
- You can decide which rules, allow or deny, are processed first — with the Order directive.
- You can apply security to the entire site, specific files and directories, or files and directories that match regular expressions.
- If you set security for a particular directory, that directory's subdirectories inherit the same security.
- You can control who receives access or is denied access by hostname, IP address, or IP range.

By default, Apache implements the following security directives to the entire site:

```
Order allow,deny
Allow from all
```

This grants all clients access to the entire site. Notice a few exceptions in the configuration file (httpd.conf), including the following:

- All files that begin with .ht are denied to everyone. This protects .htaccess and .htpasswd files that are used to control access on a directory basis. (For more information on .htaccess files, see the section "Securing Directories with .htaccess," later in this session.)
- Server status and configuration reports are set to deny from all, except clients within your domain. (The status and configuration report sections are commented out; you must uncomment the lines and enter your domain in the directives to enable.)
- Proxy server directives are also set to deny from all, except clients within your domain. (This section is also commented out; you must uncomment the section and enter your domain in the directives to enable.)

Again, one very important way you can help ensure the security of your Web site is by keeping current with the most current stable Apache releases. Newer releases will fix known vulnerabilities that can be exploited by hackers.

Securing the Entire Site

Securing the entire site managed by Apache is straightforward and requires changing only two lines of the httpd.conf file. Simply find every occurrence of these lines:

```
Order allow,deny
Allow from all
```

Change them to the following (where *ip/netmask* is an IP address and netmask that defines the subnet of your network):

```
Order deny,allow
Deny from all
Allow from ip/netmask
```

This limits access to clients within your network. If you need to restrict access further, use a different netmask to mask just the clients whom you want to have access, or specify each individual IP address that should have access:

```
Allow from IPaddr1 IPaddr2 IPaddr3 ...
```

Separate each host IP or hostname with a space.

You can also use any of the techniques described in the directory sections that follow on the entire site by applying the information to the DocumentRoot Order, Allow, and Deny directives.

**20 Min.
To Go**

Securing Individual Directories

You sometimes want to deny access to individual directories. You have two ways to do this: specify the directories in the httpd.conf file with <Directory> directives or use .htaccess files.

Securing Directories with <Directory>

Using <Directory> directive tags in the httpd.conf file, you can specify special directives for specific directories on the server. For example, consider the following httpd.conf code snippet:

```
<Directory "/var/www/html/specialfiles">
  Order deny,allow
  Deny from all
  Allow from management.com
</Directory>
```

The preceding code sets the security for the specialfiles directory to deny from all, except clients from management.com. (For more information on Order, Allow, and Deny, refer to Session 5.)

Securing Directories with .htaccess

Another way to secure specific directories is by placing a special file in the directory. This file, named .htaccess, contains access directives that apply to the directory in which the file is stored. However, such override access must first be granted in the httpd.conf file.

Security via .htaccess **should be used only when you do not have access to the** httpd.conf **file. Most, if not all, server security should be taken care of in the main configuration file. Users without admin access are prime candidates for using** .htaccess **files because their limited access won't allow them to edit the main Apache configuration file. The system administrator needs to make the changes outlined below to allow overrides, but then normal users can secure their directories with appropriate** .htaccess **files.**

In the httpd.conf file, several lines resemble the following:

```
AllowOverride None
```

These lines appear in various directory containers (directive tags). Those respective directories do not allow their security settings to be overridden. To allow the override, change the None to one or more of the following options:

- AuthConfig — allows authorization directives to be overridden
- FileInfo — allows document type directives to be overridden
- Indexes — allows directory indexing directives to be overridden
- Limit — allows control access directives to be overridden

- Options — allows directory option directives to be overridden
- All — allows all directives to be overridden

In this case, you only need Limit overrides; specifying All would be overkill. In the httpd.conf file, change the AllowOverride directive for the DocumentRoot to the following:

```
AllowOverride Limit
```

Now, suppose that the following .htaccess file were stored in the /var/www/html/specialfiles directory:

```
Order deny,allow
Deny from all
Allow from 192.168.1.25
```

Once this file is in place, only clients from IP 192.168.1.25 can access the directory. Again, you can use any combination of the Order, Allow, and Deny directives and their respective options to allow or deny access, as required.

Although you can allow overrides from the DocumentRoot, **doing so is unwise. It is better practice to keep the** DocumentRoot **security intact and specify additional security for other directories in additional** <Directory> **sections. For example, using the** specialfiles **example, leave the** DocumentRoot **override alone and add the following lines to** httpd.conf **to allow only the** specialfiles **directory** Limit **to be overridden:**

```
<Directory "/var/www/html/specialfiles">
   AllowOverride Limit
</Directory>
```

Securing Directories with Authentication Control

Limiting access by IP or hostname isn't always practical. For example, suppose your sales force needs access to /var/www/html/sales, but you want to keep everyone else out. You don't want to add every salesperson's IP address to an Allow directive and also account for traveling or otherwise changing IPs or hostnames. Instead, what if you could assign to all your salespeople a username and password that they had to enter each time they accessed the sales directory? Using Apache authentication, this is quite easy.

Apache authentication makes use of special files, usually named .htpasswd. These files contain encoded usernames and passwords that are matched against user input when a protected directory is accessed. To create the .htpasswd file, you need to use the htpasswd program (htpasswd.exe on Windows). This program is usually stored where the Apache binary is stored.

The syntax for using this program is as follows:

```
htpasswd [-c] passwordfile username
```

The -c parameter must be used to create the *passwordfile* before you can add usernames to it. (You can add a username at the same time you create the file.)

For example, suppose you want to create a new password file for the sales force. You could use the following command to create a new .htpasswd file:

```
htpasswd -c /var/www/html/sales/.htpasswd
```

Then you would use the htpasswd program to add as many users as you need:

```
htpasswd /var/www/html/sales/.htpasswd username
```

The command prompts you to enter and confirm a password for each user. If you'd rather, you can specify the –b parameter and add the password to the command line, as in the following example:

```
htpasswd -b /var/www/html/sales/.htpasswd username password
```

You can use any file name for your password file. However, because files that begin with .ht are explicitly protected by the Apache server's configuration, .htpasswd makes a good choice.

Now that you have the password file, you need an appropriate section in the httpd.conf file to use it. In the httpd.conf file, add the following <Directory> section:

```
<Directory "/var/www/html/sales">
   AuthName "Sales Force"
   AuthType Basic
   Require valid-user
   AuthUserFile /var/www/html/sales/.htpasswd
</Directory>
```

These same directives, sans the <Directory> container, can also be used in a .htaccess file, which is placed in the directory to be protected. Note that Auth overrides need to be allowed in the directory (via appropriate AllowOverride directives in the httpd.conf file) in order for the .htaccess file to actually work.

This section uses the following directives:

- AuthName — This directive passes the specified text to the client. The text appears in the Authentication dialog box so the user knows what authorization information is required (in this case Sales Force authorization). If this same AuthName is used in another area of the Web site, the client can try the same previously used credentials before prompting the user.

- AuthType — This sets the authorization scheme to either Basic or Digest.

- Require — This directive tells the server what type of requirements the user must meet to gain access to the resource. In this case, the user's credentials must validate against the authentication file (.htpasswd) — in other words, the user must be a valid user.

- AuthUserFile — This directive specifies the path and filename of the authentication file to match a user's credentials against. You must give the full path to the file using the system's regular file system, not the Apache DocumentRoot. For example, specifying `specialfiles/.htaccess` does not work; nor does `./.htaccess`.

With these directives in place, you can restart the server and test your security. When you access the sales directory, a dialog box prompts you for your Sales Force credentials, as shown in Figure 6-1.

Figure 6-1 *The credentials dialog box supplied by HTTP authentication*

If the credentials supplied match those in the password file, the user is granted access. If the credentials don't match, an Authorization Required page is generated by the server and sent to the client, as shown in Figure 6-2.

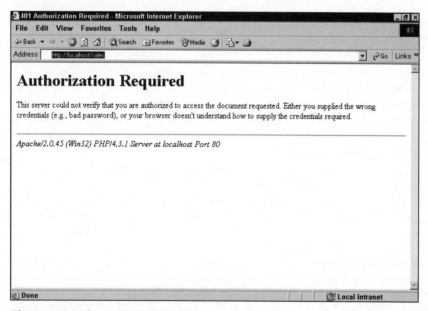

Figure 6-2 *The Authorization Required page informs the user that the credentials entered cannot be authenticated.*

Securing Script Access

Almost every system administrator who runs a Web server accessible to the public has seen log entries like the following:

```
<IPAddr> - - [24/Apr/2003:16:22:22 -0500] "GET /cgi-
bin/formmail.pl?email=<emailaddr>&subject=<domain>/cgi-
bin/formmail.pl&message=rockstar&recipient=<emailaddr> HTTP/1.0" 404 289
"-" "Mozilla/4.0 (compatible; MSIE 6.0; Windows NT 5.1)"
```

The `<IPAddr>`, `<emailaddr>`, **and** `<domain>` **tags have been inserted in the sample log entry to protect the innocent and the guilty.**

This log entry documents an attempt to find an unsecured copy of a form mail script. If this request were successful, the location of the script would be mailed back to the hacker so he or she could use it to send spam or malicious e-mail.

Scripts such as `formmail.pl` were once plentiful on the Internet. Web administrators would use these scripts to give visitors to their site the capability to send e-mail from a Web form. However, hackers soon realized that the scripts could enable open e-mail gateway support, enabling the hacker to send anonymous e-mail through the script. This would allow hackers to masquerade as other users, use your server for spamming, and more. Today, scripts such as `formmail.pl` are infamous for the security risks they present.

Many scripts with large security vulnerabilities still exist, and many of these scripts are used without adequate caution by Web developers. You should take a few precautions to ensure that you are not victimized by such scripts:

- **Don't implement any script you are unsure about.** Check out every script you put into place for vulnerabilities and security holes — especially if the script(s) access the raw file system.

- **Ensure that no scripts run as the** `root` **or Administrator user.** If a security issue exists with a script, it would be disastrous to allow someone exploiting that issue access to the administrator account!

- **Don't allow users of your Web server to implement any script without your express permission (and check it yourself).** Many scripts are available on the Internet and can be installed by simply copying them to the appropriate `cgi-bin` directory. However, most of the scripts that are freely available were not written with strict security in mind. Be sure to check for any security holes before allowing users to implement their own scripts.

- **Remove any unneeded script directories from the file system and the Apache configuration file.** Most administrators recommend removing the `ScriptAlias` `cgi-bin` from the Apache configuration file and naming your script directories something other than `cgi-bin`, or at least not placing them so prominently at the root of every domain.

- **Ensure that dangerous scripts have restricted access.** Using the methods described earlier in this session, protect script use by unwanted users by restricting access to the directories or to individual files.

No set of rules can render a Web server's scripts hazard-free, but the guidelines outlined here are a very good start.

Many Internet service providers (ISPs) choose to allow their users to run third-party scripts. If you run a service for other users and choose to let them run third-party scripts, ensure that each user's account can do limited damage and that a user cannot access the root **or Administrator account.**

Performing a Security Audit

A full security audit is beyond the scope of this book. If you want to give your server the full treatment, you can find several good articles on the subject, complete with step-by-step instructions and auditing tools.

When looking for security advice, trust the experts. Look for helpful tips from folks such as THAWTE (www.thawte.com**), CERT (**www.cert.org**), and third-party sites such as SecuritySpace (**www.securityspace.com**).**

You should perform some key tasks on a regular basis to ensure the security of your Web server:

- Access your server from outside its home network. Be sure to try to access areas that should be inaccessible to the Internet at large.
- Review the server logs. If you use scripts that could be a security risk, parse the logs for accesses of the scripts and ensure that logged users have the proper access and that the scripts aren't being used maliciously.
- Review the main Apache configuration file, httpd.conf. Research and then remove or comment out any section you do not understand or any section that is no longer needed.
- Review the file structure of your Web site. Remove any unused directories, resist storing non-Web-related files in the Web structure, and keep the clutter to a minimum.
- Generate a list of executable files within the Web file structure (for example, files with .pl, .cgi, and .php extensions). Review the list and quarantine or remove any suspicious files.
- Ensure that the underlying operating system file system and the Web file structure do not overlap any more than necessary. For example, never place and access a document, password file, or executable outside of the Web file structure. Doing so opens an exploitable hole in the underlying operating system files. One exception might be PHP include scripts or other files that you want to be accessed only by PHP — place such files in a directory protected from outside users but accessible to the user under whom the PHP process runs.

Done!

REVIEW

In this session, you learned more about Apache security and how to provide basic security for your Web server and underlying network. You started with a review of the Web's vulnerabilities and Apache's basic security structure. You then learned how to secure the entire site, as well as individual directories, by limiting access in a variety of ways. Lastly, you examined how to limit script access and how to perform a basic security audit.

QUIZ YOURSELF

1. Why is it important to keep Apache up-to-date? (See "The Web — A Great Security Hole" and "A Review of Apache Security.")

2. How would you restrict the entire site to access from a single IP, a range of IPs, and a list of IPs? (See "Securing the Entire Site.")

3. What hostnames would the directive `Allow from management.com` allow access to? (See "Securing Directories with <Directory>.")

4. When is the only time you should use .htaccess files? (See "Securing Directories with .htaccess.")

5. What directive is necessary to allow .htaccess to modify security? (See "Securing Directories with .htaccess.")

6. What command creates password authentication files, and what are its parameters? (See "Securing Directories with Authentication Control.")

7. Why is the `formmail.pl` script dangerous? (See "Securing Script Access.")

8. What are some sites that provide good security advice? (See "Performing a Security Audit.")

The Basics of MySQL

Session Checklist

✔ Understanding more about MySQL

✔ Examining the MySQL configuration options

✔ Learning about database structure

✔ Using the MySQL monitor

**30 Min.
To Go**

Database applications are among the most complex applications you can use. However, if you use them well, they are also the most powerful. MySQL strives to be easy to use without sacrificing any of its innate power and offers several features and interfaces to help you use it effectively. This session provides an introduction to using MySQL, its configuration, and the MySQL monitor.

Understanding MySQL

MySQL comes from a long line of Structured Query Language (SQL — pronounced "sequel") databases. SQL was developed as a standard and structured way of querying databases. Dating back to the mid-'70s, SQL has become the standard database query language and is used (at least as an option) in every modern database.

According to its founders, MySQL was originally created to provide economical access to high-quality software. Embracing the open source model, MySQL AB (the company behind MySQL) has delivered on its promise, creating a modular, powerful, and reliable database. Boasting some 4 million active installations worldwide, MySQL is the most popular open source database.

MySQL makes a great partner for Apache and PHP for providing Web-accessible data.

What's New in MySQL 4.0?

MySQL 4.0 brings powerful new features to the popular database server. Among the most important additions are the following:

- The InnoDB storage engine. InnoDB, modeled after Oracle, provides row-level locking, multiple isolation levels, automatic recovery, and full ACID (Atomicity, Consistency, Isolation, and Durability) guarantees.
- Improvements in the query optimizer to provide faster sorting with large queries
- More options have been moved to configuration files. Instead of having to be compiled in, now you only have to restart the engine rather than perform a full compile to tweak certain settings.
- Support for multiple-table deletes
- Enhancement of the replication system to alleviate some of the load on master and slave servers

In addition, several "under the hood" improvements generally make MySQL more stable and powerful.

Full coverage of the InnoDB storage engine is beyond the scope of this book. However, more information can be found in the *MySQL Bible*, by Steve Suehring (Wiley Publishing), or on the MySQL Web site (www.mysql.com).

Configuring MySQL

As installed, MySQL should be ready to go. However, the following section reviews its configuration for later use.

This session assumes that you installed MySQL from the MySQL AB-supplied RPMs (server and client) or from the Windows binary installer. If you installed MySQL using a different method, you may need to search for some of the files described in this session, and some of the default configuration options on your system may differ from those presented here.

MySQL Linux Configuration

MySQL ships with several preconfigured configuration file templates. These files represent different MySQL server configurations, indicating the amount of resources it consumes when running. Table 7-1 summarizes the four different templates, usually installed to the directory /usr/share/mysql.

Table 7-1 *MySQL Configuration Files*

File	Usage
my-huge.cnf	Systems with 1–2GB of memory, running mainly MySQL
my-large.cnf	Systems with 512MB of memory, running mainly MySQL
my-medium.cnf	Systems with 32–64MB of memory, running mainly MySQL, or systems up to 128M of memory running MySQL with other programs
my-small.cnf	Systems with less than 64MB of memory, on which MySQL is run sparingly or the server needs to consume as few resources as possible

Most users want to use the medium configuration, but you need to decide which configuration suits your needs. Copy the appropriate configuration file to the MySQL data directory, usually /var/lib/mysql, and name it my.cnf.

> **The exact path to the MySQL data directory is usually contained in the comments at the beginning of each configuration file template.**

Configuring the server using the appropriate template should be as much configuration as needed, assuming that your needs are relatively meager — that is, you are not setting up a replication server or don't need to tweak the configuration to squeeze out more performance for a specialized application. After you have deployed a MySQL application, it may be worth reading through the my.cnf file and tweaking some of the settings. Visit the MySQL Web site (www.mysql.com) for information on each parameter — its function and suggested settings — before you change the file.

> **Always make a backup of the current configuration file before you change it, in case you need to revert to its settings.**

Windows MySQL Configuration

Windows versions of MySQL ship with several different binaries, as summarized in Table 7-2.

Table 7-2 *Binaries Shipped with Windows Versions of MySQL*

Binary	Use
mysqld	General use. Includes full debugging and automatic memory allocation checking, symbolic links, InnoDB, and BDB tables.
mysqld-opt	Optimized binary with InnoDB enabled.

Continued

Table 7-2   *Continued*

Binary	Use
mysqld-nt	Optimized binary for Windows NT/2000/XP. Includes named pipes.
mysqld-max	Optimized binary with support for symbolic links, InnoDB, and BerkeleyDB tables.
mysqld-max-nt	Similar to mysqld-max, but includes support for named pipes.

Your needs dictate which version of the MySQL binary you run. If you are using Windows NT, 2000, or XP, you should run one of the NT-optimized binaries. The first time you run WinMySQLAdmin (as discussed in Session 3) it configures the MySQL configuration file (my.ini) for you. If you need to edit the configuration file, you can also use WinMySQLAdmin, as shown in Figure 7-1.

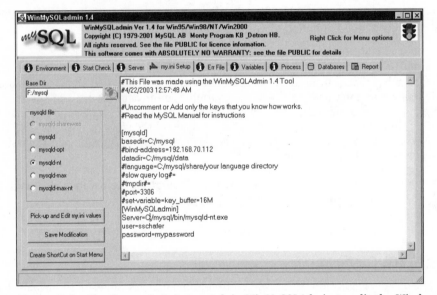

Figure 7-1 *Use the* my.ini Setup *tab in WinMySQLAdmin to edit the Windows MySQL configuration file.*

 You can find WinMySQLAdmin in the MySQL installation directory's bin subdirectory; it's usually also on the Start menu under Startup. If it is already running, a stoplight appears in the system tray — click the light and choose Show me to display the graphical interface.

If, for some reason, the WinMySQLAdmin program doesn't create the configuration file for you, copy the appropriate configuration template (my-small, my-medium, my-large, or my-huge) from the MySQL installation directory to your Windows or WINNT directory and name the file my.ini. You can then use WinMySQLAdmin to edit the file, if necessary.

*20 Min.
To Go*

Building Blocks of Databases

You should understand the basics of databases before you begin using MySQL. This section describes the basic structure of databases and related terms.

A database is a collection of data. This data can be subdivided into discrete pieces, and you need to understand each of these pieces and how it fits into the whole. This discussion is modeled around a customer orders database, containing customer contact information, customer orders, customer invoices, and customer payments.

This example does not attempt to conform to "good" database design — it is intended to be instructional only. Good database design is discussed in Session 12.

Tables

A database table is a collection of related data. For example, in our customer orders database, each of these distinct entities is a separate table:

- Customer contact information
- Customer orders
- Customer invoices
- Customer payments

This database component is called a table because it is conceptually composed of rows and columns, just like a table of data. For example, take a closer look at one of the tables, customer contact information. You would store the following customer information in this table:

- Name
- Shipping address
- Phone number

An example of actual data follows:

- Joe Public
- 123 Main Street, Somewhere, U.S.
- 555-555-1234

However, you would likely have more than one customer. Another customer's data might resemble the following:

- Jane Doe
- 456 North Ave, Somewhere, U.S.
- 555-555-5678

Putting these two customers and the name of the data together in a conceptual container gives you something similar to what is shown in Table 7-3.

Table 7-3 *Conceptual Data Container*

Name	Address	Phone Number
Joe Public	123 Main Street, Somewhere, U.S.	555-555-1234
Jane Doe	456 North Ave, Somewhere, U.S.	555-555-5678

Records (Row)

A *record* is a group of data about an individual entity, such as a customer. The term *record* is generic in data processing, although some writers (including those who wrote the MySQL documentation) prefer the word *row* when the record is part of a relational database table. For example, looking at Table 7-3, each row constitutes a record. Joe Public's record consists of the data shown in Table 7-4.

Table 7-4 *Joe Public's Data (Record)*

Name	Address	Phone Number
Joe Public	123 Main Street, Somewhere, U.S.	555-555-1234

Fields

Database records are comprised of individual pieces of data known as *fields*. The original lists of data stored in the sample table — name, address, and phone number — are fields. The easiest way to think of a field is to picture a paper form — each blank on the form would be a field (first name, middle initial, last name, street address, city, state, zip code, phone number, and so on). Referring to the conceptual container shown in Table 7-1, you can see that the fields are defined in distinct columns. MySQL also calls its fields *columns*.

In a real database, you would want to subdivide the name into separate fields for first name and last name and subdivide the address into at least street, city, and zip code. Reasons for this include easier lookup, sorting, and processing of stored data, which becomes quite apparent as you continue to work with MySQL.

Putting It All Back Together

Now that database, table, record, and field have all been defined, you can put them back together to complete the picture, as shown in Figure 7-2.

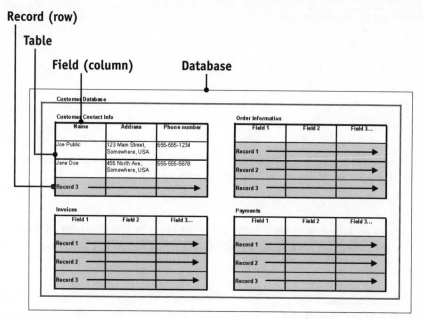

Figure 7-2 *The complete database picture*

This visual representation illustrates how a database is a collection of tables, which contain several records, made up of several fields.

Of course, an actual database would contain more fields to tie the tables together. For example, each customer would have a customer number. The customer numbers would be used to identify their records in the other tables. For example, each invoice record would also have a customer number field corresponding to the customer to whom that invoice was sent. This componentization and effort not to store data in more than one place (not storing the customer's name, address, and so on in the invoice table) is part of good database design.

Running the MySQL Server

10 Min. To Go

Before you proceed with the rest of this session, you need to ensure that the MySQL server is running:

- Windows users should click the WinMySQLAdmin icon and choose Show me to bring up the graphical interface. If the stoplight is green, the server is running.

  Note: If WinMySQLAdmin is not running, start it from the Start menu (All Programs ⇨ Startup) or by double-clicking it in Windows Explorer.

  If the MySQL server is not running, right-click anywhere on the WinMySQLAdmin interface and choose Win NT ⇨ Start the Service. (Notice that this option is a bit different if you are running on Windows 95, 98, or ME.)

- Linux users should use ps to determine if the server is running. Use the following command:

  ```
  ps -A | grep "mysqld"
  ```

If the server is running, the ps command outputs lines similar to the following:

```
1114 tty1    00:00:00 mysqld_safe
1130 tty1    00:00:00 mysqld
```

If you need to start the server, use the following command:

```
mysqld_safe --user=mysql &
```

Depending on your installation, you may need to specify the location of the mysql_safe script, as shown in the following example:

```
/usr/local/mysql/bin/mysqld_safe
```

If you installed from MySQL AB-supplied RPMs or the Windows binary installer, the server should automatically start when you boot your machine.

Using the MySQL Monitor

Session 3 introduced the MySQL monitor. The monitor provides a command-line-like interface for MySQL.

Before you use the monitor on Linux, you should set the root password for MySQL (if you haven't already). To set the password, use the mysqladmin command by issuing the following at a shell prompt (where <password> is the password you want to use for the root user):

```
<path>/mysqladmin -u root password <password>
```

You may need to supply the full path to the mysqladmin command. After you have set the password, you can start the monitor with the following command on Linux:

```
mysql -p
```

On Windows, omit the -p parameter.

More about MySQL security is covered in Session 8.

The monitor prompts you for the password, if necessary, and then displays something similar to the following:

```
Welcome to the MySQL monitor.  Commands end with ; or \g.
Your MySQL connection id is 4 to server version: 4.0.12

Type 'help;' or '\h' for help. Type '\c' to clear the buffer.

mysql>
```

The `mysql>` is the monitor prompt. At this prompt, you enter commands to the database server. Commands follow a particular syntax and must end with a semicolon (`;`).

To work with a particular database, you would first need to tell MySQL which database to use. For example, MySQL installs with a database named `test`. To use this database, you issue the following command:

```
use test;
```

The monitor replies with the following:

```
Database changed
```

From here, you can create tables, query data, update data, and even remove entire tables or the database.

 MySQL commands are covered in-depth in the next session.

The `test` database does not include any tables. You can determine this by issuing the following command:

```
show tables;
```

If the database contains tables, the monitor displays a list of all the tables contained in the database. In this case, the monitor responds with the following:

```
Empty set (0.00 sec)
```

Create a database and a table for your customer contact information, as outlined earlier in this session. Follow these steps to create the database and table:

1. Type the command `create database customer_orders;` and press Enter. The monitor should respond with Query OK, 1 row affected (0.00 sec).

2. You must select the new database before working with it, so type use `customer_orders;` and press Enter. You should get the Database changed acknowledgment.

3. To add a table, you need to define the various fields within the table in a fairly strict syntax. Type the following, on separate lines as listed, and press Enter after the semi-colon (and notice that the monitor prefixes the second and subsequent lines with `->` until you finish the command):

    ```
    CREATE TABLE customers (
      id int(11) NOT NULL AUTO_INCREMENT,
      name varchar(30),
      address varchar(100),
      phone char(12),
      PRIMARY KEY (id)
    );
    ```

    The monitor should respond with Query OK, 0 rows affected (0.00 sec).

MySQL data types are covered in the next session.

4. Now use the show tables; command. The monitor should show the customers table, as shown in the following listing:

```
+---------------------------+
| Tables_in_customer_orders |
+---------------------------+
| customers                 |
+---------------------------+
1 row in set (0.00 sec)
```

5. To see more information on a specific table, use the describe command. For example, type the command describe customers;. The monitor responds with the structure of the customers table:

```
+---------+--------------+------+-----+---------+----------------+
| Field   | Type         | Null | Key | Default | Extra          |
+---------+--------------+------+-----+---------+----------------+
| id      | int(11)      |      | PRI | NULL    | auto_increment |
| name    | varchar(30)  | YES  |     | NULL    |                |
| address | varchar(100) | YES  |     | NULL    |                |
| phone   | varchar(12)  | YES  |     | NULL    |                |
+---------+--------------+------+-----+---------+----------------+
4 rows in set (0.00 sec)
```

6. Exit the monitor by using the quit; command.

Done!

REVIEW

In this session, you learned a bit more about MySQL, including what key features have been added in version 4.0. You then reviewed the MySQL configuration files and different server levels. Basic database structure and using the MySQL monitor to create your first database and table were also covered.

QUIZ YOURSELF

1. What does the acronym ACID stand for? (See "What's New in MySQL 4.0?")

2. If you are running MySQL on Linux with 512M of RAM, which server configuration template (small, medium, large, or huge) should you use? (See " MySQL Linux Configuration.")

3. What binary should you run on a Windows 2000 server? (See "Windows MySQL Configuration.")

4. Why are database tables called *tables*? (See "Tables.")

5. How can you tell if the MySQL server is running? (See "Running the MySQL Server.")

6. What MySQL monitor command shows you the structure of a table? (See "Using the MySQL Monitor.")

MySQL Security

Session Checklist

✔ Setting the root and administrator password

✔ Introduction to the MySQL privileges system

✔ Understanding the role of tables in the `mysql` database

✔ Using the GRANT command

✔ Using the REVOKE command

**30 Min.
To Go**

As with any server application, it pays to secure MySQL. Luckily, MySQL has fairly robust security and a flexible privileges system. As installed, an individual can gain access to the MySQL server only through anonymous access from the server console or through the root account — which initially has no password. You can quickly set a password for the root user and add additional users with only the privileges you want them to have. This session walks you through the MySQL privileges system, including setting up new users.

Setting the Root Password

Initially, MySQL has a root (administrator) account, with no password set for the account. Using the `mysqladmin` command at a server console, set the root password as follows:

```
mysqladmin -u root password <password>
```

Change *<password>* to the password you want for the root account. After running this command, you can log into the MySQL server as the root user only with the password you specified.

If the mysqladmin **command is not in the system path, you need to specify the full path to the command, as shown in the following example:**

```
/usr/local/mysql/bin/mysqladmin
```

You can also set other user passwords with the mysqladmin command. Simply replace root with the user for whom you want to set the password. Notice that if the user doesn't exist, the appropriate entries are added to the MySQL privileges tables, but no rights to any databases are granted. (Granting rights is covered in the section "Setting and Changing User Privileges," later in this session.)

An Overview of the MySQL Privileges System

MySQL uses two methods for assigning privileges to control access to the SQL server and the data stored there.

The first method of privilege control is specifying who has access to connect to the server. If you don't have access, you cannot connect, do any querying, change data, and so on. MySQL tracks users by the following information:

- The hostname of the system from which the user is connecting
- The username the user specifies
- The password the user specifies

All of this information must match information stored in the MySQL privileges tables or the user is not allowed to connect. For example, suppose I tried to connect to my MySQL server from a remote computer. If I'm using the MySQL monitor to connect to a server at IP address 192.168.1.5, I'd use a command line similar to the following:

```
mysql -p -h 192.168.1.5 -u sschafer
```

The monitor would ask me for my password (because I didn't supply it with the -p parameter) and then try to connect to the MySQL server. If my username or host hasn't been added to the privileges database on the MySQL server, or if my password doesn't match the data in the server's privileges database, I am denied access with a message similar to the following (when connecting from a machine with an IP address of 192.168.1.10):

```
ERROR 1045: Access denied for user: 'sschafer@192.168.1.10' (Using
password: YES)
```

Notice that the error isn't specific — it doesn't tell me which piece of authentication failed. This deters hackers from realizing what pieces of the authentication puzzle they might have solved. I can ensure that I have the privileges to attach to the database by running the correct sequence of parameters through mysqladmin on the server:

```
mysqladmin -u sschafer@192.168.1.10 password <password>
```

This would ensure that I had a user record, host record, and correct password to connect to the MySQL server. If you want a user to be able to log in on the same machine that is running the MySQL server, use localhost as the hostname.

To test connections to your MySQL server, install a basic copy of MySQL on another machine or copy the `mysql` **program (the MySQL monitor) to another machine. Notice that, in the latter case, the dependencies for running** `mysql` **must be met on the other machine or the program cannot run.**

Notice that MySQL stores "%" in the Host column if you don't specify a hostname when creating a privileges record for a user. This enables the user to connect from any host. If you want to restrict the user to a particular host, be sure to specify a hostname when creating the privileges record for that user.

The MySQL Privileges Database

**20 Min.
To Go**

MySQL maintains a special database, aptly named `mysql`, where it stores administrative information such as authorized users, authorized hosts, and privileges for databases, tables, and columns.

You can view the names of these databases by running the MySQL monitor (as an administrator) and issuing the following commands:

```
USE mysql;
SHOW TABLES;
```

The MySQL monitor responds by listing the tables in the `mysql` database:

```
+-----------------+
| Tables_in_mysql |
+-----------------+
| columns_priv    |
| db              |
| func            |
| host            |
| tables_priv     |
| user            |
+-----------------+
6 rows in set (0.00 sec)
```

These tables each store privilege data — each table stores data specifically for the component for which it is named. However, don't get too caught up in the functionality of these tables and the specific data they contain — all of that is automated with a few commands. You should never edit these tables by hand; let MySQL maintain them for you.

If you are curious about the structure and data stored in these tables, run a `describe <tablename>` **command for each.**

Setting and Changing User Privileges

Besides controlling who has access to the database server, MySQL also controls what information, commands, and procedures users have access to.

Table 8-1 lists the data privileges that users can be granted.

Table 8-1 *User Privileges*

Privilege	Rights
ALL	Grants all of the privileges
ALTER	The right to modify meta data, altering table structure
CREATE	The right to create databases and tables
CREATE TEMPORARY TABLES	The right to use the CREATE TEMPORARY TABLE command
DELETE	The right to delete data (records)
DROP	The right to delete tables and databases
FILE	The right to read and write files (dump data to and from MySQL)
GRANT	The right to GRANT privileges to other users (only those privileges held by the user can be granted to others)
INDEX	The right to add or delete indexes
INSERT	The right to add data (records)
LOCK TABLES	The right to lock tables accessible by the SELECT command
SELECT	The right to use SELECT on tables
SHOW DATABASES	The right to list all databases with the SHOW DATABASES command
UPDATE	The right to use the UPDATE command and thereby modify data

The GRANT and REVOKE commands, covered in the next two sections, control these privileges.

The GRANT Command

User data privileges are given to users with the MySQL GRANT command. This command has the following syntax:

```
GRANT [privileges] ON [database].[table] TO [username][@host];
```

You can use the asterisk character as a wildcard to signify all databases or all tables. For example, specifying customerorders.* **would specify all tables within the** customerorders **database.**

For example, to grant only SELECT rights to user sschafer on all tables in the customerorders database, you would use the following command:

```
GRANT SELECT ON customerorders.* TO sschafer@localhost;
```

To grant several privileges within one command, list all the privileges separated by commas. For example, to add SELECT and INSERT rights, you would use the following command:

```
GRANT SELECT, INSERT ON customerorders.* TO sschafer@localhost;
```

If you want a user to be able to log in from a foreign host (a computer other than the one running MySQL), specify the fully qualified domain name or IP address of that host instead of localhost. **If you don't specify a hostname, MySQL places the wildcard character (%) in the host column — which enables the user to log in from any host.**

Notice that this command granted the SELECT and INSERT right to *all* tables in the customerorders database. If you wanted to restrict the rights to particular tables, you would use a command similar to the following:

```
GRANT SELECT, INSERT ON customerorders.customerdata,
customerorders.invoices TO sschafer@localhost;
```

Notice how each table is explicitly listed, separated by commas.

After using GRANT to add users and/or privileges, you need to tell MySQL to reload the permissions table into memory. Otherwise, subsequent logins are compared against old grant data. To reload the permissions table, use the following command:

```
FLUSH PRIVILEGES;
```

Unless specific privileges have been granted to a user, that user cannot use the specific commands granted by that privilege. Therefore, it is important to consider all the privileges a user might need and include them in one or several GRANT commands. Likewise, don't use GRANT with the ALL privilege unless all rights are absolutely necessary.

You can perform three operations with the same GRANT command: creating a user, assigning a password, and granting rights. If the user doesn't exist, the GRANT command creates a corresponding record. If you append the IDENTIFIED BY parameter to the GRANT command, you can also set a password for the user. Using the last example, you can also set a password for the sschafer@localhost user with the following command:

```
GRANT SELECT ON customerorders.customerdata, customerorders.invoices
 TO sschafer@localhost IDENTIFIED BY "somepassword";
```

The preceding example would add or change the password for sschafer@localhost to "somepassword."

The REVOKE Command

The MySQL REVOKE command is used to remove rights from users. It follows a similar syntax to that of the GRANT command:

```
REVOKE [privileges] ON [database].[table] FROM [username][@host];
```

For example, to remove UPDATE privileges from all databases for a particular user, you use the following command:

```
REVOKE UPDATE ON *.* FROM [username][@host];
```

To ensure that you are explicitly setting only the privileges you want, performing a command similar to the following before issuing a GRANT command (or commands) for a user is prudent:

```
REVOKE ALL ON <database>.* FROM <username>@<host>;
```

This command helps ensure that you are starting fresh and don't inadvertently allow any other rights to the user that you don't want the user to have.

Column Privileges

Besides database and table privileges, MySQL also enables you to set explicit privileges on a column basis. To select specific columns with the GRANT or REVOKE commands, list the columns after the privileges using the following syntax:

```
GRANT [privileges] (column list) ON ...
```

For example, to grant SELECT privileges on only the name, address, and phonenumber columns in the customerorders database's customerdata table, you would use the following:

```
GRANT SELECT (name, address, phonenumber) ON customerorders.customerdata
TO username@hostname;
```

Similarly, to revoke the SELECT privileges on those columns, you would use the following:

```
REVOKE SELECT (name, address, phonenumber) ON customerorders.customerdata
FROM username@hostname;
```

Updating Privileges

When you change a user's privileges, the data in the mysql database is changed immediately. However, the server reads the database only occasionally. To ensure that the server immediately recognizes the privileges, issue the following command after changing privileges with GRANT or REVOKE:

```
FLUSH PRIVILEGES;
```

Because of the serious nature of this command (reloading privileges), this command itself is privileged and should be performed only by a system administrator.

Done!

REVIEW

This session provided an overview of the MySQL privilege system. You learned how the system works, how to create a user, how to assign a user password, and how to assign and revoke rights to a user.

QUIZ YOURSELF

1. What is the default root/administrator password? (See "Setting the Root Password.")
2. What do the two levels of privilege systems control? (See "An Overview of the MySQL Privilege System.")
3. What do the mysql -p, -h, and -u parameters specify? (See "An Overview of the MySQL Privilege System.")
4. In what database are the MySQL privilege tables stored? (See "The MySQL Privileges Database.")
5. What does the DROP privilege enable a user to do? (See "Setting and Changing User Privileges.")
6. How do you specify multiple tables in a single GRANT command? (See "The GRANT Command.")
7. What command should you execute before any GRANT commands to ensure that a user has only the privileges you set? (See "The REVOKE Command.")

Working with Data

Session Checklist

✔ Creating and dropping databases

✔ Creating, modifying, and dropping tables

✔ Modifying the structure of columns

✔ Displaying more information about databases and tables

A variety of commands create, modify, and maintain the databases, tables, and columns stored in MySQL. This session covers the most popular commands to create databases and tables, including those commands to modify each.

30 Min.
To Go

You can use multiple interfaces to issue the commands covered in this session to MySQL. The easiest way to follow along with this session is by using the MySQL monitor, `mysql`.

Creating Databases

To create a database in MySQL you use the `CREATE DATABASE` command. This command has the following syntax:

```
CREATE DATABASE <database_name>;
```

The database name can be almost any sequence of characters and can include numbers. It is best to stay away from special symbols in the name of a database, including slashes (/ and \), dashes (—), spaces ( ), quotes (" and '), and underlines (_).

On Linux systems, database names are case-sensitive. Windows does not have this restriction, but you must use the same case throughout individual queries.

It is best to be deliberate with the case of your database names and stick to that usage whether you are on Linux or Windows. One method of capitalization is to use initial caps to distinguish separate words in your database names (for example, `CustomerOrders`).

Dropping Databases

You can use the `DROP DATABASE` command to remove an entire database from MySQL. The `DROP DATABASE` command has the following syntax:

```
DROP DATABASE <database_name>;
```

The removal of the data is instantaneous and irreversible. Be sure you don't miss the data, and make a backup before dropping a database, just in case. The MySQL utility `mysqldump`, covered in Session 12, makes backing up databases a snap.

Creating Tables

The `CREATE TABLE` command is used to create tables inside a database. The `CREATE TABLE` command has the following syntax:

```
CREATE TABLE <table_name> (
    <column_name>  <column_type>  <column_attribute>,
    <column_name>  <column_type>  <column_attribute>,
    <column_name>  <column_type>  <column_attribute>,
    ...
    PRIMARY KEY(<column_name>),
    INDEX index_name(<column_name>))
    TYPE=<table_type>;
```

The `table_name` can be almost any sequence of characters. However, as with database names, it's wise to stay away from special characters and MySQL keywords. The same rules apply for naming columns. Note that you can define one or many columns in the same `CREATE TABLE` command. If you need to add more columns later, you can do so with the `ALTER TABLE` command, which is covered in the section "Altering Tables," later in this session.

When you create a table, you can optionally assign a primary key and an index. Both allow for faster searching of the data within the table. Indexing and primary keys are covered in the section "Column Indexes and Primary Keys," later in this session.

A table's primary key, by definition, is also an index.

Lastly, you can define the table's type. MySQL supports the following table types:

- ISAM
- MyISAM
- BDB
- Heap
- InnoDB
- Gemini

The two most popular table formats are MyISAM and InnoDB. The MyISAM format is the default table format and is used if you don't specify a table format. The InnoDB format is a new, robust table type that supports various kinds of data locking to support transaction management. Data locking and transaction management both provide means to protect data from being updated while your program works on it.

 Each table type has its own advantages and disadvantages. I suggest that you familiarize yourself with the specifics of table types before using non-MyISAM tables. Check out the MySQL AB Web site (`www.mysql.com`**) for more information on the various table types.**

Column Attributes

Several attributes can modify the behavior of a standard column type when specified in a `CREATE TABLE` command. These attributes are summarized in Table 9-1.

Table 9-1   *Column Attributes*

Attribute	Use
auto_increment	The `auto_increment` attribute tells MySQL to store the next available value in the column when data is entered. For example, if you define a column as follows: `id   int(4)   auto_increment   not null` MySQL stores the first record with a value of 1 in this field, the second record with a value of 2, and so on. Note that this column must be defined as unique or as a primary key.
default *value*	The `default` attribute is used to specify what value should be used in a column if a value isn't specified when a row is created. For example, the following causes 0 to be inserted in the column `AmtOverdue` if a value isn't specified for that column when new row data is inserted into the table: `AmtOverdue  FLOAT  default 0`

Continued

Table 9-1   *Continued*

Attribute	Use
not null	The not null attribute tells MySQL that a null value is not allowed in the column. Don't mistake zero (0) for a null value — a field with zero in it is not null. Null means "no value."
primary key	The primary key attribute defines the column as a primary key for the table. Note that columns defined as primary keys must have a unique value stored in the column for each row. Hence, this attribute is often used with auto_increment to create a unique key.
unsigned	The unsigned attribute is used with numeric columns to ensure that the values of the column remain positive (not allowing a negative sign). Not all numeric columns support the unsigned attribute; see the section "Numeric Column Types," later in this session, for more information on unsigned.
zerofill	The zerofill attribute is used with numeric columns to add leading zeros to the data stored in the column.

Column Data Types

MySQL supports three column types: text, numeric, and date. Each type of column has several different variations, as covered in the following sections.

Text Column Types

Eight types of columns are suitable for storing text strings.

CHAR

```
CHAR(length)
```

The CHAR column type is used to store character strings of a finite length. This type has a fixed length that can be no more than 255 characters. In other words, if you define a column as CHAR(12), it always stores 12 characters, filling in spaces if necessary up to the 12 characters. Notice that the space fill is truncated from the result when the column's value is retrieved.

VARCHAR

```
VARCHAR(max_length)
```

The VARCHAR column type is like the CHAR type except that it stores only the amount of data required — it does not fill up the space to the maximum character limit. Like CHAR, VARCHAR columns are limited to 255 characters.

Data stored in VARCHAR columns have an extra character (byte) appended to the data; this character donates the size of the data. For example, the word *the* would be stored as four bytes, one for each letter and another with the value of 3. That last value tells MySQL that the actual length of the field is three bytes (*the*). The length character is not returned with the data when the column values are accessed.

Also notice that data stored in VARCHAR form may require more time to be processed than data stored in CHAR.

TINYTEXT

```
TINYTEXT
```

The TINYTEXT column type is a variable-length text type capable of storing up to 255 characters. It is equivalent to a VARCHAR(255) column type.

MEDIUMTEXT

```
MEDIUMTEXT
```

The MEDIUMTEXT column type is used for storing textual data and has a maximum length of 16,777,215 characters.

LONGTEXT

```
LONGTEXT
```

The LONGTEXT column type is used for storing textual data and has a maximum length of 4,294,967,295 characters.

ENUM

```
ENUM(value1, value2, value3...)
```

The ENUM (enumerated) column type is used to store textual data, but accepts only the values specified when it is created. For example, you could specify values of Y and N (for Yes or No), or perhaps TRUE and FALSE.

Typically, you would use programming techniques to enforce limits on the type of data allowed in a column, instead of using ENUM. However, you sometimes need to protect a column's integrity from multiple sources, including those outside of your control. In those cases, use ENUM.

SET

```
SET(value1, value2, value3...)
```

The SET column type enables one or more of the values specified to be stored in the column. However, storing multiple values in one field within a database is generally a bad idea, so avoid using SET columns.

Numeric Column Types

Seven types of columns are suitable for storing numeric values.

Most numeric column types can be defined as signed (allowing negative numbers) or unsigned (positive numbers only). Unsigned numeric columns can store larger numbers, at the expense of not allowing negative values.

Most numeric column types also allow you to zerofill them. This causes the database to add zeros to the left of the number up to the display size. For example, if you store the number 5 in a numeric column with a display size of 10, the number would be stored and displayed as 0000000005. Zero fill is usually used for account numbers, invoice numbers, and the like. Notice that zero fill numbers are always unsigned.

INT

```
INT(display_size) [unsigned] [zerofill]
```

The INT (integer) column type can be used to store integers between 0 and 4,294,967,295 if unsigned, or −2,147,483,648 and 2,147,483,647 if signed.

 An unsigned INT column type is often used with the auto_increment column attribute to create an automatic primary key for the table.

TINYINT

```
TINYINT(display_size) [unsigned] [zerofill]
```

The TINYINT column type can be used to store integers between 0 and 255 when unsigned, or −128 and 127 when signed.

MEDIUMINT

```
MEDIUMINT(display_size) [unsigned] [zerofill]
```

The MEDIUMINT column type can be used to store integers between 0 and 1,677,215 when unsigned, or −8,388,608 and 8,388,607 when signed.

BIGINT

```
BIGINT(display_size) [unsigned] [zerofill]
```

The BIGINT column type can be used to store integers between 0 and 18,446,744,073,709,551,615 when unsigned, or –9,223,372,036,854,775,808 and 9,223,372,036,854,775,807 when signed.

FLOAT

```
FLOAT(precision) [zerofill]
```

The FLOAT column type (when defined with this syntax) can be used to store single- and double-precision floating-point numbers. This type cannot be unsigned. You can specify up to 24 for the precision of a single-precision floating point, and between 25 and 53 for a double-precision floating-point number.

```
FLOAT[(display_size,decimals)] [zerofill]
```

The FLOAT column type (when defined with this syntax) can be used to store single-precision floating-point numbers. The range of numbers this type can store is -3.402823466E+38 to -1.175494351E-38, 0, and 1.175494351E-38 to 3.402823466E+38.

DOUBLE

```
DOUBLE[(display_size[,decimals])] [zerofill]
```

The DOUBLE column type can be used to store double-precision floating-point numbers in the range of –1.7976931348623157E+308 to –2.2250738585072014E-308, zero, and 2.2250738585072014E-308 to 1.7976931348623157E+308.

Avoid testing FLOAT **and** DOUBLE **columns for equality following any calculations using these types. Although the result might be defined as equal mathematically, the binary arithmetic involved may not be sufficiently precise to compare as equal.**

DECIMAL

```
DECIMAL[(display_size[,decimals])] [zerofill]
```

The DECIMAL column type stores floating-point numbers as strings, one character for each digit, negative sign, and decimal point. This type's range is the same as that of a DOUBLE type. If the value stored is zero, no decimal point is stored. The default display width of a DECIMAL column is 10, with a default decimal display of 0.

Date Column Types

MySQL has five column types suitable for storing date values.

20 Min. To Go

The advantages of storing dates in a column with a date format (instead of text format) are that you can specify the date format and perform date calculations without changing the data type.

DATE

```
DATE
```

The DATE column type can be used to store dates in the format YYYY-MM-DD. This type can store values between 1000-01-01 and 9999-12-31.

DATETIME

```
DATETIME
```

The DATETIME column type can be used to store a date and time in the format YYYY-MM-DD HH:MM:SS. This type can store values between 1000-01-01 00:00:0) and 9999-12-31 23:59:59.

TIMESTAMP

```
TIMESTAMP(size)
```

The TIMESTAMP column type can be used to automatically store the last date and time a record was updated (whether the data is new or just changed). The size parameter defines how many characters of the format YYYYMMDDHHMMSS are stored in the field. For example, if you specify a size of 4, only the year (YYYY) is stored. The default size is 14 (all characters).

TIME

```
TIME
```

The TIME column type can be used to store a time value in the format of HH:MM:SS. The acceptable range for this type is between –838:59:59 and 838:59:59.

YEAR

```
YEAR[(2|4)]
```

The YEAR column type can be used to store a value representing a year. The allowable range for a two-digit year is 1970 through 2069, and for a four-digit year is 1901 to 2155. Notice that you can specify whether you want the date stored in two-digit or four-digit format. If you use the two-digit format, MySQL prepends 19 for values between 70 and 99, and 20 for values between 00 and 69 when data is returned from the column.

 Although you can store a date in two-digit format, Y2K showed the folly of doing so.

Column Indexes and Primary Keys

MySQL can create indexes on columns. This enables a column to be accessed with the aid of the index, to speed data access and retrieval. MySQL support indexes up to 16 individual columns. You can specify the index when using the CREATE TABLE or ALTER TABLE commands. The INDEX parameter in the CREATE TABLE command has the following form:

```
INDEX <index_name> (<column_name>)
```

Supplying a name for the index is not mandatory, but it is highly recommended.

For example, if you plan on searching frequently for data in a column named ordernumber, you could create an index by using the following in a CREATE-TABLE command:

```
INDEX idx_ordernum (ordernumber)
```

Primary keys are a special type of index. A primary key is a special column that acts as a unique key for each row (record) in the table. Because primary keys need to be unique, a common practice is to use an auto incremented column as the primary key to ensure that the value in the column is unique.

Although creating a primary key is not necessary, it is highly recommended. Without a primary key, there is no way to uniquely identify single records in a table when you try to manipulate them.

You can define a primary key by adding PRIMARY-KEY to the column attributes or in a separate declaration in the CREATE-TABLE command. For example, the following two CREATE TABLE commands accomplish the same thing:

```
CREATE TABLE CUSTOMER (
    id  INT(4) AUTO_INCREMENT NOT NULL PRIMARY KEY
);
```

and

```
CREATE TABLE CUSTOMER (
    id  INT(4) AUTO_INCREMENT NOT NULL,
    PRIMARY KEY (id)
);
```

Notice the use of the NOT NULL parameter. This ensures that the primary key column never contains a null value.

Altering Tables

After a table is created, you can make changes to its structure or column definitions with the ALTER TABLE command. The ALTER TABLE command has several different forms, each of which is discussed in the following sections.

Changing a Table's Name

Changing a table's name is a simple task with ALTER TABLE, but it should not be performed without serious consideration of the impact the change may have to programs and users that use the database. Programs and users that expect to be able to query a CustomerData table cannot automatically adjust if the name of the table changes to CustData.

To change a table's name, use ALTER TABLE with the following syntax:

```
ALTER TABLE <table_name> RENAME <new_table_name>;
```

Adding Columns

You can also use the ALTER TABLE command to add additional columns to a table. To add a column to a table, use ALTER TABLE with the following syntax:

```
ALTER TABLE <table_name> ADD COLUMN <column_name>
  <column_type> <column_parameters>;
```

 Adding columns to tables can also have detrimental effects on users and programs that use the database. Careless access methods that do not specify the order of the columns returned by a query might expect the columns in a different order than what is returned when new columns are added.

You can also specify where in the table structure you want the column to be added: as the first column, the last column, or positioned relative to another column. By default, a new column is added to the end of the column list.

To position a column where you want it, you would append one of the parameters from Table 9-2 to the ALTER TABLE command.

Table 9-2 *Column Positioning Parameters*

Parameter	Effect
FIRST	Causes the added column to appear first in the column list
LAST	Causes the added column to appear last in the column list
BEFORE column_name	Causes the added column to appear in the column list *before* the column specified
AFTER column_name	Causes the added column to appear in the column list *after* the column specified

For example, to specify that an added column should be placed before the column CustomerBalance, you would use the following form of the ALTER TABLE command:

```
ALTER TABLE <table_name> ADD COLUMN <column_name> <column_type>
  <column_parameters>  BEFORE CustomerBalance;
```

Changing Column Definitions

The ALTER TABLE command makes it easy to alter a column's name and definition. To change a column's name, you would use the ALTER TABLE command with the CHANGE directive. The command has the following syntax:

```
ALTER TABLE <table_name> CHANGE <old_column_name>
<new_column_name> <column_attributes>;
```

You must redefine the column's attributes when you change its name, even if they do not change.

If you want to change a column's type, simply add the new type and appropriate attributes to the ALTER TABLE command:

```
ALTER TABLE <table_name> CHANGE <old_column_name>
<new_column_name> <column_type> <column_attributes>;
```

If you don't want to change the column's name, you need to specify the same name as the old and new column name. Alternatively, you can use the MODIFY parameter instead of the CHANGE parameter and specify the name only once:

```
ALTER TABLE <table_name> MODIFY <column_name> <column_type>
  <column_attributes>;
```

When you change a column's type, MySQL converts the data in the column to the new type as best as it can. You should make a backup and sample the data after such a change in case the results are not what you expected.

10 Min. To Go

Dropping Columns

You can also remove a column and its data from a table using the DROP COLUMN parameter of the ALTER TABLE command. Such an ALTER TABLE command has the following syntax:

```
ALTER TABLE <table_name> DROP COLUMN <column_name>;
```

Removal of the data is instantaneous and irreversible. Be sure you don't miss the data, and make a backup before dropping columns, just in case.

Changing Primary Keys and Indexes

You can also use ALTER TABLE commands to add or drop indexes and define additional primary keys. The following ALTER TABLE lines show the syntax for each:

```
ALTER TABLE DROP INDEX <index_name>;
ALTER TABLE ADD INDEX <index_name>(<column_name>);
ALTER TABLE ADD PRIMARY KEY(<column_name>);
```

Dropping Tables

If you ever want to delete an entire table, you can use the DROP TABLE command. The DROP TABLE command has the following syntax:

```
DROP TABLE <table_name>;
```

The table is dropped from the currently active database. It is wise to precede any DROP TABLE command with an appropriate USE command to ensure that you are dropping the table from the correct database.

Again, the removal of the data is instantaneous and irreversible. Be sure you don't miss the data, and make a backup before dropping tables, just in case.

Informational Commands

A series of commands in MySQL enables you to see more information about the databases, tables, columns, and even indexes stored within MySQL. Table 9-3 summarizes the commands and their output.

Table 9-3 _Informational Commands_

Command	Output
SHOW DATABASES;	Lists all the databases accessible to the current user
SHOW TABLES;	Shows a list of all the tables in the current database that are accessible to the current user
DESCRIBE <table_name>;	Displays the specifics of the table named table_name in the current database, including the column names, types, and any attributes. (The DESCRIBE command is a synonym for the SHOW COLUMNS FROM command.)
SHOW INDEX FROM <table_name>;	Displays all index information for the table named table_name
SHOW TABLE STATUS;	Displays more information about the tables in the current database, such as number of rows, date when the table was created, and so on
SHOW CREATE TABLE <table_name>;	Displays the TABLE CREATE command, which can be used to duplicate the structure of the table named table_name

Done!

REVIEW

In this session, you learned how to manipulate the structure of MySQL databases. You learned how to create a database and the tables within databases. You then learned how to modify the structure of a table, its columns, and how to get more information about each element of a database. The next session shows you how to query a database to retrieve information from it.

QUIZ YOURSELF

1. Are database names case-sensitive on Linux? On Windows? (See "Creating Databases.")

2. How long does it take after a DROP DATABASE command for MySQL to remove the specified database? (See "Dropping Databases.")

3. What does the auto_increment column attribute do? (See "Column Attributes.")

4. How long can data stored in a VARCHAR column be? (See "Text Column Types.")

5. What is the range of numbers that can be stored in a TINYINT column if it is unsigned? (See "Numeric Column Types.")

6. Can you store a two-digit date in a YEAR column? (See "Date Column Types.")

7. What ALTER TABLE parameter is used to rename a table? (See "Changing a Table's Name.")

Queries

Session Checklist

✔ Understanding queries

✔ Using INSERT to add data

✔ Using SELECT to retrieve data

✔ Using DELETE to delete data

✔ Using UPDATE to update data

**30 Min.
To Go**

Queries are the backbone of SQL databases. Most of the work you do with the database is accomplished through various queries, including INSERT, DELETE, UPDATE, and SELECT. This session leads you through the basics of queries, including understanding what queries are and how to use each type to manipulate the database.

Sample Data

The database used in this session is a simple computer inventory database to track the combination of computers, keyboards, mice, and monitors. The database consists of the following tables:

- `inventory.computers`

```
CREATE TABLE computers (
  comp_id INT(5) UNSIGNED ZEROFILL NOT NULL DEFAULT '00000',
  comp_make VARCHAR(25) DEFAULT NULL,
  comp_model VARCHAR(10) DEFAULT NULL,
  comp_cpu CHAR(2) NOT NULL DEFAULT '',
```

```
        comp_speed INT(4) NOT NULL DEFAULT '0',
        comp_mem INT(4) NOT NULL DEFAULT '0',
        comp_HD INT(4) NOT NULL DEFAULT '0',
        comp_CD ENUM('CD','DVD','CDRW','CDR','CDRW/DVD') DEFAULT NULL,
        comp_location VARCHAR(10) DEFAULT NULL,
        comp_ts TIMESTAMP(10) NOT NULL,
        PRIMARY KEY  (comp_id)
    ) TYPE=MyISAM;
```

● inventory.keyboards

```
    CREATE TABLE keyboards (
        kbd_id INT(5) UNSIGNED ZEROFILL NOT NULL DEFAULT '00000',
        kbd_type CHAR(3) NOT NULL DEFAULT 'PS2',
        kbd_model VARCHAR(5) NOT NULL DEFAULT '104',
        kbd_comp INT(5) UNSIGNED ZEROFILL NOT NULL DEFAULT '00000',
        kbd_ts TIMESTAMP(10) NOT NULL,
        PRIMARY KEY  (kbd_id)
    ) TYPE=MyISAM;
```

● inventory.mice

```
    CREATE TABLE mice (
        mouse_id INT(5) UNSIGNED ZEROFILL NOT NULL DEFAULT '00000',
        mouse_type CHAR(3) NOT NULL DEFAULT 'PS2',
        mouse_model VARCHAR(5) NOT NULL DEFAULT '2BS',
        mouse_comp INT(5) UNSIGNED ZEROFILL NOT NULL DEFAULT '00000',
        mouse_ts TIMESTAMP(10) NOT NULL,
        PRIMARY KEY  (mouse_id)
    ) TYPE=MyISAM;
```

● inventory.monitors

```
    CREATE TABLE monitors (
        mon_id INT(5) UNSIGNED ZEROFILL NOT NULL DEFAULT '00000',
        mon_size TINYINT(2) NOT NULL DEFAULT '0',
        mon_features VARCHAR(40) DEFAULT NULL,
        mon_comp INT(5) UNSIGNED ZEROFILL NOT NULL DEFAULT '00000',
        mon_ts TIMESTAMP(10) NOT NULL,
        PRIMARY KEY  (mon_id)
    ) TYPE=MyISAM;
```

To follow along with the SELECT **examples in this session, download the complete database from the companion Web site for this book, and perform the queries using the MySQL monitor. See Appendix B, "What's on the Companion Web Site," for more information.**

Understanding Queries

Queries are the backbone of any SQL-based database. The *structured query language* (SQL) was created to help define a consistent interface for data stored in a database. MySQL was created to bring a cheaper, faster, SQL-compliant database to market, and it adheres to most SQL rules for its queries.

Although MySQL adheres to most SQL conventions, you do find notable differences between the two. These differences are highlighted in the MySQL documentation available at the MySQL AB Web site: www.mysql.com. **However, the number of differences is diminishing as MySQL becomes more compliant and the SQL standard a little more lax.**

In fact, MySQL depends on queries for most everything it does. You may have noticed responses such as Query OK, 1 row affected (0.02 sec) to query actions such as creating a database or table, actions that don't add rows to your tables. The row affected messages are because of the way in which MySQL stores its own information, within internal databases. Used to manipulate the databases, commands such as CREATE DATABASE are simply shortcuts that track the settings and configuration of your tables.

Adding Data with INSERT

The INSERT query enables you to add data to an existing table. A typical INSERT query has the following format:

```
INSERT into <table_name>
  (<column_list>)
  VALUES
  (<value_list>);
```

Suppose that you wanted to add a new computer to your inventory database. The following query would add the data shown in Table 10-1:

```
INSERT INTO computers
  (comp_id,comp_make,comp_model,comp_cpu,comp_speed,comp_mem,
   comp_HD,comp_CD,comp_location)
  VALUES
  (02210,'Compumate','A','P3',1600,512,
   40,'DVD','C124');
```

Table 10-1   *Data for New Computer*

comp_id	comp_make	comp_model	comp_cpu	comp_speed
002210	Compumate	A	P3	1600

comp_mem	comp_HD	comp_CD	comp_location	comp_ts
512	40	DVD	C124	N/A

Notice that the values for the columns are in the exact same order as the column names. In addition, notice that the comp_ts (TIMESTAMP) column and value are not listed because MySQL manages TIMESTAMP values itself. If you needed to specify a value, you could specify 0.

Only the first TIMESTAMP **column in a table is managed by MySQL. Additional** TIMESTAMP **columns require more hands-on management by your application(s). If you want to ensure that the** TIMESTAMP **is correct, always manually store the current value when inserting or updating a row — use** now() **as the column value for the current time.**

Any strings within the column values need to be enclosed in single quotes. If a string contains a single quote (for example, the name O'Hern), you need to *escape* the quote in the string.

To escape a quote, you precede it with a backslash character (\). This tells MySQL to treat the quote as part of the column's value. For example, to store a value such as O'Hern, you would use the following text in the value list:

    'O\'Hern'

The SQL standard supports only single quotes to delimit string values in queries, but MySQL supports both single and double quotes ("). If you don't mind using nonstandard SQL statements, you can use a different type of quote to avoid escaping quotes in your strings. However, the better strategy, for consistency, is to stick with single quotes and escape when necessary.

The order in which you supply the column list and values doesn't matter as long as they match each other — in number of entries and order.

You can omit the (column_list) parameter from the INSERT query if you specify a value for every column in the database, in the exact order in which they appear in the database. Similarly, you can specify a subset of the columns in the column list with matching value list entries — any column not specified is stored with its default value where appropriate.

You can use an alternative syntax for the `INSERT` query by using the `SET` keyword., as shown in the following example:

```
INSERT INTO <table> SET <column1> = <value1>, <column2> = <value2>...;
```

You might find this alternative use more convenient.

Although omitting the column list from an `INSERT` query is not recommended, you can determine the order of a table's columns with the `DESCRIBE TABLE` command.

Examine the following `INSERT` queries with their resulting errors:

```
INSERT INTO computers
   (comp_id,comp_make,comp_model,comp_cpu,comp_speed,comp_mem,
   comp_HD,comp_CD,comp_location)
   VALUES
   (02211,'Compumate','A','P3',1600,512,
   40,'DVD','C124',now());
ERROR 1136: Column count doesn't match value count at row 1
```

In the preceding query, only nine columns were listed, but 10 values were given.

```
INSERT INTO computers
   VALUES
   (02211,'Compumate','A');
ERROR 1136: Column count doesn't match value count at row 1
```

In the preceding query, all column values needed to be listed because the column list wasn't specified.

```
INSERT INTO computers
   VALUES
   (02211,'A','P3','Compumate',1600,512,
   40,'DVD', now(), 'C124');
Query OK, 1 row affected (0.00 sec)
```

The preceding query succeeded, but the data is mangled because the order of the column values did not match the order of the columns in the database. Table 10-2 shows the data as it was stored in the database.

Table 10-2 *Errant Data Caused by Column Mismatch*

comp_id	comp_make	comp_model	comp_cpu	comp_speed
02211	A	P3	Co	1600

comp_mem	comp_HD	comp_CD	comp_location	comp_ts
512	40	DVD	0	0000000000

20 Min.
To Go

Selecting Data with SELECT

The SELECT query is the heart of retrieving SQL stored data. You use the SELECT query to select data from the database and display or parse it accordingly. The following sections describe in detail how to use SELECT, starting with a simple query to return all data from a table and working up to selecting data that matches specific criteria.

The Basics of SELECT

The basic form of the SELECT statement is as follows:

```
SELECT <column_list> FROM <table_name>;
```

You can specify one or more columns in the column list, or use an asterisk (*) to return all columns. For example, the following query returns all column values for all records in the monitors table:

```
SELECT * FROM monitors;
```

mon_id	mon_size	mon_features	mon_comp	mon_ts
00461	17		02210	20030713221811
00436	17		01347	20030713221850
00499	15		06073	20030713221855
00656	17	LCD	09307	20030713221857
00236	20	DUAL	01523	20030713222055
00428	17		07065	20030713221852
00007	20		07185	20030713222255
00603	15		09894	20030713222255
00184	20		09569	20030713221855
00239	21		08036	20030713221860
00255	17		08057	20030713221825
00851	15	LCD	05654	20030713221895
00417	20	DUAL	09834	20030713222355
00887	17		07743	20030713221825
00578	17		02559	20030713221785
00355	15		08316	20030713221955
00214	17		09499	20030713221865
00795	20		00946	20030713221855
00448	21		04070	20030713221165
00058	20	DUAL	09144	20030713222055
00167	22		05212	20030713222215
00741	21		03663	20030713221805
00605	22		05295	20030713221757
00300	19	LCD	04780	20030713221885
00450	19	LCD	00000	20030713221858

25 rows in set (0.00 sec)

If you want to see only specific columns, you can specify that just those columns be listed, as shown in the following query, for which only the columns mon_id and mon_comp are specified and listed:

```
SELECT mon_id, mon_comp FROM monitors;
+--------+----------+
| mon_id | mon_comp |
+--------+----------+
|  00461 |    02210 |
|  00436 |    01347 |
|  00499 |    06073 |
|  00656 |    09307 |
|  00236 |    01523 |
|  00428 |    07065 |
|  00007 |    07185 |
|  00603 |    09894 |
|  00184 |    09569 |
|  00239 |    08036 |
|  00255 |    08057 |
|  00851 |    05654 |
|  00417 |    09834 |
|  00887 |    07743 |
|  00578 |    02559 |
|  00355 |    08316 |
|  00214 |    09499 |
|  00795 |    00946 |
|  00448 |    04070 |
|  00058 |    09144 |
|  00167 |    05212 |
|  00741 |    03663 |
|  00605 |    05295 |
|  00300 |    04780 |
|  00450 |    00000 |
+--------+----------+
25 rows in set (0.00 sec)
```

Choosing Specific Rows with WHERE

Returning all rows from a database table isn't very useful. Thankfully, the SELECT query includes a method for selecting specific data — the WHERE clause. The basic syntax of a SELECT query with a WHERE clause is as follows:

```
SELECT <column_list> FROM <table_name/list> WHERE <condition>;
```

You can use simple numeric and string comparisons in the condition. For example, to display the IDs of only the 17-inch monitors in the monitors table, you could use a query like the following:

```
SELECT mon_id FROM monitors WHERE mon_size = '17';
+--------+
| mon_id |
+--------+
|  00461 |
|  00436 |
|  00656 |
|  00428 |
|  00255 |
|  00887 |
|  00578 |
|  00214 |
+--------+
8 rows in set (0.01 sec)
```

Table 10-3 summarizes the operators that can be used in WHERE conditions.

Table 10-3   *Operators Used In WHERE*

Operator	Meaning
=	Equal to
!= or <>	Not equal to
>	Greater than
<	Less than
>=	Greater than or equal to
<=	Less than or equal to

To display all monitors 20 inches or larger, you could use the following query:

```
SELECT mon_id,mon_size FROM monitors WHERE mon_size >= '20';
+--------+----------+
| mon_id | mon_size |
+--------+----------+
|  00236 |       20 |
|  00007 |       20 |
|  00184 |       20 |
|  00239 |       21 |
|  00417 |       20 |
|  00795 |       20 |
|  00448 |       21 |
|  00058 |       20 |
|  00167 |       22 |
|  00741 |       21 |
|  00605 |       22 |
+--------+----------+
11 rows in set (0.00 sec)
```

The WHERE clause also supports a BETWEEN operator, to help specify a range of values to select. For example, the following query selects all monitors between 18 and 21 inches:

```
SELECT mon_id,mon_size FROM monitors
  WHERE mon_size BETWEEN '18' and '21';
+--------+----------+
| mon_id | mon_size |
+--------+----------+
|  00236 |       20 |
|  00007 |       20 |
|  00184 |       20 |
|  00239 |       21 |
|  00417 |       20 |
|  00795 |       20 |
|  00448 |       21 |
|  00058 |       20 |
|  00741 |       21 |
|  00300 |       19 |
|  00450 |       19 |
+--------+----------+
11 rows in set (0.01 sec)
```

The BETWEEN operator is inclusive; that is, it includes any data equal to the two values.

Using LIKE to Find Data

So far, you've seen how the WHERE clause can find data using equal and not-equal operators. The WHERE clause has another operator that enables you to search substrings within data. This operator, LIKE, can be used with two wildcard characters to search for specific strings in columns. The syntax of a WHERE clause that uses LIKE is as follows:

```
...WHERE <column> LIKE '<string>'
```

You can use the following two wildcard characters with LIKE:

- A percent sign (%), which matches zero or more characters
- An underline (_), which matches one character

For example, to find all computers in Building C, you would use the following query:

```
SELECT comp_id FROM computers WHERE comp_location LIKE 'C%';
+---------+
| comp_id |
+---------+
|   02210 |
|   01347 |
|   06073 |
|   09307 |
```

```
|   08036 |
|   09834 |
|   07743 |
+---------+
7 rows in set (0.00 sec)
```

Using Complex Expressions with WHERE

You can use modifiers such as AND, OR, and NOT to build complex expressions for use with the WHERE clause. For example, if you wanted to select all "Custom" computers in Building C, you could use AND in a query similar to the following:

```
SELECT comp_id, comp_make, comp_location FROM computers
  WHERE comp_make = "Custom" AND comp_location LIKE 'C%';
+---------+-----------+---------------+
| comp_id | comp_make | comp_location |
+---------+-----------+---------------+
|   09834 | Custom    | C200          |
|   07743 | Custom    | C200          |
+---------+-----------+---------------+
2 rows in set (0.00 sec)
```

If need be, you can use parentheses to adjust the evaluation precedence of a complex WHERE clause. For example, if you wanted to select all computers in Building C or all Pentium III computers that *do not* have DVD drives, you would use the following query:

```
SELECT comp_id,comp_CD,comp_location FROM computers
  WHERE comp_location LIKE 'C%' OR
  (comp_cpu = "P3" AND comp_CD NOT LIKE '%DVD%');
```

 Bracketing a string in percent signs causes LIKE to find matches no matter where the substring appears in the data — at the start of a field, in the middle of a field, or at the end of a field.

Ordering Results with ORDER BY

Data returned from a query is typically returned in the order in which the data is encountered in the database. Therefore, the order in which the data appears can be quite random. However, you can control how the data is sorted with the ORDER BY clause.

The ORDER BY clause accepts one or more columns to sort by:

```
...ORDER BY <column1> [DESC], <column2> [DESC]...
```

For example, if you wanted to find all computers in Building C, sorted by their IDs, you would use the following query:

```
SELECT comp_id,comp_location FROM computers
  WHERE comp_location LIKE 'C%'
  ORDER BY comp_id;
```

```
+---------+----------------+
| comp_id | comp_location  |
+---------+----------------+
|   01347 |           C033 |
|   02210 |           C124 |
|   06073 |           C224 |
|   07743 |           C200 |
|   08036 |           C250 |
|   09307 |           C224 |
|   09834 |           C200 |
+---------+----------------+
7 rows in set (0.00 sec)
```

By default, ORDER BY sorts results in ascending order. The ORDER BY clause also accepts an optional DESC argument that specifies a sort in descending order. For example, if you wanted your last query to return results in descending order, you would use the following:

```
SELECT comp_id,comp_location FROM computers
   WHERE comp_location LIKE 'C%'
   ORDER BY comp_id DESC;
```

As previously mentioned, you can specify more than one column to sort by. This is useful when columns can contain the same values. For example, you could sort all "Super-puters" by model, CPU, speed, and finally memory:

```
SELECT comp_id,comp_model,comp_cpu,comp_speed,comp_mem
   FROM computers
   WHERE comp_make = "Super-puter"
   ORDER BY comp_model, comp_cpu DESC,
   comp_speed DESC, comp_mem DESC;
```

```
+---------+------------+----------+------------+----------+
| comp_id | comp_model | comp_cpu | comp_speed | comp_mem |
+---------+------------+----------+------------+----------+
|   05212 | SE         | P4       |       2000 |      512 |
|   03663 | SE         | P4       |       2000 |     1000 |
|   00946 | XL         | P4       |       2400 |     1000 |
|   04070 | XL         | P4       |       2400 |     1000 |
|   09144 | XL         | P4       |       2400 |     1000 |
|   05295 | XL         | P4       |       2400 |     1500 |
|   04780 | XS         | P4       |       2400 |     1000 |
+---------+------------+----------+------------+----------+
7 rows in set (0.00 sec)
```

Limiting Results with LIMIT

Occasionally, you need to limit the results returned from a query. For those cases, you can add the LIMIT clause to your query. The LIMIT clause has the following syntax:

```
...LIMIT [<start_record>,] <number_of_records>
```

For example, if you wanted to see the three fastest computers, you could use the following query:

```
SELECT comp_id FROM computers ORDER BY comp_speed DESC LIMIT 3;
+---------+
| comp_id |
+---------+
|   00946 |
|   04070 |
|   09144 |
+---------+
3 rows in set (0.00 sec)
```

The optional <start_record> parameter tells the query what result to begin with when returning results. As is usual with programming, the first record in the return set is referred to by the number 0. Using the preceding query as an example, if you wanted to return the records starting with the fifth record, you would adjust your query thus:

```
SELECT comp_id FROM computers ORDER BY comp_speed DESC LIMIT 5,3;
```

The LIMIT clause is very valuable for stepping through return sets several records at a time. For example, you can run one query with "LIMIT 0,5", a second with "LIMIT 5,5", a third with "LIMIT 10,5", and so on, to display results five records at a time. Keep this technique in mind for later sessions where you use PHP with this very technique.

Notice that, if the result set is less than the specified LIMIT, the full result set is returned.

10 Min.
To Go

Selecting from More Than One Table

As you may have guessed from the basic SELECT syntax covered earlier in this session, you can select data from more than one table. This is usually advantageous because a well-designed database doesn't duplicate data between tables, causing you to gather the data yourself.

For example, assume that you need to know the location of all three-button mice. You can do a SELECT on the mice table to find all three-button mice (mouse_model = "3B") with the following query:

```
SELECT * FROM mice WHERE mouse_model = "3B";
+----------+------------+-------------+------------+----------------+
| mouse_id | mouse_type | mouse_model | mouse_comp | mouse_ts       |
+----------+------------+-------------+------------+----------------+
|    00345 | PS2        | 3B          |      06073 | 20030713222055 |
|    00303 | PS2        | 3B          |      08057 | 20030713222116 |
|    00356 | USB        | 3B          |      08316 | 20030713222065 |
|    00944 | USB        | 3B          |      05295 | 20030713221975 |
|    00670 | PS2        | 3B          |      04780 | 20030713222057 |
|    00324 | USB        | 3B          |      00000 | 20030713222060 |
+----------+------------+-------------+------------+----------------+
6 rows in set (0.01 sec)
```

However, the mice table lists only the computer to which the individual mice are attached, not the location. You could use six more SELECT statements to find the location:

```
SELECT comp_location FROM computers WHERE comp_id = "06073";
+---------------+
| comp_location |
+---------------+
|          C224 |
+---------------+
1 row in set (0.00 sec)

SELECT comp_location FROM computers WHERE comp_id = "08057";
+---------------+
| comp_location |
+---------------+
|          A021 |
+---------------+
1 row in set (0.00 sec)
...
```

However, you can see how labor-intensive this could be, especially with large data sets. An easier way is to combine the data being selected, as shown in the following query:

```
SELECT computers.comp_location FROM computers, mice
   WHERE mice.mouse_model = "3B"
   AND mice.mouse_comp = computers.comp_id;
+---------------+
| comp_location |
+---------------+
|          C224 |
|          A021 |
|          B125 |
|         ITLAB |
|         LAB01 |
+---------------+
5 rows in set (0.00 sec)
```

Notice how each column name includes the table name as well. Specifying columns in this way ensures that MySQL knows exactly what column from what table you want to draw information. For example, suppose you have two tables with columns named color. How would MySQL determine which table's column you wanted returned from a SELECT statement like the following?

```
SELECT color FROM table1, table2...
```

Actually, MySQL wouldn't even try to determine which you wanted. Instead, the SELECT statement would generate an error:

```
ERROR 1052:  Column: 'color' in field list is ambiguous
```

In our case, no two columns from different tables are named the same. However, it's good practice to specify the table name or an alias for it along with the column name when working with multiple tables.

The following query doesn't produce exactly what you want:

```
SELECT computers.comp_location FROM computers, mice
  WHERE mice.mouse_model = "3B"

  AND mice.mouse_comp = computers.comp_id;
```

The "3B" mouse that isn't attached to a computer (ID 00324) wasn't included in the query. Because there isn't a computer with an ID of "00000," you can't use that query to return that mouse, too.

Selecting data from two or more tables is known as a *join*. In database terms, there are two types of joins: *inner joins* and *outer joins*. MySQL supports both join types, which are covered in Session 12.

Deleting Records with DELETE

Just as queries can be used to insert records, queries can also be used to delete records. The DELETE query has the following syntax:

```
DELETE FROM <table_name/list> [WHERE <conditions>];
```

For example, to delete all keyboards not attached to a computer from the keyboard table, you would use the following query:

```
DELETE FROM keyboards WHERE kbd_comp = "00000";
```

Delete operations are instantaneous and cannot be undone. Review your DELETE queries closely before using them and keep backups of your data just in case. *Always* supply a WHERE clause with your DELETE queries. The following query, for example, results in the deletion of all the data in the table:

```
DELETE FROM table;
```

As with SELECT queries, you can build very elaborate WHERE clauses to control what records are selected for deletion, and use LIMIT clauses to control how many are deleted at one time.

Updating Records with UPDATE

To update records in a database, you could remove a record and reinsert it with the new data. However, you could also use an UPDATE query to update the data selectively. An UPDATE query has the following syntax:

```
UPDATE <table_name> SET <colname>=<value>, <colname>=<value>...
WHERE <condition>
```

For example, if the computer with ID 08316 moves to location A225, the following query updates that computer's record accordingly:

```
UPDATE computers SET comp_location='A225' WHERE comp_id='08316';
Query OK, 1 row affected (0.00 sec)
Rows matched: 1  Changed: 1  Warnings: 0
```

As with SELECT and DELETE, WHERE conditions in UPDATE queries can be quite complex, if necessary. In fact, it is imperative that the WHERE condition be very specific and construed to match *only* the records you want updated. If the query matches more than one record, *all* the records matched are updated as specified by the update's SET clause.

Using a table's primary key in the UPDATE WHERE clause is often best, because you know the key is unique.

 Be sure to pay attention to the response generated for your query. In the preceding example, "Changed: 1" in the response shows that only one record was changed.

One other feature of UPDATE is its capability to use current column values in its operation. For example, suppose that the computer with ID 08057 has 256MB of RAM added to it. To update the computer's record, you could execute a SELECT to find the current value and issue an UPDATE with that value plus 256, or use a query like the following:

```
UPDATE computers SET comp_mem = comp_mem + 256 WHERE comp_id = '08057';
```

Done!

REVIEW

This session covered the main uses of queries, including inserting, deleting, selecting, and updating data. You reviewed each of these queries, including their options, caveats, and unique uses. The next few sessions wrap up the tutorial on MySQL and continue on to PHP before describing how to use the two technologies together.

QUIZ YOURSELF

1. How many column values must you specify if you don't specify any columns in the column list of an INSERT query? (See "Adding Data with INSERT.")
2. What does "escaping a quote" mean? (See "Adding Data with INSERT")
3. What column(s) are returned if you specify an asterisk (*) in your SELECT query? (See "The Basics of SELECT.")
4. What operators can be used with WHERE clauses? (See "Choosing Specific Rows with WHERE" and "Using Complex Expressions with WHERE.")
5. How many characters are matched with the underscore character (_) in a LIKE clause? (See "Using LIKE to Find Data.")
6. How do you specify that results should be sorted in descending order? (See "Ordering Results with ORDER BY.")

7. What is the maximum number of records returned if you use a LIMIT 0,10 clause? (See "Limiting Results with LIMIT.")

8. How do you specify the table from which a column should be taken? (See "Selecting from More Than One Table.")

9. How soon after a DELETE query does MySQL delete the specified records? (See "Deleting Records with DELETE.")

PART

II

Saturday Morning
Part Review

1. Why are Web servers such a security risk?
2. How do you determine whether the MySQL database server is running on your platform (Windows or Linux)?
3. How many columns can be used with ORDER BY to sort the output of a MySQL query?
4. Name a few Web sites that provide reliable security information.
5. What PHP command can you use to show almost every configuration option of your PHP installation?
6. What makes Apache one of the most secure Web servers available?
7. Define a column used to automatically generate a seven-digit serial number that is also the primary key for the table in which it is stored.
8. Can a hacker use a Web server to access a system's underlying file system?
9. Why should you restrict access to all files on your Web server that begin with .ht?
10. Describe two methods to secure a directory from everyone outside of the Apache server's domain.
11. What does SQL mean and why is it important to databases?
12. In what directory can you expect to find most CGI scripts?
13. How do you define a primary key when creating a table? What's the first line of authentication defense for MySQL?
14. What are the minimum security privileges a user needs to access and select data from a MySQL database?
15. What's the best character-based column type to use for storing a single letter?
16. What year does 1 represent when stored in a column defined as YEAR(2)?
17. How do you add a column to the middle of a table's structure?
18. Is MySQL 100 percent SQL-compliant?

19. When do you *not* need to specify column names in an INSERT statement?

20. In what order does MySQL return column values in response to a SELECT * statement?

21. Will a MySQL query with WHERE item LIKE 'cam%' find a record for which the item column contains "Camera"?

PART

III

Saturday
Afternoon

Session 11
Troubleshooting MySQL Commands and Queries

Session 12
Advanced MySQL Concepts

Session 13
Getting Ready to Use PHP

Session 14
PHP Basics

Session 15
Program Flow

Session 16
PHP Functions

Troubleshooting MySQL Commands and Queries

Session Checklist

✔ Learning more about the MySQL monitor

✔ Informational MySQL commands

✔ Troubleshooting queries

**30 Min.
To Go**

No matter how robust your database is or how skilled you become at SQL, you always encounter a few problems in the data or your queries that are tough to track down. This session describes various ways you can retrieve more information about your databases and how you can troubleshoot queries.

The MySQL Monitor

The best tool for debugging MySQL is the MySQL monitor. The monitor was introduced in Session 3 and has been used in several subsequent sessions.

The monitor is a program that gives you command-line-like access to MySQL and the data it stores. You can examine databases, run queries, and even remove entire tables or databases.

The MySQL monitor is a powerful but dangerous tool. Make sure that your database(s) are securely backed up before performing any operations in the monitor that could erase valuable data.

The following sections show you how to use the monitor effectively.

Running the Monitor

The monitor program is stored where all the MySQL executable files are stored on the system. On Windows systems, this is usually the bin subdirectory of the mysql directory. On Linux, the monitor is usually stored in a system binary directory such as /usr/bin. If you can't find the monitor (mysql on Linux, mysql.exe on Windows), use your operating system's search feature to find it.

The basic syntax for running the monitor is as follows:

```
mysql -p [-u <user_name>]
```

The -p parameter should be mandatory whenever you run the monitor. This parameter causes the monitor to ask for a password — a password on each account should also be mandatory.

Optionally, you can use the -u parameter to connect as a different user.

A password may not be necessary if you are running the monitor on the same Windows system where the MySQL server is running. Windows versions of MySQL do not use passwords for a console user on the server machine.

MySQL Monitor Basics

The monitor essentially gives you command-line access to the server. Each command is entered at the mysql> prompt and should be terminated by a semicolon (;). Table 11-1 lists some of the most common commands.

Table 11-1 *Common Monitor Commands*

Command	Use
SHOW DATABASES;	Lists all databases
USE <database>;	Specifies that you want to use the database specified by <database>
SHOW TABLES;	Lists all tables in the current database
DESCRIBE <tablename>;	Lists details (column names, types, options) of the specified table
SHOW CREATE TABLE <tablename>;	Shows the command used to create the table <tablename>
SHOW TABLE STATUS LIKE '<expression>';	Shows the status of tables that match <expression> (using standard LIKE clause format)
QUIT;	Exits the monitor

The current user's rights affect the results of most monitor commands. For example, the SHOW TABLES command shows only the tables to which the current user has rights. In addition, note that most commands operate on the current database only. Commands that support table names as arguments enable you to specify the database. For example, the command DESCRIBE test.users; describes the users table in the test database no matter what the active database is.

The monitor caches commands in a command history buffer much like most operating system consoles. You can use the up arrow to display and repeat previous commands. You can also use the right and left arrows to move around within a previous command to edit it accordingly. These features come in handy when you encounter a typo in a long command.

Linux users can use another feature of the monitor — the external editor command. Entering the command edit spawns the editor specified in the $EDITOR environment variable. You can then use the editor to construct a command for the monitor. When you save the file and exit the editor, the resulting text is sent to the monitor. You may need to press Enter to actually end the line and execute the text.

Logging the Monitor Session

**20 Min.
To Go**

You can use the tee command to set a log file and begin logging all monitor activity to that file. The file is created in the current directory and logs everything that you see on-screen — what you type and what the monitor responds with.

The syntax of the tee command is as follows:

```
tee [logfile]
```

Notice that you must specify the log file name the first time you use the tee command. You can suspend writing to the log file with the notee command. A subsequent tee command begins logging again. You can suspend or enable logging as often as you like, or specify another log file name with the tee command to begin logging to a different file.

Piping Files to the Monitor

You can use the operating system's file redirection feature to "feed" a command sequence to the monitor. The syntax for this use is as follows:

```
mysql [parameters] <file_to_feed
```

Suppose, for example, that you had a file named create_db.sql with the following contents:

```
CREATE DATABASE test;
USE test;
```

```
CREATE TABLE users (
  username VARCHAR(20),
  password VARCHAR(20)
);
```

The following command line would start the monitor, create the `test` database and the users table, and then exit the monitor:

```
mysql -p <create_db.sql
```

This feature is very useful for restoring data or duplicating databases when coupled with the `mysqldump` **command, covered in the next session.**

One benefit of this usage is that you can take complex operations, store them in a file using your favorite editor, and perform the operations with one command.

The monitor can also load files from its prompt with the `source` **command. Type** `source` **at a prompt, followed by a file name to load and execute.**

Troubleshooting Queries

Because queries are the main interface into your data, it is important to ensure that they do what you want them to do — especially if they are destructive, such as UPDATE or DELETE. This section outlines some methods to help troubleshoot your queries.

Format Your Queries with Line Breaks

One of the easiest ways to spot a problem in a query is to separate the various clauses by line breaks and include separating spaces in list elements. For example, consider the following query formatted two different ways:

```
SELECT comp_id,comp_cpu,comp_speed,mouse_type FROM computers,mice WHERE
mouse_comp = comp_id AND comp_location LIKE "A%";

SELECT comp_id, comp_cpu, comp_speed, mouse_type
  FROM computers, mice
WHERE
  mouse_comp = comp_id
AND
  comp_location LIKE "A%";
```

Obviously, the second query is easier to read and, hence, easier to troubleshoot.

Try SELECT

You can transform most non-SELECT queries into an equivalent SELECT query. For example, consider the following DELETE query:

```
DELETE FROM computers WHERE comp_make = "Custom"
  AND comp_location LIKE 'C%';
```

This query's intent is to delete all "Custom" computers currently located in Building C. However, what about a custom computer at the collocation facility, the location of which is stored as "Colo"? This query would also delete that computer. By translating the query into the following equivalent SELECT query, you can verify what information is actually affected by the DELETE:

```
SELECT * FROM computers
  WHERE comp_make = "Custom" AND comp_location LIKE 'C%';
```

Always survey the potential effects of a new DELETE or UPDATE query before actually running it. When in doubt, run the equivalent SELECT first.

**10 Min.
To Go**

Simplify Your Query

Once you get used to extending your query's scope with complex WHERE clauses, you find that the query's power is equally matched by the damage it can cause. Before constructing complex WHERE clauses, take the time to experiment with each section of the clause before adding the next. For example, consider the DELETE query discussed in the last section:

```
DELETE FROM computers WHERE comp_make = "Custom"
  AND comp_location LIKE 'C%';
```

Before submitting this query, you could run a simplified SELECT query such as the following:

```
SELECT comp_id,comp_make,comp_location FROM computers
ORDER BY comp_make;
```

This query, when run against the sample inventory database, yields the following results:

```
+---------+------------+---------------+
| comp_id | comp_make  | comp_location |
+---------+------------+---------------+
|   02210 | Compumate  | C124          |
|   01347 | Compumate  | C033          |
|   06073 | Compumate  | C224          |
|   09307 | Compumate  | C224          |
|   01523 | Compumate  | A125          |
|   07065 | Compumate  | A003          |
|   07185 | Compumate  | A122          |
|   09894 | Compumate  | B022          |
|   09569 | Compumate  | B022          |
|   08036 | Compumate  | C250          |
```

```
|   08057 | Compumate   | A021    |
|   05654 | Custom      | A122    |
|   09834 | Custom      | C200    |
|   07743 | Custom      | C200    |
|   02559 | Custom      | A010    |
|   08316 | Custom      | B125    |
|   09499 | Custom      | B126    |
|   05021 | Custom      | ITLAB   |
|   00946 | Super-puter | LAB05   |
|   04070 | Super-puter | LAB06   |
|   09144 | Super-puter | LAB07   |
|   05212 | Super-puter | A300    |
|   03663 | Super-puter | A310    |
|   05295 | Super-puter | ITLAB   |
|   04780 | Super-puter | LAB01   |
+---------+-------------+---------------+
25 rows in set (0.00 sec)
```

In this limited data set, it is trivial to find the records that match the complex DELETE query — namely, the following:

```
|   09834 | Custom      | C200    |
|   07743 | Custom      | C200    |
```

However, in more extensive data sets, you might choose to export the results to a file to print or use an editor to find affected records.

Once you know what records should be affected by the query, you can add the necessary WHERE clause to verify:

```
SELECT * FROM computers
  WHERE comp_make = "Custom" AND comp_location LIKE 'C%';
+---------+-----------+------------+----------+------------+----------+---
------+---------+---------------+------------+
| comp_id | comp_make | comp_model | comp_cpu | comp_speed | comp_mem |
comp_HD | comp_CD | comp_location | comp_ts    |
+---------+-----------+------------+----------+------------+----------+---
------+---------+---------------+------------+
|   09834 | Custom    | 1          | P3       |        900 |      512 |
60 | CD      | C200          | 0000000000 |
|   07743 | Custom    | 1          | P3       |        866 |      384 |
60 | CDRW    | C200          | 0000000000 |
+---------+-----------+------------+----------+------------+----------+---
------+---------+---------------+------------+
2 rows in set (0.01 sec)
```

Finally, you can form the query in its DELETE form, confident that it affects only the records you intend:

```
DELETE FROM computers WHERE comp_make = "Custom"
  AND comp_location LIKE 'C%';
```

This technique makes sense only for limited data sets or when spot-checking query effects. The bottom line is don't run a complex, destructive query without first checking its result set.

Done!

REVIEW

This session showed you a few ways to troubleshoot MySQL. It reviewed the MySQL monitor and described some additional commands for retrieving information about databases and their contents. It then covered a few techniques to troubleshoot queries, including reformatting the query, simplifying clauses, and using SELECT to ascertain what records a query affects. The next session covers a few more advanced techniques you can use with MySQL. The next few sessions thereafter dive into PHP.

QUIZ YOURSELF

1. Where is the MySQL monitor stored on your system? (See "Running the Monitor.")
2. What MySQL command can you use to display the command used to create a specific table? (See "MySQL Monitor Basics.")
3. How can you log the MySQL monitor session to a specific file? (See "Logging the Monitor Session.")
4. Why should you try a SELECT before using a complex DELETE or UPDATE? (See "Try Select.")

Advanced MySQL Concepts

Session Checklist

✔ Counting result sets

✔ Working with inner joins and outer joins

✔ Normalizing databases

✔ Backing up and restoring MySQL databases

**30 Min.
To Go**

U p to this point, you have learned the MySQL basics: how to create a database, populate it, and get results. A few more concepts are essential to getting the most out of
a MySQL database, from designing potential problems out of the database to combining several tables in queries. It's also important to have at least a rudimentary backup system in place just in case the worst happens. This session covers these advanced concepts.

Counting Result Sets

Sometimes you need to know only how many rows a specific query returns — the actual data
isn't important. The MySQL count() function comes in handy in such cases.

The count() function is typically used in place of the column list in a query. For example, to count how many records are in the computers table of your inventory database,
you would use the following:

```
SELECT count(*) FROM computers;
+----------+
| count(*) |
+----------+
|       25 |
+----------+
1 row in set (0.00 sec)
```

The advantage to using count() is that you don't need to return the entire data set and manually count the rows; you can simply ask MySQL to count them for you.

You can also use count() to tally combinations culled by a query. For example, to find out how many Compumate computers have each speed of processor, you would use the following:

```
SELECT comp_make,comp_speed,count(*)
   FROM computers
   WHERE comp_make = "Compumate"
   GROUP BY comp_make,comp_speed;
+------------+------------+----------+
| comp_make  | comp_speed | count(*) |
+------------+------------+----------+
| Compumate  |       1000 |        3 |
| Compumate  |       1400 |        2 |
| Compumate  |       1600 |        6 |
+------------+------------+----------+
3 rows in set (0.00 sec)
```

When using count() in this manner, you also need to specify how you want the results grouped, so MySQL knows what you want counted. You can use the GROUP BY clause to group the returned data set accordingly.

Note

Two other useful MySQL accounting functions are min() **and** max(). **These functions are used similarly to** count(). **For example, the following query shows the maximum** cpu_speed **stored in the** computers **table:**

```
SELECT max(comp_speed) FROM computers;
```

Using SELECT with More Than One Table

So far, you've seen how to use SELECT to pull data from a single table. Session 10 touched on how to use multiple tables in a SELECT query. This section covers the concept of *joins* (joining more than one table's query results) in more depth.

Specifying Columns from Multiple Tables

As briefly discussed in Session 10, you must be careful when specifying columns from multiple tables in the same query. In a perfect world, no two tables would have the same column name; however, in practice it happens quite frequently.

For example, suppose you had an orders database with the tables shown in Table 12-1.

Table 12-1 *Tables in the orders Database*

Table Name	Purpose
Customers	Storing customer information such as name, address, phone number, and so on

Table Name	Purpose
Products	Storing product information such as description, price, special shipping information, and so on
Orders	Storing orders generated by customers

The orders table would conceivably consist of the following columns:

- order_number — A sequential number to identify the order
- customer_number — A unique number identifying the customer who ordered
- product_number — A unique number to identify the product ordered
- quantity — The number of product_number ordered

Although order_number and quantity exist only in this one table, customer_number would probably be used in the customers table, and product_number would likely be used in the products table. Hence, the following query would cause ambiguity:

```
SELECT customer_name, customer_address FROM customers,orders
  WHERE customer_number = customer_number;
```

MySQL wouldn't know from which table to sample the customer_number values. However, if you specified the tables in the query, you would avoid any ambiguity:

```
SELECT customer_name, customer_address FROM customers,orders
  WHERE customers.customer_number = orders.customer_number;
```

To avoid potential ambiguity and confusion, always use table names with the column names in multiple-table queries.

20 Min. To Go

The Equi-Join

MySQL supports *equi-joins* (also known as *inner joins*), whereby you select data based on two columns, each from a separate table, being equal. For example, using the sample inventory database, the following query would return the location of the computer to which mouse "00411" is attached:

```
SELECT computers.comp_id,computers.comp_location
  FROM computers,mice
  WHERE computers.comp_id = mice.mouse_comp
  AND mice.mouse_id = "00411";
+---------+---------------+
| comp_id | comp_location |
+---------+---------------+
|   07743 | C200          |
+---------+---------------+
1 row in set (0.00 sec)
```

MySQL also supports using the keywords INNER JOIN to construct such a query. The preceding sample query rewritten using INNER JOIN, could be the following:

```
SELECT computers.comp_id,computers.comp_location
   FROM computers
   INNER JOIN mice ON computers.comp_id = mice.mouse_comp
   WHERE mice.mouse_id = "00411";
```

Notice how the joined table (mice) and the condition of the join (computers.comp_id = mice.mouse_comp) move to the INNER JOIN clause. Only the final selection criteria (mice.mouse_id = "00411") stay in the WHERE clause.

The advantage of using INNER JOIN is two-fold:

- It forces more structure on the join query syntax.
- It clearly shows that an inner join is being specified.

The Outer Join

A potential problem exists with inner joins when there isn't at least one matching record in the first table for every record in the second. For example, you might think that the following query would list every computer in inventory:

```
SELECT computers.comp_id,mice.mouse_comp
   FROM computers,mice
   WHERE mice.mouse_comp = computers.comp_id
   ORDER by computers.comp_id;
```

However, this query returns the following data set:

```
+---------+------------+
| comp_id | mouse_comp |
+---------+------------+
|   00946 |      00946 |
|   01347 |      01347 |
|   01523 |      01523 |
|   02210 |      02210 |
|   02559 |      02559 |
|   03663 |      03663 |
|   04070 |      04070 |
|   04780 |      04780 |
|   05212 |      05212 |
|   05295 |      05295 |
|   05654 |      05654 |
|   06073 |      06073 |
|   07065 |      07065 |
|   07185 |      07185 |
|   07743 |      07743 |
|   08036 |      08036 |
|   08057 |      08057 |
|   08316 |      08316 |
```

```
|   09144   |     09144   |
|   09307   |     09307   |
|   09499   |     09499   |
|   09569   |     09569   |
|   09834   |     09834   |
|   09894   |     09894   |
+---------+------------+
24 rows in set (0.00 sec)
```

However, counting the rows in the computers table yields different results:

```
SELECT count(*) FROM computers;
+----------+
| count(*) |
+----------+
|       25 |
+----------+
1 row in set (0.00 sec)
```

This is because one computer ("05021") does not have a mouse associated with it. To view all the computers via their mouse connections, you would use a *left outer join*, also commonly referred to as a *left join*:

```
SELECT computers.comp_id,mice.mouse_comp
  FROM computers
  LEFT OUTER JOIN mice ON mice.mouse_comp=computers.comp_id;
+---------+------------+
| comp_id | mouse_comp |
+---------+------------+
|   00946 |     00946  |
|   01347 |     01347  |
|   01523 |     01523  |
|   02210 |     02210  |
|   02559 |     02559  |
|   03663 |     03663  |
|   04070 |     04070  |
|   04780 |     04780  |
|   05021 |      NULL  |
|   05212 |     05212  |
|   05295 |     05295  |
|   05654 |     05654  |
|   06073 |     06073  |
|   07065 |     07065  |
|   07185 |     07185  |
|   07743 |     07743  |
|   08036 |     08036  |
|   08057 |     08057  |
|   08316 |     08316  |
|   09144 |     09144  |
|   09307 |     09307  |
|   09499 |     09499  |
|   09569 |     09569  |
```

```
|   09834 |     09834 |
|   09894 |     09894 |
+---------+-----------+
25 rows in set (0.00 sec)
```

Another type of query exists, known as a *right outer join*. However, this type of query can always be rewritten as a left join, so that type of query isn't discussed here.

A left join displays results even when there isn't a corresponding match between the joined table and the main (FROM) table. It produces NULL columns in the result set when the joined table could not provide data.

Database Normalization

Relational database construction should be a very deliberate and precise operation. However, a database is often constructed ad hoc; columns, tables, and even entire databases are added to the system as they are needed without much consideration about how they fit into or affect the whole.

Before creating a database, it pays to spend time on its design, ensuring that the resulting database is complete, soundly designed, and free from subtle problems.

One process of eliminating problems in database design is known as *normalization*. Normalization typically includes five *forms,* or steps, that should be taken to ensure that the resulting database is free from problems (typically referred to as *anomalies*). However, the first three forms are the most important and hence are covered here.

Database design is both an art and a science. You can learn much more information about the subject — much of which is beyond the scope of this book. If you do want to learn more about database design and normalization, pick up a copy of a dedicated MySQL or database design book. Some good candidates include *MySQL Bible*, by Steve Suehring (Wiley Publishing); *MySQL Enterprise Solutions*, by Alexander "Sasha" Pachev (Wiley Publishing); and *Database Design and Development: An Essential Guide for IT Professionals*, by Paulraj Ponniah (Wiley Publishing).

First Normal Form

The first normal form asserts that the database observe the following rules:

- Be free of repeated data
- Have separate tables for sets of related data
- Identify related data with a unique key.

The first rule — remaining free of repeated data groups — means that table structures such as the ones shown in Table 12-2 should be avoided.

Table 12-2 *Repeating Data Table: Orders*

Column	Use
order_id	Identifies order
product_1	First product ordered
qty_product1	Quantity of first product ordered
product_2	Second product ordered
qty_product2	Quantity of second product ordered
product_3	Third product ordered
qty_product3	Quantity of third product ordered

Notice how the groups of product data are repeated. What happens when someone orders four products? Do you add two more columns to the table to accommodate that order?

The best way to fix this problem is to move the product and quantity into their own rows, such as shown in Table 12-3.

Table 12-3 *Nonrepeating Data Table: Orders*

Column	Use
order_id	Identifies (links to) order
product	Product ordered
quantity	Quantity of product ordered

In theory, you could build a primary key on order_id and product, because there should not be an instance where two rows have the same values in both columns. This satisfies the third rule — a unique key for each row.

Second Normal Form

The second normal form asserts that separate tables be used for data that applies to multiple records.

For example, the mice and keyboards tables in the inventory database violate this form. The input device specifics are stored in the device tables despite the fact that those specifics apply to multiple records.

To fix this problem, you need to create mice_type and keyboard_type tables that contain the specifics and link them to the mice and keyboards tables. For example, examine the mice_type table:

```
CREATE TABLE mice_type (
  mouse_type_id INT(5) UNSIGNED ZEROFILL NOT NULL AUTO_INCREMENT,
  mouse_interface ENUM('USB','PS2') DEFAULT 'PS2',
  mouse_buttons TINYINT(2) NOT NULL DEFAULT '2',
  mouse_scroll ENUM('Y','N') DEFAULT 'Y',
  mouse_manufacture VARCHAR(20) NOT NULL DEFAULT '',
  PRIMARY KEY (`mouse_type_id`)
);
```

Whenever a new, unique mouse is purchased, a record is added to the mice_type table to describe that mouse. The mice table then appears as follows:

```
CREATE TABLE mice (
  mouse_id INT(5) UNSIGNED ZEROFILL NOT NULL DEFAULT '00000',
  mouse_type INT(5) UNSIGNED ZEROFILL NOT NULL;
  mouse_comp INT(5) UNSIGNED ZEROFILL NOT NULL DEFAULT '00000',
  mouse_ts TIMESTAMP(10) NOT NULL,
  PRIMARY KEY (`mouse_id`)
);
```

Each physical mouse would have an entry in the mice table, and its corresponding mouse_type column would match the appropriate mouse_type_id value from the mice_type table. For example, Tables 12-4 and 12-5 show the related records for a Logitech, two-button scroll mouse:

Table 12-4 *mice_type Record*

Column	Value
mouse_type_id	00003
mouse_interface	PS2
mouse_buttons	2
mouse_scroll	Y
mouse_manufacture	Logitech

Table 12-5 *mice Record*

Column	Value
mouse_id	00234
mouse_type	00003
mouse_comp	00549
mouse_ts	<timestamp>

> Columns such as mouse_type **in the** mice **table are commonly referred to as** *foreign keys* **because they are essentially keys into another table.**

Third Normal Form

The third normal form asserts that no columns be stored in tables that don't depend on that table's key. This means that if data in a table is not directly related to the table's key, you need to separate it out into its own table.

For example, suppose that you store the company name, address, and so on with customer contact data and regularly do business with many employees of different companies. If a company moves or changes its phone number, you would have many records to update. Instead, you could store the company name, address, and so on in a separate table and store a key to that table with your customer contact data. In other words, when you have a one-to-many relationship, you should examine moving the "one" to its own table.

Backing Up and Restoring MySQL Databases

10 Min. To Go

You can use a quick, easy method to back up a database in a form that is easy to restore. This method uses the utility program mysqldump.

The mysqldump program resides in the same directory as the mysqld and mysql executables. This utility's main function is to simply dump the contents of a database in MySQL command form. For example, the following command line dumps the sample inventory database:

```
mysqldump -p inventory
```

Notice the use of the -p parameter — its use is exactly like that of the MySQL monitor and results in the user being prompted for his or her password.

The output of this command resembles the following:

```
-- MySQL dump 9.07
--
-- Host: localhost    Database: inventory
---------------------------------------------------------
-- Server version      4.0.12


--
-- Table structure for table 'computers'
--

CREATE TABLE computers (
  comp_id int(5) unsigned zerofill NOT NULL default '00000',
  comp_make varchar(25) default NULL,
  comp_model varchar(10) default NULL,
  comp_cpu char(2) NOT NULL default '',
  comp_speed int(4) NOT NULL default '0',
  comp_mem int(4) NOT NULL default '0',
```

```
    comp_HD int(4) NOT NULL default '0',
    comp_CD enum('CD','DVD','CDRW','CDR','CDRW/DVD') default NULL,
    comp_location varchar(10) default NULL,
    comp_ts timestamp(10) NOT NULL,
    PRIMARY KEY  (comp_id)
) TYPE=MyISAM;


--
-- Dumping data for table 'computers'
--


INSERT INTO computers VALUES
(02210,'Compumate','A','P3',1600,512,40,'DVD','C124','0000000000');
INSERT INTO computers VALUES
(01347,'Compumate','A','P3',1600,512,40,'DVD','C033','0000000000');
INSERT INTO computers VALUES
(06073,'Compumate','A','P3',1600,512,40,'DVD','C224','0000000000');
INSERT INTO computers VALUES
(09307,'Compumate','A','P3',1600,512,40,'DVD','C224','0000000000');
INSERT INTO computers VALUES
(01523,'Compumate','A','P3',1600,512,40,'DVD','A125','0000000000');
INSERT INTO computers VALUES
(07065,'Compumate','B','P3',1000,256,30,'CD','A003','0000000000');
INSERT INTO computers VALUES
(07185,'Compumate','B','P3',1400,256,30,'CD','A122','0000000000');
INSERT INTO computers VALUES
(09894,'Compumate','C','P3',1000,128,30,'CD','B022','0000000000');
...
```

Each table in the database has its structure and data dumped in turn. The data is dumped in a format that is easy to re-import into MySQL — using this one file you can recreate and repopulate the database.

To get the most use out of the data dump, you should use your operating system's redirection capability to store the dump in a file. For example, the following command line stores a dump of the inventory database in a file named inventory-backup.sql:

```
mysqldump -p inventory >inventory-backup.sql
```

To create the best format for later restoration, use the following extended command line:

```
mysqldump -p --add-drop-table --databases inventory >inventory-backup.sql
```

Specifying the --databases parameter causes mysqldump to add appropriate CREATE DATABASE and USE commands to the top of the output file.

The --add-drop-table parameter causes mysqldump to insert a DROP TABLE command before each CREATE TABLE command. This ensures that the table is removed before it is recreated and restored by the rest of the dump file.

If it later becomes necessary to restore this snapshot of the database, you simply can feed this file to the MySQL monitor, as described in Session 11:

```
mysql -p <inventory-backup.sql
```

Setting Up a Script to Dump to a File

Set up a simple script to regularly dump the database to a file. It's best if you can add the current date to the filename and run it through a compression program (such as ZIP) after the information is dumped. A basic Linux script to accomplish this is as follows:

```
# Set variables
DBNAME="<database_name>"
DATE=`date -I`
BAKDIR="<directory_to_store_backup>"
BAKFILE="$BAKDIR/$DATE-$DBNAME-Backup.sql"
# Remove any backups more than 14 days old
rm `find  $BAKDIR/*.sql.gz -ctime +14`
# Dump database
mysqldump --user=<user> --password=<password>  \
  --add-drop-table --databases $DBNAME >$BAKFILE
# ZIP dump file

gzip $BAKFILE
```

This script results in a file such as 2003-05-03-inventory-Backup.sql.gz being stored for each day the script is run. To use this script, simply replace the values in corner brackets (for example, *<database_name>*) with the appropriate values and ensure that the user you specify has appropriate rights to dump the data. To make the script even more useful, add it to your crontab to automatically back up the database at specified intervals.

This method is simple, but not perfect. If the database is in use when mysqldump **is invoked, you have no guarantee that the data dumped will match the data in the database — especially if the database undergoes frequent changes when in use.**

Done!

REVIEW

This session finishes the basic tutorial sessions on MySQL. In this session, you learned how to count result sets, use a query to combine information from multiple tables, and start on the right foot by designing a problem-free database. You also learned how to back up and restore a MySQL database — you should do the former often just in case you have to do the latter. The next few sessions cover PHP.

QUIZ YOURSELF

1. What is the purpose of the count() function? (See "Counting Result Sets.")
2. How do you specify the table from which a particular column should come? (See "Specifying Columns from Multiple Tables.")
3. Why is an inner join also referred to as an equi-join? (See "The Equi-Join.")
4. What is another name for an outer join? (See "The Outer Join.")
5. How many forms does normalization have? (See "Database Normalization.")
6. What is the purpose of the --add-drop-table parameter when using mysqldump? (See "Backing Up and Restoring MySQL Databases.")

Getting Ready to Use PHP

Session Checklist

✔ Reviewing the Apache configuration for PHP

✔ Understanding how PHP works

✔ Using PHP from the command line

**30 Min.
To Go**

The next several sessions cover PHP scripting, including programming conventions such as variables, program flow, how to work with HTML files, normal file system files, and more. However, before jumping into actual scripting, you need to ensure that PHP is set up for use with Apache and learn a bit about alternative ways to run scripts through the PHP interpreter.

Reviewing Apache and PHP Configuration

You set up and configured PHP at the end of Session 2. However, before you start working extensively with PHP programs, it is wise to ensure that PHP is properly configured with Apache. The next few sections review the setup for Windows and Linux.

Unless you need to set up PHP with Windows, skip ahead to the section "Reviewing Linux PHP Setup."

Reviewing Windows PHP Setup

Windows uses a .dll file to parse PHP scripts. This file is installed as an Apache 2.0 module that is called when Apache encounters a file identified by defined PHP MIME types.

The module used for PHP 4 is named php4apache2.dll and is installed with PHP. (If you are using Apache 1.*x*, the module is named php4apache.dll instead.) This module is typically found in the following directory:

```
<php_directory>\sapi\php4apache2.dll
```

For Apache to load modules, it must have module support. The modules you want Apache to use are placed in the Apache configuration file with the following syntax:

```
LoadModule <module_structure> <module_file>
```

The `<module_file>` parameter must include the full path to the module file or be relative to the configuration file's `ServerRoot` setting. In addition, each module's structure must be referenced by its correct name — you cannot use any name you choose.

The following information must be included in the Apache configuration file (typically `httpd.conf`) for PHP 4.*x* to work in module form:

- The modules section of the configuration file must include the following line:

  ```
  LoadModule php4_module modules/libphp4.so
  ```

- The MIME type section of the configuration file must include the following line:

  ```
  AddType application/x-httpd-php .php .phtml
  ```

  Optionally, you can add more extensions to the end of the type if you want other files to be run through the PHP engine.

- Although optional, a good idea is to add `index.php` to the end of the `DirectoryIndex` line in the configuration file. This ensures that `index.php` is one of the files that is returned when a client accesses a directory without specifying a file.

 See Session 5 for more information about Apache's configuration files.

You need to restart the server if the configuration file is changed. Restart the server by using the Apache Service Monitor.

Unless you need to set up PHP with Apache on Linux, skip ahead to the section "Command-Line PHP."

**20 Min.
To Go**

Reviewing Linux PHP Setup

Linux uses an Apache module to parse PHP scripts. This module is called when Apache runs into the MIME types you defined for PHP.

The module used for PHP 4.*x* is named `libphp4.so` and is typically installed in the Apache modules directory. On a Red Hat system, where Apache is installed via RPM, the Apache modules directory is `/etc/httpd/modules`.

 Other locations for the Apache modules **directory include** `/usr/lib/`
`apache/<version>/libphp4.so`, `/etc/apache/modules`, **and so on. If in
doubt, search for files that end in** `.so`.

For Apache to load modules, it must be compiled with module support. Then the modules you want to load are placed in the Apache configuration file with the following syntax:

```
LoadModule <module_structure> <module_file>
```

The Apache configuration file is typically `httpd.conf`.

Notice that the `<module_file>` parameter must include the full path to the module file or be relative to the configuration file's `ServerRoot` setting. In addition, each module's defined module structure(s) must be referenced by its correct name — you cannot use any name you choose.

The following information must be included in the Apache configuration file for PHP 4.*x* to work in module form:

- The modules section of the configuration file must include the following line:

  `LoadModule php4_module modules/libphp4.so`

- The MIME type section of the configuration file must include the following line:

  `AddType application/x-httpd-php .php .phtml`

  Optionally, you can add more extensions to the end of the type if you want other files to be run through the PHP engine.

- Although optional, it's a good idea to add `index.php` to the end of the `DirectoryIndex` line in the configuration file. This ensures that `index.php` is one of the files that is returned when a client accesses a directory without specifying a file.

See Session 5 for more information about Apache's configuration files. You need to restart the server if the configuration file is changed. Restart the server with the appropriate `init` **script or use the** `apachectl` **program:**

`apachectl restart`

Understanding How PHP Works with Apache

Apache uses MIME types to determine how to serve up specific files. For example, look at the PHP MIME type definition in the Apache configuration file:

`AddType application/x-httpd-php .php .phtml`

Whenever Apache is asked to serve up a file with a `.php` or `.phtml` extension, it identifies the file as a PHP file and utilizes the appropriate module (the PHP module) to help serve it. In PHP's case, the module provides communication with the PHP engine. The engine executes the PHP code and directs any output back to Apache for forwarding to the client.

Command-Line PHP

10 Min.
To Go

You can also run PHP from the command line. This is useful for testing your scripts by evaluating their actions and output outside of the Web server. This can help you identify errors in the script, as opposed to those caused by the Apache server or the user's client.

PHP can be a powerful scripting language. Future sessions describe how to use PHP with the file system to accomplish various tasks, such as moving files and so on, which are useful for a command-line script.

To run PHP 4.x at the command line, you simply run the PHP 4.x executable.

On Windows, the PHP 4.x executable is php.exe and is stored in the main PHP directory.

On Linux, the PHP 4.x executable is php and is often stored in a common PHP executable directory, such as /usr/local/php/bin. On some systems, PHP is stored in a more generic binary directory such as /usr/bin.

Running the PHP executable places you in the PHP interpreter's interactive mode, from which you can enter PHP code. For example, run the PHP executable and type the following into the interpreter:

```
<?php
  echo "hello world \n";
?>
```

After entering the code, press Ctrl+D to exit the interpreter on Linux, or press Ctrl+Z to exit the interpreter on Windows. At this point, PHP executes the code and should respond with the following:

```
Content-type: text/html
X-Powered-By: PHP/4.3.1

hello world
```

Of course, this isn't a very useful way to use PHP, typing all your code manually into the interpreter. If you make a typo, correcting it is nearly impossible after you press Enter on the line where you made the mistake. A more effective way to use the interpreter is via your operating system's redirect functionality — entering your code in a file and redirecting it through the interpreter.

For example, place the sample code in a file named sample.php:

```
<?php
  echo "hello world \n";
?>
```

Now, redirect it into the PHP interpreter using a command line similar to the following:

```
php <sample.php
```

The interpreter processes the file, displays any output, and exits the interpreter mode:

```
Content-type: text/html
X-Powered-By: PHP/4.3.1

hello world
```

Notice the HTML header that is automatically output by the PHP interpreter. This is one of the automatic functions of PHP that makes it well suited for Web server deployment.

If the output from the script is lengthy, you can redirect it to a text file for evaluation in your favorite text editor:

```
php <sample.php >output.txt
```

PHP as a Command-Line Scripting Language

You can also use PHP as a command-line script utility. Although this is easier in Linux, Windows can also take advantage of PHP as a command-line scripting utility.

When using Linux, simply begin a script file with the following line:

```
#! /usr/bin/php
```

Be sure to use the correct path to the PHP executable on your system if the preceding instance is not the correct one. This line tells Linux to use the PHP executable to interpret the rest of the file. The rest of the file should include PHP code, and the file should have executable permissions for all users you want to have access to the script.

For most command-line scripting applications, you do not want PHP to output the HTTP headers. To stop the header output, append `-q` to the end of the first line, as follows:

```
#! /usr/bin/php -q
```

This parameter (quiet mode) suppresses the automatic HTTP headers.

When using Windows, you must associate .php files with the PHP executable. To do so, follow these steps:

1. Create a file on the Windows desktop with a .php extension. (Although the file can be blank, actually creating a script is best — use the sample script from earlier in this session.)

2. Double-click the file. Windows displays the Open With dialog box, as shown in Figure 13-1.

3. Make sure that the Always Use this Program to Open These Files checkbox is checked and click the Other button. Windows displays a File Manager interface, as shown in Figure 13-2.

Figure 13-1   *The Open With dialog box enables you to associate programs with particular extensions.*

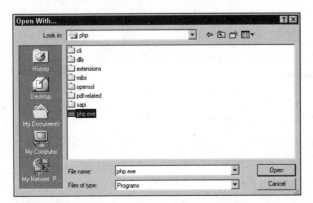

Figure 13-2   *Use the File Manager interface to select the PHP executable.*

4. Use the File Manager interface of the dialog box to locate and select the PHP executable. Click Open after you have selected the php.exe file.

5. Click OK in the Open With dialog box to select the PHP Script Interpreter as the program to handle .php files.

Thereafter, whenever you click a .php file, Windows uses the interpreter to execute the script contained in the file.

This method of using PHP in Windows is not ideal because you cannot view output created by the script — Windows closes the output window as soon as the script is complete.

Done!

REVIEW

This session covered some basics about PHP setup and alternative ways to run the PHP interpreter. After completing this session, you should be confident that Apache and PHP are set up to work with each other, and you can begin scripting Web content. The next several sessions cover how to script in PHP. Later sessions cover how to integrate PHP scripts into MySQL.

QUIZ YOURSELF

1. How does Apache use MIME type definitions? (See "Reviewing Windows PHP Setup" and/or "Reviewing Linux PHP Setup.")

2. What is the LoadModule line's format in the Apache configuration file? (See "Reviewing Windows PHP Setup" and/or "Reviewing Linux PHP Setup.")

3. Why would you add additional file types to the PHP MIME definition? (See "Reviewing Windows PHP Setup" and/or "Reviewing Linux PHP Setup.")

4. What are the advantages of using PHP on the command line? (See "Command-Line PHP.")

PHP Basics

Session Checklist

✔ Basic PHP script syntax

✔ Using PHP variables

✔ Using print and echo statements

✔ Working with data types

✔ Understanding assignment, comparison, and logical operators

**30 Min.
To Go**

Before you begin coding in PHP, you need to understand a few basic premises of the language. This session introduces you to a PHP script's basic form, including how to place comments within your code to help you and others understand it. It then covers variables, data types, and operators as a precursor to the next session.

Basic Script Syntax

PHP scripts are stored in plaintext format and follow a specific syntax. The following sections introduce you to PHP's scripting structure and syntax.

PHP Beginning and Ending Tags

All PHP code needs to be enclosed within beginning and ending tags. The PHP beginning tag is <?php and the ending tag is ?>. For example, examine the following basic PHP script:

```php
<?php
  echo "Hello world. \n";
?>
```

Notice how the first line contains the beginning tag and the last line contains the ending tag. Because of PHP's interpretation of white space (generally ignored), you could just as easily use the following:

```
<?php  echo "Hello world. \n";  ?>
```

However, this format isn't as clear because the beginning and ending tags appear on the same line. Using the first form, in which the beginning and ending tags are distinct, is best.

You can turn PHP processing on and off within a script by closing and reopening the PHP tags. For example, if you wanted to embed some complex HTML within a script (or embed simple scripts within HTML), you could do something like the following:

```
<?php
    [php code here]
?>
    [HTML code here]
<?php
    [more php code here]
?>...
```

You can turn PHP processing on and off as many times as you like within one script, providing you insert a beginning tag and ending tag for each occurrence.

Command Termination Character

PHP understands the semicolon character as the end of the current command. For example, the echo line in the sample in the preceding section ends with a semicolon. Technically, because the line is the last in the script, PHP recognizes the end of the line when it encounters the PHP ending tag (?>).

PHP's Use of White Space

PHP ignores white space, treating all manner of white space as the equivalent of a single space, including the following:

- Carriage returns
- Line feeds
- Blank lines
- Tabs
- Spaces

Therefore, the following scripts are all equally valid:

```
<?php
  echo "Hello world. \n";
?>


<?php  echo "Hello world. \n";  ?>
```

and

```php
<?php

  echo "Hello world. \n";

?>
```

Because of PHP's liberal interpretation of white space, you should let readability of your code guide your use of white space. It's generally better to follow these simple rules when formatting your code:

- Use liberal white space within lines. Separate key elements of equations and function calls with spaces. Enter a space on either side of an equal sign, after each comma in function parameters, and so on.
- Use liberal white space between significant sections of code. For example, between a section that sets up variables and a section that begins processing, insert at least one blank line to delimit the two sections. (You also want to insert comments accordingly, but that is covered in the next section.)
- Break any line that exceeds approximately 70 characters into multiple lines. This keeps your code from scrolling off the screen in 80-column editors and keeps intelligent editors from auto-breaking lines — perhaps incorrectly.
- Indent subordinate lines of code or continuations of lines. For example, consider the following echo line:

```php
echo "The quick brown fox jumped over the lazy dog. The quick brown fox
jumped over the lazy dog. The quick brown fox jumped over the lazy dog.
The quick brown fox jumped over the lazy dog.";
```

This line is clearer in the following format:

```php
echo "The quick brown fox jumped over the lazy dog. The quick brown
    fox jumped over the lazy dog. The quick brown fox jumped over the
    lazy dog. The quick brown fox jumped over the lazy dog.";
```

It's quickly apparent that all lines comprise one single command. (Subordinate lines are covered in the next session, along with commands such as if.)

Commenting Code

PHP supports the use of comments in its code. Comments are nonexecuted lines that are meant to be human readable, that is, lines to annotate the code. You can insert comments in your code several ways:

- A line that begins with a pound sign (#) or a double-slash (//) is treated as a comment. All text after the # or // is ignored up to the next line break.
- Multiline comments can be inserted between /* and */ tags. This is useful when using large blocks of text in comments.
- A double-slash can be used at the end of a command to comment that command. PHP ignores all text between the double-slash and the end of the line.

The following are all examples of valid comments:

```
# Begin code segment

  // Output "Hello world." and a line break

  echo "Hello world. \n"; // Output "Hello world."

/*
This is a block of comment text.
This is a block of comment text.
This is a block of comment text.
*/
```

Use comments liberally *while you write your code*. Often, commenting as you write code seems like a hassle, and you might think that going back and commenting your code later is easier. Resist this temptation — you may not remember what specific lines in your code actually do.

Of course, commenting every line isn't necessary. Add explanations to each section of code and to complex lines or equations. Starting your PHP scripts with a comment block similar to the following is also a good idea:

```
/*
  sample.php - A simple script to say "hello world"
  Written by: Steve Schafer
  Last updated: 5/15/03
*/
```

This block helps you identify your scripts, who wrote them, and when they were last updated. Although it may not sound important now, it will after a few months of development — trust me.

 If you plan to do a lot of development, you may also want to invest time (and perhaps money) in a content versioning system to help track code development. Linux and Windows users alike should investigate CVS (www.cvshome.org**) or Subversion (**http://subversion.tigris.org/**).**

PHP Variables

PHP denotes variables with a dollar sign. Variable names can be any length and contain numbers, letters, or underscores. Variable names must start with a letter or an underscore — they cannot start with a number. Examples of valid variables include the following:

```
$name
$_code_ptr
$first_and_last_name
$SubTotal
$log99
```

You can use variables to store text, integers, or floating-point values. Because PHP variables are untyped, you can store any type of data in any variable and even store multiple types of data in the variable. For example, any of the following values can be stored in a variable:

```
"Amy Libler"  (text)
123  (integer)
49.95  (floating point)
"$99.95"  (text, due to non-number character "$")
```

You can store values in variables in numerous ways, with the most common being direct assignment with the equal sign (=). For example, if you wanted to assign "Geoff" to the variable $name, you would use the following code:

```
$name = "Geoff";
```

Notice that you enclose "Geoff" in quotes because it is a text string. If you wanted to assign a number to a variable, you would omit the quotes (or it would end up being a string variable):

```
$price = 12.67;
```

If you then wanted to assign another variable to the same value, you could use variables on both sides of the equal sign:

```
$new_price = $price;
```

PHP 4 includes a new variable assignment method: *by reference.* **This method enables you to assign a variable to another variable's value. To do so, you prefix an ampersand (&) to the source variable. For example, the following would assign variable** $metoo **to the value of the variable** $mefirst:

```
$metoo = &$mefirst;
```

Thereafter, any change to one of the variables also changes the other in the same way.

PHP includes a multitude of built-in functions to determine the type of a particular variable and to transfer a variable value from one type to another.

See Session 16 or the online PHP documentation (available at www.php.net**) for more information on PHP functions.**

Determining a variable's type and converting the value to another type can be important — not doing such checks and conversions can have adverse results. However, PHP does some intelligent conversions for you. For example, consider the following code:

```
$price_one = 125.45;
$price_two = "56.78";
$total = $price_one + $price_two;
```

Despite the fact that $price_two is a text string, the value of $total contains the value 182.23. However, if $price_two contained any nonnumeric characters (for example, "$56.78"), PHP would have ignored it in the calculation and $total would have been 125.45.

You can use variables in output as well. For example, suppose you append the following line of code onto the preceding code:

```
print $total;
```

PHP would respond by outputting the value of $total, or "182.23." If you change the value of $total, subsequent print $total; statements would output the new value.

 The print **statement is covered in detail in the following section.**

print and echo

PHP has two similar, built-in functions for outputting data: print and echo. Both have a similar syntax:

```
print <string>
echo <string1>[, <string2>, ...]
```

However, the two functions have a few notable differences:

- Print can be used only to output a single string, whereas echo can output several strings separated by commas. Notice that echo outputs all of its arguments appended together without any interleaving spaces or other characters.
- Print supports *here document* syntax, described in the section "Here Document Output," later in this session.
- Print is a true function; it returns TRUE if the output was successful, FALSE if the output was not successful.

Both functions support variables in their parameters. For example, the following code outputs "The total is: 182.23":

```
$price_one = 125.45;
$price_two = 56.78;
$total = $price_one + $price_two;
print "The total is: $total";
```

Quoting Output

Generally, you want to use double quotes to enclose the arguments for print and echo. Double quotes enable the text within the quotes to be evaluated — something important when embedding variables in your output. Single quotes cause the text within to be output verbatim, without any evaluation.

For example, consider the following two pieces of code:

```
print "The total is: $total";
print 'The total is: $total';
```

Supposing that $total is equal to 33.55, the first line predictably outputs the following:

```
The total is: 33.55
```

However, the second line doesn't evaluate $total as a variable; it simply outputs the text within the single quotes verbatim:

```
The total is: $total
```

Escape Characters

Both print and echo also support the use of *escape characters* in their output. Escape characters are used for two purposes:

- To insert otherwise confusing characters into the output. For example, if you put a double quote (") in the output (already enclosed in double quotes), print and echo could confuse this with the end of that parameter.
- To insert special, nontypeable characters, such as a newline, a tab, and so on

Escape characters begin with a backslash (\) and have one character after them, indicating the character the escape represents. Table 14-1 lists some common escape characters.

Table 14-1 *Common Escape Characters*

Escape Character	Output
\n	Newline (line feed)
\r	Carriage return
\t	Tab
\\	Backslash
\$	Dollar sign
\"	Double quote
\'	Single quote

An example of using escape characters with print follows:

```
print "One line\nanother line\n\tthird line, indented";
```

This code would produce the following output:

```
One line
```

```
another line
    third line, indented
```

If you try the preceding example and view the results in a browser, you might be surprised that the output looks more like this:

```
One line another line third line, indented
```

This is because your browser treats the output as standard HTML, condensing the white space into a single space. If you use your browser's View Source command, you see that the text is formatted as specified.

The quote escape characters (\" and \') are useful if you need to insert a double quote inside of double-quoted text or a single quote within single-quoted text. For example, consider the following line:

```
$text = "She said, \"It was a dark and stormy night.\"";
```

The quotes around the phrase need to be escaped so that they aren't confused with the quotes surrounding the full sentence.

Here Document Output

Outputting blocks of text using print is not always convenient. Your options are to place the entire block in a long string (optionally using escape characters to format it) or use several print statements. However, print supports *here document syntax* for just such cases.

A print statement using here document syntax looks like the following code:

```
print <<<END
<html>
  <body>
      This is a sample HTML page.
  </body>
</html>
END;
```

Essentially, this syntax tells PHP to output everything between the <<<END and END; tags, just as it appears. Keep the following in mind when using here document:

- No semicolon is at the end of the opening print line.
- The here document tag (END, in the preceding example) can be any text that is valid for a variable name. (See "PHP Variables," earlier in this session.)
- The ending tag must appear flush left, without any spaces or other indentation.
- You can include variables, escape characters, and other normal constructs used in print statements in a here document block.

PHP Data Types

**20 Min.
To Go**

PHP supports several distinct types of data. This section details the various types and their use, how to operate on them, and ways to convert between them.

The Different Data Types

Table 14-2 lists the various data types supported by PHP.

Table 14-2 *PHP Data Types*

Type	Description	Examples
Integer	A whole number without a decimal point	123, -234, 0
Double	A floating-point number	3.14159, -33.4, 0.0
String	A series of characters	"Jim Dandy", "221B Baker Street", "23.45"
Boolean	True or False	TRUE, FALSE
Null	The literal value NULL	NULL
Array	A collection of like-typed variables	["Apple","Pear","Banana"]
Object	Programmer-defined class, incorporating values and functions	N/A
Resources	References to external resources (such as databases)	N/A

Arrays are covered in the next section, "PHP Arrays."

If you assign a value to a variable, PHP makes a *best guess* at the type the variable should be. For example, consider the following line of code:

```
$variable = 44.55;
```

In this case, PHP types the variable as double, because it was assigned a value that was a number and included a decimal.

However, what if you were to quote the value as shown in the following line of code?

```
$variable = "44.55";
```

In this case, PHP would type the variable as a string, simply because of the surrounding quotes.

A variable's type has some effect on PHP's capability to contextually convert the variable's type when necessary. When in doubt, always test and/or convert a variable's type to what you need. (See the section "Changing Data Types," later in this session, for more information on testing and converting types.)

PHP Arrays

Arrays are constructs that enable you to group related information together — typically, for indexed access. In PHP, you must declare a variable an array and optionally define its contents. For example, if you wanted to store a selection of car manufacturers in an array, you could use the following line:

```
$car_make = array ("Chevrolet", "Ford", "Honda", "Mitsubishi");
```

Thereafter, you would reference the individual values by suffixing the variable name with a number in brackets, corresponding to the number of the element you want. For example, to reference Ford, you would use one (1) as the index, as in the following line:

```
print $car_make[1];
```

This would output Ford.

As is typical in programming, the first element in an array is element zero (0), not element one (1). For example, the following line would output "Chevrolet":

```
print $car_make[0];
```

In PHP, arrays are typically associative, meaning that they use keys instead of numbers to reference array elements. For example, consider the following array definition:

```
$car = array ("make" => "Mitsubishi", "model" => "Eclipse Spyder",
    "year" => "2002", "color" => "Red", "mileage" => 35234);
```

Notice how each key is the equivalent of a variable name (and follows the same naming conventions as variables), which is followed by the key reference assignment operator (=>), and then by the value.

If you wanted to access the mileage for this car, you would use the following:

```
$car["mileage"]
```

This method of accessing array values is particularly useful when working with databases in which the key names correspond to field names. You can find more information on using arrays with databases in Session 23.

Changing Data Types

PHP does a decent job of automatically converting data types, as necessary, to accomplish what you tell it to do. However, sometimes you must be exact with your data types and manually convert from one type to another.

Testing Data Types

The PHP function gettype() returns the type of variable. For example, the following code would output "double":

```
$number = 44.55;
print gettype($number);
```

Several other functions, one per type, test for specific data types:

- is_integer() returns TRUE if the variable tested is an integer.
- is_double() returns TRUE if the variable tested is a floating-point number.
- is_boolean() returns TRUE if the variable tested is a boolean value.
- is_string() returns TRUE if the variable tested is a character string.

Many other is functions determine a variable's type and potential use. See the PHP documentation for more information.

These functions can be used in conditional statements — if the type isn't what is expected, the code can convert the variable type, as necessary. For more on conditional statements, see the next session.

Converting Types

The easiest way to ensure that a variable is the type you want is to use the settype() function. The settype() function takes a variable name and a type as arguments. For example, if you wanted to ensure that the variable $number was a floating-point number, you would use the following line of code:

```
settype($number, "float");
```

The settype() function returns TRUE if the conversion was successful, FALSE if it was not. The function accepts integer, float, double, string, and boolean as arguments.

Older versions of PHP (pre-version 4.2) used double. Newer versions of PHP use float but still support double.

The settype() function converts most values as you would expect. Numeric values of zero (0) are evaluated as boolean FALSE; any other value is evaluated as TRUE. Note that you shouldn't use numeric data types when you want a boolean evaluation; use a boolean type instead.

Operators and Expressions

**10 Min.
To Go**

PHP supports several different types of operators that can be used in simple or complex expressions. This section covers the most frequently used operators in several categories.

Assignment Operator

The assignment operator was previously mentioned in the "PHP Variables" section, earlier in this session. This operator, an equal sign (=), is used to assign a specific value to a variable. For example, the following code assigns the numeric value 3.14 to the variable $short_pi:

```
$short_pi = 3.14;
```

 You can specify the exact type you want a variable to be by adding the type in parentheses between the equal sign and the value. For example, to ensure that $short_pi is typed as a floating point (double), use the following:

```
$short_pi = (double) 3.14;
```

Notice that this usage supports the usual types — integer, float/double, boolean, and so on.

The assignment operator can also be used with more complex assignments, in which the value of the assignment needs to be evaluated from one or more variables. For example, consider the following lines of code:

```
$total = $first_price + $second_price;

$total = $total + ($total * $tax);

$total = cos($length);
```

All of these lines are valid assignment statements.

Arithmetic Operators

PHP supports the usual set of arithmetic operators for addition, subtraction, division, and multiplication. In addition, PHP supports an operator for modulus (division remainder) and a combination assignment operator for each arithmetic operator. Table 14-3 summarizes the arithmetic operators and their combination assignment operators.

Table 14-3 *Arithmetic Operators*

Operation	Operator	Combo-Assignment
Addition	+	+=
Subtraction	-	-=
Multiplication	*	*=
Division	/	/=
Modulus	%	%=

The combination assignment operators take a value and apply it to the current value of the variable being assigned. For example, the following results in $number equaling 12 (10 + 2):

```
$number = 10;   // Set $number to 10
$number += 2;   // Add 2
```

Notice that the value on the right side of the equal sign can be an expression such as *($alpha + 20 * $beta)* and doesn't need to be a single number or value.

Integer values have two additional shortcut assignment operators: one to increment the integer value and another to decrement it. These shortcuts use double operators directly after the variable name, as follows:

```
$number++;   //increment $number
$number--;   // decrement $number
```

This method is generally used in counting loops as shortcuts for the following lines:

```
$number = $number + 1;   //increment $number
$number = $number - 1;   //decrement $number
```

Concatenation Operator

Occasionally, combining two or more strings into one is necessary. PHP supports the concatenation operator, a period ("."), for this task. For example, consider the following code:

```
$first_name = "Steve";
$last_name = "Schafer";
$full_name = $first_name . " " . $last_name;
print $full_name;
```

This code outputs Steve Schafer, the combination of the value in $first_name, a space, and the value in $last_name. Notice that adding the space between the words was necessary or the code would have output SteveSchafer.

The concatenation operator is commonly used in print statements to append values only for printing. For example, if you used $full_name only for printing purposes, and you didn't need to retain the $full_name for any other purpose, you could have concatenated the required values in the print statement itself:

```
$first_name = "Steve";
$last_name = "Schafer";
print $full_name . " " . $last_name;
```

Comparison Operators

PHP supports several different comparison operators, summarized in Table 14-4.

Table 14-4 *Comparison Operators*

Operator	Meaning
==	Equal to
!=	Not equal to
>	Greater than (left greater than right)
<	Less than (left less than right)
>=	Greater than or equal to
<=	Less than or equal to
===	Identical (equal to and same type)

Notice the use of double and triple equal signs for two of the operators. A single equal sign is an assignment operator; two and three equal signs are comparison operators. Be very careful not to misuse them, as it is easy to do. The identical operator evaluates as TRUE only if the two values being compared are truly identical — that is, the same value and the same type. For example, the following evaluates as FALSE because one value is a double and the other is a string:

```
3.14 === "3.14";
```

Comparison operators are typically used in conditional statements. Conditional statements are covered in Session 15.

Logical Operators

PHP supports several logical operators that you can use to create more complex comparisons. For example, you may want to make a decision based on the following conditions: a customer is male and living in Maryland. To build an expression to evaluate these conditions, you would use the and operator:

```
($sex == "M") and ($state == "MD")
```

Each logical operator operates on two values. Table 14-5 summarizes the logical operators.

Table 14-5 *Logical Operators*

Operator	Meaning
!	Not. Reverses the boolean value.
&&	Synonym of and. Evaluates to TRUE only if both values are TRUE.
||	Synonym of or. Evaluates to TRUE if either value is TRUE.
xor	Xor. Evaluates to TRUE only if one or the other value is TRUE, but evaluates to FALSE if both are TRUE.

Operator Precedence

PHP follows the general arithmetic rules of precedence when evaluating complex expressions. For example, in the following expression, PHP performs the division first, and then the addition, despite the order of the operators:

```
$number = 35 + 12 / 6;
```

This causes $number to be 37 (35 + 2), not 7.83 (47 / 6).

Generally speaking, PHP evaluates operators in the following order, from left to right:

- Multiplication, division, or modulus
- Addition, subtraction, or concatenation
- Greater or less than
- Equivalency
- Logical operators

You can force PHP's order of precedence with the use of parentheses; doing so is often a good idea to ensure that the operation is carried out with the precedence you intend. Using the preceding example, you can force PHP to do the addition first if you add parentheses around the addition operation:

```
$number = (35 + 12) / 6;
```

Done!

REVIEW

This session introduced you to the basics of PHP. You learned how to tell the processor where the script starts and stops using PHP beginning and ending tags. You also learned about variables and how to output data from PHP using print and echo. The session then moved on to cover the data types PHP supports and how to build expressions using different types of operators. The next session, "Program Flow," builds on this information, showing how PHP scripts can make decisions and execute code according to the decisions made.

QUIZ YOURSELF

1. How many times can you start and stop PHP processing within a script? (See "PHP Beginning and Ending Tags.")
2. What is the PHP command termination character and how is it used? (See "Command Termination Character.")
3. How can you add a comment to the end of a command line? (See "Commenting Code.")
4. Is $99_red_balloons a valid variable name? (See "PHP Variables.")
5. How many strings can print output with one command? (See "print and echo.")
6. What is the *here document* print syntax used for? (See "Here Document Output.")
7. What is the function is_string() used for? (See "Testing Data Types.")
8. What does the statement $number++; do? (See "Arithmetic Operators.")

Program Flow

Session Checklist

✔ Working with programming blocks

✔ Using conditional statements

✔ Understanding loop structures

**30 Min.
To Go**

Without conditionals and loops, programming tools would be fairly useless. Conditionals lend intelligence to programs, enabling them to execute code (or not) based on run-time data and conditions. Loops provide a way to execute the same code repeatedly while a certain condition exists or until a certain condition exists. This session introduces you to conditional structures, such as the if statement, and loop structures, such as while and for. Session 16 introduces the breadth of functions built into PHP, and subsequent sessions teach you how to wrap all this together into useful programs.

Programming Blocks

Before you dive into conditionals and loops, you need to understand *programming blocks* in PHP. A programming block is a sequence of statements enclosed in braces. These blocks generally occur around conditionals and loops.

Blocks are delimited by braces ({ and }). They are commonly used to group lines of code together to be executed if a condition is true or as part of a loop. For example, take a look at the following code:

```
if ($number <= 10) {
  print "$number \n";
  $check = $number;
  $catalog = "Home Gadgets";
}
```

In this case, the block of code starts right after the closing parenthesis of the second line and ends on the last line. PHP executes all lines in between the braces (the `print` and two assignment statements) if the conditional statement (`if`) evaluates as TRUE.

The formatting of blocks is subjective. I prefer to start blocks on the line where the conditional or loop ends; others prefer to start the block on the line following the conditional or loop, as follows:

```
if ($number <= 10)
{
  print "$number \n";
  $check = $number;
  $catalog = "Home Gadgets";

}
```

Feel free to experiment with the placement and format of the braces and the indentation of the code within. Whatever you decide, be consistent.

If this concept seems a bit vague right now, it becomes clearer as you work through this session and the related conditional and loop constructs.

Conditional Statements

PHP has two main conditional statements: `if` and `switch`. `if` evaluates an expression and executes code based on whether the expression is TRUE or FALSE. `switch` compares a variable against several expressions and executes the code that corresponds to the expression that was matched.

The following sections cover `if` and `switch` in detail.

General if Structure

As previously mentioned, the `if` statement evaluates one expression and executes code based on the boolean value of that expression. The `if` statement has the following syntax:

```
if (expression) {
   code to do if expression = TRUE
}
```

The expression you use with an `if` conditional can be as simple or as complex as you like. The following are all valid expressions:

```
(TRUE)
```

```
($value)
```

```
($number > 2)
```

```
(($zip == "24560") && ($first_name == "John"))
```

```
!($zip == "45667")
```

Remember that the code in the if block executes only if the expression evaluates to TRUE. If the expression evaluates to FALSE, the entire block is skipped, and code execution continues with the first line after the if block.

If you have only one statement to execute with an if statement, you can skip the braces and even include the statement on the same line with the if, as shown in the following example:

```
if ($state == "MD") print "Maryland \n";
```

This holds true for most of the conditional and loop structures covered in this session.

else and elseif

Sometimes, you want one block of code to execute if an expression evaluates to TRUE and another block to execute if the expression evaluates to FALSE. In this case, you could use two if statements similar to the following:

```
if (expression) {
  <code to execute if expression = TRUE>
}
if !(expression) {
  <code to execute if expression = FALSE>
}
```

However, this code tends to be messy and can be plagued with errors. Consider what would happen if the first loop expression evaluates to TRUE and the code block changes the conditions so that the second loop expression also evaluates as TRUE. Both blocks of code would then execute.

The correct way to handle this is using the else statement. The else statement adds "otherwise do this" functionality to an if statement. An if statement with an else has the following syntax:

```
if (expression) {
  <code to execute if expression = TRUE>
} else {
  <code to execute if expression = FALSE>
}
```

Again, the placement and format of the block braces are subjective. I prefer the preceding format, but others might want the braces around the else to look more like this:

```
}
else
{
```

The execution of an `if` or `else` is straightforward, but it always helps to see an example. Consider the following code:

```
if ($state == "MD") {
  print "The customer is in Maryland \n";
} else {
  print "The customer is not in Maryland \n";
}
```

The `if` statement controls which `print` statement is executed. If the value of the `$state` variable is MD (the two-letter state abbreviation for Maryland), the code outputs The customer is in Maryland. If the value of the `$state` variable is not MD, the code outputs The customer is not in Maryland.

However, what if you had more conditions? For example, what if you wanted to print another message for another state? That's where the `elseif` option for the `if` statement comes in handy:

```
if ($state == "MD") {
  print "The customer is in Maryland \n";
} elseif ($state == "NV") {
  print "The customer is in Nevada \n";
  } else {
    print "The customer is not in Maryland or Nevada \n";
  }
```

This structure is a bit more complex. If `$state` equals `"MD"`, the in Maryland message is printed and the rest of the lines are ignored. If `$state` does not equal `"MD"`, the `elseif` expression is evaluated.

If `$state` is equal to `"NV"`, the in Nevada message is printed. If `$state` is not equal to `"NV"`, the `else` is executed and the not in Maryland or Nevada message is printed. (If the `elseif` block is executing, you know that `$state` does not equal `"MD"`.)

Multiple Choice with switch

Building on the example in the preceding section, suppose you wanted to print similar messages for all states for which you had customers. Even if you had customers in only five States, the `if/elseif/else` structure would quickly become unwieldy.

For cases such as this, you should use the PHP `switch` command.

The `switch` command has the following syntax:

```
switch (expression) {
  case <expression_1>;
    <code to execute if expression = expression_1>
  break;
  case <expression_2>;
    <code to execute if expression = expression_2>
  break;
  case <expression_3>;
```

```
  ...
  break;
  default:
    <code to execute if expression does not match any case>
}
```

For example, assume that you have customers in the following five States: Maryland (MD), Nevada (NV), Colorado (CO), California (CA), and New York (NY). The following `switch` structure prints the correct message based on the value of `$state`:

```
print "The customer is ";

switch ($state) {
  case "MD";
    print "in Maryland";
  break;
  case "NV";
    print "in Nevada";
  break;
  case "CO";
    print "in Colorado";
  break;
  case "CA";
    print "in California";
  break;
  case "NY";
    print "in New York";
  break;
  default;
    print "not in a valid State ($state).";
}

print "\n";
```

Don't let the additional `print` statements cloud the example; just concentrate on the `switch` structure in the middle of the code. The value of `$state` is evaluated and matched against the first `case` expression (MD). If the expression matches the `switch` expression, that `case` block is executed. If no case is matched, the `default` block is executed, printing the `not in a valid State` message.

Notice that, once a match is found, every `case` thereafter is executed if no `break` statements are encountered. This is the reason for the `break` statements at the end of each `case` code block. The `break` statement causes code execution to "break" out of the current loop or conditional structure. More information on `break` is contained in the section "Breaking and Continuing Code," later in this session.

You seldom want several `case` blocks to execute for one expression. Therefore, ending each `case` block with a `break` is a good habit.

The additional `print` **statements were added to adhere to good coding prac-tices — try never to duplicate effort. In every case, you want to start the output with** `The customer is`, **so add a** `print` **statement outside of the** `switch` **structure to avoid having to add it to each** `print` **statement inside the structure. The same is true for the last** `print` **statement — in every case, you want to end your output with a new line, so add the requisite** `print` **statement outside of the** `switch`.

20 Min.
To Go

Understanding Loops

Programming loops provide a mechanism for repeating code until a specific condition occurs. Usually, these loops are dependant on a certain number of iterations controlled by an integer value — but sometimes other, perhaps complex conditions trigger the end of the loop.

The following sections discuss each of PHP's loop structures.

while Loop

The `while` loop is perhaps the simplest of the PHP loop constructs. A `while` loop has the following syntax:

```
while (expression) {
   repeat this code while expression is TRUE
}
```

For example, if you wanted to print the numbers between 1 and 10, inclusive, you could use the following code:

```
$number = 1;
while ($number <= 10) {
   print "$number \n";
   $number++;
}
```

Start by setting $number to 1, and then define the `while` loop to run until $number is greater than 10. Because $number is less than or equal to 10, the loop runs at least once. Inside the loop, print the current value of $number and then increment $number.

The loop then repeats, starting again with the evaluation of the `while` expression (is the value in $number less than or equal to 10?). This process repeats until $number is greater than 10. At that point, the loop is skipped, and code execution continues on the first line after the loop.

Notice that the `while` expression controls the first loop iteration. If this expression eval-uates to FALSE, the loop does not run — not even once.

Take care to ensure that something inside the `while` loop influences the evaluation of the `while` expression to prevent the loop from executing forever. For example, if you omit-ted the $number increment line, the variable $number would *never* be greater than 10, and the loop would never end.

do while Loop

Occasionally, you encounter situations in which you want a loop to execute at least once. In those cases, you should use a do while loop instead of a plain while. The do while loop has the following syntax:

```
do {
    repeat this code while following expression = TRUE
} while (expression);
```

The evaluation of this loop's expression is exactly opposite that of a plain while; the evaluation happens at the end of the loop instead of at the beginning. This ensures that the loop runs at least once. However, once the expression evaluates as FALSE, the loop stops executing, and the code execution continues on the first line after the loop.

Just as with a while, take care to ensure that the expression eventually evaluates as FALSE so that the loop ends.

10 Min.
To Go

for Loop

When you need symmetry between the loop and a particular variable or fine control over the loop itself, you can use a for statement. The for statement has the following syntax:

```
for (expression1; expression2; expression3;) {
    code
}
```

When the for loop is first executed, expression1 is evaluated. This happens once and is unconditional.

At the beginning of each iteration, expression2 is evaluated — if it evaluates as TRUE, the loop's code block is executed. At the end of the iteration, expression3 is evaluated, and the loop process starts over with the evaluation of expression2.

For example, suppose that you wanted to print the numbers 1 through 10. The following for loop does just that:

```
for ($number = 1; $number <= 10; $number++;) {
    print "$number \n";
}
```

Now apply the description of the for process as follows:

1. At the beginning of the loop, the first expression is evaluated. This results in $number being set to 1.

2. At the beginning of each iteration, the second expression is evaluated. If it evaluates to TRUE (it does, 1 <= 10), the loop is executed.

3. The loop's code block (the print statement) is executed.

4. At the end of the loop, the third expression is evaluated. This results in $number being incremented.

5. The process repeats, starting with Step 2, until the second expression evaluates to FALSE.

This structure of a for loop is perhaps the most frequently used structure, executing a loop a given number of times. However, you can do more with for expressions. For example, the following code prints all the even numbers between 2 and 100 by adding 2 to $number with each loop iteration:

```
for ($number = 2;  $number <= 100;  $number = += 2;) {
   print "$number \n";
}
```

As with other loops, you should take care not to adversely affect the loop variables within the loop itself. For example, changing the value of $number within the loop would affect the expression(s) controlling the for loop itself.

Breaking and Continuing Code

Occasionally, you need to change the execution of a loop, driven by a condition within the loop itself. For example, suppose that you want to print all the even numbers between 2 and 100 (inclusive), but want to skip the number 50. You could place an if statement within a for, as shown in the following code:

```
for ($number = 2;  $number <= 100;  $number += 2;) {
   if ($number != 50 ) { print "$number \n"; }
}
```

This example would indeed print all even numbers between 2 and 100 except for 50. The logic doesn't exclude 50; it simply executes if the number isn't 50. You can accomplish the same thing by skipping all subsequent statements in the current iteration of the loop. Using a continue statement, you can stop the current iteration and have the loop continue with the next iteration:

```
for ($number = 2;  $number <= 100;  $number = $number + 2;) {
   if ($number = 50 ) { continue; }
   print "$number \n";
}
```

When $number is equal to 50, the IF expression evaluates as TRUE and the continue is used to skip to the next loop iteration, skipping the print statement entirely.

What if you wanted to discontinue the loop entirely if a specific condition were met? In that case, you would use the break command instead of continue. For example, suppose that you wanted to stop a while loop if $counter were ever equal to or greater than 205. The following code snippet does just that:

```
while ($number < 10) {
   if ($counter >= 205) { break; }
   repeat this code otherwise
}
```

Notice that break and continue can be used with any loop structure discussed here.

Both break and continue accept an optional parameter to indicate how many loops should be broken out of. For example, the following break breaks out of the for (loop #1) *and* the switch (loop #2):

```
switch ($number) {
  case 2;
    for ($counter = 1;  $counter <= 200; $counter++) {
      // Break out of two loops (for and switch) if
      //  expression = TRUE
      if (expression) { break 2; }
      ...
    break;
    case ...
```

Done!

REVIEW

This session introduced you to methods used to give programs intelligence (conditionals) and showed you how to save programming effort by repeating blocks of commands (loops). Both concepts are fairly elementary in nature but they form the basis of programming's true power. Future sessions show you how to put this knowledge to good use in complete programs.

QUIZ YOURSELF

1. How do you delimit a programming code block in PHP? (See "Programming Blocks.")
2. What is the fundamental difference between the else and elseif statements? (See "else and elseif.")
3. Why should you usually include a break at the end of each case of a switch? (See "Multiple Choice with switch.")
4. Is the loop expression evaluated before or after iterations in a while loop? (See "while Loop.")

PHP Functions

Session Checklist

✔ Understanding functions

✔ Using built-in functions

✔ Defining your own functions

30 Min. To Go

F unctions enable you to perform miracles on data. PHP has a function for just about anything, from converting data to performing complex mathematical operations. If PHP doesn't provide a function to do what you want, you can even create your own functions to compensate.

Functions enable you to encapsulate commonly used code in a central place and return singular values from complex operations. This session delves into functions, both built-in and user defined.

Understanding Functions

Functions are special groups of code that perform a useful task, and usually return a value related to that task. Functions also accept an argument (or several) to aid in their work.

Throughout earlier sessions, you have been introduced to many internal PHP functions. Although you haven't been exposed to the internal code of these functions, you have used the values they return. For example, the `date()` function takes a timestamp and a format parameter and returns the date specified by the timestamp parameter in the format specified by the format parameter.

For example, the following code prints the current date in a traditional long format (month, day, year):

```
print date("F j, Y");
```

Examining the documentation for the date() function on the PHP Web site
(www.php.net), you see that its syntax is as follows:

```
string date ( string format [, int timestamp])
```

Notice that the function returns a string. You can either use the string directly (as with
print() in the first example) or capture it in a string variable for continued use:

```
$longdate = date("F j, Y");
```

In addition, notice that the timestamp parameter is optional — if you don't include it,
the current system date and time is used.

You can also nest functions within larger operations, such as in the following:

```
$longdate = date("F j, Y", strtotime("+2 week"));
```

PHP follows typical rules of evaluation precedence when dealing with nested functions,
working from inside out. In the preceding example, PHP would evaluate the strtotime()
function first and pass its return value to date() as the timestamp argument — generating
a date two weeks from the current date in the specified format and storing it in the variable
$longdate. The following code would be equally valid:

```
$tempdate = strtotime("+2 week");
$longdate = date("F j, Y", $tempdate);
```

However, the first line of code is unnecessary, as you probably don't need the value of
$tempdate except in the next line within the date() function. A few good guidelines for
nesting functions within functions versus intermediary use of variables follow:

- Use whichever method makes the code more legible. Although it may not be necessary to store intermediary values in variables, a long line of nested functions may be
  hard to decipher.
- If you need a value for several different reasons or functions, store it in a variable
  once and reuse the variable. This can make your code quite a bit faster because the
  function doesn't have to run each time you need the value. It can also make your
  code more reliable if there's a possibility that the function's value may unexpectedly
  change between calls. (Consider what happens when the date("F j, Y") example
  is run once at 11:59 p.m. and again at 12 a.m.)
- Conversely, if you need the value of a function to be dynamic, do not store its
  return value in a variable; instead, embed or nest the function, as necessary.

Built-in PHP Functions

PHP has a built-in function for just about anything you ever need — for returning data,
converting data, interfacing with other technologies, and more. In fact, PHP lists 113 categories of functions, from Apache to Zlib Compression.

The PHP Web site (www.php.net) is the best resource for information on PHP functions. The search feature on the main page (as shown in Figure 16-1) can be used to quickly find details about specific functions, to look up functions that deal with specific technologies or types of data, or to locate additional documentation about PHP.

Search feature

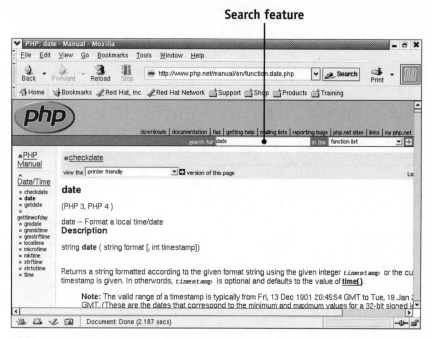

Figure 16-1   *The PHP Web site includes a comprehensive search feature.*

Enter search terms in the Search For text box and use the In The pull-down list to select where you want to search. For example, to find more information on the date() function, search for date in the function list. If you want to find functions that deal with compression, search for compression in the function list. To find more information on superglobals, search for superglobal in the online documentation.

User-Defined Functions

Occasionally, you find that you need to create your own functions. The main reason to create functions is to reuse code — when you find yourself using the same lines of code more than once, putting those lines in a function usually pays. The following sections explain how to define your own functions in PHP.

Function Definition

The syntax for defining a function in PHP is as follows:

```
function function_name([argument1, argument2...]){ code }
```

The code for the function is placed between the braces and is executed every time the function is called. The arguments can be used when calling the function, with their values used inside the function's code; or, if the function doesn't need arguments, they can be omitted from the definition. (See the section "Function Arguments," later in this session, for more information on arguments.)

For example, suppose that you routinely need a date two weeks in the future. Your function definition would resemble the following:

```
function twoweeks() {   }
```

Because you don't need the time frame to be variable (it's always two weeks), the function doesn't need any arguments. If you wanted the time frame to be variable, you could define the function with an appropriate argument:

```
function xweeks($numweeks) {   }
```

Function definitions are generally placed as a group, near the beginning of a script, before general code. Versions of PHP prior to version 4.0 *required* that a function definition appear before it was called. Version 4.0 removed this restriction, but it is still good programming style to define a function prior to its use.

Returning a Value from a Function

**20 Min.
To Go**

Returning a value from a function is accomplished with the `return` statement. This statement takes one argument and returns the value of that argument. For example, to return the value TRUE, the appropriate `return` statement would be as follows:

```
return(TRUE);
```

Notice that the argument can be a single value, a variable, or even a compound expression. For example, to return the date two weeks from the current date, you could simply use the following:

```
return(date("F j, Y", strtotime("+2 week")));
```

Alternatively, you could store the return value in a string and return the string's value:

```
$longdate = date("F j, Y", strtotime("+2 week"));
return($longdate);
```

Guidelines for when to use a compound expression or a single value are similar to the guidelines for nesting functions, as discussed in the section "Understanding Functions," earlier in this session. Basically, do whatever makes your code more legible.

Last, remember that you can choose to omit the `return()` statement, causing your function to return NULL. For example, if you want to create a function to output the tags to start a Web page, you don't need anything returned:

```
function pagestart() {
print <<<HMTL
<html>
  <body>
```

```
HTML;
}
```

Function Arguments

You can define your function with or without arguments. You can also define the arguments you choose to use in a variety of ways. The following sections discuss the various ways to define and use function arguments.

Default Argument Definition and Use

By default, arguments are pretty basic creatures. You define them as variables in your function's definition and use them as variables in your function's code. For example, if you wanted to define a function that returned a date *x* number of weeks in the future, you could define and use the following function:

```
function xweeks($numweeks) {
    $longdate = date("F j, Y", strtotime("+$numweeks week"));
    return($longdate);
}
```

Notice how you define $numweeks as an argument simply by including it in the function definition and use it like any other variable within the function's code.

If you want to define more arguments, simply include them in the definition, separated by commas. For example, if you want the format to also be variable, you can use a second argument:

```
function xweeks($numweeks,$format) {
    $longdate = date($format, strtotime("+$numweeks week"));
    return($longdate);
}
```

To use your function, call it just as you would a built-in function, supplying the same number of arguments as in the definition:

```
print xweeks(3,"m/d/Y");
```

The preceding code prints the day three weeks from the current day, in the format *mm/dd/yyyy*.

Optional Arguments

If you define arguments for a function, you need to supply at least that number of arguments when calling the function. You can supply more arguments (which are generally ignored by the function), but supplying less generates an error similar to the following:

```
<b>Warning</b>:  Missing argument 2 for xweeks()
 in <b>/var/www/html/functest.php</b> on line <b>4</b><br />
```

Optional arguments are sometimes useful. For example, suppose that you want to specify a default date format for your xweeks() function and, therefore, don't require a format to be passed to the function when it is called.

In such a case, define the argument with an equal sign and its default value. For example, if you wanted your default format to be "F j, Y" in your xweeks() function, you would define the function as follows:

```
function xweeks($numweeks,$format = "F j, Y") {
   $longdate = date($format, strtotime("+$numweeks week"));
   return($longdate);
}
```

Then, if the function call does not include a value for $format, the default ("F j, Y") is used. Notice that a function can be defined with only one optional argument — such a function can be called with no arguments without generating an error.

Functions fill their parameters from the calling list from left to right, so you need to define any optional parameters last in the function definition.

The functions func_num_args() and func_get_arg() can determine the number and value of arguments passed to a function. Using these functions, you can retain the value of additional arguments passed to a function, above and beyond the number of arguments defined for the function.

10 Min.
To Go

Call by Reference

Typically, arguments passed to functions are called by value; that is, the value of the argument is passed on to the function, but if the value of the argument is changed in the function, it doesn't affect the argument used in calling the function. For example, consider the following code:

```
<?php

function evalnums($num1,$num2) {
   $num1 = $num1 * 2;
   $num2 = sqrt($num2);
   return($num1+$num2);
}

$a = 21;
$b = 9;

print "Eval: ".evalnums($a,$b)."\n";
print "A: $a   B: $b \n";

?>
```

As you might expect, this code prints the following:

```
Eval: 45
A: 21    B: 9
```

Notice that the values of $a and $b did not change, despite the fact that the arguments changed inside the function.

Occasionally, you want the argument changes inside the function to affect the calling values as well. In that case, you would preface the argument with an ampersand (&) in the function definition. Using the preceding example, you can modify the function accordingly:

```php
<?php

function evalnums(&$num1,&$num2) {
   $num1 = $num1 * 2;
   $num2 = sqrt($num2);
   return($num1+$num2);
}

$a = 21;
$b = 9;

print "Eval: ".evalnums($a,$b)."\n";
print "A: $a   B: $b \n";

?>
```

Now the code prints the following:

```
Eval: 45
A: 42   B: 3
```

Notice how the changes to $num1 and $num2 within the function were reflected on the variables used to call the function. This technique is referred to as calling *by reference* because the call to the function references the actual variables and not just their values.

Variable Scope

As you might have gathered, variables inside a function are local only to that function; they do not affect variables outside the function — unless you call a function by reference or use one of the techniques described in this section.

For example, consider this code:

```php
<?php
   function declare_var() {
      $x = 10;
   }

$x = 30;
print "$x \n";
```

```
declare_var();
print "$x \n";

?>
```

The preceding example prints the following:

```
30
30
```

Even though the same variable name appears inside and outside the function, "**$x**" actually refers to two separate variables — one with *global scope* and the other with *local scope* inside the variable.

Notice that global scope does not include the inside of functions — it means within the main code of the script. To use an otherwise global variable inside a function, you must declare it as global using the `global` function. The syntax of the `global` function is simple:

```
global $variable;
```

The following code modifies the preceding example to add a global declaration to the function:

```php
<?php
  function declare_var() {
    global $x;
    $x = 10;
  }

$x = 30;
print "$x \n";
declare_var();
print "$x \n";

?>
```

Now the **$x** variable inside the function references the same variable outside the function, the function changes the value of **$x** globally, and the script prints as follows:

```
30
10
```

Each time a function runs, it reinitializes the values of its local variables; that is, the local function variables do not maintain their values between function calls. However, you can use the `static` function to declare a variable that keeps its value between calls. The format of the static function is as follows:

```
static $variable = value;
```

This line should be placed at the beginning of the function, before you actually work with the variable. This causes the variable to be set with an initial value and declared as static. Every subsequent function call ignores this line, but the variable maintains its value between calls.

Done!

REVIEW

This session covered the ins and outs of functions. You learned how to use PHP's built-in functions and how to find out more information about those functions when you need it. You also learned how to define your own functions and the various ways you can define and use function arguments. The next few sessions show you how to use PHP with files, HTML, and HTML forms.

QUIZ YOURSELF

1. What does the date() function do? (See "Understanding Functions.")
2. What are the reasons for and against nesting functions in expressions? (See "Understanding Functions.")
3. How many arguments must a user-defined function have? (See "Function Definition.")
4. If you don't use the return() statement in your user-defined function, what value does it return? (See "Returning a Value from a Function.")
5. How do you define a default for a function argument? (See "Optional Arguments.")
6. If a variable isn't declared inside a function but is used in the main body of a script, can you reference its value? (See "Variable Scope.")

PART

III

Saturday Afternoon
Part Review

1. What use is the SHOW CREATE TABLE command in the MySQL monitor?
2. What's a good format to use for entering the following query?

   ```
   "SELECT comp_id, comp_cpu, comp_speed FROM computers, mice WHERE
   mouse_comp = comp_id AND mouse_type != "PS2" AND comp_location = "B%";"
   ```

3. What does the "%" character mean in a query's WHERE element?
4. What commands can be used to quickly back up and restore a database?
5. How many document (MIME) types can you add to the following httpd.conf line?

   ```
   AddType application/x-httpd-php
   ```

   What, if any, is the disadvantage of adding more types?
6. Does the function call dothis() pass any arguments to the function? What happens if the function has arguments defined?
7. What is a procedure to find out more information about the SWFSprite() PHP function?
8. Give an example of how the MySQL monitor can help you troubleshoot MySQL.
9. How many arguments must be included in a user-defined function definition?
10. If you want to return a value from a complicated mathematical operation from a function, what are two ways you can do that? What is the best way?
11. How do you pipe files to the monitor? Why would you want to?
12. Define a function that takes two arguments, one optional with a default value of "" that creates the beginning tags for an HTML document, including <head> and <title> tags, and an optional list of options for the <body> tag.
13. How can you determine how many parameters were passed to a function?
14. What's the advantage(s) of using PHP as a command-line scripting language?

15. If a variable, $num, is defined and assigned a value in the main body of the script, what does the following function print?

```
function printval($val) {
    static $num=20;
    $num++;
    $temp = $val + $num;
    print $temp;
}
```

16. What is the difference between the `else()` and `elseif()` functions?

17. When do you use the `break()` function within a `switch()` function element?

18. What does an inner or equi-join do?

19. Write a function to expand the state abbreviation (for example, `.IN`) to its full name (`.Indiana`).

20. What is the minimum number of times a `do...while()` loop will execute?

21. What is the difference between the `break()` and `continue()` keywords?

22. How much white space will PHP actively ignore in your scripts?

23. Is the variable $100percent a legal variable name? If not, why?

24. What is the main difference between the `print()` and `echo()` keywords?

25. When should you use the \ escape character?

26. What does the following expression return?

```
12 % 9
```

27. How do you output multiple strings with `print()`?

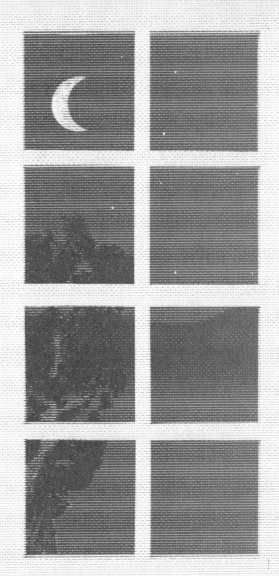

Session 17
Working with Files

Session 18
HTML Constructs

Session 19
Working with Forms

Session 20
Multiple-User Considerations in PHP

Working with Files

Session Checklist

✔ Accessing text and binary files

✔ Opening, reading, writing to, and closing files

✔ File locking and related information

✔ Working with directories

30 Min.
To Go

PHP is a well-rounded programming language. As such, it incorporates many functions to access a variety of data formats — from plaintext files to data stored in a database. This session covers how to use PHP to read and write to files on the system's file system; work with directories; and gather information about a file or directory.

File Operations with PHP: The Good and the Bad

PHP offers a wealth of file-related functions to do just about anything with the file system that you could do at the command line. You can add, rename, move, read, and even delete files and directories. This functionality lends a lot of power to PHP scripts.

However, there is a dark side to this power — namely, the possible compromise of system security. You open a potential security hole any time you allow Web script access to the underlying file system. Hackers can utilize such holes to do all kinds of unscrupulous things to your system — implant viruses or back doors, delete key files, and so on.

At the risk of being an alarmist, I recommend very limited use of PHP file operations. Storing data by more secure means (such as in MySQL) is generally preferred and much safer, due to the various levels of security that must be bypassed before someone could abuse the system.

When you do need to access files using PHP methods, follow these simple guidelines:

- Limit access to potentially harmful scripts.
- Limit your access to select directories on the system.
- Regularly monitor the directories for unusual activity.
- Monitor the system for unusual activity and files.
- Ensure that the directories have limited permissions (usually just permissions for the user ID under which the Web process is running).
- Install virus and intrusion-detection software, as appropriate.

The PHP file functions are extremely useful when using PHP for command-line scripting. Such use is generally safe, assuming you limit access to the scripts accordingly. See "PHP as a Command-Line Scripting Language" in Session 13 for more information on using PHP for command-line scripting.

Accessing Files with PHP

PHP follows general program conventions when dealing with file operations. Follow these three steps to access files:

1. Open file for access.
2. Perform desired operations (reading/writing).
3. Close file.

The following sections review each of these steps in more detail.

Opening a File

Before you can work with a file, PHP must open it. Opening a file associates a resource variable with the file on disk and readies the operating system to read and/or write to the file. The basic use of the open() function follows this syntax:

```
$resource_variable = fopen(filename, 'mode');
```

The valid modes with which you can open a file include those shown in Table 17-1.

Table 17-1 *File Open Modes*

Mode Identifier	Meaning
r	Opens a file for *reading* only. The file pointer is placed at the beginning of the file. Returns FALSE if the file does not exist.
r+	Opens a file for *reading* and *writing*. The file pointer is placed at the beginning of the file. Returns FALSE if the file does not exist.

Mode Identifier	Meaning
w	Opens a file for *writing* only. If the file exists, it is cleared of content and the file pointer is placed at the beginning of the file. If the file does not exist, it is created and the file pointer is placed at the beginning of the file.
w+	Opens a file for *reading* and *writing*. If the file exists, it is cleared of content and the file pointer is placed at the beginning of the file. If the file does not exist, it is created and the file pointer is placed at the beginning of the file.
a	Opens a file for *writing* only. The file pointer is placed at the end of the file. If the file does not exist, it is created.
a+	Opens a file for *reading* and *writing*. The file pointer is placed at the end of the file. If the file does not exist, it is created.
t	Treats the file as a text file. This identifier should appear at the end of the mode, such as "w+t".
b	Treats the file as a binary file. This identifier should appear at the end of the mode, such as "w+b".

The modes that attempt to create a file might not always succeed. Their success depends on the operating system and file system allowing the file to be accessed and optionally written. Appropriate rights for the user that the Web server runs must be set. For example, if a file is specified in a directory that is read-only, the operation fails and fopen() **returns** FALSE.

In addition, most files should be opened in binary mode (specify b at the end of the mode identifier). Opening a binary file in text mode can have unexpected results due to additional line breaks and the mishandling of extended characters. The reverse, opening a text file in binary mode, is usually not a problem.

Notice that the a modes place the file pointer at the end of the file. This provides an easy way to append information to the end of a file — simply open the file with one of the a modes and write the data. The new data is placed at the end of the file.

If the file open operation succeeds, the fopen() function returns TRUE. If the file open operation does not succeed, the fopen() function returns FALSE. You can use this behavior as simple error checking, as shown in the following example:

```
if ($file = fopen("datafile.txt","rb")) {
   ...do file stuff...
} else {
   print "File does not exist \n";
}
```

Closing a File

Make sure that you close any files that you open. On most systems, final data isn't written to a file until it is closed. Although PHP tries its best to close all open files at the end of a script, relying on PHP to do this work can produce unpredictable results.

You close a file using the fclose() function. This function has the following syntax:

```
fclose($file_variable);
```

As with other file functions, fclose() returns TRUE if the operation is successful and FALSE if the operation is not successful.

Reading from or Writing to a File

As mentioned in the section, "Opening a File," earlier in this session, you can open a file for read access, write access, or both. Typically, you use only read or only write, seldom using a file for both operations simultaneously (though it does happen).

Writing to a File

Writing to a file is as simple as directing output to the file resource variable instead of the standard output (a console or Web page). The fwrite() function is typically used to accomplish file writing. The fputs() function (an alias of fwrite()) can also be used.

The fwrite() function has the following syntax:

```
fwrite($file_variable, <string_to_write>);
```

The following script creates a new file named test.txt that contains 10 lines, each line with a single number, 1000 through 1010:

```php
<?php

if ($file = fopen("test.txt","wb")) {
  for ($i=1000; $i<=1010; $i++) {
    fwrite($file, $i."\n");
  }
} else {
  print "File cannot be opened."
}
?>
```

Notice the use of the concatenation operator and the newline character in the fwrite() function. Without the newline, the code would have placed all the numbers consecutively, without line breaks, as follows:

```
10001001100210031004100510061007100810091010
```

 Replacing a malfunctioning fwrite() **with an equivalent** print() **is an easy way to check a script's file output. The standard output of the** print()**closely resembles the output to a file of** fwrite().

As with other file operations, if fwrite() fails to write to a file, it returns FALSE.

Reading from a File

You can use two methods to read data from a file. Which method you should choose depends on the type of file you are accessing and how you want to access it.

The first method is to read entire lines by using the fgets() function. This function is typically used with text format files and has the following syntax:

```
$line = fgets($file_variable[,<byte_length>]);
```

This function reads data from the current position in the file to whichever of the following comes first:

- The amount of data specified by <byte_length> (default: 1024 bytes)
- A newline
- The end of the file

A *newline* is both a concept and a literal character. On the Linux platform, a "new line" in a file is indicated with a Ctrl+J key combination, which is ASCII character 10 (commonly known as a *linefeed*). On Windows platforms, a new line is indicated by Ctrl+M, which is ASCII character 13 (commonly known as a *carriage return* — you might notice that the terms are derived from the use of a typewriter). By default, PHP recognizes only the Linux case, a linefeed, as signaling a new line.

A *newline* in program-speak is the occurrence of the characters that cause a new line or the insertion of the characters into a string or file. In PHP, you can add a newline to your output by using the newline escape character \n.

For example, the following code reads the current line of the file linked to $file, up to 4096 bytes, and stores the line in the variable $line:

```
$line = fgets($file,4096);
```

The second method of reading a file reads sequences of bytes using the fread() function. The fread() function is typically used with binary files and has the following syntax:

```
$bytes = fread($file_variable,<byte_length>);
```

As does fgets(), the fread() function stops reading when the amount of data specified by <byte_length> has been read or when the end of the file is reached. However, unlike fgets(), fread() treats newlines the same as other data — fread()does not stop if it encounters a newline.

Using the example file created in the section "Writing to a File," earlier in this session, you can now run through a few examples using both methods:

```php
<?php
if ($file = fopen("test.txt","rb")) {
```

```
// Read a file and output line by line
  while (!feof($file)) {
    $line = fgets($file,4096);
    print $line."\n";
  }
  fclose($file);
} else {
  die("File cannot be opened");
}
?>
```

This code introduces a new function, feof(). The feof() function tests the specified file to see if the end of the file has been reached. The function returns FALSE if the file pointer is not at the end of the file and TRUE if it is. This function can be used with loops to read a file from beginning to end, as shown in the preceding code.

Somewhat unpredictably, the preceding code generates the following output when run from the command line:

```
1000

1001

1002

1003

1004
...
```

The double-spacing occurs because the fgets() function included the newline at the end of each line, and the example added an additional newline to the print() function.

The following example reads a file a few bytes at a time:

```
<?php
if ($file = fopen("test.txt","rb")) {
// Read a file and output 3 bytes at a time
  while (!feof($file)) {
    $content = fread($file,3);
    // print the content and its length
    print $content."-( ".strlen($content).")\n";
  }
  fclose($file);
} else {
  die("File cannot be opened");
}
?>
```

This code produces the following output when run from the command line:

```
100-( 3)
0
1-( 3)
001-( 3)

10-( 3)
02
-( 3)
100-( 3)
3
1-( 3)
004-( 3)

10-( 3)
05
-( 3)
100-( 3)
6
1-( 3)
007-( 3)

10-( 3)
08
-( 3)
100-( 3)
9
1-( 3)
010-( 3)

-( 1)
```

At first glance, the output is a bit confusing. However, the addition of the data size (strlen()) helps account for the newlines:

```
100-( 3)
0               <- Newline
1-( 3)
001-( 3)
                <- Newline
10-( 3)
...
```

Therefore, the second read and output is made up of the following three bytes:

1. The last character of 1000, namely, 0
2. A newline
3. The first character of 1001, namely, 1

Notice the last line output:

```
-( 1)
```

This is the one exception to reading and outputting three bytes. It is only one byte long because the end of the file was reached before `fread()` could read three full bytes. In short, the function is working as advertised.

> Sometimes, you might find it convenient to read an entire file into a string to work with its contents. For example, when changing the contents of a text file, you can read the contents into a string, modify the string, and rewrite the entire file by writing the single string back to the file. The following `fread()` can be used for this purpose:
>
> ```
> fread($file, filesize($filename));
> ```
>
> Notice that the parameter passed to the `filesize()` function is a string containing the path and name of the file, *not* the resource variable associated with the file. Although this technique is useful, it can also consume a lot of memory depending on the size of the file being read. It's best to use this technique only with small files.

Additional Reading and Writing Techniques

**20 Min.
To Go**

You have seen how to read files line by line and in arbitrary byte chunks. PHP includes a few more functions and techniques, which are described in the following sections.

Positioning the File Pointer

This session has mentioned the file pointer several times. The file pointer is a PHP and file-system construct that points to the place where the next data read or write takes place. Typically, the pointer is moved automatically with each read or write. However, it is sometimes advantageous to move the pointer manually to finely control where the next read or write occurs.

You can move the file pointer by using the `fseek()` function. This function has the following syntax:

```
fseek($file_variable, <position>)
```

The `<position>` parameter is an integer, specifying the number of bytes from the beginning of the file. For example, to read the third 1K chunk from a file, you would use the following code:

```
// Open the file for reading
$file = fopen("test.txt","r");
// Move the file pointer forward 2K
fseek($file, 2048);
// Read the next 1K chunk
$bytes = fread($file, 1024);
```

As with the other file functions, fseek() returns TRUE if the seek is successful, FALSE if the seek does not succeed. Notice that seeking past the end of the file is not considered an error; the file pointer is left positioned at the end of the file.

> The fseek() function has an optional third parameter, *whence*, which controls where the offset applies (from the beginning of file [default], the current position, or the end of the file). This provides even more flexibility in dynamically setting the file pointer. See the PHP documentation for more information on this parameter.

Reading a File One Character at a Time

The fgetc() function is similar to the fgets() function, except that it reads one character at a time (instead of a string) from the specified file. The following two lines are basically equivalent in function:

```
$char = fgetc($file);
$char = fgets($file, 1);
```

The advantages to using the fgetc() function are twofold: You don't need to worry about the length parameter, and what the code is doing (reading a single character) is instantly obvious.

Locking Files

Occasionally, your scripts need exclusive access to a file. This is usually the case when multiple instances of a script are running and trying to update a particular file (or files) at the same time.

To lock a file, use the flock() function. This function has the following syntax:

```
flock($file_variable, <mode>);
```

Table 17-2 describes the various options for <mode> in the flock() function.

Table 17-2   *Valid Modes for flock()*

Mode	Meaning
LOCK_SH	Shared. Other processes can read from the file but writing is prohibited.
LOCK_EX	Exclusive. No other process can read from or write to the file.
LOCK_UN	Unlock. Releases a lock.

Locking a file is important, but should be done only for finite periods of time. It's impractical to lock a file at the beginning of a script that can run for several seconds before using the file. You should lock a file immediately before you need the exclusive access and unlock it immediately afterward. Moreover, notice that closing a file does not release the lock — always unlock files that you lock.

The flock() **function does not work on some networked file systems (such as NFS) and older file systems (such as FAT). Users of those file systems should find another way to ensure exclusive access to files when required.**

Deleting Files

You can use the unlink() function to delete files. The syntax of unlink() is as follows:

```
unlink(<filename_string>);
```

For example, to delete the file /var/www/html/test.txt, you would use the following code:

```
unlink("/var/www/html/test.txt");
```

Notice that the user running the script, or the user ID under which the Apache process is running, needs to have adequate permission to delete the specified file, or the operation fails. As with all the other file functions, unlink() returns a value according to the success of the operation — TRUE if the file was deleted, FALSE if the file was not deleted.

**10 Min.
To Go**

Working with Directories

PHP also includes functions for creating, removing, and reading directories. Each of these functions is covered in the following sections.

Making Directories

You can use PHP's mkdir() function to create directories. The syntax for this function is as follows:

```
mkdir(<pathname_string>,<mode>);
```

Notice that the <mode> parameter follows Linux permission mode notation (in octal) and is ignored on Windows platforms. For example, to create the directory "/var/www/html/test" with user and world read-only, you would use the following code:

```
mkdir("/var/www/html/test",0744);
```

A full discussion of Linux permissions is beyond the scope of this book, but 0744 is the octal representation of the file permission mask for the directory being created. In the preceding case, the permission corresponds to rwxr- -r- - **or "read, write, and execute" for the owner and "only read" for everyone else.**

After this line of code is executed, the new directory's existence can be verified by the Linux ls command:

```
ls /var/www/html/test -ld
drwxr--r--    2 apache    apache        4096 May  5 13:58 /var/www/html/test
```

Notice that the owner of the directory is the user running the Apache process, in this case, apache. For mkdir() to succeed, that user must have sufficient rights to create the directory where specified.

Removing Directories

PHP also has a function for removing directories, rmdir(). The rmdir() function has the following syntax:

```
rmdir(<pathname_string>);
```

To remove the example directory from the preceding section, you would use the following code:

```
rmdir("/var/www/html/test");
```

Notice that the user running this code (the command-line user or the user under which the Apache process is running) must have sufficient rights to delete the directory for this operation to succeed. Additionally, only empty directories can be removed.

Reading the Contents of a Directory

The PHP function opendir() can be used to open a directory to read its contents. The syntax of opendir() is similar to fopen():

```
$dir = opendir(<pathname_string>);
```

After the directory is open for reading, you can use the function readdir() to actually read the contents. After you are done accessing the directory, you should close it with closedir().

For example, the following script displays the contents of the /etc directory on a Linux system:

```php
<?php

$dir = opendir("/etc");
while (!($filename = readdir($dir)) === FALSE) {
  print $filename."<br>\n";
}
closedir($dir);
?>
```

On my Red Hat system, this code generates the following listing:

```
.
..
sysconfig
X11
fstab
mtab
modules.conf
csh.cshrc
bashrc
gnome-vfs-mime-magic
profile.d
csh.login
exports
filesystems
group
host.conf
hosts.allow
hosts.deny
inputrc
...
```

 An improvement to this script, which includes showing directory items as directories, appears in the next section.|

File Information

PHP also includes several functions that you can use to determine specific things about files on the file system — whether a file exists, its size, if it is a directory, and so on. Table 17-3 details some of these functions.

Table 17-3 *File Information Functions*

Function	Use	Returns
file_exists(<*file*>)	Determines whether a file exists (name contained in string <*file*>)	TRUE if file exists, FALSE if file does not exist
is_file(<*file*>)	Determines whether the string <*file*> is a file	TRUE if the string specified is a file, FALSE if the string is not a file

Function	Use	Returns
is_dir(<path>)	Determines whether the string <path> is a directory	TRUE if the string specified is a directory, FALSE if the string is not a directory
is_readable(<file>)	Determines whether the file in string <file> is readable	TRUE if the file is readable, FALSE if the file is not readable
is_writable(<file>)	Determines whether the file in string <file> is writable	TRUE if the file is writable, FALSE if the file is not writable
is_executable(<file>)	Determines whether the file in string <file> is executable	TRUE if the file is executable, FALSE if the file is not executable
filesize(<file>)	Returns the size of the file in string <file>	Size, in bytes, of the file
filectime(<file>)	Returns the date and time the file was last changed or created	Date, in operating-system-specific format
filemtime(<file>)	Returns the date and time the file was last modified	Date, in operating-system-specific format
fileatime(<file>)	Returns the date and time the file was last accessed	Date, in operating-system-specific format.

To make the dates and/or times returned by the filetime() **functions human-readable, use the PHP** date() **function. For example, the following code formats and prints the date returned from the** filectime() **function:**

```
$timestamp = filectime("test.txt");

print date("M j, Y  h:i:s a",$timestamp);
```

An example of the preceding code's output is as follows:

```
Jan 19, 2001 11:44:44 am
```

The file functions can be quite useful, as shown in the following code, which mimics the DOS dir command's output:

```
<?php
// Directory listing script
// Output the contents of the /etc directory in
//   a format similar to the DOS dir command

// Start table
print "<table border=1 cellspacing=5> \n";
```

```
// Open directory
($dir = opendir("/etc")) or die("Cannot open '/etc'");

// Read all filenames
while (!($filename = readdir($dir)) === FALSE) {

// Start new row
  print "<tr><td>";

// Get and print the modified time and date
  $ts = filemtime("/etc/".$filename);
  print date("m/d/Y  h:i:s A",$ts);
  print "</td><td>";

  if (is_dir("/etc/".$filename)) {
        // If it is a directory, mark it as such
        //   and skip the size column
        print "DIR";
        print "</td><td> ";

  } else {
        // If it is a file, skip the directory column
        //   and output the file's size
        print "  </td><td>";
        print filesize("/etc/".$filename);

  }

  // End current column
  print "</td><td>";

  // Output the filename
  print $filename."</td>";

  // End the row
  print "</tr> \n";

}

closedir($dir);

print "</table>";

?>
```

A sample of this code's output is shown in Figure 17-1.

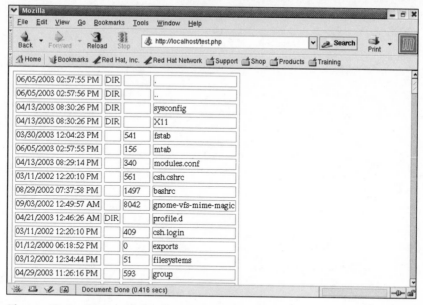

Figure 17-1 *Output of the directory listing script*

Done!

REVIEW

This session covered file operations and functions relating to file information. You learned how to open files, read and write data, and close files. It also covered how to access directories and how to get more information from files. The next session describes how to work with HTML within PHP.

QUIZ YOURSELF

1. Why should you avoid accessing files on a computer's root file system? (See "File Operations with PHP: The Good and the Bad.")

2. What mode enables you to append to a file, but not read from the file? (See "Opening a File.")

3. Why should you always close a file? (See "Closing a File.")

4. When would the fwrite() function return FALSE? (See "Writing to a File.")

5. What is the difference between the fgets() and fgetc() functions? (See "Reading a File One Character at a Time.")

6. Can you use the rmdir() function to remove a directory that still contains files? (See "Removing Directories.")

HTML Constructs

Session Checklist

✔ Understanding PHP's built-in HTML features

✔ Circumventing default HTML headers

✔ Sending additional HTTP headers

✔ Using good HTML formatting

**30 Min.
To Go**

A s I've mentioned throughout this book, PHP's heritage lends itself quite well to delivering HTML, mainly because it is simply what PHP was designed to do. As such, much of what PHP does intrinsically is automatically suited for deployment straight to a Web page. This session covers some of these intrinsic features and the best ways to use them.

The Automatic HTML Header

As you saw in Session 13, by default, PHP script output includes an HTML header. You can see this by running the following script through the PHP processor:

```php
<?php
  print "Hello world.";
?>
```

Enter the PHP processor by typing php at a system prompt. Windows users need to include the full path to php.exe if the php directory is not in the system path.

Type the preceding code and press Ctrl+D at the end (Ctrl+Z on Windows). The processor parses the code and outputs the following:

```
X-Powered-By: PHP/4.2.2
Content-type: text/html

Hello world.
```

Notice that PHP identifies itself with a `Powered-By` field and includes an appropriate `Content-type` for HTML. It also includes a blank line required by the HTML header specification.

The `expose_php` **setting in the** `php.ini` **file controls the PHP identification header. If this option is set to** `On`**, the** `X-Powered-By` **header is sent whenever a script is run. Set this option to** `Off` **to help hide the fact that PHP is running. Hiding PHP helps keep unscrupulous users from trying to exploit your system (knowing that PHP is running could open up a new bag of tricks for potential hackers).**

The option `default_mimetype` **in the** `php.ini` **file controls what default** `Content-type` **header is sent. Typically, this option is set to** `text/html` **to identify PHP output as HTML by default.**

Other Content Headers

20 Min.
To Go

You may encounter situations in which you need to supply another header to the requesting client, circumventing the default HTML header. For example, I routinely use PHP to deliver WML wireless content. WML requires the following header:

```
Content-type: text/vnd.wap.wml
```

The `header()` function enables you to send all manners of raw HTTP header content. This function's basic syntax is as follows:

```
header(<header_string>);
```

For example, I use the following `header()` function in my WML files:

```
header("Content-type: text/vnd.wap.wml");
```

As previously mentioned in Sessions 2 and 13, you can add additional file extensions to the `Addtype` **setting for PHP in the Apache configuration file. For example, I add** `.wml` **to cause all** `.wml` **files to be parsed by the PHP processor:**

```
AddType application/x-httpd-Php .php .wml
```

Using the `header()` **function completes the loop, causing the requesting clients to understand the returned content as WML.**

You can send other HTTP header information using the header() function. For example, to prevent a page from being cached by the browser, you can use the following headers:

```
// Prevent caching, HTTP/1.1
header("Cache-Control: no-cache, must-revalidate");
// Prevent caching, HTTP/1.0
header("Pragma: no-cache");
```

To control when the page expires in the cache, you can use code similar to the following:

```
header("Expires: Mon, 2 Jun 2003 05:00:00 GMT");
```

Use the PHP date() function to format the date and time for the Expires **header. If you set the date to a date and/or time that has already passed, the page expires immediately. Keep in mind that the date() function returns the server time (when not given a timestamp). Note that the client and server may be set to radically different times — this could affect the expiration of cookies and other such functions.**

Other useful headers include the Status header (for example, Status: 404 Not Found) and the WWW-Authenticate header to force the browser to open an authentication dialog box.

You *must* use any header() functions prior to outputting anything else to the browser.

Outputting HTML

Outputting HTML by using PHP is relatively easy. You simply embed any HTML tags into a print() function. However, you can use various techniques to make outputting HTML easier, and you should follow certain guidelines when printing HTML. These are covered in the next few sections.

Large HTML Blocks

You can use several methods to output large HTML blocks — large or numerous print functions, here document printing, raw HTML, and included files. The method you choose depends on whether you need any PHP features within the HTML block.

Large or numerous print() functions are the worst choice for outputting large blocks of HTML. Embedded escape characters for formatting, concatenation operators for combining disparate pieces of text, and line after line of print() functions quickly make your code complex and unreadable. For example, compare the following code to other examples in this section:

```
print "<html> \n";
print "\t<body> \n";
print "\t\tHello world. \n";
print "\t</body> \n";
print "</html> \n";
```

Here documents were covered in Session 14. They incorporate special tags surrounding large blocks of text to tell the print() function to "print everything between the tags." For example, the following code snippet outputs the raw HTML between the print() line and the HTML line:

```
print <<<HTML
<html>
  <body>
    Hello world.
  </body>
</html>
HTML;
```

The here document approach offers two distinct advantages:

- **The text is output exactly as formatted in the block.** All line breaks, indentations, and so on are preserved.
- **PHP parses the code for variables.** You can include variables in the block. They are parsed and their values sent instead of the variable names.

The other method to output large blocks of HTML is to turn PHP processing off. The following code snippet shows how this can be accomplished. Everything between the ?> and <?php tags is output verbatim to the browser:

```
<?php
    ...php code...
// Turn PHP processing off
?>
<!--This is raw HTML, no PHP processing-->
<html>
  <body>
    Hello world.
  </body>
</html>
<?php
// PHP processing is back on
    ...more php code...
?>
```

One disadvantage to this approach is that PHP does not process any of the code outside the PHP beginning and ending tags. If you include a variable in this section, it is sent verbatim; that is, $variable appears as $variable on the page.

 If the PHP option short_open_tag **is set to** On **in the** php.ini **file, you can use a short version of the** echo **function to output variables in non-PHP blocks. For example, including the following in a non-PHP block causes the value of the variable** $name **to appear in the output:**

```
<?=$name?>
```

The third way to include HTML blocks in your output is via the `include()` function. The `include()` function takes a file name as an argument and simply places the specified file's content in the script at the position of the `include()` function. For example, suppose that the file `hello.html` contained the following:

```
<html>
  <body>
    Hello world.
  </body>
</html>
```

Wherever you want this code to appear in a PHP script, you would use this `include` function:

```
Include "hello.html";
```

Notice that PHP processing is turned off for the content of the included file. Therefore, if the included file needs to include PHP functionality, it should also include PHP beginning ("<?PHP") and ending ("?>") tags.

HTML Formatting Conventions

**10 Min.
To Go**

Just as using liberal white space and good formatting in your PHP code is important, so is ensuring that any HTML output by your code follows similar good formatting.

You may have noticed the line breaks and indentations within the HTML examples earlier in this session. This was done to ensure that the HTML output by the script was readable. For example, examine the following two `print()` blocks and their resulting output:

```
Print Sample 1
print "<html><body>Hello world.</body></html>";
```

```
Output Sample 1
<html><body>Hello world.</body></html>
```

```
Print Sample 2
print "<html>\n\t<body>\n\t\tHello world.\n\t</body>\n</html>";
```

```
Output Sample 2
<html>
  <body>
    Hello world.
  </body>
</html>
```

Although both examples produce valid HTML, the latter output is much easier to debug if the script has a problem.

Here, document printing makes formatting and reading HTML output very easy. Take, for example, the following line:

```
print "<html>\n\t<body>\n\t\tHello world.\n\t</body>\n</html>";
```

It becomes the following:

```
print <<<HTML
<html>
  <body>
  Hello world.
  </body>

</html>
```

Line breaks and indentations (usually with tabs) are the hallmarks of good HTML formatting. Use line breaks liberally (even blank lines) to delimit sections of HTML code and indent tables and other nested entities.

Lastly, it's important to include HTML comments where appropriate, especially within here document print functions where you cannot use PHP comments to annotate your code. Just be sure that you don't mind the HTML comments being read by clients who view the source using their browsers.

Done!

REVIEW

This session showed you some of the functionality that makes PHP a natural for use with HTML. You saw how PHP automatically supplies headers to the browser, how you can supply your own headers, and how to best output large blocks of HTML. The next session extends this discussion, showing how easily PHP integrates with HTML forms.

QUIZ YOURSELF

1. What setting in the php.ini file controls the default content header that PHP sends? (See "The Automatic HTML Header.")

2. Why would you want to hide the X-Powered-By: PHP header? (See "The Automatic HTML Header.")

3. What is the best way to output large blocks of HTML? (See "Large HTML Blocks.")

4. Why is it important to format your HTML output? (See "HTML Formatting Conventions.")

Working with Forms

Session Checklist

✔ Understanding HTML forms

✔ Reviewing form fields

✔ Understanding how PHP handles form data

✔ Handling file uploads

**30 Min.
To Go**

HTML forms provide an excellent framework for receiving data from users. They provide a data entry GUI, rudimentary error checking, and can be used to pass the received data on to a script where the data can be parsed, stored, and so on.

This session reviews HTML forms and how PHP can be used as a form handler to receive and use the data from the forms.

Understanding How HTML Forms Work

Before delving into how PHP works with forms, you should understand how HTML forms themselves work. HTML forms enable a Web developer to design a graphical environment for Web users to input data. This environment uses fields and controls similar to those used in application program dialog boxes.

Standard HTML Form Elements

As of this writing, standard HTML supports the following form elements:

- **Text box** — A single-line, free-form text field.
- **Text area** — A multiline, free-form text field.

- **Password box** — A single-line field like a text box, but any input in a password field shows up as asterisks (to help obscure sensitive data).
- **Selection list** — A multi-field text box that enables the user to select one or more of its entries.
- **Check box** — An option that the user can select (check) or deselect (uncheck).
- **Radio button** — Usually used in groups, radio buttons enable a user to select one of several options.
- **Button** — A standard button image displaying specific text.
- **Image** — Substitutes an image for a button.
- **Hidden** — A special field that stores data invisible to the user.
- **Submit button** — A special button that causes the form to be submitted.
- **Reset button** — A special button that causes the form to be reset to default field entries.

Certain browsers support supersets of these form elements. However, this book covers only the basic form elements in the HTML 4.0 standard. The file input type, which enables users to submit a file for uploading, has also been omitted. This field type is covered in the section "File Uploads," later in this session.

If you want more information on HTML and forms, pick up a copy of *HTML 4.01 Weekend Crash Course*, by Greg Perry (Wiley Publishing).

Listing 19-1 shows a sample of each of these fields in an HTML document. Figure 19-1 shows how this code looks in a browser.

Listing 19-1   sampform.html

```
<html>
  <body>
    <form>
    <table cellspacing=20>
    <tr><td>

      <!-- Text boxes -->
      First Name: <input type=text name=fname size=20><br>
      Last Name: <input type=text name=lname size=20><p>
      <p>

      <!-- Text area -->
      Address:<br>
        <textarea name=addr cols=20 rows=4></textarea><p>
      <p>

      <!-- Password -->
      Password: <input type=password name=pwd size=20><p>
      <p>
      </td><td>
```

```
        <!-- Select list -->
        What product(s) are you<br>
        interested in? <br>
        <select name=prod[] multiple size=4>
          <option name=MB>Motherboards
          <option name=CPU>Processors
          <option name=Case>Cases
          <option name=Power>Power Supplies
          <option name=Mem>Memory
          <option name=HD>Hard Drives
          <option name=Periph>Peripherals
        </select>
        <p>

        <!-- Check boxes -->
        How should we contact you?<br>
          <input type=checkbox name=email checked> Email<br>
          <input type=checkbox name=postal> Postal Mail<br>
        <p>

        </td></tr>
        <tr><td>

        <!-- Radio buttons -->
        How soon will you be buying hardware?<br>
        <input type=radio name=buy value=ASAP>ASAP<br>
        <input type=radio name=buy value=10>Within 10 business days<br>
        <input type=radio name=buy value=30>Within the month<br>
        <input type=radio name=buy value=Never>Never!<br>
        </td><td>
        <p>

        <!-- Submit and Reset buttons -->
        <input type=submit>   <input type=reset>
        <p>

        <!-- Button -->
        <input type=button name=Leave value="Leave!">
        <p>

        <!-- Image -->
        <input type=image name=Coupon src="coupon.jpg">

        <!-- Hidden field -->
        <input type=hidden name=referredby value=Google>

        </td></tr>
      </table>
      </form>
    </body>
</html>
```

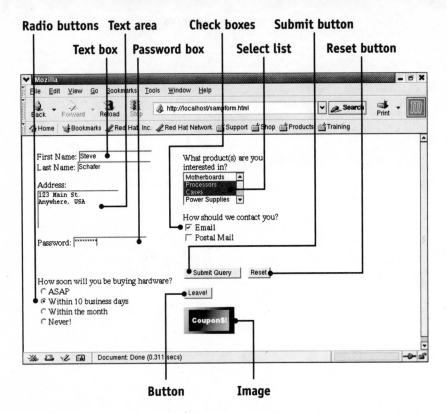

Figure 19-1   *Browser output of* `sampform.html`

Notice that each form field tag includes a `name` parameter. Scripts and form handlers use this parameter to uniquely identify each field.

Form Actions

When a user clicks the Submit button, the browser passes the data to the defined "action" in the form tag. For simplicity's sake, Listing 19-1 didn't contain several elements of the form tag. Although this code enables a form to be displayed, the form isn't very useful because it has no method to pass the input data along to an appropriate handler — making the data rather useless.

The full syntax of the form tag is as follows:

```
<form name=name action=url method=get/post >
```

The `name` parameter is helpful for identifying the form, especially when your document has several forms. The `action` parameter is a URL to a form handler. The form handler is typically a CGI program or other script that interprets the data and does something useful with it. The `method` parameter specifies how the data should be passed to the handler. The valid options for method are `get` and `post`.

The get method appends the data to the URL as name/value pairs using the following format:

```
http://url?name1=value1&name2=value2&...
```

The name/value pairs are separated from the URL with a question mark (?), and each pair is separated from the previous set by an ampersand (&).

The post method encodes the data into a separate part of the HTTP request that is passed to the handler.

Of the two, post is usually the preferred method because it is noticeably cleaner (it doesn't clutter the URL), it can hold more data, and its data handling is more robust (no messy quoting). However, not every handler can accept post data and sometimes using get is simply more convenient.

How Form Data Is Returned

**20 Min.
To Go**

The last step in this HTML form primer describes how form data is returned from a form to the handler. Table 19-1 describes the various form elements and the data they return.

Table 19-1   *Returned Form Element Data*

Element	Data Returned
Text box	The data entered into the text box.
Text area	The data entered into the text area.
Password box	The data entered into the Password box (real data, not asterisks).
Select list	A single value or an array if multiple parameters are used (but notice that an option's name is used instead of its text if the name parameter is used).
Check boxes	If checked, the contents of the field's value parameter are returned (or a generic "on", if no value was given). If the box is not checked, nothing is returned.
Radio buttons	The value or name (if no value was given) of the selected button.
Hidden	The value of the field.

Buttons and images do not return values; they must be used with scripting within the HTML document to perform actions. This would be done using a scripting language such as JavaScript. Exceptions are the Submit and Reset buttons. The Submit button causes the action of the form to take place, while the Reset button reloads the form in its default state. Both of these buttons can also be scripted — inside the HTML document — to circumvent their default behavior.

Hidden fields make convenient places to store various state data — data that helps to control scripts but which the user shouldn't see. We use this technique in later sessions. However, be careful when using hidden fields for sensitive data — remember that users can see the field definition if they choose to view your form's source.

PHP Form Data Handling

What does all this mean to PHP? If you can figure out how to get at and use the information passed from forms, you have a powerful form-handling platform at your disposal. This platform also integrates with almost every known Web and system technology, making it easy to store, retrieve, and work with form data.

Parsing $_POST

You might have noticed that the output of the phpinfo() function includes post data values in its output. Using a script with the phpinfo() function facilitates tracking form data. The data can be found in the "PHP Variables" section of the phpinfo() output under the values of $_POST or $_GET, depending on the method your form uses.

For example, this minimal script works nicely:

```
<?
  phpinfo();
?>
```

Store this code in a file named handler.php and change the form tag in the preceding example to the following:

```
<form action=handler.php method=post>
```

Filling out the form shown in Figure 19-1 and clicking the Submit button results in the information shown in Figure 19-2.

You may have noticed the brackets after the select tag's name in the example form:

```
<select name=prod[] multiple size=4>
```

These brackets force the handler to treat the value returned by the field as an array — as several values may be returned (due to the multiple parameter). However, you might also have noticed that the returned values are duplicated inside the array when PHP parses them.

The data in the prod field illuminates a bug between PHP 4.2+ and Apache 2.0+ — namely, the duplication of array elements. (Processors and Cases are duplicated in the prod array.) At the time of this writing, only one easy fix was available: using the array_unique() function to remove duplicates from the array prior to processing it. (Of course, this doesn't work if the array is *supposed* to have duplicates.) This is a known bug that one hopes will be fixed in short order.

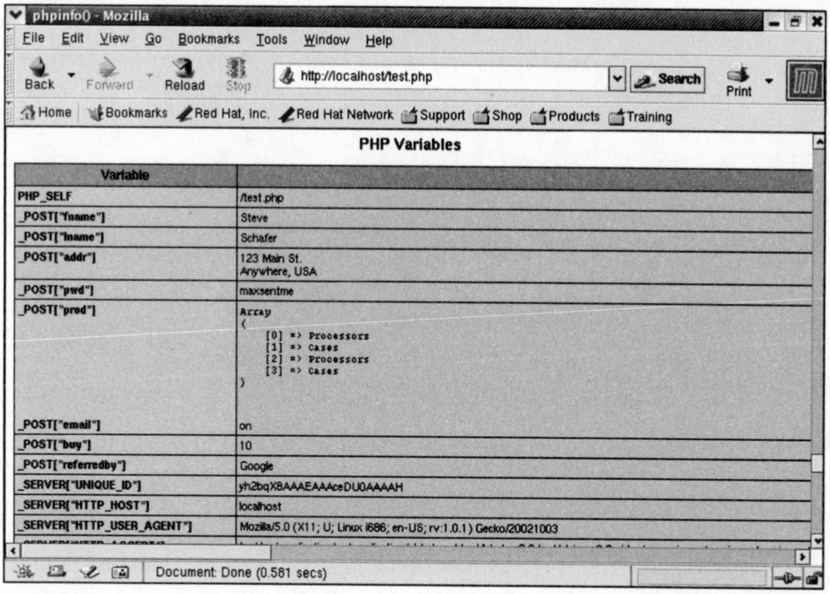

Figure 19-2 *Information from the handler on the* post *information it received.*

Notice that all of the data is stored in a **$_POST** variable. This variable is one of many *superglobal* variables built into PHP. Superglobal variables are used by PHP to store various pieces of environmental, system, and Web-related data. (Review the "PHP Variables" section of phpinfo() for more superglobals.)

Now that you know where the data is stored, how do you use it?

The **$_POST** variable is actually a keyed array — the keys are the names of the form data fields and their values are the data returned from each field. In the preceding example, **$_POST['fname']** would store **Steve**.

To get at each key/value pair, you could use a foreach() loop such as the following:

```
foreach($_POST as $key => $value) { }
```

This loop parses the **$_POST** variable into its respective keys and variables. Each iteration of the loop parses a new set of key/value pairs. Therefore, you want to change the handler.php script to the following:

```
<?php
// Generic form data parser


// Begin HTML page and field table
print <<<HTML
<html>
<body>
<table cellpadding=20 border=1>
<tr><td><b>Name</b></td>
  <td><b>Value</b></td></tr>
HTML;
```

```
// For each POST field
foreach ($_POST as $key => $value) {
  // Print the key in the first column
  print "<tr><td>$key </td>";
  print "<td>";
  // If the field is an array, parse it
  if (is_array($value)) {
    foreach ($value as $selkey => $selvalue) {
      print "$selkey : $selvalue <br>";
    }
  } else {
    // Else (not array) just print value in
    // second column
    print "$value ";
  }
  print "</td></tr>\n";

}


// Close open HTML elements
print <<<HTML
</table>
</body>
</html>
HTML;

?>
```

Notice the nested foreach() loop within the main loop. Because <select> fields are returned in arrays, you need to identify any field that is an array and parse it to get all values. Figure 19-3 shows the results of the sample data run through the new handler.

This handler is a good troubleshooting tool for forms, as is the phpinfo() **version. Consider keeping them both handy to help solve problems with your form data.**

Auto-Register Globals: Easier, But Less Secure

10 Min. To Go

An easier way for PHP to handle form data is by using the auto-register-globals functionality of the language. The php.ini file includes a setting, register_globals, that automatically registers select pieces of data as global variables. One of those pieces of data is form POST data. For example, say you have the following field in a form:

```
<input type=text name=fname size=20>
```

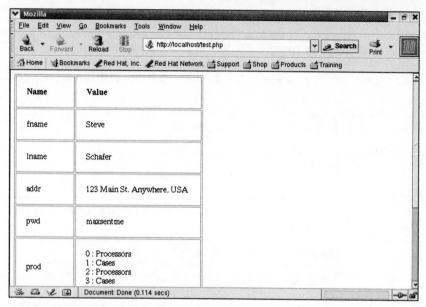

Figure 19-3   *The new handler output*

If you use a PHP script as the form handler, the variable $fname is automatically created and holds the value of the field when the form was submitted. You could then dispense with the parsing of $_POST and reference the field values directly ($fname, $lname, $pwd, and so on).

As of PHP version 4.2.0, the default for this setting is Off. The reasoning behind disabling such a useful feature has to do with security. With register_globals set to On, variables can be initialized from the URL. For example, the following URL would result in the variable $authorized being set equal to 1 in the script sample.php:

```
http://<server>/sample.php?authorized=1
```

If the code within sample.php were poorly written and the variable $authorized was used to actually authorize a user, the preceding URL could be used to gain unauthorized access. Therefore, the PHP community prefers that register_globals remains Off and that PHP coders use the superglobal variables to parse data passed to their scripts.

Working with File Uploads

Sometimes it is useful to allow users to post an actual file as data in a form. For example, you could allow prospective employees to post their resume to your company's employment site when filling out an application for a position.

The file type of the input tag has the following syntax:

```
<input type=file accept=<mime_type(s)> name=<field_name>
    value=<default_filename>
```

When placed in a form, this tag generates a text box with a Browse button.

The user can either type a file name into the text box (including a full path to a local file) or use the Browse button to spawn a File Manager window to navigate to the file. When the form is submitted, the file is sent to the handler using the HTTP POST protocol. Notice that the file_uploads setting in the php.ini file must be On for PHP to receive HTTP uploads.

PHP has a special superglobal variable to handle posted files — namely, $_FILES. Table 19-2 describes the $_FILES variable's various components.

Table 19-2   *$_FILES Components*

Component (key)	Use
name	The name of the uploaded file (what the user entered, minus the path information).
type	The MIME type of the uploaded file.
tmp_name	The temporary name of the uploaded file. (See the explanation of temporary names in the text that follows.)
error	Error code corresponding to the upload error. Error code zero (0) equals no errors.
size	Size of the file, in bytes.

The $_FILES superglobal is usually stored as a two-dimensional array. The first dimension is the filename and the second is the keys and/or values listed in Table 19-2. For example, an input file tag with the name resume **has its temporary name stored in** $_FILES['resume']['tmp_name']**.**

The PHP handler script receives the file and stores it in the directory specified by the upload_tmp_dir setting in the php.ini file. The file is given a temporary, unique name. It is the script's responsibility to do something useful with the file — move it to another directory, parse it for information, and so on.

You can control how much information can be uploaded in several ways. The upload_max_filesize **setting in the** php.ini **file has a default of 2MB. Any file over that limit causes an error. You can also place a special hidden tag before the input file tag in your HTML document, such as the following:**

```
<input type=hidden name=MAX_FILE_SIZE value=bytes>
```

This tag controls how much data the form actually passes on. Notice that unscrupulous users can view this code, save it to another file, edit it to their liking, and circumvent the limit. It's best to always have the upload_max_filesize **setting set to a reasonable limit (in the** php.ini **file or via the** ini_set() **function).**

Now you can put this together into a working example. Start with a basic upload form:

```
<html>
  <body>

  <!-- Form needs to be multipart for file upload-->
  <form action="filehandler.php" method="post"
    enctype="multipart/form-data">

    Enter file name (include full path)<br>
    or use the browse button:<p>

    <!-- Set max size to 100K -->
    <input type=hidden name=MAX_FILE_SIZE value=100000>
    <input type=file name=resume>
    <p>

    <input type=submit value=Upload>

  </form>

  </body>
</html>
```

Notice that the form needs to be specified as encoded multipart form data (enctype="multipart/form-data"). This parameter tells the handler to expect multiple parts to the submission of the form data — one of those parts is the file upload.

Then create a simple file handler (filehandler.php) to deal with the upload:

```
<?php

// Begin HTML page
print <<<HTML
<html>
<body>
HTML;

// Get the data out of the "resume" form element
$filedata = $_FILES['resume'];
$tempfile = $filedata['tmp_name'];

// Check to see if the file is indeed an upload
if (is_uploaded_file($tempfile)) {
  // Create destination path/filename (Linux format)
  $destfile = "/var/www/html/".$filedata['name'];

  // Attempt file move and report success/failure
  if (move_uploaded_file($tempfile, $destfile)) {
    print "File moved to: $destfile";
  } else {
    print "File cannot be moved to: $destfile";
```

```
    }

  } else {

    // File specified in "resume" element was
    //   not an upload, or nothing specified
    print "No uploaded file!";
  }

  // Close open HTML elements
  print <<<HTML
  </body>
  </html>
  HTML;

  ?>
```

Notice the following about the preceding example and file uploads in general:

- Always move the temporary file to a more permanent location before performing any other actions on it.
- The temporary file is deleted at the end of the handling script.
- The move_uploaded_file function replaces the destination if it exists.
- Always check the file specified with the is_uploaded_file function. Otherwise, your code might end up working with hazardous files.
- The code checks each step of the operation and responds or reports accordingly. If the file upload or move fails, the $_FILES superglobal can be further parsed for useful information to report to the system administrator or the user (for example, File was too big. Uploads have a 100K limit.)
- You probably do not want to store files using the file name included with the file. For example, what happens when a user on one platform uploads an invalid file name for your server platform? At least consider checking the file name before relying upon it.
- You can further control the type of data allowed as an upload with the accept parameter of the input file tag. This parameter accepts a comma-delimited list of MIME types that are valid uploads. If the file specified is not one of those types, the upload fails. (Notice that the MIME type doesn't fully guarantee that the data in the file matches the type.)
- Remember that the user ID under which the PHP process is running needs to have appropriate rights to the temporary directory and the destination directory in order for the upload and move to succeed.

Done!

REVIEW

This session reviewed HTML forms and showed you how to use PHP as a form handler. The techniques learned in this session are useful in later sessions and projects — where you use forms to gather information from users as well as to display data from MySQL for editing.

QUIZ YOURSELF

1. Why does the password form field print asterisks as data is entered? (See "Standard HTML Form Elements.")

2. Why should you always use name parameters in form field tags? (See "Standard HTML Form Elements.")

3. How do forms, using the GET method, pass information to their handler? (See "Form Actions.")

4. What type of variable is $_POST? (See "Parsing $_POST.")

5. What is the compelling argument against using register_globals? (See "Auto-Register Globals: Easier, But Less Secure.")

6. Why shouldn't you always store an uploaded file using the name provided by the user? (See "Working with File Uploads.")

Multiple-User Considerations in PHP

Session Checklist

✔ Understanding the challenge of multiple, concurrent users

✔ Using different methods to lock data

✔ Saving state with sessions

✔ Working with session data

**30 Min.
To Go**

When programming for the Web, you need to keep multiple, perhaps simultaneous, users in mind. What happens if two users access separate instances of your script(s) at the same time? Will the script encounter an error? Will it completely fail? Will it produce erroneous results?

This session covers some of the issues you face in dealing with multiple users and describes some of the solutions that you can use to prevent problems.

The Old Counter Example

To set the stage for the discussion, you can review the old *hit counter* example. This example has been around for almost as long as the Web and nicely illustrates the problems that can occur with multiple users.

The Problem

Suppose that you have a script for tracking how many users visit your Web site. The script is simple enough and follows this design:

1. The script is called from the main page of the site.
2. The file in which the current number is stored is opened.

3. The current number is retrieved.
4. One is added to the number.
5. The new number (current + 1) is stored in the file.
6. The file is closed.

What happens if two users access the site at the same time? Two instances of the script run, one for each user, and they both execute simultaneously — both pulling the current number and writing the change.

In the best scenario, one script makes it through Step 5 (storing the new number) before the other script reaches Step 3 (retrieving the "current" number). More likely, the reading and writing collide, causing both scripts to use the same number and write the same number to the file. The absolute worst case is that the underlying file system doesn't handle two simultaneous reads and writes, and the counter file is damaged or destroyed in the process.

How can you avoid these results?

The easiest and most widely used solution is to have the script lock the counter file until it is done with the file. This changes the program flow to the following:

1. The script is called from the site's main page.
2. The file in which the current number is stored is opened.
3. The script locks the file.
4. The current number is retrieved.
5. One is added to the number.
6. The new number (current + 1) is stored in the file.
7. The script unlocks the file.
8. The file is closed.

Now, each instance of the script ensures that it has exclusive access to the file. However, what happens if the file is locked by another instance? With the preceding sequence, the script is likely to fail with a fatal Cannot open file error.

You can add more functionality with a test to determine whether the file is locked:

1. The script is called from the site's main page.
2. The file in which the current number is stored is opened.
3. If the file is locked, the script pauses for a few milliseconds and tries Step 2 again.
4. The script locks the file.
5. The current number is retrieved.
6. One is added to the number.
7. The new number (current + 1) is stored in the file.
8. The script unlocks the file.
9. The file is closed.

Of course, this scheme could still fail in numerous ways:

- A script could fail for other reasons before unlocking the file, leaving the file locked and inaccessible indefinitely.
- Another instance of the script could sneak in between Steps 2 and 4, locking the file before the current instance can lock and read the file itself.
- Two scripts can run almost simultaneously, waiting and checking the file in concert, causing each other to fail and loop continuously.

> The last failure, two scripts running simultaneously, is known as a *race condition*. Both instances continue to race each other, forcing a *lockstep loop*. However, this has a quick fix. Instead of having the script wait for a fixed amount of time, randomize the script's waiting interval. This way, scripts running simultaneously try to re-access the locked file at different intervals.

The "So What if a Simple Counter Fails?" Argument

Bad code can cause a Web site counter to fail. This might not seem serious, but consider the consequences if the counter were used to increment customer order numbers. In the event of an error, the system could catastrophically fail, two customers could be assigned the same order number, and so on. The problem of handling multiple users is much more insidious than you might first think.

When you write code that can be used by multiple users, consider the following:

- Will each instance of the code save its own state, or will it be influenced by the other instance's state?
- What about external resources (files, operating system, and so on)? Will two instances of the code cause a conflict that needs to be resolved?
- Does the code adequately clean up after itself? If an error is encountered, does the code release locks, close open files, delete temporary files, and so forth?
- Do you need to uniquely identify each instance or even each user who accesses the code?
- What else will the code do if two instances run simultaneously?

Letting the Technology Sort It Out

Most of the technology you are using with this book has already handled the majority of problems that can result from multiple users. For example, MySQL is robust enough to handle most conflicts with internal constructs, such as table and row locking. In addition, many operating systems support the use of the flock() function, as discussed in Session 17. In short, don't reinvent the wheel if a solution is already available with the current technology.

Data Locking Schemes

**20 Min.
To Go**

Scripts that might generate simultaneous access to dynamic data should lock the data before attempting to make changes to the data. The following sections discuss several file locking methods.

Using flock()

In most cases, using the PHP flock() function on a file *before you open it* and *after you close it* is enough to maintain exclusive access. However, you also need to build a layer of error checking into your script to check for the lock — in case another instance of the script locked the file first.

The following code snippet is an example of locking a file, complete with rudimentary error checking and race condition escape:

```
while (!flock("$file",LOCK_EX)) {
  usleep(rand(1000,1000000));
}
```

This code attempts to lock the file specified in $file. If the lock cannot succeed, the while()condition evaluates to TRUE and the usleep() function is used to put the script to sleep (delay execution) for a random amount of time between 1,000 milliseconds and one full second. These numbers may need adjusting depending on your code — you should give the other code instance enough time to complete its operations and unlock the file, but you don't want to overdo it and have the code delay for longer than is needed. (One second is about the longest that you should ever delay code for file locking.) Keep in mind that the file might be unlocked by the initial instance of code and relocked by a third instance while this particular instance sleeps.

Using a Lock File

Another method commonly employed to lock files is the use of a separate lock file. This lock file is a uniquely named file that is created to signify a lock on a data file. For example, if you have a data file named data.txt, you might create a file named data.txt.lock in the same directory to signify a lock.

It's up to your code to check for this file prior to creating it and assuming a lock on the data. You can use code similar to the example from the preceding section for this method:

```
while (file_exists($file)) {
  usleep(rand(1000,1000000));
}
$lockfile = fopen($file.".lock","w+");
fclose($lockfile);
```

If the lock file already exists, the code continues to sleep for random periods of time. After the lock file is deleted (usually with the unlink() function), the code continues, creating the lock file to establish its exclusive access.

The delay between the while() **and** fopen() **functions creates the possibility that another process could create the file during the interval between when the code realizes the file doesn't exist and when it tries to create the file. In this instance, the delay should not be long enough to cause a concern, but it does emphasize that the code should not delay in creating the lock file for itself.**

Clearing Stale Locks

If you are using the lock file method of maintaining exclusive access, you can employ another level of error control to your code — stale lock checking. Using the `filectime()` function, you can determine when the lock file was last created. Subtracting the creation time from the current time gives you an idea of how long the lock file has been sitting idle. The amount of idle time should be relatively small unless another process did not properly unlock the data, causing the stale lock. The following code example determines how long the lock file has existed and stores that time, in seconds, in the `$stalechk` variable:

```
$locktime = filectime($file.".lock");
$nowtime = strtotime ("now");
$stalechk = $nowtime - $locktime;
```

You can then use this value to compare it to a reasonable margin (a few seconds) to determine whether the lock is indeed stale. If the lock appears stale, your code can delete the file and recreate it to establish the lock.

Keeping User State with Sessions

As you saw in the Session 16, certain means are available to you to keep a variable's state between functions. However, what if you wanted to keep a variable's state between scripts? Session 19 described how you can pass data to other scripts by using the GET method — adding name/value pairs to the end of URLs.

However, you have a simpler way to save state between scripts. PHP employs the use of *sessions* to store user state. Sessions are essentially uniquely named holders that keep data that you (as the programmer) specify. That data can be stored and reloaded by multiple scripts as long as the session exists.

Session Mechanics

Sessions store data in specially coded files on the server's file system. When allowed by the user's browser settings, the *session ID* — a unique identifier for each session — is stored on the user's system using cookies. If cookies are not allowed, PHP attempts to send the session ID between scripts by using POST or GET methods. Subsequent scripts then use this ID to retrieve the session data from the server.

Sessions, by default, are not automatic. Special functions must be called to start a session, save a variable's state to that session, and even to recall a session. Sessions are typically destroyed when the user exits his or her browser — or after a time specified in the `php.ini` file.

Key Session Configuration Options

**10 Min.
To Go**

You should familiarize yourself with a handful of session configuration options in `php.ini` if you intend to use sessions with your code. Table 20-1 summarizes these settings.

Table 20-1 *Key Session Configuration Options*

Option	Use
session.save_path	The path where session files are stored. This is /tmp by default. Windows users must change this to a valid path (to which PHP instances have adequate file rights) before using sessions.
session.use_cookies	Controls whether PHP attempts to store the session ID in a cookie or only use GET/POST. If this option is enabled and a cookie cannot be used, PHP falls back to GET/POST methods.
session.name	The default session name (used as the cookie name). Can be changed at runtime with the session_name() function.
session.auto_start	Controls whether sessions are automatically started at the beginning of every script. Unless you use sessions in almost every script, leave this setting disabled to save on session read and write overhead.
session.cookie_lifetime	The default time, in seconds, that a session should live. The default, zero (0), enables the session to live until the user quits the browser.
session.cookie_path session.cookie_domain	The default path and domain under which the session ID cookies should be registered.

Keep in mind that you can use .htaccess **files to override these settings for scripts in particular directories. This technique enables you, for example, to keep** session.auto_start **off for general scripts and turn it on for scripts that require it.**

Using Sessions

Using sessions requires that your scripts undertake the following activities:

- Start or resume a session
- Register key variables in the session
- Unregister variables that are no longer needed from a session
- Destroy unneeded sessions
- Manually pass the session ID to other scripts
- Optionally encode and save session data for later recall

Each of these activities is covered in the following sections.

Because sessions use cookies, most session operations must be performed prior to your script outputting anything. Cookie operations (creating a session and so on) must be performed before the HTTP header is completed and before any other data is sent. This does not affect working with the variables that are registered in the session; you can still change their values as you wish.

Starting or Resuming a Session

The session_start() function is used to start or resume a session. If PHP finds a valid session ID, that session is resumed when this function is run. If no valid session ID can be found, a new session is created when the session_start() function is run.

The format of the session_start() function is simple:

```
session_start();
```

Notice that, if an existing session is found, this function also restores any registered variables to the state of the session. If you use this function in a script that has received other data via GET or POST, any variables in the GET or POST information are overwritten by like-named variables in the session.

The session_start() function is unnecessary if you have enabled session.auto_start. In addition, the first session_register() function encountered (see the next section) automatically calls session_start() if it has not already been called.

Registering Variables with a Session

You use the session_register() function to register variables with the current session. The syntax of the session_register() function is as follows:

```
session_register('variable_name'[,'variable_name'...]);
```

One important syntactical note: The variable names specified in the session_register() command should not include the dollar sign ($). For example, to register the variable $name, you would use session_register('name') and not session_register('$name').

The session_register() function works only if the PHP register_globals setting has been enabled. If you don't have this setting enabled (Session 19 gave you a few reasons to leave it disabled), you need to use the $_SESSION superglobal array to register variables instead.

To use the $_SESSION array to register variables, you assign a variable's value to an array element keyed to the variable's name. In other words, to register $name with the session, you would use the following:

```
$_SESSION['name'] = $name;
```

Unregistering Variables with the Session

You can unregister unneeded variables and free up the resources they are using. To unregister a variable, use the session_unregister() function. The session_unregister() function has the same syntax as that of session_register() except that only one variable can be specified at a time:

```
session_unregister('variable_name');
```

This does not erase the value or the actual variable; it simply removes the variable from session tracking.

As with session_register(), you can use the session_unregister() function only if the PHP register_globals setting is enabled. If this setting is not enabled, you need to work with the superglobal $_SESSION array.

To unregister a variable using the $_SESSION array, use the unset() function on the array element you wish to unregister. For example, to unregister the aforementioned $name example registration, you would use the following:

```
unset($_SESSION['name']);
```

Always specify an array element — using unset() on the superglobal itself (unset($_SESSION)) destroys the variable's capability to track sessions.

If you are unsure whether a variable has been registered with the current session, you can check its status with one of the following two methods:

```
session_is_registered('variable_name');
```

```
isset($_SESSION['variable_name']);
```

Both methods return TRUE if the variable specified has been registered with the session. However, the former method (the session_is_registered() function) is valid only if the PHP setting register_globals is enabled. If you are not using register_globals, you must use the latter method (the $_SESSION array).

Destroying a Session

If you no longer need a session, you should destroy it and free up the resources it is consuming. To destroy a session, use the session_destroy() function. This function has the following simple syntax:

```
session_destroy();
```

This function destroys only the session; it does not alter the actual variables that were registered with it.

Manually Dealing with Session IDs

Occasionally, you need to manually pass the session ID between scripts. PHP handles the passing of the ID in most cases. However, in some instances, PHP cannot pass the data itself, so you need to step in and help.

The current session ID can be accessed with the session_id() function. Unfortunately, you have no way to tell PHP what the ID should be, so sending the ID via random fields does not work. You must send the session ID by using the field PHPSESSID or the field specified by the PHP setting session.name. Thankfully, PHP maintains a Session ID (SID), which contains all the relevant data to include in a GET URL scheme. For example, this constant might contain the following:

```
PHPSESSID=b7d59a0e3fda1f7293845f37996114f4
```

To use this constant in a URL, simply include the SID constant where PHP can evaluate it. For example, the following would be valid:

```
print "http://domain/path/file.php?".SID;
```

However, the following example would not be valid because PHP would not realize that the SID constant should be expanded instead of being included literally (the text, SID):

```
print "http://domain/path/file.php?SID";
```

Within raw HTML, you can use a construct similar to the following:

```
url=http://domain/path/file.php?<?php echo(SID);?>
```

Encoding and Saving Session Data

You may encounter situations in which saving session data for later retrieval would be advantageous (for example, when a user returns to your site). If the user quits his or her browser in between visits, the session data is lost. However, you can use the session_encode() function to encode the session data into a string and then store the string in a file, database, or other construct for later recall. The session_encode() function has the following syntax:

```
$string_variable = session_encode();
```

Later, when you retrieve the string from storage, you can restore it to the current session with the session_decode() function. This function has the following syntax:

```
session_decode($string_variable);
```

This has a similar effect to that of the session_start() function — all variables registered in the encoded string are restored to the state they were in when the string was encoded.

Done!

REVIEW

When writing code for the Web, you must consider multiple users. In fact, with popular Web sites, the number of simultaneous users can reach into the thousands, with active users in the millions.

This session showed you why you need to be concerned about simultaneous data access and saving user states. It explored methods to prevent problems with simultaneous data usage, and you learned how to use sessions to save user state between scripts. The next two sessions wrap up the PHP lessons with a session on good programming practices and another on debugging PHP code. Shortly thereafter, all three technologies are tied together — Apache, MySQL, and PHP — describing how to create dynamic, data-driven sites for the Web.

QUIZ YOURSELF

1. Why is it important to write code that cleans up after itself? (See "The 'So What if a Simple Counter Fails?' Argument.")

2. Can you rely on methods and procedures built in to PHP and MySQL to help solve multi-user issues? (See "Letting the Technology Sort It Out.")

3. Why should you have a script pause for a random amount of time while checking file locks? (See "The Problem" and "Using flock().")

4. What is a stale file lock? (See "Clearing Stale Locks.")

5. Where is session data actually stored? (See "Session Mechanics.")

6. How many variables can you unregister with one instance of the session_unregister() function? (See "Unregistering Variables with the Session.")

7. Why should you unregister unneeded variables and destroy unneeded sessions? (See "Unregistering Variables with the Session" and "Destroying a Session.")

PART

IV

Saturday Evening Part Review

1. If you write a script for a Web page, how many users will PHP allow to access the script at the same time?
2. What is the problem with relying upon `flock()` for file locking?
3. Why would you want to use `fseek()`?
4. Where is session data stored? How does PHP find the right data for the right session?
5. What is wrong with the following code?

   ```
   session_start()
   register_session('$username');
   ```
6. If register_globals is not enabled, how do you unregister the variable $password from the current session?
7. What are some reasons to destroy an active session?
8. How would you preserve a user's session from one visit to the next?
9. Why would you want to hide PHP's automatic X-Powered-By: header?
10. What is wrong with the following code fragment?

    ```
    print "Your total is: ".$total;
    header("Expires: Mon, 2 Jun 2003 05:00:00 GMT");
    ```
11. What is a good security-based reason to avoid using the GET method of transferring data?
12. Show two ways to output the following block of HTML:

    ```
    <html>
      <body>
        <table>
          <tr><td>First Name</td><td>Last Name</td></tr>
          <tr><td>$fname</td><td>$lname</td></tr>
        </table>
      </body>
    </html>
    ```

13. Why should you use the name= parameter in all HTML form fields?

14. What does the setting session.cookie_lifetime = 600 do? Why would you want to use it?

15. How would you pass the value of the $fname variable to another script using the GET method?

16. What's the difference between the HTTP GET and POST methods of sending data?

17. How do you parse information passed to a script via the POST method if register_globals is not enabled?

18. How is data from an input HTML form tag passed via POST to PHP?

19. When do you need to use the enctype= parameter with a form tag?

20. Why should you always close files that you open?

21. What is the state of the file "sample.txt" after the following code line?

    ```
    $file = ("sample.txt","w+b");
    ```

22. What is a valid reason for not reading an entire file into a string for processing?

☑ Friday

☑ Saturday

☑ **Sunday**

Part V — Sunday Morning

Session 21
Good Coding Practices

Session 22
Debugging and Troubleshooting PHP

Session 23
MySQL Through PHP

Session 24
Debugging and Troubleshooting MySQL in PHP

Session 25
Odds and Ends

Session 26
Project: Calendar I

Part VI — Sunday Afternoon

Session 27
Project: Calendar II

Session 28
Project: Content Publishing I

Session 29
Project: Content Publishing II

Session 30
Project: Building an RSS Feed

PART

V

Sunday Morning

Session 21
Good Coding Practices

Session 22
Debugging and Troubleshooting PHP

Session 23
MySQL Through PHP

Session 24
Debugging and Troubleshooting MySQL in PHP

Session 25
Odds and Ends

Session 26
Project: Calendar I

Good Coding Practices

Session Checklist

✔ Employing the right tools for writing code

✔ Using code libraries

✔ Writing effective comments and documentation

✔ Applying good habits to all code

**30 Min.
To Go**

Before you start coding larger and more complex scripts, a good idea is to cover some basic good habits for writing code in PHP. Up to this point, your code has been very simple, short, and to the point. However, in a few sessions, you start combining technologies (PHP, Apache, and MySQL) and working with much larger scripts. Even if you are an old-school programmer, browsing this session is worth your time.

If you are new to programming or even just new to PHP programming, you might find it useful to reread this session after writing a few more complex scripts and compare the suggestions in this session with your coding habits.

Building Solid Code

PHP makes Web scripting very easy — so easy, in fact, that you're often tempted to whip up a "fast-and-dirty script" whenever you encounter a Web-coding application. However, the "fast-and-dirty" route generally spawns bad code and is more trouble than it is worth. This section covers some basic guidelines you should try to follow for every script you write, in an effort to always generate solid code.

The Value of the Right Tools

PHP does not have its own Integrated Development Environment (IDE) — at least not yet. However, several separate IDEs are available for PHP, including the following:

- PHPEdit (www.phpedit.biz/products/PHPEdit/)
- IDE.PHP (www.ekenberg.se/php/ide/)
- NuSphere phpED (www.nusphere.com/)
- KPHPDevelop (www.project9.com/kphpdev/)
- Zend Studio (www.zend.com/store/products/zend-studio.php)

 See Section 9 of the PHP HOW-TO ("IDE tools for PHP") for more information on IDEs for PHP (www.linuxdocs.org/HOWTOs/PHP-HOWTO-9.html**).**

You can use just about any editor to write your scripts. However, it pays to invest in learning and using a good programming-friendly editor.

Don't settle for a plain-Jane text editor such as Windows Notepad or standard Linux vi. Instead, use an editor that handles multiple files at once, marks up code as you write, automatically indents, and perhaps even offers shortcuts for entering commonly used commands.

A good example for Windows users is TextPad, by Helios Software Solutions (www.textpad.com/). UltraEdit, by IDM Computer Solutions, Inc. (www.ultraedit.com/), is another friendly but capable programming editor. Both offer numerous features to make your coding easier, including the following:

- Simultaneous editing of several files, with up to two views per file
- A "warm start" feature to return to where your last editing session left off
- Mass text editing and formatting
- Unlimited undo capabilities
- Keystroke macros
- A text search (and optional replace) engine that supports regular expressions
- Visible bookmarks
- A built-in file manager
- DOS and Linux file formats (with appropriate newline handling)
- A binary file viewer

Many good text editors are available for Linux, mostly because the platform grew up around text editing. Many users prefer Emacs, while others swear by vim (an enhanced version of vi that does support syntax highlighting and so on). Emacs has the richest features for programmers, but vi alternatives (such as vim) are quickly catching up. Whichever editor you use, it is helpful to turn on syntax highlighting and other automatic formatting and marking features. Most of the features in the preceding list for Windows editors are available for use in Linux editors.

Syntax highlighting, whereby the editor changes the color of the code to highlight open and closed elements, is perhaps the most useful feature an editor can have.

Coding It Right the First Time Around

Taking shortcuts is tempting when coding an otherwise simple script. PHP offers you plenty of opportunities to do so, automating many tasks almost effortlessly. However, as you are likely to find, if you don't code it right the first time around, you might not get the chance (or remember) to fix it later, and that useful script can turn into your worst nightmare.

Keep the following guidelines in mind as you code your scripts:

- **Don't skimp on the documentation.** That 30-line script might be very clear now, but if you encounter a problem with it later, or if someone else needs to debug the code, you always wish that you had more information. At a minimum, always comment the beginning of code sections (functions, loops, the main body of the script, and so on).

- **Write legible, not clever, code.** It's sometimes tempting to squeeze that last bit of ingenuity into your code. Generally, however, the more ingenuity that you add, the more complexity you add, and the more likely the code is to contain errors. Unless you are coding for a school grade or the Nobel Prize, remember to KISS (Keep It Simple, Stupid). Break down complex operations into distinct steps, avoid overnesting functions, and name your variables something legible.

- **Build out.** Begin with working code and expand around it, testing as you go. This reinforces your understanding of coding principles, your understanding of the problem at hand, and your confidence in your ability to make things happen. It also helps you keep the problems you are solving at a more manageable level of complexity.

- **Add error detection and correction now.** That simple script may run for months without any problems, but what if the environment changes around it — a key data file disappears, resources move, standards change, and so on? Don't assume that every file operation will automatically succeed; test the file functions' return values to ensure that the operations do what you want.

- **Stick to your guns.** Develop some good programming habits and stick to them. Always try to do the same operations the same way to help in troubleshooting them later. I'm not saying that you should never innovate, but when you do, make sure that you do so consistently.

- **Code for your intended audience.** Although you may understand output such as A# 454 T 63, the script's audience may not. You are sure to make some last-minute changes to the code, the interface, or output presented to users; general interface work is generally easier to do up front.

The Value of Consistency

"Write consistent code," is a mantra you should live by. You may be surprised at the number of problems you can solve by using tried and true methods instead of always shooting from the hip. There isn't an expected or "right" style to adopt when coding with PHP. Some guidelines can help eliminate common mistakes and such, but no one really cares whether the opening brace of an if() function is on the same line as the if or on the line that follows. Find what you are comfortable with and stick to it.

Using Functions

If you repeat code verbatim in a script more than twice, the repeated code should be moved to a function. Using functions has multiple advantages, including the following:

- **Saving typing** — You need to type the code only once, and thereafter, you can simply type the function name.
- **Preventing typos** — That one character difference between two sections of supposedly identical code can cause a world of problems. If you type the code once and ensure that it is right, you don't need to worry about mistyping a variable name, function call, or assignment operator.
- **Increasing modularity** — Program modularity is good. As you see in the next session, modular code is much easier to read, understand, and debug.

Revisiting Old Code

**20 Min.
To Go**

As your experience with PHP grows, so do your abilities to write better scripts. When you have the time, revisiting old code is usually worth the effort. However, don't try to solve the world's problems with old scripts; just look for mistakes you used to make and correct them. This is especially important for frequently used scripts.

Of course, a script doesn't have to be months or even hours old before you revisit it. Giving a script one more look before moving on is well worth the time. You might be surprised what you find in the code you were just working with.

Think of how different preparation for Y2K would have been if programmers had fixed code as they realized the problem (several years before 2000).

Code Libraries

As you continue to program with PHP, you come to recognize code that you use repeatedly. Consider starting a common.php file that you can use as a code library for your projects.

This file can be stored in a global location and should contain any functions that you find yourself using in multiple scripts. Take care to make the library version of your functions general in nature — you might find that you need to add an argument or two to help control what the function does and when.

Common HTML tasks — opening tags for a page, common table definitions, closing tags for a page — are prime candidates for a code library.

After creating this file, you can reference it by using the include(), include_once(), require(), or require_once() function at the top of any script that needs the library.

Remember that PHP turns processing *off* for included documents. Be sure to include the appropriate PHP tags (for example, "<?php") in your library files. This behavior does have a benefit; you can create HTML template files containing pure HTML (no PHP tags) and use `include()` functions to add them to your script as raw HTML.

Commenting and Creating Documentation

Commenting code can be slightly or severely neglected. Seldom is it not neglected to some degree. At the risk of beating a dead horse, the following sections review some good strategies for commenting and documenting code.

Comment Placement

It's generally accepted practice to place comments before the code to which they refer. It's also generally accepted to place the comments at the same indentation level as that of the code to which they refer. The only exceptions to this should be out-of-the-ordinary comments, such as using horizontal lines (rules) to divide or delimit code segments.

At a minimum, you should comment code blocks. Any time you have an open brace ({) you have an opportunity to add a comment describing what that block accomplishes. If the code block is more complex, use several lines and add a variable legend.

"Look Here!" Comments

You often want to mark certain sections of your code for later perusal. For example, you might have a block of code that you feel should be better optimized, but you want to pursue that task later.

Invent a scheme for such comments and consistently use it. Many programmers use a string of characters that do not commonly appear together to call attention to these comments, such as the following:

```
// XXX  The following should be better optimized XXX
```

That way, they can quickly search through the code for the string of characters (XXX in the preceding example) to find areas of the script that need attention.

Use the `grep` command (when using Unix or Linux) or your editor's Search Files function to find all scripts with such comments in a given directory — scripts that need attention.

"War and Peace" or "Reader's Digest"?

Good coding practices incorporate a good mix of short, to-the-point comments and longer, tell-all comments. Remember that you can use C programming-style comments (/* *comment* */) to include multiple line, free-form format comments in your code.

In addition, keep in mind that you can use the standard comment format (//) to append comments to the end of lines if necessary. The key to good commenting is to include enough information to be able to quickly assess what the code does without needing to decipher the comment first. Write simply and concisely.

Using long, descriptive variable names can help alleviate the need for comments. For example, you don't need to comment a line like the following:

```
$total = $subtotal + ($subtotal * $taxrate);
```

10 Min.
To Go

Documentation

Documentation is the most overlooked part of any programming project. Although you understand what a script does and how it acts, writing it all down somewhere generally pays. You might find that the details on clever features you added today are more than a little foggy next month when you need to update the script.

Make a habit of creating a .doc file for every script of medium to large size that you write. Unless you can fit all the details of the script's operation in the opening comments (for example, Reads the record keyed by $key into form fields and displays the form), summarize the operation in the script's comments and reference the .doc file. If your script is for general consumption, adding a user section to your documentation — outlining how a user actually goes about using the script, its interface, and so on — would also be appropriate.

Creating documentation files becomes useful only if these files are actually retained past the creation of the project. The file extension .doc is simply a suggestion; many programmers place all relevant documentation inside the code, and some create external files (under various names: sometimes simply README and sometimes full Linux MAN pages). Whatever the case, you need to document more than what the code accomplishes — including the expected user experience, ties to other scripts, system requirements, and so on.

With larger scripts, writing documentation as you write the program is best. If you follow the modular approach to implementing features, you can add a section of documentation as you finish each module and/or feature.

Applying Good Coding Habits Universally

As you have seen with the scripts dealt with thus far, you also code a good bit of HTML within your PHP. Take care to apply the same concepts outlined for coding PHP to coding HTML:

- Use the same tools that you use for PHP to write your HTML. When necessary, consider using a dedicated HTML editor for more elaborate code and then cut and paste the code into your PHP script (generally in a here document print() function).
- Indent and otherwise format your HTML for maximum legibility.
- Consider building a library of HTML code for easy inclusion of common HTML blocks.

- Use HTML standards. Although most modern browsers are a bit lenient in enforcing standards (for example, quotes around every parameter value in a tag), you want to stick as close to the standards as possible to help ensure that your code runs on every platform.

- Control every aspect of the HTML page possible. The following single line of code produces a valid HTML page in Internet Explorer and Mozilla:

```
<?php print "Hello world." ?>
```

However, the preceding example is noticeably void of HTML tags. You should include all necessary tags and information (such as header definitions) within your code to help ensure that the code renders and behaves as you intended.

 The same care should be taken when structuring MySQL queries within PHP code: Don't take shortcuts, adhere to standards, and so on.

Done!

REVIEW

This session covered some basic good coding habits that you should use when coding PHP scripts. It reviewed code formatting, tools, scripting habits, and some modular coding techniques. It then described practices for commenting code and creating more comprehensive documentation for your scripts. Last, this session emphasized the importance of using these habits across all of your coding, including HTML and MySQL.

QUIZ YOURSELF

1. What features make a good programming-friendly editor? (See "The Value of the Right Tools.")
2. When should you add error detection and correction code to your script? (See "Coding It Right the First Time Around.")
3. After how many repetitions of verbatim code should you consider placing the duplicate code in a function? (See "Using Functions.")
4. What is a code library, and why is it useful? (See "Code Libraries.")
5. Why would you use "Look Here!" comments? (See "'Look Here!' Comments.")

Debugging and Troubleshooting PHP

Session Checklist

✔ Writing modular code

✔ Identifying problem code

✔ Printing diagnostics

✔ Diagnosing code from the command line

E ven the simplest scripts can contain errors. Sometimes the errors are simple typos or syntactical blunders. However, given the nature of programming, many errors turn out to be complex beasts that are hard to identify and fix.

**30 Min.
To Go**

Before you progress into writing longer, more complex scripts, it is wise to examine some troubleshooting tips so you can adequately debug and fix your code. This session covers various debugging techniques.

Many of the coding practices described in the previous session also help you more easily debug and solve problems in your code.

Modular Code for Easy Debugging

Writing modular code is the best way to ensure that you can easily debug and troubleshoot your code. The main idea behind modular coding is to write distinct chunks of code that perform very specific tasks and to avoid mixing too much functionality into each distinct chunk. If you code in this fashion, troubleshooting problem functionality becomes easier.

This section covers the basic principles of modular code and some techniques to help you create it.

A Nonmodular Coding Example

Suppose that you wanted to view all the document icons available in Apache. These icons are used for fancy directory listings. They supply iconic graphics that show the type of each file in the directory.

These files can be accessed through the Web with the /icons/ alias and are typically stored in the icons directory under the Apache directory (/var/www/icons on Red Hat 8).

The following script (iconview.php) prints the icons to an HTML file within a table for viewing:

```php
<?php

// Set up globals
//  Note that directories may be different on your system
$fdir = "/var/www/icons";
$wdir = "/icons/";
$files = array();

// Start HTML page
print <<<HTML
<html>
  <body>
HTML;

// Open directory
($dir = opendir($fdir)) or die("Cannot open \"$dir\"");

// Keep track of # of graphics
$grphnum = 0;

// Read all files
while (!($file = readdir($dir)) === FALSE) {
  // Only process .GIF and .PNG files
  if (strpos($file,".png") || strpos($file,".gif")) {
    $grphnum++;
    $files["$grphnum"] = $wdir.$file;
  }
}
closedir($dir);

// Sort files in ascending order
array_multisort($files,SORT_ASC,SORT_STRING);

// Start first row
print "\t<table border=1>\n";
print "\t<tr height=\"60\">\n";

// Print 5 per row
$perrow = 5;

for ($x = 1; $x <= $grphnum; $x++) {
```

```
// Put image in cell
print "\t\t<td><img src=".$files["$x"]." width=\"50\"></td>\n";
// Every $perrow graphics, break row
if (($x % $perrow) == 0) {
  print "\t</tr>\n\t<tr height=\"60\">\n";
}
}

// Close row & table accordingly
if (($x % $perrow) != 0) {
  print "\t\t<td> </td>\n\t</tr>\n";
} else {
  print "\t</tr>\n";
}

// Close table
print "\t</table>\n";

// Close other open tags
print <<<HTML
  </body>
</html>
HTML;

?>
```

The output of this code is shown in Figure 22-1.

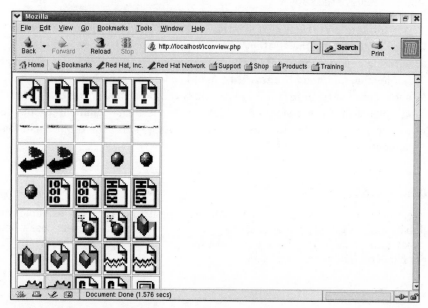

Figure 22-1 *Output of the* `iconview.php` *script*

Windows users need to modify the $fdir variable accordingly for their platform.

However, this script wasn't written with modularity in mind. It is a simple script that places all functionality in the main program body. (The next section explains how to rewrite this code with modularity in mind.)

Modular Coding Techniques

20 Min. To Go

The following sections cover a few techniques that you can use to help modularize your code.

Use Functions

Previous sessions have mentioned that functions save time, lend consistency, and save on duplicating code. They can also be a great aid to modular coding.

Placing distinct features and functionality within a user-defined function enables you to easily evaluate that functionality and even replace it with debugging code if necessary. It also helps organize your code into distinct chunks and usually helps your train of thought regarding the code.

Replacing a function with another similar function that contains debugging code is also very easy. For example, you could copy a function, add debugging code to the copy, and comment out the original. When you find the problem, you make the appropriate changes to the original and remove the copy.

Don't delete problematic code or make drastic changes without a backup copy of the code. One strategy is to make a copy of the code and place it within a comment for preservation. Then if you find that you are chasing a red herring and need to revert to the old code, you can simply move the commented section back into place. However, do remove code that is inside comments after your program is fully tested, as such "commented-out" code can be very confusing to someone who drops by your code later (including yourself).

Using Global Variables

Typically, avoid hard-coding values that you might later want to change. For example, consider the globals used in the preceding example — variables were used in every case where you might want to later make a change, from path names and file names to how many graphics to include on one line of the table.

Group Global Variable Declarations

One distinct problem with the example shown earlier in this session is that the global declarations are separated in the code. Early on, for example, you have the following cluster:

```
// Set up globals
$fdir = "/var/www/icons";
$wdir = "/icons";
$files = array();
```

Later in the code, you have these two declarations:

```
$grphnum = 0;
$perrow = 5;
```

I see no reason why the latter two declarations can't be moved to the top of the script with the other declarations.

Placing all the declarations together gives you a snapshot of the script's operation.

A Modular Code Example

The following listing shows the example `iconview.php` script written in a modular fashion:

```php
<?php

// Set up globals
$fdir = "/var/www/icons";
$wdir = "/icons/";
$files = array();
$grphnum = 0;
$perrow = 5;


// Start or stop a HTML file
function startstopHTML($startstop) {
  if ($startstop == "start") {
// Start HTML page
print <<<HTML
<html>
  <body>
HTML;
  } else {
// Close HTML page
print <<<HTML
  </body>
</html>
HTML;
  }
} // End startstopHTML()
```

```php
// Store all graphics in $dir to array $files
function getgraphics($fdir, $wdir, &$files) {
  // Open directory
  ($dir = opendir($fdir)) or die("Cannot open \"$dir\"");
  $grphnum = 0;
  // Read all graphic files
  while (!($file = readdir($dir)) === FALSE) {
    // Only process .GIF and .PNG files
    if (strpos($file,".png") || strpos($file,".gif")) {
      $grphnum++;
      $files["$grphnum"] = $wdir.$file;
    }
  }
  closedir($dir);

  // Sort files in ascending order
  array_multisort($files,SORT_ASC,SORT_STRING);

  return($grphnum);
}  // End getgraphics()


// Print table of graphics from array $files
function printgraphics($files, $grphnum, $perrow) {
  // Start first row
  print "\t<table border=1>\n";
  print "\t<tr height=\"60\">\n";

  for ($x = 1; $x <= $grphnum; $x++) {
    // Put image in cell
    print "\t\t<td><img src=".$files["$x"]." width=\"50\"></td>\n";
    // Every $perrow graphics, break row
    if (($x % $perrow) == 0) {
      print "\t</tr>\n\t<tr height=\"60\">\n";
    }
  }
  // Close row & table accordingly
  if (($x % $perrow) != 0) {
    print "\t\t<td> </td>\n\t</tr>\n";
  } else {
    print "\t</tr>\n";
  }

  // Close table
  print "\t</table>\n";
} // End printgraphics()


// Main program body

startstopHTML("start");
```

```
$grphnum = getgraphics($fdir, $wdir, $files);

printgraphics($files, $grphnum, $perrow);

startstopHTML("stop");

?>
```

Notice how all the different pieces of functionality were moved to distinct user-defined functions. However, they weren't broken down to a very fine grain — operations such as sorting the array were left within the getgraphics() function instead of being broken out into their own functions.

You can also shorten the main body of the script by nesting the getgraphics() **call within the** printgraphics() **call. However, doing so makes the** printgraphics() **call harder to read and follow.**

Dividing and Conquering

You can usually determine which *part* of your code is causing a problem. Identifying the exact problem, however, can be a bit tricky. In such cases, try separating out some of the code and testing it in a vacuum, without the other code in the process.

Typically, this means commenting out known good sections of code and using troubleshooting techniques on the rest. However, sometimes it means commenting out questionable sections and then adding them back in one section at a time until the problem section is identified.

For example, in the iconview.php example, if a problem arises with the final output, you can comment out the body of the printgraphics() function (or just not call it) and run some checks on the getgraphics() function to ensure that the file names were being retrieved correctly.

You would then return to calling the printgraphics() function but would comment out the section where the <IMG> tags were inserted into the table cells. This would ensure that the HTML coding wasn't at fault. Lastly, you would return the code to its normal state, perhaps with some extra troubleshooting statements around the <IMG> tag section.

Independently verifying a script's HTML also helps. For example, if you have a large block of HTML within a here document print() function, you can cut and paste that code into a separate file and load it into a browser to ensure that it works as intended.

In fact, you're generally better off doing the opposite — writing the HTML, verifying it in a browser, and then cutting and pasting it into your script.

Error Control and Processing

PHP has a host of functions and mechanisms to help control how errors are handled in your code. By using these functions, you can increase or decrease the amount of errors reported, intercept errors you want to handle in the code, and so on.

Controlling the Error Level

The PHP error_reporting() function controls which errors are reported at run time. This function takes one argument as either a bitmapped value corresponding to the error levels you want returned or a string of named constants corresponding to the error levels you want returned. Table 22-1 lists the bitmapped values and their named constant counterparts.

Table 22-1   *Values for the error_reporting() Function*

Value	Constant
1	E_ERROR
2	E_WARNING
4	E_PARSE
8	E_NOTICE
16	E_CORE_ERROR
32	E_CORE_WARNING
64	E_COMPILE_ERROR
128	E_COMPILE_WARNING
256	E_USER_ERROR
512	E_USER_WARNING
1024	E_USER_NOTICE
2047	E_ALL

See the PHP documentation on error code constants (www.php.net/manual/en/ref.errorfunc.php#errorfunc.constants**) for more information on what kinds of errors fall into each category.**

For example, if you want to report run-time errors and warnings, you can use either of the following two formats:

```
// Note that level 3 = level 2 + level 1
error_reporting(3);
```

```
// Note each error level constant should be listed,
//   separated by a vertical bar (|)
error_reporting(E_ERROR | E_WARNING);
```

If you do not want any errors reported, use a zero in the error_reporting() call:

```
// No error reporting
error_reporting(0);
```

Sending Errors to a File or E-mail Address

You can use the error_log() function to send specifics about an error to a file or e-mail address. This function is handy for production scripts whereby the user, not the programmer, experiences the errors firsthand. The error_log() function has the following syntax:

```
error_log(<error_message> [, <message_type>[, <message_destination>[,
    <extra_headers>]]]);
```

The first parameter, <error_message>, is a string containing the type and description of the error. For example, you could send Unable to open file *filename* as the error text, replacing *filename* with the name of the file that could not be opened.

The second parameter, <message_type>, tells the error_log() function what type of error to send, text to a file or text to e-mail. This argument supports the values contained in Table 22-2.

Table 22-2 *Valid Values for the <message_type> Argument of error_reporting()*

Value	Meaning
0	Sends the error text to the system's logger or the file name in the error_log directive (contained in the php.ini file)
1	E-mails the error text to the address specified in the <message_destination> argument. This mechanism uses the same routines as the mail() function.
2	Sends the error text through the remote debugging interface. This requires that remote debugging be enabled. The <message_destination> argument is used to specify the IP address (and, optionally, the port) to which the information should be sent.
3	Appends the error text to the file name specified in <message_destination>

The following code snippets provide examples of each type of error reporting via the error_log() function. In each case, the variable $errtext is assumed to hold the text of the error that occurred.

```
// Send the error to the system logger (error_log directive not set)
error_log($errtext, 0);
```

```
// Send the error to specific error log
//  (error_log directive set to file, e.g. /var/log/php.error)
error_log($errtext, 0);

// Send the error via email to sschafer@example.com
error_log($errtext, 1, sschafer@example.com);

// Send the error to a remote debugger at 192.168.1.10
error_log($errtext, 2, "192.168.1.10");

// Append the error to the file "/var/log/php.error"
error_log($errtext, 3, "/var/log/php.error");
```

A few things are necessary to keep in mind regarding the functionality of error_log():

- Method 0 (send to error_log or system logger) depends on quite a few settings in the php.ini file. Look in the configuration file (php.ini) for information on each directive (for example, log_errors_max_len, which sets the maximum length of each error).
- Method 1 (e-mail) depends on quite a few outside influences to be able to actually send the e-mail. For example, PHP under Windows requires that a mail transfer agent (MTA) — a mail server — be listening at the destination to which the e-mail is sent.
- Method 2 (remote debugging) requires that you set up a remote debugging session — explaining the details of such is outside the scope of this book.
- Method 3 (append to file) requires that PHP be able to actually write to the file specified.
- All of these methods are influenced by the log_errors and error_reporting directives. Remember that you can use the ini_set() function or specific error functions (for example, error_reporting()) to change these directives at run time.

When you're logging errors, the error text needs to contain all the pertinent information about the specific error. For example, an error that simply states Could not open file **is relatively useless. You should also include the current date and time in the error text so that you know when the error occurred.**

Custom Error Handling

So far, you have seen how to change the error reporting level and where errors are reported. The real meat of PHP's error functions is encapsulated in the set_error_handler() function. This function enables you to define your own error handler. This is important for creating recovery code for otherwise catastrophic errors — rebuilding a damaged file or recovering data.

The set_error_handler() function has the following syntax:

```
set_error_handler(<function_name>);
```

For example, if you wanted all errors passed to a function named err_handler(), you would specify that function with set_error_handler():

```
set_error_handler("err_handler");
```

The set_error_handler() **function returns the previous error handler. The complementary** restore_error_handler() **function reinstates the previous error handler, whether it is the internal PHP handler or a user-defined handler. (The** restore_error_handler() **function takes no arguments — PHP remembers the previous handler.)**

The error-handling function needs to accept at least two arguments, the code of the error that was generated and the text of the error that was generated. As of PHP version 4.3, three other parameters can be handled by an error-handling function: the file name of the script in which the error occurred, the line number on which the error occurred, and an array that points to the active symbol table (script variables and status) at the time the error occurred.

User-defined error handlers cannot handle the following types of errors: E_ERROR, E_PARSE, E_CORE_ERROR, E_CORE_WARNING, E_COMPILE_ERROR **and** E_COMPILE_WARNING. **See the PHP documentation for information on these errors.**

You define an error-handling function just as you would define any other function. The following code snippet shows the beginning of a sample error handler:

```
function err_handler($errno, $errtext, $errfile, $errline, $errcontext) {
    <code to handle error here...>
```

What you do inside the error handler is up to you. You can perform different actions based on the type of error, the content of the error text, and so on. However, remember that your function is now handling the error entirely — be sure to output as much useful information as possible to help debug the error.

Keep in mind that you can call the error-handling function manually — you don't need to generate an error. This is useful if a noncode error is generated (invalid user input and so on) — you can use the same code to report the error. If you ever need to generate an actual error, you can use the PHP trigger_error() **function.**

Print Everything

Whenever a problem occurs in the code, printing all suspect variables usually helps identify the culprits. For example, when writing the example for this session, I ran into a problem for which the output resembled what is shown in Figure 22-2.

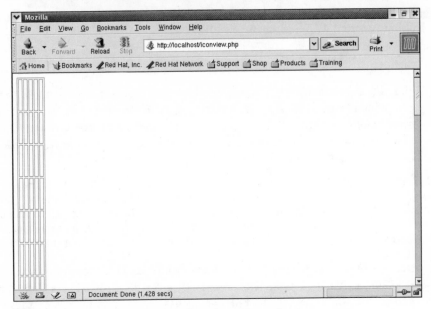

Figure 22.2   *Erroneous output from* `iconview.php`

To quickly verify that the file names were being retrieved correctly, I added the following code between the `getgraphics()` and `printgraphics()` function calls:

```
foreach ($files as $key => $value) {
  print "$key : $value<br>";
}
```

This resulted in the output shown in Figure 22-3, from which I could quickly check the file names stored in the `$files` array — finding the missing / between the path and file names.

The preceding code shows you how to parse a keyed array into its subparts. Using the `var_dump()` function is an easy way to dump information about variables. The `var_dump()` function takes one or more expressions as arguments and "dumps" their details to the standard output. When you simply need a variable's details (in no particular format), use `var_dump()`. For example, the preceding code example becomes the following:

```
var_dump($files);
```

When you are dealing with complex operations, outputting all related variables before and after the operation often helps. Generally, you easily spot the problem — typically, it's a simple case of a variable being set to a wrong value.

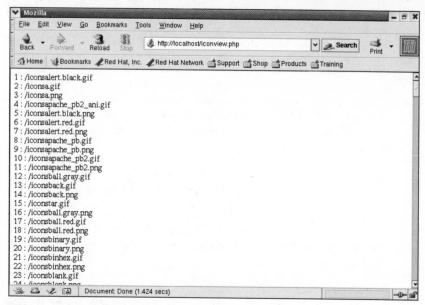

Figure 22-3 Diagnostic output from `iconview.php`

Sometimes adding diagnostic output into the script's regular output is pro-
hibitive — such as when the regular output is highly stylized or formatted.
In such cases, you can use PHP's file output features to print the diagnostic
information to a file. In fact, it's usually advisable to keep a diagnostic
library handy. The library should contain functions to open, write to, and
close a diagnostic file. You can then add the library to a script by using the
`include()` function and add calls to its functions in appropriate locations in
your code.

You may decide that it is worthwhile to make your debugging code conditional on the presence of a *$debug* variable that is set *to* TRUE only if you
want debug output.

Command-Line PHP

Don't forget that you can run your scripts from the command line. This technique is covered
in Session 13. The advantage of doing diagnostic work from the command line is that you
remove the HTTP delivery of your script's output from the mix. In addition, remember that,
from the command line, you can pipe a script's output to a file and then load that file into
an editor or browser to check it.

You can use several command-line switches with the PHP executable to help diagnose your code. Some of these switches are described in Table 22-3.

Table 22-3 *PHP Command-Line Switches*

Switch	Use
-s	Displays (in HTML) a color-highlighted version of the script's source. This option is useful for checking your script's syntax if you aren't using a syntax-highlighting editor.
-c	Specifies an alternative location for the php.ini file. This is useful for checking the configuration of PHP as a whole — you can copy php.ini, change a few options, and see how it affects your script.
-d	Changes configuration directives. This option is handy for changing only a few options. The format for this option is as follows: -d configuration_directive[=value]
-l	Performs a syntax check on the specified script. If no errors are found, PHP responds with a No syntax errors detected message. If PHP finds any errors, they are output accordingly.
-i	The equivalent of using the phpinfo() function. Although this produces a fairly large HTML file, it is generally better for diagnosing global problems — making the phpinfo() function Web-accessible (inside a script) presents a few security problems and should be used sparingly.
-r	Executes code passed as an argument, without the need for a full script file or PHP beginning and ending tags. This is useful when you want to check the output of a particular PHP function, a long equation, or other *single* PHP operation. This option cannot be used with most of the other command-line options.

Done!

REVIEW

As a prelude to more complex coding, the last two sessions detailed methods for writing good code and troubleshooting errors. In this session, you learned how to modularize your code and the advantages of doing so. You also learned various troubleshooting techniques to employ when you encounter errors. The next few sessions combine the PHP and MySQL technologies; you learn how to troubleshoot their interaction and begin coding applications employing all you've learned thus far.

QUIZ YOURSELF

1. What is the main advantage of modular code? (See "Modular Code for Easy Debugging.")

2. How do functions help you modularize code? (See "Use Functions.")

3. What is the disadvantage to hard-coding file names directly into file functions? (See "Using Global Variables.")

4. Why would you use the -d PHP command-line option instead of the -c option? (See "Command-Line PHP.")

MySQL Through PHP

Session Checklist

✔ Connecting to and disconnecting from MySQL

✔ Selecting a database

✔ Using queries

✔ Working with result sets

**30 Min.
To Go**

I've spent a good portion of this book touting how easy it is to work with MySQL through PHP. In this session, you find out just how easy it is. It starts with connecting to a MySQL server and selecting a database and finishes by showing how to query a database and then transverse and parse the result set returned by the query.

Connecting to and Disconnecting from the MySQL Server

Before you can talk to MySQL databases, you must connect to the server on which they reside. Much like opening and closing data files, the connection to a MySQL must be initiated, used, and then appropriately closed.

The next few sections describe how to connect to and disconnect from a MySQL server.

Connecting to the MySQL Server

Before you can have PHP interact with MySQL, you must connect to the server. The PHP function mysql_connect() accomplishes this. The mysql_connect() function's basic syntax is as follows:

```
mysql_connect(<server>, <username>, <password>);
```

The `mysql_connect()` function returns a resource or link to the server connection. Typically, you want to assign that link to a resource variable so that you can reference it in other functions:

```
$link = mysql_connect("server","username","password");
```

You can use the `mysql_connect()` function to connect to any accessible MySQL server — the server doesn't have to be running on the same machine as the PHP engine.

The server name, username, and password are passed as strings. For example, to connect to the server running on the local host with the username Sam and the password xtrvv5, you would use the following code:

```
$link = mysql_connect("localhost","Sam","xtrvv5");
```

Take care when deciding which user to specify when connecting to the database. You want to specify a user who has sufficient privileges to the data that you want to access but not more access than required (for security and safety reasons). Consider creating a new user for these cases instead of using an existing user.

If the connection is not successful, the `mysql_connect()` function returns FALSE. You should always include a check in your code to determine whether the connection was successful and report an error if it was not. An example of such code follows:

```
$link = mysql_connect("localhost", "Sam", "xtrvv5")
        or die("Could not connect! Error:  " . mysql_error());
```

The `mysql_error()` function returns the last error reported by MySQL and should usually be included in your error reporting.

If the username and/or password parameters are not included in the `mysql_connect()` function call, PHP substitutes the user under which the PHP engine is running and an empty password.

Disconnecting from the MySQL Server

Just as when using files, make sure that you close MySQL connections after you are through with them. Although PHP should close any open connections when the script ends, a good practice is to have your script close anything that it opens.

To close a MySQL link, use the `mysql_close()` function. This function has the following syntax:

```
mysql_close(<link_variable>);
```

For example, to close the database linked to the $link variable, you would use this code:

```
mysql_close($link);
```

The `mysql_close()` function returns TRUE or FALSE according to the success or failure of the close operation.

Selecting a Database

Just as when you are using MySQL interactively, you must select a database before you can begin performing database operations. The `mysql_select_db()` function is used to select a database after you are connected to a server. The basic syntax of the `mysql_select_db()` function is as follows:

```
mysql_select_db("<database_name>",<database_link>);
```

> **Specifying the link in the `mysql_select_db()` function is optional, but recommended. If you omit the link from the function call, PHP uses the last link created.**

As with many access functions, the `mysql_select_db()` function returns TRUE if the operation was successful, FALSE if it was not. Always include basic error handling for this function, such as the following:

```
mysql_select_db("inventory",$link)
        or die("Could not open database inventory!
        Error:  " . mysql_error());
```

> **Containing your database name, parameters, and so on within variables is helpful. That way, you can easily use those values in your error messages. For example, if you store "inventory" in $dbname, the preceding code becomes the following:**
>
> ```
> mysql_select_db($dbname,$link)
>         or die("Could not open database $dbname!
>
>         Error:  " . mysql_error());
> ```

Querying the Database

20 Min. To Go

Now that you are connected to the server and have selected a database, how does PHP actually work with MySQL? Simply put, it works exactly as it did in earlier sessions when you used the MySQL console — it submits SQL queries to the server to perform functions and return data.

The main PHP function that you use to pass queries to the MySQL server is the aptly named `mysql_query()` function. This function has the following basic syntax:

```
mysql_query("query_text",database_link);
```

The `query_text` parameter can be any valid query and *should not* end with a semicolon. The optional (but recommended) `database_link` parameter should be the variable linked to the MySQL connection. Like other MySQL functions, the mysql_query() function returns a resource value of FALSE if the query causes an error.

To use this function to query your connection to the local host server with the inventory database selected, you would use code similar to the following:

```
$result = mysql_query("SELECT * FROM computers",$link)
        or die("Query error!  Error:  " . mysql_error());
```

Storing your query in a variable and passing the variable to the mysql_query() **and** die() **functions is useful. For example, examine the following:**

```
$query = "SELECT * FROM computers";
$result = mysql_query($query,$link)
          or die("Query error!  Query: $query

        Error:  " . mysql_error());
```

The value returned from the mysql_query() function is a resource pointer to the result set returned from the query. You can access this result set several ways — the most popular methods are outlined in the next few sections.

Returning the Result Set Row by Row

Using the mysql_fetch_row() function, you can retrieve the returned result set row by row. The syntax of the mysql_fetch_row() function is as follows:

```
$array_var = mysql_fetch_row($result_var);
```

You must then parse the elements in the array to retrieve each column's value.

As with most MySQL functions, mysql_fetch_row() **returns** FALSE **if unsuccessful — if no data is returned, for example. You can use this behavior to add error checking to your code, branching accordingly if the returned result set is empty.**

For example, the following code snippet prints out all the rows of the return set referred to by $result:

```
while ($line = mysql_fetch_row($result)) {
  foreach($line as $key => $value) {
    print "$line[$key]";
  }
}
```

The major problem with this method of parsing return sets is that you must know the order in which the columns are returned. For example, consider the following two queries:

```
SELECT * FROM mice WHERE mouse_type = "USB";
```

and

```
SELECT mouse_id, mouse_model, mouse_comp
   FROM mice WHERE mouse_type = "USB";
```

The first query returns the columns in the order they appear in the database — which you may not know. The second query specifies the columns to return and, as such, sets the order in which they are returned. If you decide to parse the return result set row by row, be sure to use a query that controls the order of the columns returned.

Resetting the Result Set Pointer

At times, you need to manually control which row of the returned result set the MySQL functions operate on. For example, if you need to work through the set twice, you need to reset the row pointer back to the first row after the first pass.

You can use the `mysql_data_seek()` function for this purpose. The function has the following syntax:

```
mysql_data_seek($result_var, <row_number>);
```

The rows of a returned result set are numbered starting at zero (0). Therefore, to reset the pointer back to the beginning, you would use code similar to the following:

```
mysql_data_seek($result, 0);
```

The `mysql_num_rows()` function can be used to ascertain how many rows the returned result set actually contains. You can use this value to ensure that calls to the `mysql_data_seek()` function stay within the bounds of the result set.

Returning the Result Set in an Associative Array

You can use the `mysql_fetch_array()` function to return each row in an associative array. The `mysql_fetch_array()` function has the following syntax:

```
$array_var = mysql_fetch_array($result_var, <return_type>);
```

The `<return_type>` parameter accepts one of the values listed in Table 23-1.

Table 23-1 *Return Type Values for mysql_fetch_array()*

Value	Use
MYSQL_NUM	Returns the array with numeric keys
MYSQL_ASSOC	Returns the array with associative keys, where the keys are the names of the columns to which they refer
MYSQL_BOTH	Returns the array with both numeric and associative keys (default)

Using the `mysql_fetch_array()` function increments the result set pointer by one. If you need to work through the entire result set a second time, use the `mysql_data_seek()` function to reset the pointer back to row 0.

The array in which you store the MySQL return set needs to be parsed accordingly. For example, the following loop prints each column name and value in the return set:

```
$row = mysql_fetch_array($result,MYSQL_ASSOC)
foreach($row as $column => $value) {
  print "Column: $column   Value: $value";
}
```

As a reminder, the `inventory.mice` table has the following columns:

`mouse_id, mouse_type, mouse_model, mouse_comp, mouse_ts`

The advantage to using the MYSQL_ASSOC option is that the column name is attached to the value, so sorting out which value refers to which column is automatic. For example, to access the mouse_comp column, simply access the `'mouse_comp'` array element:

```
$array['mouse_comp']
```

Just like the other MySQL functions in PHP, `mysql_fetch_array()` returns FALSE if the operation cannot be completed — in other words, if the result set is empty or no more rows are there to return. You can use this behavior to test the row before parsing it.

Working with Result Sets

The best way to understand result sets and how to work with them is to actually play with appropriate code. The following listing shows the script `queryhandler.php`:

```php
<?php

// queryhandler.php - Query handler
//  Accept a query, run it against the inventory
//  database and print results


// Opens the DB, performs the query
//  and return the results
function doquery($query) {
  // Get rid of pesky smart quotes
  $query = stripslashes($query);
  $db = "inventory";
  // Do the query
  $link = mysql_connect("localhost","Sam","xtrvv5")
    or die("Could not connect to server! Error: ".mysql_error());
  mysql_select_db($db,$link)
```

```
      or die("Could not select $db! Error: ".mysql_error());
    $result = mysql_query($query,$link)
      or $result = "Query Error!<p>Query: $query<p>Error: ".mysql_error();
    mysql_close($link);
    // Return the results
    return($result);
  }

  // Parse the result set ($result) into a table
  function parseresults($result) {
    // Test for empty result set
    // If there is data, do the header (column names) row
    if ($line = mysql_fetch_array($result,MYSQL_ASSOC)) {
      print "<table border=1 cellpadding=3>\n<tr>";
      // Parse the column names
      foreach($line as $key => $value) {
        print "<td><b>$key</b></td>";
      }
      print "</tr>\n";
      // Reset data pointer
      mysql_data_seek($result,0);
      // Step through the data rows
      while ($line = mysql_fetch_row($result)) {
        print "<tr>";
        // Print each value in its own cell
        foreach($line as $key => $value) {
          print "<td>$line[$key] </td>";
        }
        print "</tr>\n";
      }
      print "</table>\n";
    } else {
      // If mysql_fetch_array fails, report empty set
      print "Empty result set.<p>";
    }
  }

  // Display the form
  function displayform($result) {
  print <<<HTML
  <html>
  <body>
    <form action="$PHP_SELF" method="POST">
      Enter your query below. Remember, no semicolon at
      the end!<p>
      <input type="hidden" name="cmd" value="doquery">
      <input type="text" name="query" size="80" value="$query"><p>
      <input type="submit">
      <p><hr>
  HTML;

    // Parse the results if $result actually points
```

```
  //  to a resource (result set), else just print
  //   the value of $result
  if (is_resource($result)) {
    parseresults($result);
  } else {
    print "$result<p>\n";
  }

print <<<HTML
    <p>
  </form>
</body>
</html>
HTML;
}


// Main program body

// First time through ($cmd <> "doquery" and
//  no query to run), don't run the query
if ($_POST["cmd"] == "doquery") {
  $query = $_POST["query"];
  if (!($query == "")) {
    $result = doquery($query);
  }
}

// Display the form (and results of prev query)
displayform($result);

?>
```

This script uses the same user Sam **and password** xtrvv5 **used earlier in this session. Before this script can work, you must assign** Sam **the appropriate privileges to the** inventory **database or replace the credentials with a user who has such privileges.**

This script displays a simple form that enables the user to enter a query to be run against the inventory database. When the form is submitted, the script calls itself, runs the query, and redisplays the form along with the query results from the previous query.

The MySQL connection and querying are all done in the doquery() function, and the handling of the returned result set is taken care of by the parseresults() function. To avoid declaring any global variables, the code passes the required values between functions (for example, $results).

The script uses the superglobal $PHP_SELF as the form's action, which results in the script calling itself when the form is submitted. The $PHP_SELF variable is an excellent tool when you need to refer to the current script, no matter where it is located or has been moved to.

The return result set is parsed by returning an associated array (via the mysql_fetch_array() function) and moving column by column through each row in the set. An associative array is used in the first step so that the script can parse the column values (keys in the array) and use them for the column headers in the HTTP table. The result set pointer is then reset to the first row (using the mysql_data_seek() function) and the set is parsed into correct columns one row at a time.

Figures 23-1 and 23-2 each show a sample of running queryhandler.php. Figure 23-1 shows a query entered into the form's text box, and Figure 23-2 shows the result set returned from the query.

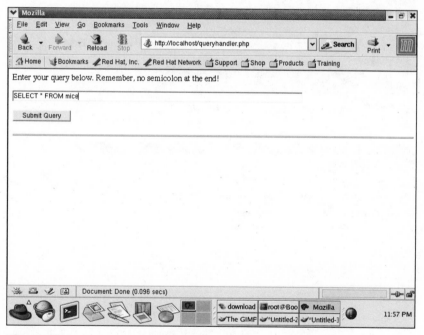

Figure 23-1   *A query entered into the* queryhandler.php *form*

Try a few queries of your own to see how the data is returned.

Almost every MySQL operation can be accomplished through the query interface, and every result returned from the query is returned as a table (or an empty result set). For example, a query from which you wouldn't expect return data in table form is SHOW CREATE TABLE mice. However, Figure 23-3 shows that the data was indeed returned in table form.

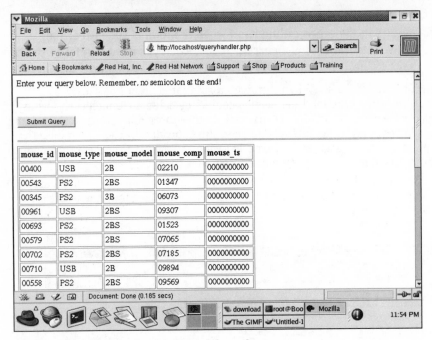

Figure 23-2   *The result set returned from the query*

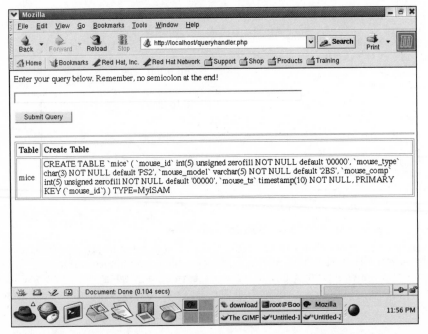

Figure 23-3   *The result set returned from the query — in table format*

Because almost all data is returned in table form, you can use the same techniques for parsing just about anything that comes back in a result set.

Determining Affected Rows

10 Min. To Go

MySQL INSERT, UPDATE, and DELETE queries can all affect several rows. However, these types of queries don't normally return enough information for you to determine how many rows they affected — information that could be useful to your script.

The mysql_affected_rows() function returns the number of rows affected by the last INSERT, UPDATE, or DELETE query. The syntax of this function is as follows:

```
mysql_affected_rows($link_variable)
```

The mysql_affected_rows() function cannot be used with SELECT queries. However, the mysql_num_rows() function can be used to return the number of rows in a given result set — effectively telling you how many rows were affected by the SELECT query. The syntax of the mysql_num_rows() function is as follows:

```
mysql_num_rows($result_variable)
```

These functions have myriad uses, from supplying the bounds for parsing routines to verifying that a query did its job correctly.

Letting MySQL Do Some Work

When you use queries and parse return sets, remember that MySQL has its own robust set of functions that you can rely upon. For example, consider the following points:

- Use the MySQL's SORT and GROUP BY clauses to help organize the returned result set.
- Instead of parsing a large result set and using PHP to search for a few matching values, use MySQL's WHERE clause to preparse the data for you.
- Use the LIMIT clause to control how many rows are returned at one time.

You can use the pg_free_result() **function to free the memory being used by a returned result set. The data for all return sets is released at the end of a script. However, when dealing with large result set rows and long scripts, you might want to free the memory sooner.**

Other MySQL Functions

PHP offers several other MySQL functions. Although you can accomplish most of your work through the query interface, where appropriate, consider using the specialized functions described in Table 23-2 instead.

Table 23-2 *Other MySQL Functions*

Function	Use
mysql_change_user()	Changes the active (logged in) MySQL user
mysql_create_db()	Creates a new database
mysql_drop_db()	Drops a database
mysql_errno()	Returns the numeric value of the last MySQL operation
mysql_error()	Returns the text value of the last MySQL operation
mysql_fetch_field()	Returns an object containing information about the next column
mysql_fetch_object()	Returns an object containing the return result set of the last query
mysql_pconnect()	Opens a persistent link to MySQL; a persistent connection is not automatically closed at the end of the script, and it remains open for future use
mysql_ping()	Tests the connection to the server; if the connection is down, PHP tries to reestablish it
mysql_stat()	Returns an array of server status information

Done!

REVIEW

This session provided your first glimpse of using MySQL through PHP. Dealing with MySQL is only a bit more complex than dealing with the data files covered in Session 17. You learned how to connect to and disconnect from a MySQL server, select a database, query the database, and parse data returned from your queries.

The next few sessions cover more troubleshooting and security information — information that is important to know before embarking on larger scripting projects.

QUIZ YOURSELF

1. What defaults does PHP use for the username and password parameters in the mysql_connect() function? (See "Connecting to the MySQL Server.")
2. How can you determine which error was generated when trying to select a database with the mysql_select_db() function? (See "Selecting a Database.")

3. What is wrong with submitting the following query via `mysql_query`?
   SELECT * FROM employees WHERE firstname LIKE "Sam%";
   (See "Querying the Database.")

4. Of what use is the `$PHP_SELF` superglobal variable? (See "Working with Result Sets.")

5. How can you determine how many records were deleted with a DELETE query? (See "Determining Affected Rows.")

Debugging and Troubleshooting MySQL in PHP

Session Checklist

✔ Turning off error reporting in production scripts

✔ Avoiding common errors

✔ Error testing, trapping, and reporting

**30 Min.
To Go**

Debugging MySQL problems in PHP is not much different from doing so directly with MySQL (see Session 11). However, with PHP you are another layer away from MySQL and don't have the immediate feedback you get with tools such as the MySQL console. This session offers helpful techniques for troubleshooting your MySQL code in PHP.

Turning Off Verbose Error Reporting

You usually want to turn off verbose error reporting in production scripts. The main reason for this has to do with security — you don't want users seeing too much of the "man behind the curtain." For example, PHP usually outputs something similar to the following if it fails to connect to a database:

```
Warning: Access denied for user: 'username@localhost' (Using password:
YES) in /var/www/html/errortest.php on line 11
Warning: MySQL Connection Failed: Access denied for user:
'username@localhost' (Using password: YES) in /var/www/html/errortest.php
on line 11
```

These errors are generally reported directly to the user's browser window, as shown in Figure 24-1.

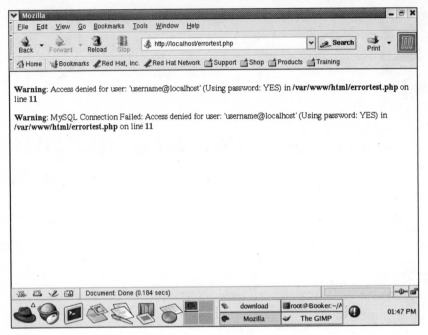

Figure 24-1 *PHP errors reported in the browser window*

These error messages are very helpful for debugging purposes, but they could give an unscrupulous user way too much information about your system and code. Several things are obvious:

- The system is running Linux.
- The script runs from the directory /var/www/html.
- The user who tried connecting to the MySQL server was *username@localhost*.
- The user was trying to connect by using a password.

With this information, someone quite possibly could compromise your system. Therefore, you're best off using the error_reporting() function to set reporting to 0 in production scripts — especially scripts that access MySQL or other servers. (See Session 22 for more information on PHP error reporting.)

Avoiding Common Errors

**20 Min.
To Go**

Sometimes the error you encounter is caused by something simple that takes only moments to fix. Some of the more common errors are listed here:

- If the magic_quotes_gpc setting is on in the php.ini file, PHP automatically escapes quoted data received via GET, POST, or cookies. For example, consider the following text:

```
Here's "Johnny!"
```

If `magic_quotes_gpc` is on, that text is translated to the following:

```
Here\'s \"Johnny!\"
```

If the escaped text is passed to MySQL, it might cause an error. It's advisable to use the `stripslashes()` function or another method to clean up a query string before it is sent to MySQL — or be prepared to deal with possible escaped text coming out of MySQL and handle it appropriately.

- A corollary to the previous point is not adequately dealing with quote characters in PHP variables that are used in queries. Although MySQL permits double quotes in queries, you're better off sticking with single quotes when constructing queries in PHP. That way, less conflict arises between quotes in your code, such as the following:

```
$query = "SELECT * FROM employees WHERE firstname LIKE 'Sam%'";
```

- Variables can also wreak havoc with queries. Be sure to watch how you quote variables — remember that, in PHP, single-quoting a variable results in the variable name, not the value, being used. In addition, ensure that you leave space around variable names when including them in a query.

- Ensure that the machine running the PHP code has appropriate access to the MySQL server and database, especially if MySQL is running on another machine. A common deployment error occurs when the code is developed on a machine that is also running MySQL but is then deployed on a machine that connects to the MySQL server remotely. Be sure to change your server parameters in the `mysql_connect()` function calls and ensure that you grant appropriate MySQL privileges to a user on the PHP host and use that user in your connections.

- Typos in database, table, or field names are another persistent problem. It helps to have the output of a MySQL `SHOW TABLE CREATE` command for each table in the database(s) you are working with. That way, you have all the table and field names handy for reference.

- Mishandling of result sets is another common problem. The query might be functioning as advertised, but your code can't interpret the data returned. In such cases, it again pays to run the query through the MySQL console to evaluate what it returns. Keep in mind that the `mysql_fetch` functions all have different uses and can return different data. In addition, functions such as `mysql_fetch_array()` can return data differently than you intended — for example, if any fields in the return data set have the same name, the keys of the returned array might not be what you expected.

- Misunderstanding queries is probably the most prevalent error encountered when building a query with PHP code. Try building the query, printing it to the browser or a file, and then cutting and pasting it into the MySQL console to check its functionality.

Error Testing, Trapping, and Reporting

Because you are another technical layer away from MySQL, it is vital that you code test for errors and trap and report any errors that occur when PHP accesses MySQL. The next few sections cover the various pieces of the error-handling process.

Error Testing and Trapping

Every MySQL function in PHP returns enough information to indicate whether an error occurred during its operation. For example, the mysql_connect() function returns FALSE if it fails the connection. Whenever you use MySQL functions, wrapping them inside an error-checking routine such as the following is good practice:

```
$link = mysql_connect("localhost", "username", "password")
    or die("Cannot connect to database.");
```

If the mysql_connect() function returns FALSE (could not connect), the script has hit a fatal error — you can't work with the database if you can't connect to the server. The script ends and outputs the message in the die() function.

However, what if the error is not fatal or you want to know when the code fails? In such cases, actually trapping the error and doing some processing of it instead of just killing the script outright is a good idea.

Using the die() function does qualify as error trapping, but it doesn't give you the chance to actually handle the error. The or construct of the assignment operator enables you to call any function, not just the die() function. Therefore, you can call your own comprehensive function to handle the error accordingly. For example, consider this code fragment:

```
function  MySQL_error_handler($errortext,$fatality) {
   ... handle error reporting ...
   if ($fatality) { die(); }
}
...
$link = mysql_connect("localhost", "username", "password")
    or MySQL_error_handler (mysql_error(),TRUE);
```

The function MySQL-error-handler() takes two arguments — the error text to report and whether the error is fatal (should end the script). In the previous code example, if the script cannot connect to the server, the error handler is passed the mysql_error() value and a fatality of TRUE, because without the connection the script shouldn't continue.

Error Reporting

In Session 22, you learned how to report PHP errors to more than just the browser window. You should employ those same techniques when dealing with MySQL functions. However, what information should you report? The PHP error alone does not give you enough information. It's best to include the output of mysql_error() and perhaps mysql_errno().

As you saw in the previous session, including the offending (or last used) query's text is also advisable.

As mentioned in the previous session, try to keep your query text in a variable so that it is easy to pass to an error handler or otherwise report it.

Testing Queries and Functions

10 Min.
To Go

When encountering errors with your queries, you should usually print the offending query so that you can cut and paste it into the MySQL console. Typically, the error is readily apparent, but you may find that you need to break the query down and troubleshoot it further, as discussed in Session 11. Once you have the query functioning in the monitor, you can return to your PHP code and emulate the fix there.

An even more generic way to handle debugging around the MySQL calls is to embed all MySQL function calls within your own user-defined functions. This way, `mysql_query` can become `my_query` and `mysql_fetch_assoc` can become `my_fetch_assoc`, as shown in the following example:

```
function my_query ($query, $fatality) {
    global $debug;
$result = mysql_query ($query) or MySQL-error-handler(mysql_error(),TRUE);
    if ($debug) echo "Query processed: $query<BR>";
    return($result);
}

function my_fetch_assoc ($result) {
global $debug;
    $return_value = mysql_fetch_assoc ($result);
    if ($debug) var_dump ($return_value);
    return($return_value);
}

$debug=TRUE;
$query = "select comp_id, comp_make, comp_cpu from computers order by
comp_id";
$result = my_query($query);
while ($computers=my_fetch_assoc($result)) {
        $comp_id = $computers['comp_id'];
        $comp_make = $computers['comp_make'];
        $comp_cpu = $computers['comp_cpu'];
        echo "Computer #$comp_id is a $comp_make with a $comp_cpu cpu.\n";
}
```

The preceding example uses the value of the `$debug` variable to control whether debugging information is output or not. You can turn debugging on or off by setting the value of the `$debug` variable accordingly.

Done!

REVIEW

This session reviewed a few common problems when accessing MySQL through PHP and described a few techniques you can use to troubleshoot any additional problems you might encounter. Using this session and the two previous troubleshooting sessions (Session 11 and Session 22) should round out your troubleshooting skills in both technologies as well as in combination with one another.

The next session covers additional server security and administrative issues.

QUIZ YOURSELF

1. Why and when should you turn off verbose error reporting? (See "Turning Off Verbose Error Reporting.")
2. Which functions can you call with the assignment operator's or construct? (See "Error Testing and Trapping.")
3. How should you construct your own debugging variables, and what should they control? (See "Testing Queries and Functions.")

Odds and Ends

Session Checklist

✔ Finding PHP libraries

✔ Using PHP help sites

✔ Getting PHP object-oriented support

✔ Monitoring Apache log files

✔ Virtual hosting with Apache

**30 Min.
To Go**

Before moving on to larger projects, a few odds and ends can help round out your understanding of PHP to ensure that you get the most out of your PHP programming for use on the Web and with other technologies such as MySQL.

This session covers where you can find libraries to help you with your PHP projects, where you can go for help from others in the PHP community, using objects in PHP, and monitoring Apache log files. Last, it covers how to run Apache as a virtual host server, serving up multiple domains from one computer.

PHP Libraries

One of the things that makes languages such as Perl and Java popular is the vast number of libraries and prefabricated code available for both languages. A Perl module for just about any function or task you need is available from repositories such as the Comprehensive Perl Archive Network (commonly known as CPAN) at `www.cpan.org`. Many sites offer Java applet repositories, such as the following:

- `www.javaboutique.com`
- `www.jars.com`
- `www.gamelan.com`

However, PHP programmers aren't left out in the cold — thanks to PEAR and sites such as PHPBuilder.com, both of which are covered in the following sections.

What Is PEAR?

PHP Extension and Application Repository (PEAR) can be found at `http://pear.php.net`. PEAR was created to provide the following benefits to PHP programmers:

- A structured library of open source PHP code
- A system for package maintenance and code distribution
- A standard style for PHP code
- PHP Foundation Classes (PFC)
- PHP Extension Code Library (PECL)
- A Web site and other online resources to support the PHP coding community

 You can find more information on any of these benefits on the documentation pages of the PEAR site (`http://pear.php.net/manual/en/ introduction.php`**).**

All code in the PEAR library is licensed under an open source license, although any specific license is up to the individual contributor. Each contribution to the library must adhere to the PEAR coding standards and each project and/or package has its stability, releases, license type, and code history listed in the library.

Within the PEAR library, you can find (as of this writing) 193 packages across 31 different categories. Packages are available for Internationalization, Authentication, HTML, XML, Image tools, and more.

If you need code for a particular task, check out the PEAR library.

 Keep in mind that you must adhere to the license for individual packages if you use their code. Before using any code, make sure that you have read and understand all the licensing conditions for the package(s) you use.

PHPBuilder.com

PHPBuilder.com (`www.phpbuilder.com`) is another site with an impressive library of code — 835 pieces of code across 16 categories. Code for File Management, Networking, Math Functions, Auctions, and more can be found in the PHPBuilder.com libraries. Most of the code is free, although some restrictions may be noted in the code.

PHPBuilder.com also has several other assets for the PHP coder, such as news, documentation, and articles.

PHP Classes Repository

PHP Classes Repository (`www.phpclasses.org`) is mirrored all around the world and has many searchable object-oriented classes of code that have been contributed by a variety of authors. Although the packages are individually licensed, many use the GNU General Public License (GPL).

New York PHP Components

The New York PHP group (`www.nyphp.org`) offers PHP components at a Web site that is just getting started as of this writing (`http://pcoms.net`).

Object-Oriented PHP

**20 Min.
To Go**

One of the criticisms of PHP is that it doesn't have true object-oriented support. Such criticisms are usually leveled by C++ or Java programmers who are used to object-oriented programming.

PHP does offer base-level, object-oriented support. You can define classes, objects, and methods to use in the same way you use them in other languages. However, PHP wasn't designed as an object-oriented language from the ground up, so its object support isn't as robust as other languages that were designed to be object-oriented from the beginning. Instead, PHP was designed to be easy to learn and use and well integrated with Web technologies.

Personally, I've not found the utility for objects in any of the PHP scripts I've written. Most scripts are simple enough that object creation and manipulation seems like unnecessary overhead. However, I do realize that larger applications can benefit from the use of objects.

PHP 5 (in beta test and available as such to the public as of this writing) has more in the way of object-oriented support than previous versions, so the trend in PHP is following trends in other languages.

The bottom line is that, if you are adept at object-oriented programming, you are likely to find PHP a mixed bag — it has enough support to enable you to use objects, but you might find its support lacking.

Monitoring Apache Traffic

Any public Web site should have its traffic monitored. Apache does a great job of tracking all access, errors, and content it serves and storing it all in its log files. However, reading a log file — even a modest one — can be tedious and unproductive.

Thankfully, several tools are available to monitor traffic on Apache. Most tools work off the Apache log files and can be used to view retroactive traffic. The following sections cover three of the most popular open source tools — Analog, Webalizer, and Advanced Web Statistics (AWStats).

Analog

The maintainers of Analog hail it as "the most popular log file analyser [sic] in the world." Whether this claim is actually true or not, many sites all around the world use Analog. Written in C, Analog is highly portable.

The main advantage to Analog is its capability to quickly process many different log file formats. This enables Webmasters to compile data from log files on demand. Analog also supports 31 different languages.

It can display 45 different reports, including quick summaries of activities, actual hosts that connected to your site, search terms used to find your site, most common files requested, and more. Another advantage to Analog is the amount of customization that you can add to its reports.

Analog is available for multiple platforms from the main Analog Web site (www.analog.cx). Binaries are available for both Linux and Windows, and full source is available if you need to compile your own copy.

 Analog is one of the few log analyzers that automatically analyzes archived logs — even logs that have been compressed by a log-rotating program. By specifying a log file name with a wildcard in its configuration file, such as access.log*, **Analog analyzes** access.log **as well as archived logs such as** access.log.3.gz.

Figure 25-1 shows a sample of the output from Analog.

```
Mar 2003: 16663:   810: ████████████████████
Apr 2003: 15423:   821: ████████████████████
May 2003: 14765:   849: ████████████████████
Jun 2003: 14634:   862: ████████████████████
Jul 2003:     6:     2: ▪

Busiest month: Feb 2003 (1,016 requests for pages).
```

Daily Summary

(Go To: Top: General Summary: Monthly Report: Daily Summary: Hourly Summary: Domain Report: Organization Report: Referring Site Report: Browser Summary: Operating System Report: Status Code Report: File Size Report: File Type Report: Directory Report: Request Report)

This report lists the total activity for each day of the week, summed over all the weeks in the report.

Each unit (▪) represents 30 requests for pages or part thereof.

```
day: #reqs: #pages:
---: ------: -------:
Sun: 18971:   1183: ████████████████████████████████████████
Mon: 20026:   1237: ██████████████████████████████████████████
Tue: 20473:   1188: ████████████████████████████████████████
Wed: 20861:   1198: ████████████████████████████████████████
Thu: 21877:   1149: ██████████████████████████████████████
Fri: 23770:   1200: ████████████████████████████████████████
Sat: 19128:   1042: ███████████████████████████████████
```

Figure 25-1   *Sample output from Analog*

Webalizer

Webalizer is similar to Analog, providing fast processing of log files into HTML reports. Also written in C, Webalizer is highly portable, and binary versions are available for download for Windows and Linux from the Webalizer Web site (`www.webalizer.com`). Webalizer supports 33 different languages and has a multitude of configuration options for customizing the reports it generates.

Figure 25-2 shows a sample of the output from Webalizer.

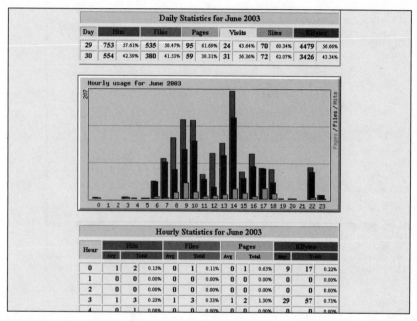

Figure 25-2 *Sample output from Webalizer*

AWStats

Advanced Web Statistics (AWStats) is another popular open source Apache log analyzer. AWStats is written in Perl and runs on any platform running Perl.

Perl is available from several different sources. You can download a copy for most platforms from CPAN (`www.cpan.org`). Most Linux distributions include a packaged version of Perl in their distribution as well.

As do the other two programs, AWStats supports multiple languages (36), can be configured to read almost any log file format, and is open source, with full source code available.

AWStats runs either from the command line or from administrative pages as a CGI program. Unlike the other two analyzers just described, it is preferable to run AWStats on a regular basis, reading the log files as they are generated instead of after the fact. The advantage to this approach is that your statistic pages are kept relatively up-to-date automatically, but the downside is that AWStats wasn't written for speed, so analyzing old logs can take a while.

Figure 25-3 shows a sample of the output from AWStats.

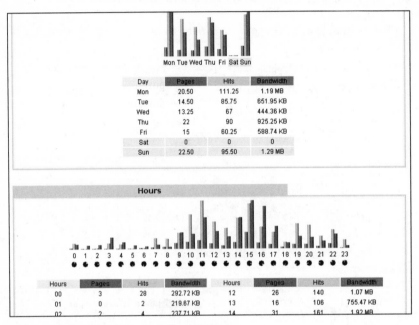

Figure 25-3 *Sample output from AWStats*

Finding the Right Log Analyzer

All three programs covered in this session provide detailed logs that you can use to help troubleshoot your site, fine-tune your server, or just provide raw statistics. All in all, they provide fairly equal features and reporting.

How do you determine which tool is right for you?

My advice is to run at least two tools, even if you run one of them only occasionally. Running more than one helps you get a better view of your data, seeing it from multiple perspectives. Visit all three sites and view the sample reports to ensure that each tool provides the data you need.

If you don't have Perl installed and don't want the increased overhead of installing it, you don't want to run AWStats. If you want a fast analyzer that also handles archived logs, run Analog. If you want ease of setup with the most complete reports "out of the box," run Webalizer.

Several other commercial log file-analyzing programs are available, such as Webtrends' Log Analyzer series of programs (www.netiq.com/products/log/ default.asp**). However, for general use, the open source tools listed in this session work quite well.**

Virtual Hosting with Apache

Apache supports virtual hosting — that is, serving content from multiple Web sites from one machine. You can use several methods to enable Apache to work with virtual hosts; the method that you use depends on the resources at your disposal.

For example, suppose that you had the following three domains that you wanted to serve up from the same computer:

- acmepencils.ned
- academyprocessing.ned
- luckylottowinner.ned

I have done my best to use nonexistent domains in this section. However, to ensure that these domains are not real, I've specified a fictitious top-level domain, .ned **(nonexistent domain) for each.**

If you have three IPs assigned to one computer, you can assign each domain its own IP and configure Apache to monitor each IP appropriately (see the next section). However, if you have only one IP address to use, you must configure Apache to share that IP over the three domains and process requests appropriately.

This session does not cover the configuration of Domain Name Services (DNS). No matter what method you use to provide virtual hosts, your domains must be set up correctly to map to the appropriate IP address(es).

Monitoring Several IP Addresses

To enable Apache to monitor several IP addresses, you must include several Listen directives in the Apache configuration file. For example, the following would set Apache up to listen to port 80 on the three IP addresses listed (192.168.0.20-22):

```
Listen 192.168.0.20
Listen 192.168.0.21
Listen 192.168.0.22
```

If you are using a nonstandard port, you must specify the port number in the Listen line as well, such as in the following:

```
Listen 192.168.0.21:8080
```

Monitoring One IP Address

If you are using only one IP address to serve several domains, you must include a NameVirtualHost line in your Apache configuration file that lists the IP address. For example, if you were serving several virtual domains on the IP address 192.168.0.21, you would add the following line to your configuration file:

```
NameVirtualHost 192.168.0.21
```

This one line enables you to serve several domains through the one IP.

If you are using this method of virtual hosting, you must also include a matching Listen **directive in the configuration file. For example, using the IP address** 192.168.0.21, **you would need these two lines:**

```
Listen 192.168.0.21
NameVirtualHost 192.168.0.21
```

**10 Min.
To Go**

Setting Up Virtual Hosts

No matter which method of hosting you use — single IP or multiple IP — the configuration of the virtual hosts is the same:

```
<VirtualHost  ipaddress:port>
    ServerName servername
    ...additional directives for host...
</VirtualHost>
```

The IP address in the opening VirtualHost tag needs to match the IP address you are using for that virtual host. If you have only one IP, that entry in the VirtualHost tag is the same for all virtual hosts. The ServerName directive should refer to the fully qualified domain name of the server (for example, www.acmepencils.ned).

You can add any additional Apache configuration directives between the VirtualHost **tags. Notice that these directives affect *only* the virtual host being defined — any missing, necessary directives are taken from the general directives in the rest of the configuration file. Therefore, including a unique** DocumentRoot, **and perhaps unique log file directives, is usually advisable.**

Because you can use other Apache directives within the VirtualHosts containers, keep in mind that you can constrain or restrict what features each site has. For example, you can add PHP support to only those sites that you want to offer such support, while omitting PHP support from any sites you don't want to offer PHP support.

If a site is commonly accessed by other fully qualified names, you can include those names in a ServerAlias **directive. For example, if** www.acmepencils.ned **is also accessed as just** acmepencils.ned, **you would include this** ServerAlias:

```
ServerAlias acmepencils.ned
```

You can include as many aliases on one line as you like, separated by spaces.

Putting It All Together

The next two sections provide an example of how you could set up the Apache log file using the sample domains discussed earlier, on multiple IP addresses and one IP address.

Three Domains, Three IP Addresses

The following configuration file snippet configures acmepencils.ned on IP address 192.168.0.20, academyprocessing.ned on IP 192.168.0.21, and luckylottowinner.ned on IP address 192.168.0.22. Each virtual host has its own DocumentRoot under the /var/www/ht-docs/ directory and its own error and access logs (named appropriately for each host).

```
Listen 192.168.0.20
Listen 192.168.0.21
Listen 192.168.0.22

<VirtualHost 192.168.0.20>
   ServerName www.acmepencils.ned
   ServerAlias acmepencils.ned
   DocumentRoot /var/www/ht-docs/acmepencils.ned
   ErrorLog /var/log/apache/acmepencils.ned-error.log
   CustomLog /var/log/apache/acmepencils.ned-access.log combined
</VirtualHost>

<VirtualHost 192.168.0.21>
   ServerName www.academyprocessing.ned
   ServerAlias academyprocessing.ned
   DocumentRoot /var/www/ht-docs/academyprocessing.ned
   ErrorLog /var/log/apache/academyprocessing.ned-error.log
   CustomLog /var/log/apache/academyprocessing.ned-access.log combined
</VirtualHost>

<VirtualHost 192.168.0.22>
   ServerName www.luckylottowinner.ned
   ServerAlias luckylottowinner.ned
   DocumentRoot /var/www/ht-docs/luckylottowinner.ned
   ErrorLog /var/log/apache/luckylottowinner.ned-error.log
   CustomLog /var/log/apache/luckylottowinner.ned-access.log combined
</VirtualHost>
```

Three Domains, One IP Address

The following configuration file snippet configures all three domains — acmepencils.ned, academyprocessing.ned, and luckylottowinner.ned — on IP address 192.168.0.20. Each virtual host has its own DocumentRoot under the /var/www/ht-docs/ directory and its own error and access logs (named appropriately for each host).

```
Listen 192.168.0.20
NameVirtualHost 192.168.0.20

<VirtualHost 192.168.0.20>
  ServerName www.acmepencils.ned
  ServerAlias acmepencils.ned
  DocumentRoot /var/www/ht-docs/acmepencils.ned
  ErrorLog /var/log/apache/acmepencils.ned-error.log
  CustomLog /var/log/apache/acmepencils.ned-access.log combined
</VirtualHost>

<VirtualHost 192.168.0.20>
  ServerName www.academyprocessing.ned
  ServerAlias academyprocessing.ned
  DocumentRoot /var/www/ht-docs/academyprocessing.ned
  ErrorLog /var/log/apache/academyprocessing.ned-error.log
  CustomLog /var/log/apache/academyprocessing.ned-access.log combined
</VirtualHost>

<VirtualHost 192.168.0.20>
  ServerName www.luckylottowinner.ned
  ServerAlias luckylottowinner.ned
  DocumentRoot /var/www/ht-docs/luckylottowinner.ned
  ErrorLog /var/log/apache/luckylottowinner.ned-error.log
  CustomLog /var/log/apache/luckylottowinner.ned-access.log combined
</VirtualHost>
```

Done!

REVIEW

This session wrapped up basic coverage of the technologies (Apache, MySQL, and PHP) by describing a few more reference and code library sites for PHP and a few tricks to add to your Apache kit — namely, how to analyze Apache log files and host virtual domains.

The remaining sessions in this book cover various projects, including a simple date manipulation calendar script and a content management system.

QUIZ YOURSELF

1. What are some of the benefits to PHP programmers that can be found on the PHPBuilder.com Web site? (See "PHPBuilder.com.")

2. What is the advantage of a standard coding style for the PEAR library? (See "What is PEAR?")

3. Why should you use more than one log file analyzer? (See "Finding the Right Log Analyzer.")

4. What are the two methods for virtual hosting? (See "Virtual Hosting with Apache.")

Project: Calendar I

Session Checklist

✔ Describing the project

✔ Pseudocoding the project

✔ Understanding the final code

**30 Min.
To Go**

O ne useful utility to have on hand is a dynamic calendar. You can use it to enable Web users to select a date, as an organizational tool for data, and so on. PHP's date functions make it ideal for use with date-intensive operations. This session shows you how to build a simple calendar using PHP and HTML tables and forms.

Project Description

This project creates a dynamic calendar displayed in HTML. The calendar does the following:

- Initially displays the current month if no parameters are passed to the script
- Accepts POST and GET parameters to control what it displays
- Highlights the current day
- Enables moving forward and backward by month
- Includes a method to return to the current month
- Includes enough space for adding data for each day if required by later specifications
- Provides an option to display a miniature format for small, pop-up use

Taking Stock of Assets in PHP

Several attributes make PHP ideal for a project such as this, but two in particular stand out — robust date handling and ease of integration with forms. Each of these assets is covered in the following two sections.

Robust Date Handling

Currently, PHP has several date handling functions and 13 individual time and date functions. The two most powerful functions are date() and getdate().

The date() function returns the date specified by a timestamp parameter in a format specified by another parameter. If no timestamp is given, the date() function operates on the current date.

This function is very useful for displaying various information about a date — day, month, year, a.m. or p.m., weekday, and so on. You can also use it to display a highly formatted string of information about the date. For example, on June 17, 2003, date('M') returns Jun, whereas date('D, F j, Y (\d\a\y z of 365)') returns Tue, June 17, 2003 (day 167 of 365).

The various format characters for the date() **function are explained in detail in the online PHP function reference (**www.php.net**).**

The getdate() function is also quite useful for retrieving detailed data about a current date. This function takes an optional timestamp parameter and returns an associative array containing the following information about the specified date:

- Seconds
- Minutes
- Hours
- Day of the month
- Day of the week (numeric)
- Month (numeric)
- Year (in four digits)
- Day of the year
- Day of the week (full text)
- Month (full text)

This function stores all the preceding information for later access by other portions of the script.

Various other functions provide services such as retrieving the current time in various formats and generating a timestamp from various textual representations of a date.

Integration with Forms

With PHP's handling of GET and POST data, you can easily construct a form that can be used to display and control the calendar. The form contains information about the current display (so that the script knows what is and/or was displayed) as well as controls to move forward and backward by month. The form recursively calls the script, which determines what month to display (same, current, next, or previous) and then redisplays the calendar using the new month.

Pseudocoding Our Calendar

Before you start coding, you should understand what is actually involved in constructing a dynamic calendar. The next few sections divide the calendar into its various technical components:

- The table to contain the calendar
- The form to automate the controls
- The data to pass between iterations
- The code to tie it all together

Pseudo-Table

You can use a simple seven-column table to display a calendar for any month. Of course, the number of rows (weeks) needed changes month-to-month, but that variable is one of the reasons to use a script language to help display the calendar.

Figure 26-1 shows a mockup of a calendar for June 2003 in a browser.

Figure 26-1 *Calendar mock-up showing June 2003*

The HTML code for the sample table is as follows:

```html
<table border=1>
<!-- Controls and calendar title (month) -->
<tr>
  <td colspan="2" align="left">
    Prev
  </td>
  <td colspan="3" align="center">
    <strong>
      June 2003
    </strong>
  </td>
  <td colspan="2" align="right">
    Next
  </td>
</tr>
<!-- Day of week header row -->
<tr>
  <td width="100"><center><b>Sunday</b></center></td>
  <td width="100"><center><b>Monday</b></center></td>
  <td width="100"><center><b>Tuesday</b></center></td>
  <td width="100"><center><b>Wednesday</b></center></td>
  <td width="100"><center><b>Thursday</b></center></td>
  <td width="100"><center><b>Friday</b></center></td>
  <td width="100"><center><b>Saturday</b></center></td>
</tr>
<!-- Calendar (days) start here -->
<tr>
  <td align="right" valign="top" height="100">1</td>
  <td align="right" valign="top" height="100">2</td>
  <td align="right" valign="top" height="100">3</td>
  <td align="right" valign="top" height="100">4</td>
  <td align="right" valign="top" height="100">5</td>
  <td align="right" valign="top" height="100">6</td>
  <td align="right" valign="top" height="100">7</td>
</tr>
<tr>
  <td align="right" valign="top" height="100">8</td>
  <td align="right" valign="top" height="100">9</td>
  <td align="right" valign="top" height="100">10</td>
  <td align="right" valign="top" height="100">11</td>
  <td align="right" valign="top" height="100">12</td>
  <td align="right" valign="top" height="100">13</td>
  <td align="right" valign="top" height="100">14</td>
</tr>
<tr>
  <td align="right" valign="top" height="100">15</td>
  <td align="right" valign="top" height="100">16</td>
  <td align="right" valign="top" height="100">17</td>
  <td align="right" valign="top" height="100">18</td>
  <td align="right" valign="top" height="100">19</td>
```

```
   <td align="right" valign="top" height="100">20</td>
   <td align="right" valign="top" height="100">21</td>
 </tr>
 <tr>
   <td align="right" valign="top" height="100">22</td>
   <td align="right" valign="top" height="100">23</td>
   <td align="right" valign="top" height="100">24</td>
   <td align="right" valign="top" height="100">25</td>
   <td align="right" valign="top" height="100">26</td>
   <td align="right" valign="top" height="100">27</td>
   <td align="right" valign="top" height="100">28</td>
 </tr>
 <tr>
   <td align="right" valign="top" height="100">29</td>
   <td align="right" valign="top" height="100">30</td>
   <td align="right" valign="top" height="100"> </td>
   <td align="right" valign="top" height="100"> </td>
   <td align="right" valign="top" height="100"> </td>
   <td align="right" valign="top" height="100"> </td>
   <td align="right" valign="top" height="100"> </td>
 </tr>
 </table>
```

Notice the use of size parameters in the table to help maintain the square aspect of the cells, and the `align` parameters to help align the text within the cells. In addition, note the filler cells at the end of the table.

 June happens to start on a Sunday, so no filler cells appear in the first date row, but remember that filler cells might be required for other months. For example, May 2003 starts on a Thursday, so the first row of that month needs filler cells for Sunday through Wednesday.

Pseudo-Form

The form needs to include controls to move the calendar backward and forward by month, and data holders for persistent data.

The pseudocode of the form resembles the following:

```
<form action=[the calendar script] method=post>
  <input type=hidden [name and values of persistent data]>
  <table [to contain calendar]>
  <input type=submit name=Prev> [move backward]
  [Month & Year]
  <input type=submit name=Next> [move forward]
  [Calendar grid]
  </table>
</form>
```

Data and State

You also need a way to preserve state between calls to the script so that the script can adequately adjust to display the right month. This can be handled by passing a minimum amount of data — namely, the following:

- Month last displayed
- Year last displayed
- Action to take

For example, if the script displays December 2003 and the user clicks the Next button, the script does the following:

1. Takes the month last displayed (December).
2. Adds a month (January).
3. Determines that the year should change (December to January).
4. Takes the last year displayed (2003).
5. Adds a year (2004).
6. Displays the appropriate month (January 2004).

You can use hidden fields to save the state and form controls to pass commands.

You can also use sessions to maintain the state of the calendar, but because you need a form for the controls, you might as well use the form to maintain the state (via hidden fields).

One other piece of information that you should consider passing is a control value that assures your script that it has been called from a reliable source (namely, itself) and can find all the data it needs to function. You can also use this control value to tell the script to display the miniature form of the calendar.

All of this information can be passed transparently to the user via POST. However, you should also consider allowing other access to the script's dynamic display functionality via GET. That way, other processes can call the script and request that a particular month be displayed without worrying about all the POST variables. In fact, the GET data doesn't need to be very elaborate; it can consist of just a month and year in the form "*m-y*".

Pseudo-PHP

**20 Min.
To Go**

Now that you have all the supporting code, mechanisms, and technology lined up, you can draft an outline of your code's operation. The PHP code needs to follow these steps:

1. Determine whether there is POST and/or GET data.
2. If POST data exists, update the date according to POST data.
3. If GET data exists, check for the valid date.
4. If no data or bad GET data exists, set the date to the current date.

5. Print HTML headers.

6. Set month and days of the week to full text or abbreviations, depending on the status of the $calendar variable.

7. Print the month header, form controls, and day-of-week (DOW) table headers.

8. If the first day of the month does not equal the current DOW, print a blank cell and increment DOW until it does.

9. Print the first day of the month.

10. Print each day, starting a new row after every Saturday.

11. If the last day of the month does not equal Saturday, print blank cells until DOW equals Saturday.

12. Close HTML tags.

Calendar Code

Now to examine the actual code that results from this planning. This section provides the final code and walks you through it, explaining each part.

Calendar.php

The following listing shows the final calendar code. (Notice that the numbers at the beginning of each line are not part of the code — they appear here to aid in the discussion that follows the listing.)

```
1.   <?php
2.
3.   /* Calendar.php
4.   Display a calendar and allow user to move forward and backward
5.     through months via form controls.
6.
7.   $month = last month displayed
8.   $year = last year displayed
9.   $calendar = TRUE if this script is calling, "mini" to
10.    display miniature calendar
11.
12.   Form control (POST) Next = Next month
13.   Form control (POST)  Prev = Previous month
14.
15.   GET variable "display" overrides display - date to display
16.     passed in (m-y) format (e.g., June 2003 = "?display=6-2003")
17.
18.   */
19.
20.   // Globals for easy reference
21.   global  $month, $year, $calendar;
22.
23.   // Get the variables from POST or GET
24.   function get_vars($type) {
```

```
25.     global $month, $year, $calendar;
26.     // Get POST vars
27.     if ($type == "POST") {
28.       foreach($_POST as $key => $value) {
29.         $$key = $value;
30.       }
31.     } else {
32.       // GET data is in different format for
33.       //   simple calling, "display=m-y"
34.       // Put the mdy into array $dt
35.       $dt = explode("-",$_GET['display']);
36.       // If a valid date was passed, assign it to vars
37.       if (checkdate($dt[0],1,$dt[1])) {
38.         // Rearrange date to ISO 8601 format (yyyy-mm-dd)
39.         //   and get timestamp ($ts)
40.         $ts = strtotime($dt[1]."-".$dt[0]."-1");
41.         $month = date('n',$ts);
42.         $year = date('Y',$ts);
43.       } else {
44.         // Not a valid date, use today
45.         $month = date('n');
46.         $year = date('Y');
47.       }
48.       // Get calendar value if passed
49.       if (isset($_GET['calendar'])) {
50.         $calendar = $_GET['calendar'];
51.       } else {
52.         // Set to default
53.         $calendar = "TRUE";
54.       }
55.     }
56.   }
57.
58.
59.   // Set up the date to display
60.   function set_date() {
61.
62.     global $month, $year, $calendar;
63.
64.     // If GET n/v pairs exist, they override POSTS
65.     if (!empty($_GET)) {
66.       get_vars("GET");
67.
68.     } else {
69.       // If $calendar is set then we can assume that
70.       //   this call is under control of this script
71.       //   (or a well-behaved handler)
72.       if (!isset($_POST["calendar"])) {
73.
74.         $calendar = "TRUE";
```

```
75.
76.        // Set today
77.        $month = date('n');
78.        $year = date('Y');
79.
80.      } else {
81.
82.        // Get POST data
83.        get_vars("POST");
84.
85.        // If Next, then move month forward
86.        if ($_POST["Next"] == ">>") {
87.          $month = $month + 1;
88.          if ($month == "13") {
89.            $year = $year + 1;
90.            $month = 1;
91.          }
92.        }
93.
94.        // If Prev, then move month backward
95.        if ($_POST["Prev"] == "<<") {
96.          $month = $month - 1;
97.          if ($month == "0") {
98.            $year = $year - 1;
99.            $month = 12;
100.          }
101.        }
102.      }
103.    }
104. }
105.
106.
107. // Display the calendar form
108. function display_cal($month,$year,$calendar) {
109.
110.    // Determine today to mark it accordingly
111.    $today = date("n-j-Y");
112.
113.    // Build calls to script, include calendar var if
114.    //    it has been set (!= default TRUE)
115.    $this_script = $_SERVER['PHP_SELF'];
116.    if ($calendar != "TRUE") {
117.      $reset_script = $this_script."?calendar=".$calendar;
118.    } else {
119.      $reset_script = $this_script;
120.    }
121.
122.    // Get timestamp for first day of current month/year
123.    $timestamp = strtotime($year."-".$month."-01");
124.    // What's the last day of this month? (28-31)
```

```
125.    $lastday = date('t',$timestamp);
126.    // What weekday does the first fall on?
127.    $wkday = date('w',$timestamp);
128.
129.    // Set monthtext and dow display according to size
130.    //   of calendar
131.    if ($calendar != "mini") {
132.      // Not mini-cal, use full text
133.      $tblsize = 100;
134.      $dow = array("Sunday","Monday","Tuesday","Wednesday",
135.                   "Thursday","Friday","Saturday");
136.      $monthtext = date('F',$timestamp);
137.    } else {
138.      // Mini-cal, use single char days and 3 char month
139.      $tblsize = 20;
140.      $dow = array("S","M","T","W","T","F","S");
141.      $monthtext = date('M',$timestamp);
142.    }
143.
144.
145. // Print calendar header info
146. print <<<HTML
147. <html>
148. <title>Calendar</title>
149. <body>
150.
151. <form action="$this_script" method="post">
152.
153. <!-- Script control vars -->
154. <input type="hidden" name="calendar" value="$calendar">
155. <input type="hidden" name="month" value="$month ">
156. <input type="hidden" name="year" value="$year">
157.
158. <!-- Month header with Prev/Next buttons -->
159. <table border=1>
160. <tr>
161.   <td colspan="2" align="left">
162.     <input type="submit" name="Prev" value="<<">
163.   </td>
164.   <td colspan="3" align="center">
165.     <strong>
166.     <a href="$reset_script".$getdata>$monthtext $year</a>
167.     </strong>
168.   </td>
169.   <td colspan="2" align="right">
170.     <input type="submit" name="Next" value=">>">
171.   </td>
172. </tr>
173. <!-- Day of week header row -->
174. <tr>
```

```
175.    <td width="$tblsize"><center><b>$dow[0]</b></center></td>
176.    <td width="$tblsize"><center><b>$dow[1]</b></center></td>
177.    <td width="$tblsize"><center><b>$dow[2]</b></center></td>
178.    <td width="$tblsize"><center><b>$dow[3]</b></center></td>
179.    <td width="$tblsize"><center><b>$dow[4]</b></center></td>
180.    <td width="$tblsize"><center><b>$dow[5]</b></center></td>
181.    <td width="$tblsize"><center><b>$dow[6]</b></center></td>
182. </tr>
183. <!-- Calendar starts here -->
184.
185. HTML;
186.
187.    // Skip days of week up to first day of month
188.    print "<tr> \n";
189.    for ($x = 0; $x < $wkday; $x++) {
190.      print "\t<td align=\"right\"
     valign=\"top\" height=\"$tblsize\">";
191.      print " ";
192.      print "</td>\n";
193.    }
194.
195.    // Step through month, 1st through last day (28, 30, or 31)
196.    //   Print table cell for each
197.    for ($x = 1; $x <= $lastday; $x++) {
198.    // Close row after each Sat, start next row with Sunday (0)
199.      if ($wkday == "7") {
200.        print "</tr>\n<tr>\n";
201.        $wkday = 0;
202.      }
203.      print "\t<td align=\"right\"
     valign=\"top\" height=\"$tblsize\">";
204.      // If this is today, highlight it with red font
205.      if ($today == $month."-".$x."-".$year) {
206.        print "<font color=\"#ff0000\">"; }
207.      print "$x";
208.      if ($today == $month."-".$x."-".$year) {
209.        print "</font>"; }
210.      print "</td>\n";
211.      $wkday++;
212.    }
213.
214.    // Close out row
215.    while ($wkday < 7) {
216.      print "\t<td align=\"right\"
     valign=\"top\" height=\"$tblsize\"> </td>\n";
217.      $wkday++;
218.    }
219.
220. // Close open tags and page
221. print <<<HTML
```

```
222. </tr>
223. </table>
224.
225. </form>
226.
227. </body>
228. HTML;
229.
230. }
231.
232.
233. // Main program body
234. // Set the dates to display
235. set_date();
236. // Display the calendar
237. display_cal($month,$year,$calendar);
238.
239. ?>
```

Figure 26-2 shows the normal calendar. Figure 26-3 shows a sample of the calendar in mini-mode.

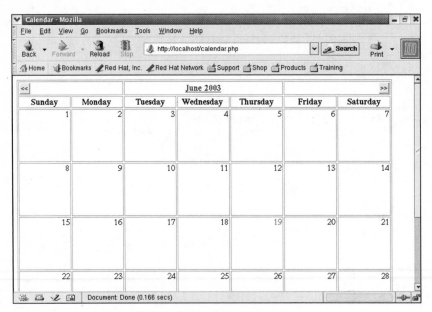

Figure 26-2   *Sample of the calendar script output*

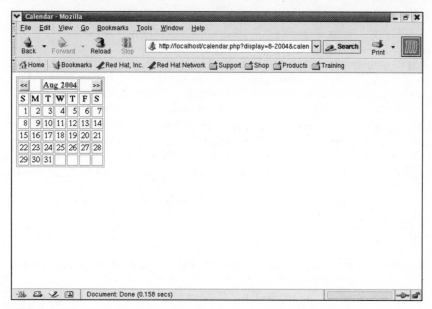

Figure 26-3   Sample of the calendar script output in mini-mode

Explaining the Code

**10 Min.
To Go**

Lines 3–18 comprise a standard documentation block explaining what the script does and the variables involved.

Lines 20 and 21 list the global variables used throughout the script. This line is unnecessary from a technical sense, but is included to help document the code.

Lines 23–56 comprise the get_vars() function. This function takes one argument ($type), which tells it from which type of arguments to get the variables. POST variables are assumed to be passed from a previous run of the script and include all the global variables and the script control used to submit the form during the last run. However, only one GET variable ($date) should hold a date in the form m-y.

If the function is told to return POST values ($type = "POST"), a simple foreach() is used to return all POST data into equivalent variables (for example, the POST month value is stored in $month). The function uses slightly more complex means to return GET data because it must also check the data for a valid date. Line 35 places the GET display value into the array; $dt--$dt[0] should equal the value of the month, and $dt[1] should equal the value of the year. The date is checked to verify that it is a valid date (line 37) and then converts to ISO 8601 format for conversion into standard formats.

> **Note**
>
> The user is allowed to enter the date in the form m-y — which isn't constrained to a format supported by strtotime() — for convenience sake. In addition, lines 40–42 aren't strictly necessary (you could just assign the values of the $dt array elements), but they provide another level of error control by running the dates through consistent formatting with the date() function.

If the GET data doesn't supply a valid date, lines 44–46 assign the current date to the variables. Last, the GET value of calendar is stored in the $calendar variable if it is passed (Lines 48–53).

Lines 59–104 comprise the set_date() function, which adjusts the $month and $year values according to what control (if any) was used during the last script iteration. If GET values exist, they override any POST values. Either way, the script appropriately calls get_vars() to return the values (lines 64–66 for GET and lines 72–104 for POST).

The POST value of calendar needs to be set in order for the script to parse the POST variables. If this value has not been set, the script assumes that it has been incorrectly called by some other process or that this is its first time running and sets the date to the current date (lines 72–78). Lines 85–99 adjust the date according to whether the Next or Prev control was used.

Lines 107–230 display the actual form. Appropriate values are set in lines 110–142, including the following:

- Today's date ($today) for marking it appropriately in the calendar
- An appropriate GET structure to enable a mini calendar to stay in that form when the reset URL is used ($reset_script)
- The last day of the month ($lastday) and the day of week on which the first day of the month falls ($wkday)
- The cell size ($tblsize; 100 for standard, 20 for mini)
- Day of week text (full text for standard, one-letter abbreviations for mini)

Notice the use of tabs and newlines within the print() **functions to format the HTML code for legibility purposes.**

Header HTML data and calendar rows are printed in lines 146–185. The state controls (form hidden fields) are printed on lines 154–156. Lines 159–172 print the calendar header rows (month title, day of week row), including the calendar controls.

Lines 187–193 print blank cells up to the first day of the month (for example, if the first falls on a Wednesday, the code prints three blank cells for Sunday–Tuesday).

Lines 195–212 step through the days of the month, printing one cell for each day, marking the current date with a red font, and printing one week per table row.

Lines 214–218 complete the last row of the calendar with blank cells, if necessary, and lines 220–228 close out the last week (row) with blank cells.

Lines 233–237 comprise the main body of the program, which is made up of two function calls.

Done!

REVIEW

This session showed how to create a simple dynamic calendar that enables the user to move forward and backward by months and can be displayed in a miniature format. The session reviewed what PHP lends to the project and outlined the expectations for the finished script. It then showed the pseudocode for all the various components followed by the finished script. The next session adds appointment capability to the calendar using a MySQL database.

QUIZ YOURSELF

1. What is the primary difference between the PHP date() and getdate() functions? (See "Robust Date Handling.")

2. Why should you use a form to control the script? (See "Integration with Forms.")

3. Why do you need filler cells in the calendar? (See "Pseudo-Table.")

4. What two methods can you use to save the state of the calendar between script iterations? (See "Data and State.")

5. What does the calendar script display if the date passed in GET values is invalid? (See "Explaining the Code.")

6. Where and how is the get_vars() function called? (See "Calendar Code" and "Explaining the Code.")

PART

V

Sunday Morning
Part Review

1. What does PHP do with open files at the end of a script?
2. What is a PHP IDE and what is its value?
3. What is virtual hosting?
4. What is the minimum amount of comment documentation you should add to your code?
5. Are there any disadvantages to using functions?
6. Why do you need PHP beginning and ending tags (<?php and ?>) in PHP files that are attached to other files with one of the include() functions?
7. How should you format HTML in your PHP scripts?
8. If you know a particular section of code is bad, how should you go about troubleshooting it?
9. If printing diagnostic information or error messages to the screen is problematic, what can you do with this valuable information so that you can use it to troubleshoot your scripts?
10. What does the PHP command line parameter -r do?
11. What kind of variable does the PHP mysql_connect() function return? What about the PHP mysql_query() function?
12. What does the following code do?
    ```
    die("Error: ".mysql_error($link2));
    ```
13. What types of data are returned by the mysql_fetch_array() function?
14. Why would you use the pg_free_result() function?
15. Why should you use single quotes instead of double quotes when constructing queries in PHP?

16. What does the `magic_quotes` PHP setting do?

17. What is the advantage to creating a pseudo-form for a PHP project?

18. Why should you group your global variable definitions together? Where should the definitions be placed?

Sunday
Afternoon

Session 27
Project: Calendar II

Session 28
Project: Content Publishing I

Session 29
Project: Content Publishing II

Session 30
Project: Building an RSS Feed

Project: Calendar II

Session Checklist

✔ Understanding the scope of the project

✔ Defining the database

✔ Defining the code

✔ Coding the project

**30 Min.
To Go**

I n the last session, you learned how to use PHP to serve up dynamic content in the form of a calendar. This calendar could have several uses — from simply viewing the days month by month to selecting dates for input. However, to make the calendar more useful, you need to tie in other technologies.

This session integrates a simple MySQL database, enabling the calendar to store and maintain appointments.

Defining the Project

This project enables the calendar to store daily appointments. More specifically, you want the calendar to be able to do or offer the following:

- Store appointments in half-hour increments
- Show a day view with all appointments for the given day
- No limit on the length of an appointment (within current day)
- Enable the user to easily edit appointments
- Check for various errors in data input
- Check for conflicting appointments
- Supply easy navigation between functions

None of this functionality is in the calendar created in the last session, so you must supply code for each item in the preceding list.

Database Definition

The database for this project is relatively simple, incorporating only one table. You need to store the following data:

- Appointment date
- Appointment starting time
- Appointment ending time
- Subject of the appointment (short display)
- Any notes for the appointment
- A timestamp for checking the appointment's last modification

The following commands, issued at the MySQL monitor prompt, create your database and assign appropriate rights to the webuser user, which is used in the code:

```
CREATE DATABASE calendar;
USE calendar;
CREATE TABLE `appts` (
    `idx` int(10) unsigned NOT NULL auto_increment,
    `date` date default NULL,
    `begtime` time default NULL,
    `endtime` time default NULL,
    `subj` varchar(40) default NULL,
    `notes` text,
    `ts` timestamp(10) NOT NULL,
    PRIMARY KEY  (`idx`)
) TYPE=MyISAM;
GRANT ALL ON calendar.* TO "webuser" IDENTIFIED BY "webster";
FLUSH PRIVILEGES;
```

You use an auto-incremented index (idx) to easily reference each appointment. You could also use combinations of the date and time fields, but a single numeric field tends to simplify indices. In larger-scale applications, you may choose to create additional columns and indexes to speed access to the data via different methods.

Web and Flow Design

Now you need to rough out the Web forms used in your project and the functional flow of the program(s) themselves. The following sections cover building the Web side of the project and defining the flow for the project.

Web Design

You need two new Web pages for your project. One displays a full day's worth of appointments, and the other enables the user to edit an appointment.

Figure 27-1 shows a mock-up of the day-view page.

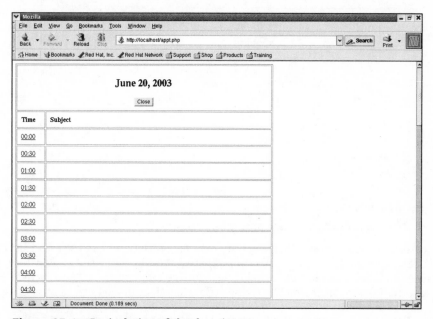

Figure 27-1   *Basic design of the day-view page*

The day view displays the full day from midnight to midnight in half-hour increments. The user can click a time in the left column to set an appointment or edit an appointment already scheduled for that time. Appointments that exceed a half-hour slot have +++ displayed in subsequent slots.

Although using an HTML form for this page is tempting, it is unnecessary and serves only to complicate the code. All the navigation is driven by hyperlinks and the necessary data passed via GET by appending name/value pairs to the hyperlinked URLs. However, to include a Close button, you need to include minimal form tags for good HTML coding.

Although additional form elements might make the code more complex, they can also make the page more attractive. In this case, I choose simplistic code over design, but you should make your own appropriate choices when developing applications.

Figure 27-2 shows a mock-up of the appointment editing form.

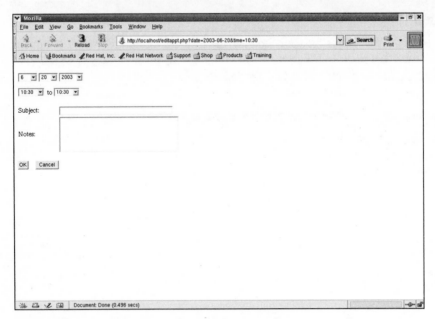

Figure 27-2   *Basic design of the appointment editor*

In this case, you need a form to help simplify data entry. The user can use select lists to choose the date, starting time, and ending time. These fields should be self-explanatory, so you don't need to label them, but do include labels for the two text fields. Also include space for an error message in the middle of the form where it is unlikely to be missed.

I chose to implement the functions by using pop-up windows (using the `target="_blank"` parameter in anchors). For example, clicking a date on the calendar opens a new browser instance with the day view. This enables the user to see the application much like a standard GUI application — substituting browser windows for pop-up dialog boxes and application windows. Moving between elements (to check a daily schedule while entering a new appointment) is as easy as switching windows or closing the newly opened element.

In a world of pop-up advertising, this might not be the most agreeable choice for your users, who might consider pop-up windows inherently evil instead of helpful. Use your best judgment regarding interface design when creating your own applications.

Application Flow

Our application functions as follows:

**20 Min.
To Go**

1. The user clicks a date on the displayed calendar to see and then possibly edit appointments for that day.

2. The day view appears for that day, listing all pre-entered appointments.

3. Each appointment can be edited by clicking any time slot that it spans.

4. A new appointment can be entered by clicking an appropriate time slot.

5. The data for the appointment is entered or edited with the appointment editing form.

6. The data is submitted for storage in the database — a special variable indicates whether the data overwrites an existing appointment or constitutes a new appointment.

7. Basic error checking is run against the data. If any errors are encountered, the form is displayed again, with the data entered plus an error message.

8. If the data is successfully stored, the user is informed and returned to the day view.

9. At any point, users can close the various windows themselves.

In some cases, all of the functionality can be built into one script. (One such monolithic script is developed for editing content in Session 28.) However, three distinct scripts are used here:

- Your existing `calendar.php` script, with a few modifications
- An `appt.php` script for displaying the day view (appointments)
- An `editappt.php` script for editing individual appointments

Coding the Application

Having only one database with only one table makes data handling relatively straightforward. Some queries are a bit complex — the conflict-checking queries come to mind — but you don't need to construct query joins or manually combine data.

The following sections detail how to code the three scripts mentioned in the last section.

Calendar.php

The calendar script was not set up to handle appointments; it was a simple display-only model. However, the changes needed to make it work with this new project are very simple.

Construct a valid name/value pair for inclusion in the hyperlink and surround your numeric date display with the appropriate anchor tags to make it a hyperlink. The following code snippet shows the additional code in bold. (This code replaces lines 203–211 in the final `calendar.php` code listing in the previous session.)

```
print "\t<td align=\"right\"
valign=\"top\" height=\"$tblsize\">";
    $nvdate = $year . "-";
    if (strlen($month) == 1) { $nvdate = $nvdate . "0"; }
    $nvdate = $nvdate . $month . "-";
    if (strlen($x) == 1) { $nvdate = $nvdate . "0"; }
    $nvdate = $nvdate . $x;
```

```
PRINT "<a href=\"./appt.php?date=$nvdate\" target=\"_blank\">";
// If this is today, highlight it with red font
if ($today == $month."-".$x."-".$year) {
  print "<font color=\"#ff0000\">"; }
print "$x";
if ($today == $month."-".$x."-".$year) {
  print "</font>"; }
print "</a></td>\n";
$wkday++;
```

The variable $nvdate (name/value date) is used to hold the date in *YYYY-MM-DD* format — which the appt.php script requires. That value is included with the name date in the hyperlink. It's as simple as that.

This change affects the functionality of the calendar. If you need simple display-only functionality, you probably want to create a new script with the appointment functionality — leaving the original calendar script alone. Alternatively, you can use the $calendar variable in the calendar.php **script to control whether the dates are hyperlinked to** appt.php **or not and then call the calendar with the appropriate option(s) corresponding to the functionality you need.**

Appt.php (Day View)

This script is simple in nature but needs to account for a few appointment eventualities, such as appointments that span several half-hour time slots.

The script should accept a single argument — the date to display in *YYYY-MM-DD* format. It then needs to look up all appointments for that day and display them chronologically, with links to the editappt.php script.

The following listing shows the full code for appt.php. (Notice that the numbers at the beginning of each line are not part of the code. They exist to aid in the discussion following the listing.)

```
1.    <?php
2.
3.    // List globals for reference
4.    global $link,$date;
5.
6.    // Get the variables from GET
7.    function get_vars() {
8.      foreach($_GET as $key => $value) {
9.        global $$key;
10.       $$key = $value;
11.     }
12.   }
13.
14.   // Open connection to DB
15.   function open_db() {
16.
```

```
17.     $db = "calendar";
18.
19.     $link = mysql_connect("localhost","webuser","webster")
20.       or die("Could not connect to server! Error: ".mysql_error());
21.
22.     mysql_select_db($db,$link)
23.       or die("Could not select $db! Error: ".mysql_error());
24.
25.     return($link);
26.   }
27.
28.   // Get all appts for $date
29.   function get_day($date) {
30.
31.     global $link;
32.
33.     $query = "SELECT * FROM appts WHERE date = '".$date."' ORDER
    BY begtime";
34.
35.     $result = mysql_query($query,$link)
36.       or die("Query Error!<p>Query: $query<p>Error:
    ".mysql_error());
37.
38.     // Return the results
39.     return($result);
40.
41.
42.   // Display the date appt/agenda form
43.   function display_day($date) {
44.
45.     global $link;
46.
47.     // Set up long text for day and $PHP_SELF
48.     $datetext = date("M d, Y",strtotime($date));
49.     $this_script = $_SERVER['PHP_SELF'];
50.
51.   // Print day header info
52.   print <<<HTML
53.   <html>
54.   <title>$date</title>
55.   <body>
56.
57.   <form>
58.   <table border="1" width="640" cellpadding="10">
59.
60.   <tr><td colspan="2">
61.     <center><h2>$datetext</h2>
62.     <input type="button" value="Close" onclick="self.close();">
63.     </center>
64.   </td></tr>
65.
66.   <tr>
```

```
67.    <td width="10%"><b>Time</b></td>
68.    <td width="80%"><b>Subject</b></td>
69.   </tr>
70.
71.   HTML;
72.
73.    // Init vars
74.    $result = get_day($date);
75.    $subs = array();
76.    $notes = array();
77.    $begtime = array();
78.    $endtime = array();
79.
80.    // Parse each return, store in arrays where key = begtime
81.    while ($line = mysql_fetch_array($result,MYSQL_ASSOC)) {
82.      $tmptime = substr($line[begtime],0,5);
83.      $begtime[$tmptime] = $tmptime;
84.      $endtime[$tmptime] = substr($line[endtime],0,5);
85.      $subs[$tmptime] = $line[subj];
86.      $notes[$tmptime] = $line[notes];
87.    }
88.
89.    // Init vars for time display
90.    $sttm = strtotime("00:00");
91.    // carry = whether time should display an appt carried
92.    //   over from prev time
93.    $carry = FALSE;
94.
95.   for ($x = $sttm; $x <= ($sttm + (1800*47)); $x=$x+1800) {
96.
97.    $tm = date("H:i",$x);
98.
99.   print <<<HTML
100.  <tr>
101.    <td>
102.    <a href="editappt.php?date=$date&time=$tm"
       target="_blank">$tm</a>
103.    </td>
104.    <td>
105.
106.  HTML;
107.
108.    // End of a carryover appt?
109.    if ($tm == $tmptime) {
110.      $carry = FALSE;
111.    }
112.
113.    // Appt exists for current time slot and is not
114.    //   a carry over
115.    if (isset($subs[$tm]) && !$carry) {
116.      print $subs[$tm];
117.      // If begtime != endtime then appt carries over into
```

```
118.     //   subsequent time slot(s)
119.     if ($endtime[$tm] != $begtime[$tm]) {
120.       $tmptime = $endtime[$tm];
121.       $carry = TRUE;
122.     }
123.   } elseif ($carry) {
124.     // Display "+++" mark to show carry over
125.     print "    +++";
126.   } else {
127.     print " ";
128.   }
129.   print "</td>\n</tr>\n";
130. }
131.
132. print <<<HTML
133. </table>
134. </body>
135. </html>
136. HTML;
137. }
138.
139.
140. // Main program body
141.
142. // Get vars
143. get_vars();
144. // Open DB
145. $link = open_db();
146. // Set current date
147. $date=date("Y-m-d");
148. // Display date
149. display_day($date);
150.
151. ?>
```

Notice the technique to autoregister globals used in the get_vars()
function. By using the double-dollar sign, you can use functions such as
global() **in a dynamic function, passing values that correspond to variable**
names instead of hard-coding the variable names. If you are working with a
script that has security concerns, you want to further parse the variables
returned from GET **and** POST **to ensure that only the variables you want**
returned are returned. Otherwise, an unscrupulous user could pass other
values via POST **or** GET **to override other script variables that you don't want**
them to affect.

The script opens the database and performs a query to find all appointments that occur
on that day. The details about each appointment are stored in keyed arrays for easy reference by time (lines 73–87). For example, the variable $subs[13:00] contains the subject of
the appointment with a beginning time of 1:00 p.m. (13:00). As you step through the day,
half-hour at a time, you can instantly reference any information tied to that day.

The script outputs the table containing the day view, stepping through the times in half-hour increments (starting at line 95, notice that 30 min = 1800 seconds). Each time entry is set up as a hyperlink to the editappt.php script.

The $carry variable controls whether an appointment should "carry over" time slots. If an appointment has different beginning and ending times, $carry is set to TRUE (lines 119–121), and the carryover text (+++) is displayed in subsequent time slots. When the ending time for the appointment is reached ($tmptime == $tm, line 108), $carry is reset to FALSE and the script returns to the normal processing of appointments.

Editappt.php (Edit Appointment)

10 Min. To Go

This script performs the only database writing in the project. It also performs the following functions:

- Looks up any appointment for the date/time specified
- Breaks data into fields for display or sets fields to defaults
- Enables users to edit data
- Accepts data submission and checks for errors
- Encodes data back into the DB field form and stores it in the database

The following listing shows the full code for editappt.php:

```
1.    <?php
2.
3.    // List globals for reference
4.    global $link, $result,
5.            $time, $date, $idx,
6.            $submit_err, $cmd;
7.
8.    // Return the variables from GET
9.    function get_vars() {
10.     global  $date, $time, $submit_err;
11.     foreach($_GET as $key => $value) {
12.       $$key = $value;
13.     }
14.   }
15.
16.   /* Return the variables from POST -- doing this AFTER processing
         GET   variables ensures that POST variables are not altered by
         the URL */
17.   function post_vars() {
18.     foreach($_POST as $key => $value) {
19.       global $$key;
20.       $$key = $value;
21.     }
22.   }
23.
24.   // Open connection to DB
```

```
25.    function open_db() {
26.
27.      $db = "calendar";
28.
29.      $link = mysql_connect("localhost","webuser","webster")
30.        or die("Could not connect to server! Error:
       ".mysql_error());
31.
32.      mysql_select_db($db,$link)
33.        or die("Could not select $db! Error: ".mysql_error());
34.
35.      return($link);
36.    }
37.
38.    // Get the appt for the specified date and time
39.    function get_appt($date,$time) {
40.
41.      global $link;
42.
43.      $query = "SELECT * FROM appts WHERE date =
       '$date ' ";
44.      $query = $query."AND (\"$time\" >= begtime AND
           \"$time\" <= endtime)";
45.
46.      $result = mysql_query($query,$link)
47.        or die("Query Error!<p>Query: $query<p>
           Error: ".mysql_error());
48.
49.      // Return the results
50.      return($result);
51.    }
52.
53.    // Print the appt form for $date
54.    function print_appt($result) {
55.
56.      global $link, $date, $time, $submit_err,
57.             $begtime, $endtime, $subj, $notes,
58.             $idx;
59.
60.      // Assemble select list "name" from first to last by step
61.      //   match = initially selected item, time = format for time
62.      function print_list($name,$first,$last,$step,$match,$time) {
63.          print "<select name=\"$name\" size=\"1\">";
64.
65.          for ($x = $first; $x <= $last; $x=$x+$step) {
66.            print "\t<option";
67.            if ($time) {
68.              $tmp = date("H:i",$x);
69.            } else {
70.              $tmp = $x;
```

```
71.            }
72.
73.            if ($tmp == $match) {
74.              print " selected"; }
75.            print ">$tmp\n";
76.          }
77.        print "</select>\n";
78.    }
79.
80.  $this_script = $_SERVER['PHP_SELF'];
81.
82.    // If this isn't a redisplay because of error, init vars
83.    if (!$submit_err) {
84.      $begtime = $time;
85.      $endtime = $time;
86.      $subj = "";
87.      $notes = "";
88.      $idx = 0;
89.      $cmd = "write";
90.
91.      // Get fields for appt, if one exists
92.      // (else use values above)
93.      while ($line = mysql_fetch_array($result,MYSQL_ASSOC)) {
94.          $begtime = substr($line[begtime],0,5);
95.          $endtime = substr($line[endtime],0,5);
96.          $subj = $line[subj];
97.          $notes = $line[notes];
98.          $idx = $line[idx];
99.          $cmd = "update";
100.      }
101.    }
102.
103. // Start form with state fields (hidden)
104. print <<<HTML
105. <html>
106. <body>
107. <form action="$this_script" method="post">
108. <input type="hidden" name="date" value="$date">
109. <input type="hidden" name="cmd" value="$cmd">
110. <input type="hidden" name="idx" value="$idx">
111. <table border="0" width="100%">
112.
113. HTML;
114.
115.    print "<tr>\n\t<td colspan=\"2\">\n";
116.
117.    // Display date in M D and Y select lists
118.    print_list("month",1,12,1,substr($date,5,2),FALSE);
119.    print_list("day",1,31,1,substr($date,8,2),FALSE);
120.    $year = substr($date,0,4);
```

```
121.    print_list("year",$year-1,$year+2,1,$year,FALSE);
122.
123.    print "<p>\n";
124.
125.    // Display beginning and ending time in two
126.    //  select lists
127.    $sttm = strtotime("00:00");
128.    print_list("begtime",$sttm,($sttm + (1800*47)),1800
129.           ,$begtime,TRUE);
130.    print " to ";
131.    print_list("endtime",$sttm,($sttm + (1800*47)),1800
132.           ,$endtime,TRUE);
133.
134.    print "\n</td>\n</tr>\n<tr>\n\t<td colspan=\"2\"> ";
135.
136.    // Print any error from last submission
137.    if ($submit_err) {
138.      print "<font color=\"red\">ERROR: ";
139.      print "$submit_err</font>\n";
140.    }
141.    print "\t</td>\n</tr>\n";
142.
143. // Display Subject and Notes
144. print <<<HTML
145. </select><p>
146. <tr>
147.   <td width="10%">Subject:</td>
148.   <td><input type="text" name="subj" value="$subj"
149.        size="40" maxlength="40"></td>
150. </tr>
151. <tr>
152.   <td>Notes:</td>
153.   <td>
154.   <textarea cols="40" rows="5" name="notes"
155.     wrap="virtual">$notes</textarea>
156.   </td>
157. </tr>
158. </table>
159. <p>
160. <input type="submit" name="OK" value="OK">
161.   
162. <input type="submit" value="Cancel" onclick="self.close()">
163.
164. </form>
165. </body>
166. </html>
167.
168. HTML;
169. }
170.
```

```
171. // Decode submission and write to DB
172. //    $cmd = whether to overwrite (rewrite) or insert (write)
173. function
     write_appt($idx,$date,$begtime,$endtime,$subj,$notes,$cmd) {
174.
175.   global $link;
176.
177.   // Check to make sure beginning time doesn't run into another
     appt
178.   $query = "SELECT idx,begtime,endtime,subj FROM appts WHERE
     date = \"$date\" AND ".
179.          "\"".$begtime."\" >= begtime AND \"".$begtime."\"
                 <=     endtime";
180.   $result = mysql_query($query,$link)
181.     or die("Query Error!<p>Query: $query<p>Error:
     ".mysql_error());
182.   // If overlap (conflict) found, display error
183.   while ($line = mysql_fetch_array($result,MYSQL_ASSOC)) {
184.     if ($line[idx] != $idx) {
185.       $errtext = "Conflict: ".substr($line[begtime],0,5)."-".
186.                 substr($line[endtime],0,5)." : ".$line[subj];
187.       return($errtext);
188.     }
189.   }
190.   // Check to make sure ending time doesn't run into another appt
191.   $query = "SELECT idx,begtime,endtime,subj FROM appts
        WHERE date = \"$date\" AND ".
192.          "\"".$endtime."\" >= begtime AND \"".$endtime."\" <=
     endtime";
193.   $result = mysql_query($query,$link)
194.     or die("Query Error!<p>Query: $query<p>Error:
        ".mysql_error());
195.   // If overlap (conflict) found, display error
196.   while ($line = mysql_fetch_array($result,MYSQL_ASSOC)) {
197.     if ($line[idx] != $idx) {
198.       $errtext = "Conflict: ".substr($line[begtime],0,5)."-".
199.                 substr($line[endtime],0,5)." : ".$line[subj];
200.       return($errtext);
201.     }
202.   }
203.
204.   // Build appropriate query
205.   if ($cmd == "update") {
206.     $query = "UPDATE appts SET
     date='$date',begtime='$begtime',endtime='$endtime',".
207.                "subj='$subj',notes='$notes' WHERE idx = '$idx'";
208.   } else {
209.     $query = "INSERT INTO appts VALUES
     ('0','$date','$begtime','$endtime','$subj','$notes','0')";
210.   }
```

```
211.
212.    // Handle query
213.    $result = mysql_query($query,$link)
214.      or die("Query Error!<p>Query: $query<p>
             Error:  ".mysql_error());
215.
216. // Close page if no errors
217. print <<<HTML
218. <html>
219. <body>
220. <form>
221. Appointment Saved.<p>
222. <input type="button" value="Close" onclick="self.close()">
223. </form>
224. </body>
225. </html>
226.
227. HTML;
228. }
229.
230. // Main program body
231.
232. $link = open_db();
233.
234. // Called with POST arguments?
235. //  (From another iteration of this script)
236. if (!empty($_POST)) {
237.
238.   $submit_err = "";
239.
240.   // Get POST data
241.   post_vars();
242.
243.   // Properly format date (leading zeros on M & D)
244.   if (strlen($month) == 1) { $month = "0".$month; }
245.   if (strlen($day) == 1)   { $day = "0".$day; }
246.   $date = $year."-".$month."-".$day;
247.
248.   // Proper date?
249.   if (!checkdate($month,$day,$year)) {
250.     $submit_err = "Invalid Date!";
251.     print_appt($result);
252.   }
253.
254.   // Valid start and end times? (start < end)?
255.   if (strtotime($begtime) > strtotime($endtime)) {
256.     $submit_err = "Invalid Start Time!";
257.     print_appt($result);
258.   }
259.
```

```
260.   // Subject exists?
261.   if (strlen($subj) == 0) {
262.     $submit_err = "Subject is Blank!";
263.     print_appt($result);
264.   }
265.
266.   // Attempt write and err on conflicting appt
267.   if (!$submit_error) {
268.     $conflict = write_appt($idx,$date,$begtime,
269.                       $endtime,$subj,$notes,$cmd);
270.     if ($conflict) {
271.       $submit_err = $conflict;
272.       print_appt($result);
273.     }
274.
275.   }
276.
277. } else {
278.   // Called with GET arguments?
279.   //   (From calendar)
280.   // Get GET data and print edit form
281.   get_vars();
282.   $result = get_appt($date,$time);
283.   print_appt($result);
284. }
285.
286. // Close DB
287. mysql_close($link);
288.
289. ?>
```

The code begins (on line 230) by opening the database connection and checking for passed data. This code needs to be able to parse data from GET *and* POST (GET data from appt.php and POST data from itself). The type of data returned dictates what the script does — GET data results in appropriate data being pulled from the database and displayed in the edit form; POST data results in an attempt to store the data in the database.

If the data is to be displayed (line 278), the data in GET contains the date and time to display. The database is queried by the get_data() function, and the result of the query is returned in the $result variable. That variable is then passed to the print_appt() function, which prints the appointment.

The nested function print_list() (within print_appt()) is a good example of how to avoid redundant code. Because each <SELECT> element is built the same way (via a sequence of values), the code to build each element is 99 percent the same. Without the print_list() function, lines 63–78 would have been duplicated five times (three date fields, two time fields). Because the function is called exclusively by the print_appt() function, I've nested it within print_appt() for clarity.

The `$submit_err` variable contains any errors that occurred during the last iteration of the script. If this variable contains a value other than FALSE, the `print_appt()` script uses current data (data contained in the last iteration) instead of getting the data from the result set in `$result` (line 83). The error is then displayed in the form (lines 136–140).

Either way, the data is broken down into distinct fields and displayed in the form (lines 117–132 and lines 147–156). When the user clicks the OK button, the form data is submitted back to this script via POST.

If the script detects POST data (line 234), it attempts to write the data to the database. The data is parsed and checked for errors (lines 243–264). If there are no errors (thus far), the function `write_appt()` is called to write the data to the database. If an error does exist, the appointment is displayed again with the appropriate error.

The `write_appt()` function does some additional error checking — namely, looking for conflicting appointments (lines 177–202) — and either writes the data or returns an error (and the form is displayed again, with the error). The value of the `$cmd` variable determines whether the `write_appt()` function updates existing data (`$cmd` = "rewrite") or inserts a new record (`$cmd` = "write") (line 205).

The Scripts in Action

Figures 27-3 through 27-7 show the scripts in action.

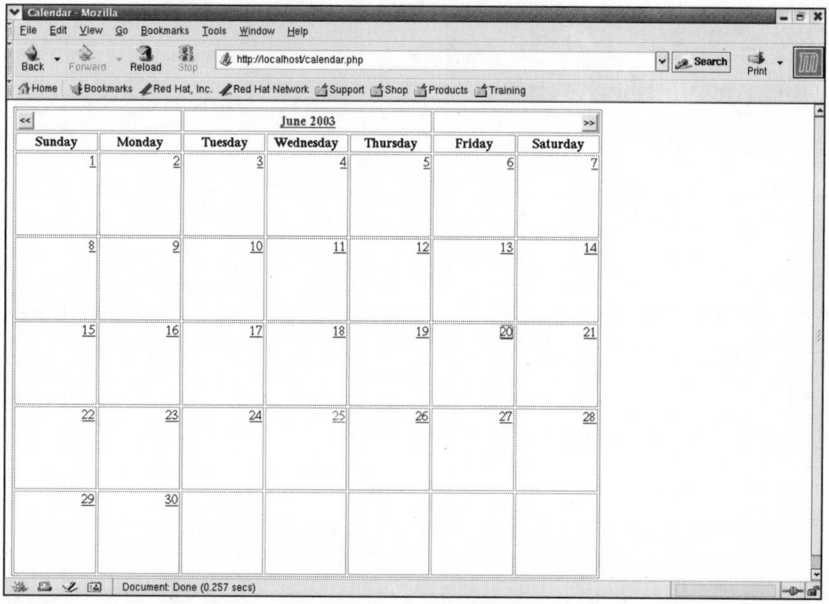

Figure 27-3 *The revised calendar with hyperlinks*

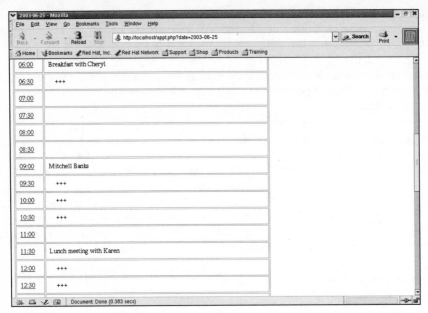

Figure 27-4   *June 25 was clicked, spawning the day view for that day.*

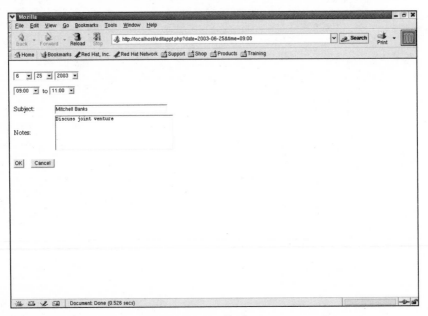

Figure 27-5   *The user clicks 09:00 to edit the 9 a.m. appointment.*

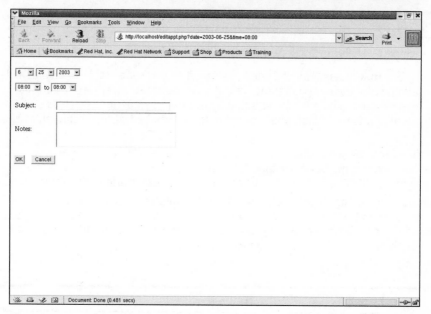

Figure 27-6 *Alternatively, the user clicks an empty time (08:00) to create a new appointment.*

Error message

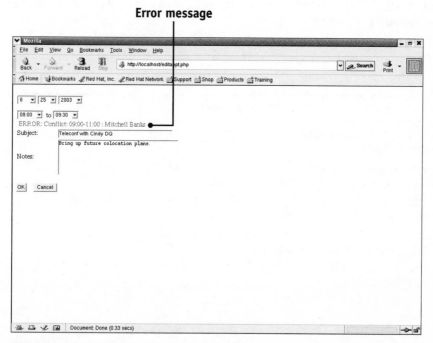

Figure 27-7 *Any errors are displayed in the data entry or edit form and the user is given a chance to correct them.*

Room for More

The project still doesn't offer several things that might be useful, such as the following:

- **Tracking multiple users.** You can add a user field to the appts table to enable multiple users to store their appointments in the same calendar. A separate user table would be necessary to help track users and appropriate permissions (such as setting appointments for other users), and a user would need to be tracked within all of the scripts.
- **Searching for appointments.** This function would be relatively simple to implement — you could build a simple form to accept text to search for and use a query with a WHERE or LIKE clause to search for the text in the appts table.
- **A calendar indicating days with appointments.** Additional code and a query could be added to the main calendar script to check each day for appointments as it is printed. If any appointments are found, an indicator could be printed in the day cell so the user knows there are appointments there.

Done!

REVIEW

This session built on the previous session and extended the calendar project. You learned how you could quickly modify an existing script to interact with other scripts, and how simple database integration lends itself to extending script functionality. After outlining the desired functionality of the extended project, the session described the modifications and new scripts necessary to achieve the goals.

The next few sessions deal with additional dynamic content and increased database interactivity.

QUIZ YOURSELF

1. Why is the date format used in the calendar.php hyperlinks so specific? (See "Calendar.php.")
2. What is the advantage of using keyed arrays to store appointment info in the appt.php script? (See "Appt.php (Day View).")
3. What does the editappt.php script assume if it detects POST data? (See "Editappt.php (Edit Appointment).")
4. What does the editappt.php script assume if it detects GET data? (See "Editappt.php (Edit Appointment).")
5. What is the $cmd variable used for in the editappt.php script? (See "Editappt.php (Edit Appointment).")

Project: Content Publishing I

Session Checklist

✔ Scoping the project

✔ Creating the database

✔ Designing the editing tools

✔ Writing all supporting scripts

**30 Min.
To Go**

One of the best uses for the combination of PHP and MySQL is deploying dynamic content. Whether you need statistical data, a graphics repository, or a current news site, you can store your content in MySQL and deploy it in various ways via PHP scripts.

This session develops a simple publishing application for a newsletter site. The site publishes a handful of small articles per day in various categories, written by various authors. The content is created and edited with PHP scripts and then stored in MySQL for later retrieval.

This session focuses on the scripts used to create and edit the content, while the next session focuses on delivering the content in various forms.

The Scope of the Project

This project creates a simple newsletter publishing system that enables multiple authors to submit stories in several categories. A few administrative tools — to add and edit authors and categories — are also required.

The Publishing System

The system creates short articles that are dynamically displayed. The articles are stored in a MySQL database where they can be retrieved by utility programs and displayed. They include attributes such as `category` and `author`.

Suppose, for example, that the following article is entered into the system:

```
Date:  February 20, 2003
Category:  Sports
Author:  Tom
Title:  Mike Tyson's Tattoo
Article:  Mike Tyson showed up to a news conference today sporting a new
tattoo he had done over the weekend. The tattoo, an interesting bit of
scrollwork over Tyson's left eye, is "not finished," according to Iron
Mike. When asked about why he got the tattoo, Tyson responded: "I did not
like the way my face was looking anyway."
```

A few simple PHP scripts can retrieve the article by date, by category, or by author. The scripts for placing the articles on Web pages are covered in Session 29.

 The next session also covers creating a textual index and enabling users to search for specific text in the article database.

Necessary Tools

To manage the system (the database of articles), the following tools are needed (and created in this session):

- A tool to enter and edit articles
- A tool to enter and edit categories
- A tool to enter and edit authors

The Publishing System Database

The publishing system database consists of three tables — authors, categories, and articles. The following sections detail each table.

The Authors Table

The system enables multiple authors to post articles. As such, a table containing the author names is needed. This table contains the author's name, a password, the author's e-mail address, and a numeric index to identify the author in other tables. The MySQL create statement for this table is as follows:

```
CREATE TABLE `authors` (
  `idx` int(10) unsigned NOT NULL auto_increment,
  `name` varchar(40) NOT NULL default '',
  `pwd` varchar(20) NOT NULL default '',
  `email` varchar(80) NOT NULL default '',
  PRIMARY KEY (`idx`)
) TYPE=MyISAM;
```

The pwd **(password) field is included for future functionality, such as authentication.**

The Categories Table

The system supports multiple categories for the articles. For example, articles about sports can be saved in a Sports category. The categories table contains the category name, a short description, and a numeric index for reference in other tables. The MySQL create statement for this table is as follows:

```
CREATE TABLE `categories` (
   `idx` int(10) NOT NULL auto_increment,
   `name` varchar(40) NOT NULL default '',
   `description` text NOT NULL,
   PRIMARY KEY  (`idx`)
) TYPE=MyISAM;
```

The Articles Table

The articles table is the heart of the system, storing all articles for retrieval via various utility programs. The articles table needs to store the following pieces of data:

- An index to uniquely identify the article
- The publication date of the article
- The category to which the article is assigned
- The author of the article
- A short title for the article
- The full text of the article
- A field to identify the article as a draft or a final copy

The MySQL create statement for this table is as follows:

```
CREATE TABLE `articles` (
   `idx` int(10) unsigned NOT NULL auto_increment,
   `pubdate` datetime NOT NULL default '0000-00-00 00:00:00',
   `cat` int(10) unsigned NOT NULL default '0',
   `author` int(10) unsigned NOT NULL default '0',
   `title` varchar(80) NOT NULL default '',
   `article` text NOT NULL,
   `publish` tinyint(1) unsigned NOT NULL default '0',
   PRIMARY KEY  (`idx`)
) TYPE=MyISAM;
```

The category and the author fields are numeric, designed to hold the index corresponding to the category or author entry in their respective tables. This adheres to good database design, as discussed in the "Database Normalization" section of Session 12.

However, this brings up an important design consideration — once created, a category or author cannot be deleted from the database. For example, suppose that the category Sports is assigned to several articles and has an index of 3. If Sports is ever deleted from the categories table, several articles reference invalid category fields. You could spend more time designing the system to handle this eventuality, but for this exercise, assume that categories and authors cannot be deleted.

20 Min.
To Go

Designing the Editing Tools

All the editing tools are created as monolithic scripts — enabling a user to perform all functions (add, edit, and search) on the individual tables. A monolithic script is fairly easy to create and operates by having itself called again with one or more status variables that tell the script what to do next.

Understanding Monolithic Scripts

Figure 28-1 shows a flowchart of the script to handle article maintenance.

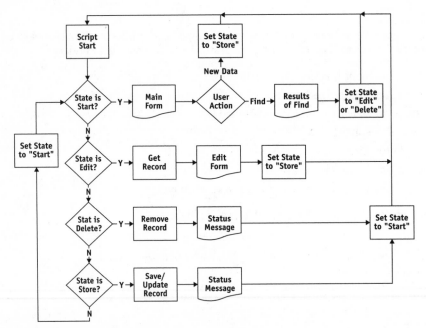

Figure 28-1 *The flowchart of a monolithic editing script*

The script maintains a state variable that tells it what to do when it is called. If the state isn't set, the script assumes that this is the first time it has been called and initializes all variables and displays the default form. The choices that a user makes in several forms determine the data that is sent via POST back to the script — each piece of data plays a part in determining the next state of the script and what it does next.

The publishing system scripts use a command variable ($cmd) to determine what the script should do during the current iteration. Several other values play an integral role in setting the $cmd variable — these values depend on what the script did in the last iteration and what the user chose to do.

Controlling State with Submit

One of the easiest ways to control state with interactive pages is by using forms and Submit button values. For example, the following form results in a Find button being displayed:

```
<form action="$_SERVER[PHP_SELF]" method="post">
  <input type="submit" name="Find" value="Find">
</form>
```

The button, although not labeled "Submit," is a form Submit button and causes the form to pass handling to the script handler (form action attribute) when clicked.

When the user clicks the Submit button, the form action causes the script to call itself by using POST to pass the value of the form fields — in this case, only the Submit button. Submit buttons send a name/value pair that consists of the values specified in their name and value attributes. For example, the preceding code causes a name/value pair of Find/Find to be sent to the script handler.

These miniforms can be placed wherever you need to make a user-inspired action accessible. Place a Find button where you want a user to be able to select the Find function, an Edit button wherever you want a user to be able to select the Edit function, and so on.

Any additional data needed by the functions should be included in the form body. For example, if you want to enable users to enter text to search for when activating the Find feature, the form could include something like the following:

```
<form action="$_SERVER[PHP_SELF]" method="post">
  <input type="text" name="findtext">
  <input type="submit" name="Find" value="Find">

</form>
```

Then, when the form is submitted, the text entered into the findtext **field is also passed to the form handler.**

A POST value reading routine can be used to gather the POST data and then evaluate it. For example, a PHP script could use code similar to the following snippet:

```
foreach($_POST as $key => $value) {
  global $$key;
  $$key = $value;
}

if ($Find == "Find") { $cmd = "Find"; }
if ($Edit == "Edit") { $cmd = "Edit"; }
...

switch ($cmd) {
```

```
   case "Find";
     ...do actions appropriate for "find"...
   break;

   case "Edit";
     ...do actions appropriate for "find"...
   break;
   ...
 }  // End of switch
```

The POST reading routine also sets additional values submitted by the form. For example, if you included the following line in your form, the global variable $findtext contains the text (if any) that the user entered into the form field:

```
<input type="text" name="findtext">
```

This ensures that only the variables you want are returned from the POST data. Those additional values can be used in the appropriate function sections of the script to facilitate the appropriate processing given the users' input.

Returning Variables from POST Data

Because these scripts can be run only by trusted individuals, you can afford to be a bit lax about your POST variable handling — it's doubtful that anyone authorized to run these scripts would attempt to sabotage them. However, in more public settings, be careful about pulling all the variables out of POST and into your script. What if someone sends a value for authorized and overrides your variable of the same name?

A suitable tactic to address this hole would be to add an argument of accepted or rejected values for the getpost() function. The code would resemble the following:

```
// Get requested variables from POST data
function getpost($varlist) {
  foreach($varlist as $variable) {
    if (!empty($_POST[$variable])) {
      global $$variable;
      $$variable = $_POST[$variable];
    }
  }
}
```

You would then call the function with a list of variables to return from the POST data whenever you need them:

```
$varlist = array("firstname", "lastname");
getpost($varlist);
```

A Basic Monolithic Editor

A template for a monolithic editor resembles the following code:

```php
<?php

// Get variable from POST data
function getpost() {
  foreach($_POST as $key => $value) {
    global $$key;
    $$key = $value;
  }
}

// Print Add/Edit form
function printform() {

  global //Add all fields for form(s) here

print <<<HTML
<html>
<body>
<!-- Add form(s) here -->
</body>
</html>
}

//MAIN PROGRAM BODY

getpost();

if ("Find" == "Find") { $cmd = "Find"; }
// Add other state switches here

// If no state is set, assume first run
if (empty($cmd)) { $cmd = "Start"; }

switch ($cmd) {

  case "Start";
    printform();
  break;

  // Add additional cases, one for each state
  case ...
  break;
}

?>
```

States for the Article Editor

The article editing script needs the following states, performing the functions described with each:

- **Start** — Displays the beginning form, an empty input form to add an article, and a small Find form enabling entry of the text argument for searching the article database.
- **Find** — Displays the results of a substring search and enables the user to pick a record to edit or delete.
- **Edit** — Displays the Edit form, a variation of the Add form with the selected record's details displayed.
- **Add/Update** — Adds a record to the database or updates an existing record and displays results of the database operation to the user.
- **Delete** — Deletes the selected record from the database and displays the results of the database operation to the user.

Although this may seem a meager set of states and functions, it performs all the operations needed. The following task examples help illustrate how operations are performed:

- **Adding an article:**
  1. The script displays the empty Start form; the user fills it out and clicks Add.
  2. The form data is passed back to the script along with values to set the state to Add or Update.
  3. The second iteration of the script stores the data in the database and displays the results to the user.
  4. The state is then set back to Start, and the beginning form is displayed again.
- **Editing an article:**
  1. The script displays the beginning Start form (which includes Find controls).
  2. The user enters text to search for in the Find field and clicks the Find button.
  3. The form data (text to search for) is passed back to the script, and the state is set to Find.
  4. The second iteration of the script uses the text the user entered to find matching articles, which are displayed in a list.
  5. The user finds the article he or she wants to edit and clicks the matching Edit button, which passes the article index back to the script and sets the state to Edit.
  6. The third iteration of the script displays the Edit form with the details from the selected record.
  7. The user edits the form and clicks Update. The edited fields are passed back to the script and the state is set to Add or Update.

8. The fourth iteration of the script stores the data in the database and displays the results to the user.

9. The state is then set back to Start, and the beginning form is displayed again.

Other functions, such as deleting an article, follow a similar path through multiple iterations of the script.

Coding the Article Editing Script

Each of the functions the editing script performs is identified by an individual state. To help modularize the development, this section breaks down the functions by state. Notice that many utility functions are not fully illustrated in this section, but they are explained in the full code listing later in this session.

The Start State

The starting state is perhaps the most simple, because it only needs to display the main form. The full code of the Start state is as follows:

```
case "Start";

    $pubdate = $today;
    printform("Add");

break;
```

The Find State

This state is more complicated than most of the other states because of the database operations and HTML output necessary to accomplish its goal of listing all matching articles. Following is the code for the Find state:

```
case "Find";

    // Get categories and authors
    $cats = getcats();
    $auths = getauths();

    // Find all occurrences of $find_text
    $query = "select * from articles where title like \"%$findtext%\"";
    $query = $query." or article like \"%$findtext%\"";
    $query = $query." order by pubdate";
    $result = mysql_query($query,$link)
        or die("Query failed:<br>$query");
```

```
    // Start form
    print "<body><html>\n";
    print "<form action=\"$this_script\" method=\"post\">\n";
    print "<table border=\"1\" width=\"75%\">";

    // Print appropriate header
    if (empty($result)) { $word = "No "; } else { $word = ""; }
    print "<h3>$word Articles Matching: \"$findtext\"</h3>\n";

    // For each article found, print mini-table
    while ($line = mysql_fetch_array($result, MYSQL_ASSOC)) {
      $article = stripslashes ($line[article]);
      $title = stripslashes($line[title]);
      $cattext = $line[cat];
      $authtext = $line[author];

print <<<HTML
<tr><td>
  <form action="$this_script" method="post">
  <input type="hidden" name="idx" value="$line[idx]">
  $auths[$authtext]
</td><td>
  $cats[$cattext]
</td><td>
HTML;

  // Print status of Publish
  if ($line[publish] == 1) {
    print "<font color=\"green\">PUBLISHED</font>";
  } else {
    print "<font color=\"red\">NOT PUBLISHED</font>";
  }
  print "</td></tr>\n";

// Print Edit/Delete controls
print <<<HTML
<tr><td colspan=2>
  $title
</td><td>
<input type="submit" name="Edit" value="Edit"> 
<input type="submit" name="Delete" value="Delete">
</td></tr>

<tr><td colspan="3">$article</td></tr>
</form>
<tr><td colspan="3" bgcolor="#000000"> </td></tr>

HTML;
    }  // End WHILE
```

```
   // Close page
print <<<HTML
   </table>
   <form action="$this_script">
   <input type="submit" name="Cancel" value="Cancel">
   </form>
   </body></html>
HTML;
   break;
```

The functionality of this state is straightforward. It begins by placing the contents of the category and author tables in associative arrays for easy access. The script then uses a SELECT query with a WHERE clause to find all articles in the article database that contain the text the user entered (now in the $findtext variable).

Matching records are then displayed in a table, as shown in Figure 28-2.

If the user doesn't enter any text before clicking the Find button, all articles in the database are displayed.

Each record is displayed in its own form, and each form has a hidden field that corresponds to that record's index. That way, when the user clicks an Edit or Delete button, the appropriate record's index is also returned in the POST data.

Last, an additional form is added to the bottom of the page to give the user a Cancel option.

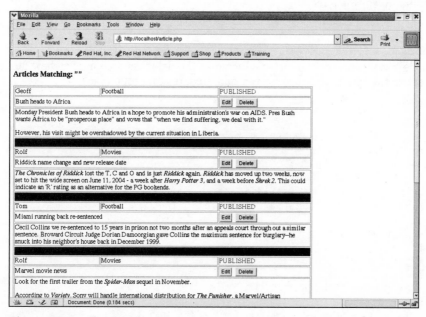

Figure 28-2 *The Find function displays all articles matching the text entered.*

The Edit State

The Edit state is marginally more complex than the Start state because it has to look up a record to populate the main form. The code for the Edit state follows:

```
case "Edit";

  $query = "select * from articles where idx = \"$idx\"";
  $result = mysql_query($query,$link)
    or die("Query failed:<br>$query");

  // Set values and display form for editing (Update)
  while ($line = mysql_fetch_array($result, MYSQL_ASSOC)) {
    $idx = $line[idx];
    $pubdate = $line[pubdate];
    $cat = $line[cat];
    $author = $line[author];
    $title = stripslashes ($line[title]);
    $article = stripslashes($line[article]);
    $publish = $line[publish];
  }
  printform("Update");

break;
```

The `printform()` function is called with the `Update` parameter. This tells the function to make certain choices regarding the way it displays the form — choices that make the form more applicable to editing a record.

The Add/Update State

The Add/Update state inserts or updates a record in the database according to how other values are set in the script. The code for the Add/Update state follows:

```
case "Add/Update";

  // Set or update pubdate
  $pubdate = $today;

  // Strip invalid HTML tags
  $title = strip_tags($title);
  $article = strip_tags($article,$valid_tags);

  // Set appropriate text for status message
  if ($Add == "Add") {
    $action = "Added";
  } else {
    $action = "Updated";
  }

  // Set publish
  if ($publish == "on") {
```

```
        $publish = 1;
    } else {
        $publish = 0;
    }

    // Form query and execute it
    if ($Add == "Add") {
        $query = "insert into articles
(idx,pubdate,cat,author,title,article,publish)";
        $query = $query." values
('0','$pubdate','$cat','$author','$title','$article',";
        $query = $query."'$publish')";
    } else {
        $query = "update articles set title='$title',article='$article',";
        $query = $query."cat='$cat',author='$author',publish='$publish' ";
        $query = $query." where idx=$idx";
    }
    $result = mysql_query($query,$link)
        or die("Query failed:<br>$query");

// Print status
print <<<HTML
<html><body>
<h3>Article $action</h3>
<form action=$this_script>
<input type=submit value=OK>
</form></body></html>
HTML;

    break;
```

The script uses the value of the $Add variable to determine if this iteration of the script should be inserting or updating a record. This value also affects the status message displayed after the database operation by setting an appropriate value in the $action variable.

As with most scripts that allow free-form text entry, it pays to have a few routines that check the text for unwanted values. In this case, you want to remove any unwanted HTML tags from the article text and description. Otherwise, an unwitting (or unscrupulous) user could place inappropriate HTML tags in the article, tags that could break the display of the article later.

This function is accomplished with the PHP strip_tags() function. Notice that the value of $valid_tags is set in the main program body for easy reference.

The Delete State

The code for the Delete state is very straightforward because it has to simply delete a record identified by its index. The code for the Delete state follows:

```
    case "Delete";
```

```
      $query = "delete from article where newsid='$idx'";
      $result = mysql_query($query,$link)
        or die("Query failed: $query");

// Print status
print <<<HTML
<html><body>
<h3>Article Deleted</h3>
<form action=$this_script>
<input type=submit value=OK>
</form></body></html>
HTML;

    break;
```

 The Delete function has no additional prompts; the article is deleted as soon as the user clicks the Delete button.

The printform() Function

The main form of the article editing script turns out to be fairly complex, only because of the select lists and other controls within the form and the several decisions that must be made depending on whether the function is displaying the form for adding a record (blank fields) or editing a record (populated fields).

Because the form is used in two different operations (start/add and edit), the code to generate the form is placed inside a function to reduce repeated code.

The code for the printform() function follows:

```
// Print the article form
//  Use "submit_text" as the name of the submit button
//  and to make decisions on language in form
function printform($submit_text) {

  global $idx, $pubdate, $cat, $author,
         $title, $article, $publish,
         $this_script;

    // Get the categories and authors
    $cats = getcats();
    $auths = getauths();

// Begin the form, print up through BODY
print <<<HTML
<html>
<head>
  <script language="JavaScript">
```

```
    function AddText(text) {
      articleform.article.value = articleform.article.value + text;
    }

    function AddURL() {
      url = urlform.url.value;
      urldesc = urlform.urldesc.value;

      at = "<a href='" + url + "' target='_blank'>" + urldesc + "</a>";
      articleform.article.value = articleform.article.value + at;

      urlform.url.value = "";
      urlform.urldesc.value = "";
    }

  </script>
</head>
<body>

HTML;

  // Print heading
  print "<h2>$submit_text Article</h2>\n";
  // If we are adding a new article, mention FIND feature
  if ($submit_text == "Add") {
    print "<br>(Use <a href=\"#find\">Find</a> to find article(s) ";
    print "for editing.)";
  }

// Print up through author/category
print <<<HTML
  <hr>
  <form name="articleform" action="$this_script" method="post">
  <input type="hidden" name="idx" value="$idx">

  <table>
  <tr><td>
  <b>Date:</b>
  </td><td>
  $pubdate
  <input type="hidden" name="pubdate" value="$pubdate">
  </td></tr>

HTML;

  // Print category select list
  if (($submit_text == "Add") || ($submit_text == "Update")) {
    print "<tr><td>\n";
    print "\t<b>Category:</b></td>\n";
    print "<td colspan=\"2\">\n";
    print "\t<select name=\"cat\" size=\"1\">\n";
```

```php
    foreach ($cats as $key => $name) {
      print "\t<option value=\"$key\"";
      // If editing, select appropriate category
      if (($key == $author) && ($submit_text == "Update")) {
        print " selected";
      }
      print ">$name";
      print "</option>\n";
    }
    print "</select>\n</td></tr>";
  }

  // Print author select list
  if (($submit_text == "Add")  || ($submit_text == "Update")) {
    print "<tr><td>\n";
    print "\t<b>Author:</b></td>\n";
    print "<td colspan=\"2\">\n";
    print "\t<select name=\"author\" size=\"1\">\n";

    foreach ($auths as $key => $name) {
      print "\t<option value=\"$key\"";
      // If editing, select appropriate author
      if (($key == $cat) && ($submit_text == "Update")) {
        print " selected";
      }
      print ">$name";
      print "</option>\n";
    }
    print "</select>\n</td></tr>";
  }

// Print subject and article text
print <<<HTML
  <tr><td>
  <b>Subject:</b>
  </td><td>
  <input type="text" name="title" value="$title" size="90">
  </td></tr></table>
  <b>Article:</b><br>
  <textarea name="article" cols="80" rows="8"
wrap="virtual">$article</textarea>

  <p>

  <input type="checkbox" name="publish"
HTML;

  // Appropriately check/uncheck Published checkbox
  if ($publish == "1") { print " checked"; }
```

```
// Print submit button and edit buttons
print <<<HTML
> <b>Publish</b><p>
  <input type="submit" name="$submit_text" value="$submit_text">
     
  <input type="reset" name="reset" value="Reset">
     
  <input type="submit" name="Cancel" value="Cancel">

  </form>
  <p>

  <!-- Buttons to add various HTML attribs -->
  <form name="edbuttons">
  <table>
  <tr><td>
  <input type=button value="BoldOn" onclick='javascript:AddText("<b>")'>
  <input type=button value="BoldOff" onclick='javascript:AddText("</b>")'>
  <input type=button value="ItalOn" onclick='javascript:AddText("<i>")'>
  <input type=button value="ItalOff" onclick='javascript:AddText("</i>")'>
  <input type=button value="UndOn" onclick='javascript:AddText("<u>")'>
  <input type=button value="UndOff" onclick='javascript:AddText("</u>")'>
  </td></tr>
  <tr><td>
  <input type=button value="LineBreak"
onclick='javascript:AddText("<br>")'>
  <input type=button value="ParaBreak"
onclick='javascript:AddText("<p>")'>
  <input type=button value="HorzLine"
onclick='javascript:AddText("<hr>")'>
  </td></tr>
  </table>
  <p>
  </form>

  <!-- Control to add URL link -->
  <form name="urlform">
  <table>
  <tr><td>
  <b>URL Description:</b>
  </td><td>
  <input type="text" size="60" name="urldesc">
  </td></tr>
  <tr><td>
  <b>URL:</b>
  </td><td>
  <input type="text" size="100" name="url">
  </td></tr>
  <tr><td>
```

```
 
</td><td>
<b>Reminder:</b>  Do not forget to add the
 protocol (ie. 'http://', 'mailto:', etc) to the URL!<br>
</td></tr></table>
<input type="button" value="AddURL" onclick="javascript:AddURL()">
</form>
</table>
<p><hr><p>

HTML;


    // If form is the Add form, show FIND tool
    if ($submit_text == "Add") {
print <<<HTML
    <a name="find"><h2>Search for Article(s)</h2></a>
    <form name="findform" action="$this_script" method="post">
    <b>Find article(s) containing this text:</b><br>
    <input type="text" name="findtext" size="90">
    <input type="submit" name="Find" value="Find">
    </form>

HTML;
    }


    // Close page
    print "</body>\n</html>";


    }
```

The select lists (category and author) are set to the correct values if a record is being edited. In addition, a handful of controls have been added to make the user's addition of HTML to the article easier. Figure 28-3 shows how the form looks in a browser.

This form includes JavaScript-enabled buttons for common editing tags (bold, italic, underline, paragraph break, and so on). When the user clicks the appropriate button, the JavaScript code adds the appropriate tag to the end of the article entry field. Although not strictly necessary, it does help the non-HTML-savvy make the most of the markup language.

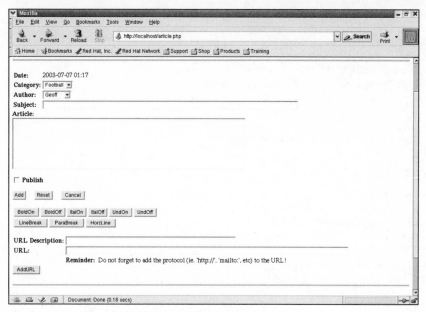

Figure 28-3   *The main article editing form*

The Finished Article Editing Script

**10 Min.
To Go**

All that is left is adding a few utility functions (retrieving POST data, loading category and author data, and so on) and tying it all together. The following listing is the finished article editing script:

```php
<?php

/*  article.php
    A tool to create and edit article
    content for the publishing system.
*/

// Add edit any tags that are valid for
//  inclusion in articles below
$valid_tags = "<a><i><b><u><p><br><hr>";


// Get variable from POST data
function getpost() {
  foreach($_POST as $key => $value) {
    global $$key;
    $$key = $value;
  }
}
```

```
// Open the pubsys database
function opendb() {
  $link = mysql_connect("localhost", "author", "newsletter")
    or die("Could not connect to MySQL");
  mysql_select_db("pubsys")
    or die("Could not select pubsys database");
  return($link);
}

// Get categories into associative array
function getcats() {
  global $link;

  $cats = array();
  $query = "select * from categories order by name asc";
  $result = mysql_query($query,$link)
    or die("Query failed:<br>$query");

  while ($line = mysql_fetch_array($result, MYSQL_ASSOC)) {
    $cats[$line[idx]] = $line[name];
  }
  return($cats);
}

// Get authors into associative array
function getauths() {
  global $link;

  $auths = array();
  $query = "select * from authors order by name asc";
  $result = mysql_query($query,$link)
    or die("Query failed:<br>$query");

  while ($line = mysql_fetch_array($result, MYSQL_ASSOC)) {
    $auths[$line[idx]] = $line[name];
  }
  return($auths);
}

// Print the article form
//   Use "submit_text" as the name of the submit button
//   and to make decisions on language in form
function printform($submit_text) {

  global $idx, $pubdate, $cat, $author,
         $title, $article, $publish,
         $this_script;

    // Get the categories and authors
    $cats = getcats();
    $auths = getauths();
```

```
// Begin the form, print up through BODY
print <<<HTML
<html>
<head>
  <script language="JavaScript">

    function AddText(text) {
      articleform.article.value = articleform.article.value + text;
    }

    function AddURL() {
      url = urlform.url.value;
      urldesc = urlform.urldesc.value;

      at = "<a href='" + url + "' target='_blank'>" + urldesc + "</a>";
      articleform.article.value = articleform.article.value + at;

      urlform.url.value = "";
      urlform.urldesc.value = "";
    }

  </script>
</head>
<body>

HTML;

  // Print heading
  print "<h2>$submit_text Article</h2>\n";
  // If we are adding a new article, mention FIND feature
  if ($submit_text == "Add") {
    print "<br>(Use <a href=\"#find\">Find</a> to find article(s) ";
    print "for editing.)";
  }

// Print up through author/category
print <<<HTML
  <hr>
  <form name="articleform" action="$this_script" method="post">
  <input type="hidden" name="idx" value="$idx">

  <table>
  <tr><td>
  <b>Date:</b>
  </td><td>
  $pubdate
  <input type="hidden" name="pubdate" value="$pubdate">
  </td></tr>

HTML;
```

```php
  // Print category select list
  if (($submit_text == "Add") || ($submit_text == "Update")) {
    print "<tr><td>\n";
    print "\t<b>Category:</b></td>\n";
    print "<td colspan=\"2\">\n";
    print "\t<select name=\"cat\" size=\"1\">\n";

    foreach ($cats as $key => $name) {
      print "\t<option value=\"$key\"";
      // If editing, select appropriate category
      if (($key == $author) && ($submit_text == "Update")) {
        print " selected";
      }
      print ">$name";
      print "</option>\n";
    }
    print "</select>\n</td></tr>";
  }


  // Print author select list
  if (($submit_text == "Add")  || ($submit_text == "Update")) {
    print "<tr><td>\n";
    print "\t<b>Author:</b></td>\n";
    print "<td colspan=\"2\">\n";
    print "\t<select name=\"author\" size=\"1\">\n";

    foreach ($auths as $key => $name) {
      print "\t<option value=\"$key\"";
      // If editing, select appropriate author
      if (($key == $cat) && ($submit_text == "Update")) {
        print " selected";
      }
      print ">$name";
      print "</option>\n";
    }
    print "</select>\n</td></tr>";
  }

// Print subject and article text
print <<<HTML
  <tr><td>
  <b>Subject:</b>
  </td><td>
  <input type="text" name="title" value="$title" size="90">
  </td></tr></table>
  <b>Article:</b><br>
  <textarea name="article" cols="80" rows="8"
wrap="virtual">$article</textarea>

  <p>
```

```
      <input type="checkbox" name="publish"
HTML;

   // Appropriately check/uncheck Published checkbox
   if ($publish == "1") { print " checked"; }

// Print submit button and edit buttons
print <<<HTML
> <b>Publish</b><p>
   <input type="submit" name="$submit_text" value="$submit_text">
      
   <input type="reset" name="reset" value="Reset">
      
   <input type="submit" name="Cancel" value="Cancel">

   </form>
   <p>

   <!-- Buttons to add various HTML attribs -->
   <form name="edbuttons">
   <table>
   <tr><td>
   <input type=button value="BoldOn" onclick='javascript:AddText("<b>")'>
   <input type=button value="BoldOff" onclick='javascript:AddText("</b>")'>
   <input type=button value="ItalOn" onclick='javascript:AddText("<i>")'>
   <input type=button value="ItalOff" onclick='javascript:AddText("</i>")'>
   <input type=button value="UndOn" onclick='javascript:AddText("<u>")'>
   <input type=button value="UndOff" onclick='javascript:AddText("</u>")'>
   </td></tr>
   <tr><td>
   <input type=button value="LineBreak"
onclick='javascript:AddText("<br>")'>
   <input type=button value="ParaBreak"
onclick='javascript:AddText("<p>")'>
   <input type=button value="HorzLine"
onclick='javascript:AddText("<hr>")'>
   </td></tr>
   </table>
   <p>
   </form>

   <!-- Control to add URL link -->
   <form name="urlform">
   <table>
   <tr><td>
   <b>URL Description:</b>
   </td><td>
   <input type="text" size="60" name="urldesc">
   </td></tr>
   <tr><td>
```

```
<b>URL:</b>
</td><td>
<input type="text" size="100" name="url">
</td></tr>
<tr><td>
 
</td><td>
<b>Reminder:</b>  Do not forget to add the
 protocol (ie. 'http://', 'mailto:', etc) to the URL!<br>
</td></tr></table>
<input type="button" value="AddURL" onclick="javascript:AddURL()">
</form>
</table>
<p><hr><p>

HTML;


  // If form is the Add form, show FIND tool
  if ($submit_text == "Add") {
print <<<HTML
  <a name="find"><h2>Search for Article(s)</h2></a>
  <form name="findform" action="$this_script" method="post">
  <b>Find article(s) containing this text:</b><br>
  <input type="text" name="findtext" size="90">
  <input type="submit" name="Find" value="Find">
  </form>

HTML;
}

// Close page
print "</body>\n</html>";


}


// MAIN PROGRAM BODY


// Get POST data
getpost();

// Direct function according to call
if ($Add == "Add") { $cmd = "Add/Update"; }
if ($Find == "Find") { $cmd = "Find"; }
if ($Edit == "Edit") { $cmd = "Edit"; }
if ($Update == "Update") { $cmd = "Add/Update"; }
if ($Delete == "Delete") { $cmd = "Delete"; }
if ($Reset == "Reset") { $cmd = "Start"; }
if ($Cancel == "Cancel") { $cmd = "Start"; }
```

```
// On first call, select START function
if (empty($cmd)) { $cmd = "Start"; }

// Clear vars on Start or Reset
if ($cmd == "Start") {
  foreach($GLOBALS as $key => $value) {
    // Protect system vars and vars used in loop
    if (($key != strtoupper($key)) &&
        ($key != "key") && ($key != "value") &&
        ($key != "cmd")) {
      unset($$key);
    }
  }
  unset($key,$value);
}

// Preset other vars & open DB
$this_script = $_SERVER['PHP_SELF'];
$today = date("Y-m-d H:i");
$link = opendb();

// Function selector
switch ($cmd) {

  // Display Add form
  case "Start";

    $pubdate = $today;
    printform("Add");

  break; // End Start

  // Display matches for $findtext
  case "Find";

    // Get categories and authors
    $cats = getcats();
    $auths = getauths();

    // Find all occurrences of $find_text
    $query = "select * from articles where title like \"%$findtext%\"";
    $query = $query." or article like \"%$findtext%\"";
    $query = $query." order by pubdate";
    $result = mysql_query($query,$link)
      or die("Query failed:<br>$query");

    // Start form
    print "<body><html>\n";
    print "<form action=\"$this_script\" method=\"post\">\n";
    print "<table border=\"1\" width=\"75%\">";
```

```
    // Print appropriate header
    if (empty($result)) { $word = "No "; } else { $word = ""; }
    print "<h3>$word Articles Matching: \"$findtext\"</h3>\n";

    // For each article found, print mini-table
    while ($line = mysql_fetch_array($result, MYSQL_ASSOC)) {
      $article = stripslashes($line[article]);
      $title = stripslashes($line[title]);
      $cattext = $line[cat];
      $authtext = $line[author];

print <<<HTML
<tr><td>
  <form action="$this_script" method="post">
  <input type="hidden" name="idx" value="$line[idx]">
  $auths[$authtext]
</td><td>
  $cats[$cattext]
</td><td>
HTML;

  // Print status of Publish
  if ($line[publish] == 1) {
    print "<font color=\"green\">PUBLISHED</font>";
  } else {
    print "<font color=\"red\">NOT PUBLISHED</font>";
  }
  print "</td></tr>\n";

// Print Edit/Delete controls
print <<<HTML
<tr><td colspan=2>
  $title
</td><td>
<input type="submit" name="Edit" value="Edit"> 
<input type="submit" name="Delete" value="Delete">
</td></tr>

<tr><td colspan="3">$article</td></tr>
</form>
<tr><td colspan="3" bgcolor="#000000"> </td></tr>

HTML;
    }  // End WHILE

  // Close page
print <<<HTML
  </table>
  <form action="$this_script">
  <input type="submit" name="Cancel" value="Cancel">
  </form>
  </body></html>
```

```
HTML;
  break;  // End Find

  // Look up article and display for editing
  case "Edit";

    $query = "select * from articles where idx = \"$idx\"";
    $result = mysql_query($query,$link)
      or die("Query failed:<br>$query");

    // Set values and display form for editing (Update)
    while ($line = mysql_fetch_array($result, MYSQL_ASSOC)) {
      $idx = $line[idx];
      $pubdate = $line[pubdate];
      $cat = $line[cat];
      $author = $line[author];
      $title = stripslashes($line[title]);
      $article = stripslashes($line[article]);
      $publish = $line[publish];
    }
    printform("Update");

  break; // End Edit

    // Add/Update and display results
    case "Add/Update";

      // Set or update pubdate
      $pubdate = $today;

      // Strip invalid HTML tags
      $title = addslashes(strip_tags($title));
      $article = addslashes(strip_tags($article,$valid_tags));

      // Set appropriate text for status message
      if ($Add == "Add") {
        $action = "Added";
      } else {
        $action = "Updated";
      }

      // Set publish
      if ($publish == "on") {
        $publish = 1;
      } else {
        $publish = 0;
      }

      // Form query and execute it
      if ($Add == "Add") {
        $query = "insert into articles
(idx,pubdate,cat,author,title,article,publish)";
```

```
            $query = $query." values
('0','$pubdate','$cat','$author','$title','$article',";
            $query = $query."'$publish')";
        } else {
            $query = "update articles set title='$title',article='$article',";
            $query = $query."cat='$cat',author='$author',publish='$publish' ";
            $query = $query." where idx=$idx";
        }
        $result = mysql_query($query,$link)
            or die("Query failed:<br>$query");

// Print status
print <<<HTML
<html><body>
<h3>Article $action</h3>
<form action=$this_script>
<input type=submit value=OK>
</form></body></html>
HTML;

    break; // End Add/Update

  // Delete selected article
  case "Delete";

    $query = "delete from article where newsid='$idx'";
    $result = mysql_query($query,$link)
        or die("Query failed: $query");

// Print status
print <<<HTML
<html><body>
<h3>Article Deleted</h3>
<form action=$this_script>
<input type=submit value=OK>
</form></body></html>
HTML;

  break; // End Delete

} // End of switch

mysql_close($link);

?>
```

Figures 28-4 through 28-7 show the script in action.

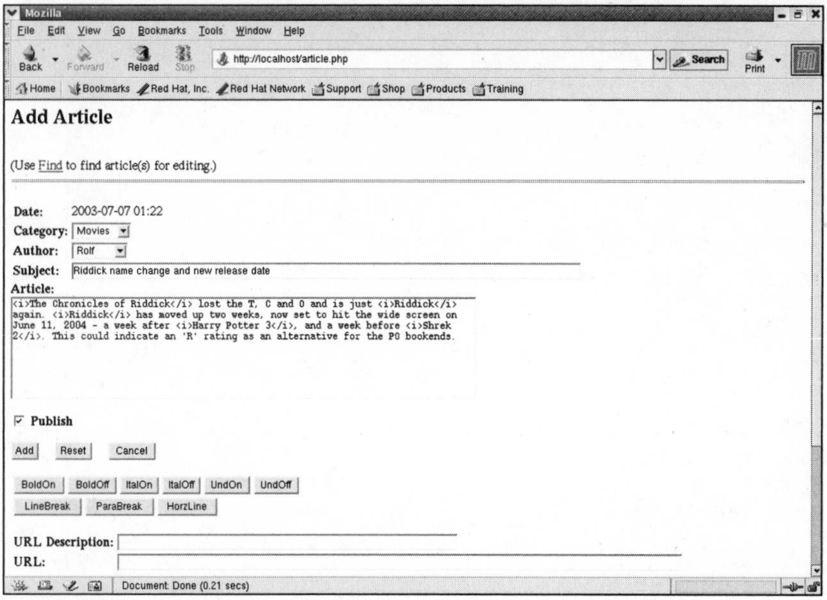

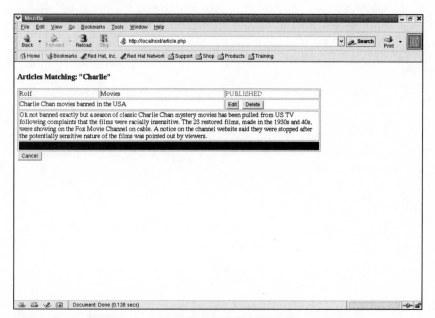

Figure 28-4 *Entering a new article*

Figure 28-5 *Finding an article containing "Charlie"*

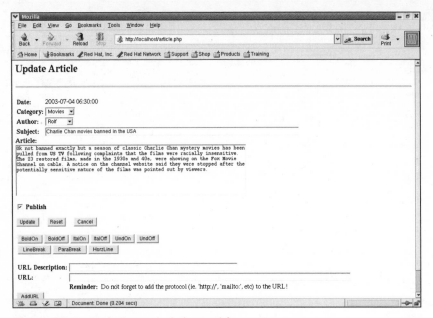

Figure 28-6   *Updating an existing article*

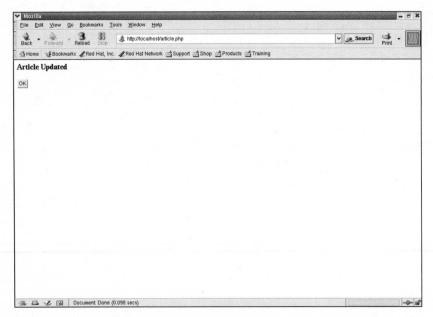

Figure 28-7   *Status after updating the article*

Category and Author Editing Scripts

You also need two additional scripts to edit the category and author information. These two scripts are much simpler than the article editing script, but they follow the same basic principles. The next two listings show the completed code for these two scripts (catmaint.php and authmaint.php):

catmaint.php

```php
<?php

/*  catmaint.php
    A tool to create and edit category information
    for the publishing system.
*/

// Get variable from POST data
function getpost() {
  foreach($_POST as $key => $value) {
    global $$key;
    $$key = $value;
  }
}

// Open the pubsys database
function opendb() {
  $link = mysql_connect("localhost", "author", "newsletter")
    or die("Could not connect to MySQL");
  mysql_select_db("pubsys")
    or die("Could not select pubsys database");
  return($link);
}

// Get categories into associative array
function getcats() {
  global $link;

  $cats = array();
  $query = "SELECT * FROM categories ORDER BY name ASC";
  $result = mysql_query($query,$link)
    or die("Query failed:<br>$query");

  while ($line = mysql_fetch_array($result, MYSQL_ASSOC)) {
    $cats[$line[idx]] = $line[name];
  }
  return($cats);
}
```

```
// Print category maint form
function printcatform($idx) {

  global $link, $this_script;

   // Add (idx=0) or Edit (idx!=0) function?
  if ($idx == "0") {
    $action = "Add New";
  } else {
    // If edit, get record to edit
    $query = "SELECT * FROM categories WHERE idx = \"$idx\"";
    $result = mysql_query($query,$link)
      or die("Query failed: $query");
    while ($line = mysql_fetch_array($result, MYSQL_ASSOC)) {
      $name = $line[name];
      $desc = $line[description];
    }
    $action = "Edit";
  }

// Output form
print <<<HTML
<body>
<html>
  <h2>Category Maintenance</h2>
  <h3>List Categories</h3>
  <form name="listcat" action="$this_script" method="post">
  <input type="submit" name="List" value="List">
  </form>
  <p>
  <h3>$action Category</h3>
  <form name="newcat" action="$this_script" method="post">
  <input type="hidden" name="idx" value="$idx">
  <table><tr>
  <td>Name:</td>
  <td><input name="name" type="text" size="40"
        maxlength="40" value="$name"></td>
  </tr><tr>
  <td>Description:</td>
  <td><textarea name="desc" cols="40"
      rows="5">$desc</textarea></td></tr>
  <tr><td> </td><td>
    <input type="submit" name="Save" value="Save">
      
    <input type="reset" name="reset">
  </td></tr>
  </table>
  </form>

  <p> </p>
  <form action="$this_script" method="post">
```

```php
    <input type="submit" name="Restart" value="Restart">
    </form>

HTML;
}

// Print list to choose record to edit
function printcatlist() {

  global $this_script;

  $cats = array();
  $cats = getcats();

print <<<HTML
<html>
<body>
<h2>Select Category to Edit</h2>
<table width="75%" border="1">

HTML;

  // Print table of entries with Edit button
  foreach($cats as $idx => $name) {
print <<<HTML
  <form action="$this_script" method="post">
  <tr><td width="10%" valign="bottom"
        align="center">
    <input type="hidden" name="idx" value="$idx">
    <input type="submit" name="Edit" value="Edit">
  </td><td>
    $name
  </td></tr>
  </form>


HTML;
  }

print <<<HTML
</table>
  <p> </p>
  <form action="$this_script" method="post">
  <input type="submit" name="Cancel" value="Cancel">
  </form>
</body></html>
HTML;
}

// MAIN PROGRAM BODY
```

```
// Get POST data and open DB
getpost();
$link = opendb();

$this_script = $_SERVER[PHP_SELF];

// Set function
if ($List == "List") { $cmd = "List"; }
if ($Edit == "Edit") { $cmd = "Edit"; }
if ($Save == "Save") { $cmd = "Save"; }
if (($Cancel == "Cancel") ||
    ($Reset == "Reset") ||
    ($Restart == "Restart") ||
    ($OK == "OK")) {
  $cmd = "Start";
}
if (empty($cmd)) { $cmd = "Start"; }

// Select and perform function
switch ($cmd) {

  case "Start";
    printcatform(0);
  break;

  case "List";
    printcatlist();
  break;

  case "Edit";
    printcatform($idx);
  break;

  case "Save";

    // $idx=0 means new record
    // $idx!=0 means update
    if ($idx == 0) {
      $action = "Saved";
      $query = "INSERT INTO categories VALUES ";
      $query = $query."(0,'$name','$desc')";
    } else {
      $action = "Updated";
      $query = "UPDATE categories SET name='$name', description=";
      $query = $query."'$desc' WHERE idx='$idx'";
    }

    // Strip HTML tags
    $name = strip_tags($name);
    $desc = strip_tags($desc);
```

```php
    $result = mysql_query($query,$link)
      or die("Query failed: $query");

print <<<HTML
<html><body>
  <h2>Category $action</h2>
  <form action="$this_script" method="post">
  <input type="submit" name="OK" value="OK">
  </form>
</body></html>
HTML;

  break;

} // End Switch

mysql_close($link);

?>
```

authmaint.php

```php
<?php

/*  authmaint.php
    A tool to create and edit author information
    for the publishing system.
*/

// Get variable from POST data
function getpost() {
  foreach($_POST as $key => $value) {
    global $$key;
    $$key = $value;
  }
}

// Open the pubsys database
function opendb() {
  $link = mysql_connect("localhost", "author", "newsletter")
    or die("Could not connect to MySQL");
  mysql_select_db("pubsys")
    or die("Could not select pubsys database");
  return($link);
}

// Get authors into associative array
function getauths() {
  global $link;

  $auths = array();
  $query = "select * from authors order by name asc";
```

```
    $result = mysql_query($query,$link)
      or die("Query failed:<br>$query");

    while ($line = mysql_fetch_array($result, MYSQL_ASSOC)) {
      $auths[$line[idx]] = $line[name];
    }
    return($auths);
  }

  // Print the author maint form
  function printauthform($idx) {

    global $link, $this_script;

    // Add (idx=0) or Edit (idx!=0) function?
    if ($idx == "0") {
      $action = "Add New";
      $pwdtext = "";
    } else {
      // If edit, get record to edit
      $query = "SELECT * FROM authors WHERE idx = \"$idx\"";
      $result = mysql_query($query,$link)
        or die("Query failed: $query");
      while ($line = mysql_fetch_array($result, MYSQL_ASSOC)) {
        $name = $line[name];
        $pwd = $line[pwd];
        $email=$line[email];
      }
      $action = "Edit";
      $pwdtext = "(Leave password blank to keep same password.)";
    }

  // Output form
  print <<<HTML
<body>
<html>
  <h2>Author Maintenance</h2>
  <h3>List Authors</h3>
  <form name="listauth" action="$this_script" method="post">
  <input type="submit" name="List" value="List">
  </form>
  <p>
  <h3>$action Author</h3>
  <form name="newauth" action="$this_script" method="post">
  <input type="hidden" name="idx" value="$idx">
  <table><tr>
  <td>Name:</td>
  <td><input name="name" type="text" size="40"
        maxlength="40" value="$name"></td>
  </tr><tr>
```

```
    <td>Password:</td>
    <td><input name="pwd" type="password" size="20"
        maxlength="40" value=""> $pwdtext</td>
  </tr><tr>
    <td>Email:</td>
    <td><input name="email" type="text" size="40"
        maxlength="80" value="$email"></td></tr>
  <tr><td> </td><td>
    <input type="submit" name="Save" value="Save">
      
    <input type="reset" name="reset">
  </td></tr>
  </table>
  </form>

  <p> </p>
  <form action="$this_script" method="post">
  <input type="submit" name="Restart" value="Restart">
  </form>

HTML;
}

// Print list to choose record to edit
function printauthlist() {

  global $this_script;

  $auths = array();
  $auths = getauths();

print <<<HTML
<html>
<body>
<h2>Select Author to Edit</h2>
<table width="75%" border="1">

HTML;

  // Print table of entries with Edit button
  foreach($auths as $idx => $name) {
print <<<HTML
  <form action="$this_script" method="post">
  <tr><td width="10%" valign="bottom"
      align="center">
    <input type="hidden" name="idx" value="$idx">
    <input type="submit" name="Edit" value="Edit">
  </td><td>
    $name
  </td></tr>
  </form>
```

```
HTML;
  }

print <<<HTML
</table>
  <p> </p>
  <form action="$this_script" method="post">
  <input type="submit" name="Cancel" value="Cancel">
  </form>
</body></html>
HTML;
}


// MAIN PROGRAM BODY

// Get POST data and open DB
getpost();
$link = opendb();

$this_script = $_SERVER[PHP_SELF];

// Set function
if ($List == "List") { $cmd = "List"; }
if ($Edit == "Edit") { $cmd = "Edit"; }
if ($Save == "Save") { $cmd = "Save"; }
if (($Cancel == "Cancel") ||
    ($Reset == "Reset") ||
    ($Restart == "Restart") ||
    ($OK == "OK")) {
    $cmd = "Start";
}
if (empty($cmd)) { $cmd = "Start"; }

// Select and perform function
switch ($cmd) {

  case "Start";
    printauthform(0);
  break;

  case "List";
    printauthlist();
  break;

  case "Edit";
    printauthform($idx);
  break;

  case "Save";
```

```
      // $idx=0 means new record
      // $idx!=0 means update
      if ($idx == 0) {
        $action = "Saved";
        $query = "INSERT INTO authors VALUES ";
        $query = $query."(0,'$name',password('$pwd'),";
        $query = $query."'$email')";
      } else {
        $action = "Updated";
        $query = "UPDATE authors SET name='$name',";
        $query = $query."email='$email'";
        if (!empty($pwd)) {
          $query = $query.", pwd=password('$pwd')";
        }
        $query = $query." WHERE idx='$idx'";
      }

      // Strip HTML tags
      $name = strip_tags($name);

      $result = mysql_query($query,$link)
        or die("Query failed: $query");

print <<<HTML
<html><body>
  <h2>Author $action</h2>
  <form action="$this_script" method="post">
  <input type="submit" name="OK" value="OK">
  </form>
</body></html>
HTML;

  break;

} // End Switch

mysql_close($link);

?>
```

Putting It all Together

So how does all of this work together as a system? You can make the scripts available and have users access them via shortcuts or create an HTML page similar to the following as a gateway into the scripts:

```
<html>
<body>
<a href="authmaint.php" target="_blank">
  Maintain Authors</a>
```

```
<a href="catmaint.php" target="_blank">
  Maintain Categories</a>
<a href="articles.php" target="_blank">
  Enter/Edit Articles</a>
</body>
</html>
```

Of course, these scripts should not be available to the general public, so it is best to place them in a special directory and protect them with Apache access control. (More information on Apache access control is available in Session 6.) This assumes that the authors can be trusted not to make mistakes with the various pieces of data (authors, categories, and articles). The next session introduces base-level authentication using PHP and describes how you can protect content on a per-author basis.

Done!

REVIEW

This session covered building tools for a simple publishing system — namely, the scripts to add and edit data in the system. It described how to design the database, scope out the tools necessary to maintain the data, and how to build the various scripts. You learned how to create a monolithic editing script and how simple forms can be used to maintain a script's state.

The next session covers how to actually deploy the stored content in various forms.

QUIZ YOURSELF

1. Why are categories stored as numbers in the `articles` table? (See "The Articles Table.")

2. What is the definition of a monolithic editing script? (See "Designing the Editing Tools.")

3. What are some of the advantages of a monolithic script? (See "Understanding Monolithic Scripts.")

4. What does a Submit button return in POST data? (See "Controlling State with Submit.")

5. What does the Add/Update function of the article editing script actually do? (See "States for the Article Editor" and "The Add/Update State.")

6. Why is the main form output contained in the `printform()` function? (See "The `printform()` Function.")

SESSION

Project: Content Publishing II

Session Checklist

✔ Methods for publishing dynamic content with PHP

✔ Sample publishing scripts

✔ Using search features

✔ Adding authentication

**30 Min.
To Go**

I n the last session, you learned how you could build a simple publishing system to enable users to add and edit content. However, that is only half the equation; you must also have methods to actually deploy (publish) that content to users on the Web.

This session continues the development of the publishing system by creating several scripts to publish the articles in a variety of forms. You also learn how to add search and authentication functionality to the system.

Methods of Publishing Dynamic Content

You have several ways to publish dynamic content using PHP scripts. Two popular methods are as follows:

- Writing a script to output a full HTML page that includes the content you wish to publish
- Writing a script that is included in an HTML page in which you want the content

The first method provides the most control over how the dynamic content is displayed but the least amount of flexibility. Any change in the overall structure of the pages in which the content appears must be made in the script.

The second method is a more practical approach — enabling the script to fit nicely within any page design and to be designed by a professional HTML page editor. However, this approach requires a few extra Apache tricks.

Both methods are outlined in the following sections.

Full Page from PHP

You have seen several instances of PHP outputting a full HTML page from the beginning <html> tag to the ending </html> tag. As described in Session 18, the easiest way to output a lot of raw HTML is by using a here document print statement. For example, the following code begins a fairly complex HTML document complete with a complicated table layout:

```
print <<<HTML
<!DOCTYPE HTML PUBLIC "-//W3C//DTD HTML 4.0 Transitional//EN">
<HTML>
<HEAD>
<META HTTP-EQUIV="Content-Type" CONTENT="text/html; charset=ISO-8859-1">
<TITLE>Newsletter - Home</TITLE>
<!-- Set Meta tags for search engine use -->
<META NAME="keywords" CONTENT="news, movies, sports, newsletter">
<LINK REL=STYLESHEET TYPE="text/css" HREF="./style.css">
<LINK REL=STYLESHEET TYPE="text/css" HREF="./site.css">
</HEAD>
<BODY>
<TABLE CELLPADDING=0 CELLSPACING=0 BORDER=0 WIDTH=748 NOF=LY>
  <TR VALIGN=TOP ALIGN=LEFT>
    <TD>
      <TABLE BORDER=0 CELLSPACING=0 CELLPADDING=0 WIDTH=170 NOF=LY>
        <TR VALIGN=TOP ALIGN=LEFT>
          <TD WIDTH=27 HEIGHT=7><IMG
SRC="./assets/images/autogen/clearpixel.gif" WIDTH=27 HEIGHT=1 BORDER=0
ALT=""></TD>
          <TD></TD>
          <TD WIDTH=35><IMG SRC="./assets/images/autogen/clearpixel.gif"
WIDTH=35 HEIGHT=1 BORDER=0 ALT=""></TD>
        </TR>
        <TR VALIGN=TOP ALIGN=LEFT>
          <TD HEIGHT=183></TD>
          <TD ALIGN=CENTER VALIGN=MIDDLE WIDTH=108>
            <A HREF="./index.php">
            <IMG ID="logo" HEIGHT=183 WIDTH=108
SRC="./assets/images/logo.gif" BORDER=0 ALT="Home">
            </A></TD>
          <TD></TD>
        </TR>
        <TR VALIGN=TOP ALIGN=LEFT>
          <TD COLSPAN=3 HEIGHT=55></TD>
        </TR>
HTML;
```

When creating complex pages to deploy via PHP, it is advisable to use a tool designed for HTML editing (Microsoft FrontPage, Macromedia Dreamweaver, and so on) to create the basic template and then import the resulting raw HTML into your script.

Wherever you need the dynamic content, you simply include the code to produce it. Alternatively, you can place the code in a separate file and use the PHP include() function to include the external script where you need it.

When using the include() function multiple times within the same script, you should ensure that the included scripts do not result in external libraries being included multiple times. For example, if you include three scripts, each of which includes a common library, that common library ends up appearing three times in the main script. To avoid this problem, consider using the include_once() function instead.

Only Dynamic Content from PHP

Several ways are available for you to utilize PHP only for the dynamic content while using other programs to maintain your HTML files. The two most popular methods — turning PHP on and off and server-side includes — are covered in the next two sections.

Turning PHP On and Off

One easy way to include PHP only for dynamic content is to use the PHP beginning and ending tags to turn PHP on only when you need it, as shown in the following HTML snippet:

```
<html>
<body>
<table>
... complex table used to format page ...
<?php
...dynamic content generated here...
?>
...continue complex table...
</table>
</body>
</html>
```

You can embed the <?php ...code...?> constructs wherever you need to generate dynamic content.

Alternatively, you can use constructs similar to the following snippet:

```
<?php  include "dynamic.php"; ?>
```

This enables the content-generating script to inhabit its own external file so that it can be independently updated. The changes appear in each file for which it is used.

Using this method, you can maintain your HTML files in the editor of your choice. You need to set the editor to output only files with a .php extension or add another extension to the Apache PHP handler. See Session 2 for details about how to add multiple extensions to the PHP handler.

Server-Side Includes

Another, perhaps more clean, method to include dynamic content scripts within HTML is using Apache's server-side includes (SSI) functionality. This functionality uses the server to do the work of the file inclusion. However, Apache must be configured to deliver server-side content.

The SSI engine (`include_mod`) is included in the base set of modules for Apache 2.0. As such, SSI functionality should be available unless you choose to compile Apache with the `--disable-include` switch (disabling `include_mod`).

To configure Apache for SSI, you should include the following lines in your Apache configuration file (usually `httpd.conf`):

```
AddType text/html .shtml
AddOutputFilter INCLUDES .shtml
```

This causes Apache to parse all files with an extension of `.shtml` through the SSI engine and assign the MIME type of `text/html` to the resulting document. Note that this causes any SSI documents to be named with an `.shtml` extension.

Although you can force Apache to process other files (such as `.html`) as SSI documents, it is not advisable. Forcing all documents through the SSI engine significantly slows your server.

Additionally, any directory in which you wish to use SSI documents must have the option `+Includes` set. Typically, this is done by including the following line in a `<Directory>` definition:

```
Options +Includes
```

However, if you allow overrides, you can also place this line in a `.htaccess` file in each directory in which you want SSI capability.

See Session 1 and Session 5 for more information on these configuration options.

After Apache is correctly configured for SSI, you can use SSI `virtual` tags to include PHP scripts in your HTML files wherever you need them.

For example, to include a script called `dynamic.php`, you would use a tag similar to the following:

```
<!--#include virtual="./dynamic.php" -->
```

This tag tells Apache to include the file `dynamic.php` and allow processing of the file as though it were served individually (allowing the PHP engine to parse it).

Most HTML editors allow manual editing of the HTML code, so you can place the SSI tags wherever you need them.

SSI is quite powerful and can be used for purposes other than simply including scripts in otherwise raw HTML files. For more information on SSI and its capabilities, visit the Apache Web site and read the SSI Tutorial (`http://httpd.apache.org/docs-2.0/howto/ssi.html`).

Publishing Scripts

The following sections provide sample scripts for publishing content from the publishing system database created in the last session. Each script displays a different view into the data and is meant to be included in a larger HTML file, as discussed in the previous section.

Common Library

All the publishing scripts use a handful of common utility functions. Instead of repeating them in each script, you can create a library named `common_pubsys.php` that contains these functions. Then, each script that needs the functions can use the PHP `include()` function to include them appropriately. The following listing shows the contents of `common_pubsys.php`:

```php
<?php

// Common pubsys functions

// Open the pubsys database
function opendb() {
  $link = mysql_connect("localhost", "author", "newsletter")
    or die("Could not connect to MySQL");
  mysql_select_db("pubsys")
    or die("Could not select pubsys database");
  return($link);
}

// Get categories into associative array
function getcats() {
  global $link;

  $cats = array();
  $query = "select * from categories order by name asc";
  $result = mysql_query($query,$link)
    or die("Query failed:<br>$query");

  while ($line = mysql_fetch_array($result, MYSQL_ASSOC)) {
    $cats[$line[idx]] = $line[name];
```

```
    }
  return($cats);
}

// Get authors into associative array
function getauths() {
  global $link;

  $auths = array();
  $query = "select * from authors order by name asc";
  $result = mysql_query($query,$link)
    or die("Query failed:<br>$query");

  while ($line = mysql_fetch_array($result, MYSQL_ASSOC)) {
    $auths[$line[idx]] = $line[name];
  }
  return($auths);
}

?>
```

Full Article

This script prints the full text and details of one specific article. The article to print is passed to the script as the index of the article via GET (usually appended to the URL):

```
<?php

/*  displayarticle.php
    Display the article specified (index via GET).
*/

include "common_pubsys.php";

// If no article idx was passed, error
if (empty($_GET[idx])) {

  die("<p>Invalid article number</p>");

} else {

  // Get index passed via GET
  $idx = $_GET[idx];

  // Open DB and init lists
  $link = opendb();
  $cats = getcats();
  $auths = getauths();

  // Get selected article (if published)
  $query = "SELECT * FROM articles WHERE idx = \"$idx\" ";
```

```
$query = $query."AND publish = \"1\"";

$result = mysql_query($query,$link)
  or die("Query failed: $query");

// If empty then no article or not published, error
if (mysql_num_rows($result) == 0) {
  die("<p>Invalid article number</p>");
}

// Parse results
while ($line = mysql_fetch_array($result, MYSQL_ASSOC)) {
  $temptime = strtotime($line[pubdate]);
  $pubdate = date("m-d-Y",$temptime);
  $pubtime = date("H:m",$temptime);
  $article = $line[article];
  $title = $line[title];
  $cattext = $line[cat];
  $authtext = $line[author];

  // Get author's email
  $query = "SELECT email FROM authors WHERE idx = ";
  $query = $query."\"$authtext\"";

  $authresult = mysql_query($query,$link)
    or die("Query failed: $query");

  $authdata = mysql_fetch_array($authresult, MYSQL_ASSOC);
  $email = $authdata[email];

// Print article
print <<<HTML
<h3>$title</h3>
<p><font size="-2"><b>Posted by:</b>
<a href="mailto:$email">$auths[$authtext]</a>
 <b>on</b> $pubdate <b>at</b> $pubtime</font><br>
$article</p>
<p><font size="-2"><b>Category:</b> $cats[$cattext]<br></font></p>

HTML;

  } // End while
} // End if

mysql_close($link);

?>
```

Figure 29-1 shows an example of the output from `displayarticle.php`.

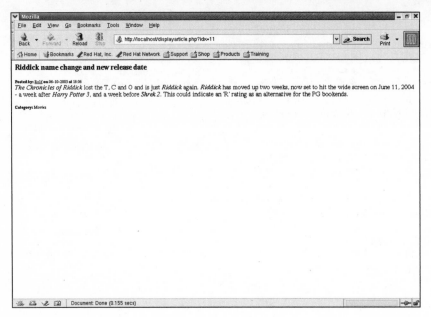

Figure 29-1   *Example of full-text article output from* `displayarticle.php`

Headlines Only

**20 Min.
To Go**

This script prints only the headlines from a given range of articles. The headlines published must come from articles that have the publish field set to 1 (publish). Each headline is a link to the full article display script, `displayarticle.php`; clicking a headline causes the full article to be displayed.

The `headlines.php` script also confines its listing to articles that were published in the last two weeks. This script can be customized to display any range of articles by changing the value of `$max_days` near the beginning of the script:

```php
<?php

/*  headlines.php
    Display headlines for published articles within
    a given timeframe.
    Article headlines are linked to displayarticle.php
    So clicking a headline will display the full article.
*/

// Set maximum number of days to display here
$max_days = 14;

include "common_pubsys.php";

// Open DB and init cutoff
$link = opendb();
```

```php
$cutoff = strtotime("-".$max_days." day");
$cutoff = date("Y-m-d H:i",$cutoff);

// Get all article titles in timeframe and that are published
$query = "SELECT idx,title FROM articles WHERE publish = \"1\"";
$query = $query." AND pubdate >= \"$cutoff\"";
$result = mysql_query($query,$link)
  or die("Query failed: $query");

// Display each article title
while ($line = mysql_fetch_array($result, MYSQL_ASSOC)) {

print <<<HTML
<a href="displayarticle.php?idx=$line[idx]" target="_blank">
  $line[title]
</a><br>

HTML;

}  // End while

mysql_close($link);

?>
```

Figure 29-2 shows an example of the output from `headlines.php`.

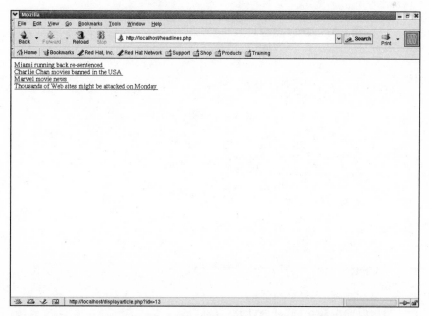

Figure 29-2   *Example of article headlines output from* `headlines.php`

Category Listings

The `categories.php` script displays all the categories that had articles posted in the given time frame. Each category is listed by name along with the headlines of the articles. The headlines are linked to `displayarticle.php`, so clicking a headline displays the entire article. As with `headlines.php`, the script's time frame can be edited by changing the value of the `$max_days` variable:

```php
<?php

/*  categories.php
    Display categories for published articles within
    a given timeframe.
    Article headlines are linked to displayarticle.php
    So clicking a headline will display the full article.
*/

// Set maximum number of days to display here
$max_days = 14;

// Set number of words per teaser here
$teaser_words = 20;

include "common_pubsys.php";

// Open DB and initialize vars
$link = opendb();
$cats = getcats();
$auths = getauths();
$cutoff = strtotime("-".$max_days." day");
$cutoff = date("Y-m-d H:i",$cutoff);

// Process each category
foreach($cats as $key => $value) {

  // Select all articles published in timeframe and
  //   in category
  $query = "SELECT * FROM articles WHERE publish = \"1\"";
  $query = $query." AND cat = \"$key\"";
  $query = $query." AND pubdate >= \"$cutoff\"";
  $result = mysql_query($query,$link)
    or die("Query failed: $query");

  // If there are articles, display them
  if (mysql_num_rows($result) != 0) {

    print "<h3>Category: $value</h3>\n<hr>\n";

    // Display each article title
    while ($line = mysql_fetch_array($result,
          MYSQL_ASSOC)) {
```

```
            $temptime = strtotime($line[pubdate]);
            $pubdate = date("m-d-Y",$temptime);
            $pubtime = date("H:m",$temptime);
            $article = $line[article];
            $title = $line[title];
            $cattext = $line[cat];
            $authtext = $line[author];

print <<<HTML
<a href="displayarticle.php?idx=$line[idx]" target="_blank">
  $line[title]
</a> (Posted by $auths[$authtext] on $pubdate $pubtime)<br>

HTML;

    }  // End while

    print "\n<hr>\n<p>\n";

  }  // End if


} // End foreach

?>
```

Figure 29-3 shows an example of the output from `categories.php`.

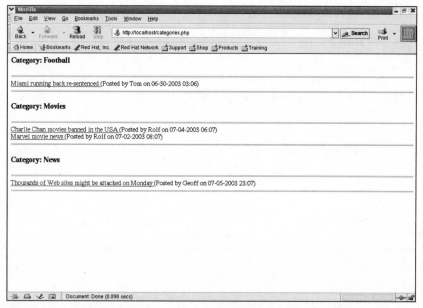

Figure 29-3   *Example of a category listing from* `categories.php`

Teasers

The teasers.php script displays the first 20 words of an article followed by a ...[more] link to display the complete article. Teasers offer users an advantage over headlines because they provide a hint of the article content, but enable users to pick the articles they are most interested in seeing in their entirety. Like the other time frame scripts, this script's time frame can be changed by modifying the value of the **$max_days** variable:

```php
<?php

/*  teasers.php
    Display teasers for published articles within
    a given timeframe. (first $teaser_words words)
    Teasers have a "[more]" link. Clicking the link
    will display the full article (via displayarticle.php)
*/


// Set maximum number of days to display here
$max_days = 14;

// Set number of words per teaser here
$teaser_words = 20;

include "common_pubsys.php";

// Open DB and initialize vars
$link = opendb();
$cats = getcats();
$auths = getauths();

$cutoff = strtotime("-".$max_days." day");
$cutoff = date("Y-m-d H:i",$cutoff);

// Get all articles within the timeframe that are published
$query = "SELECT * FROM articles WHERE publish = \"1\"";
$query = $query." AND pubdate >= \"$cutoff\"";

$result = mysql_query($query,$link)
  or die("Query failed: $query");

// Parse each article
while ($line = mysql_fetch_array($result, MYSQL_ASSOC)) {

  $title = $line[title];
  $article = $line[article];
  $cattext = $line[cat];
  $authtext = $line[author];
```

```
    // Generate teaser (1 to $teaser_words of article)
    $words = explode(" ",$article,$teaser_words);
    $teaser = "";
    for ($i = 0; $i < count($words); $i++) {
      $teaser = $teaser . $words[$i] . " ";
    }

// Print teaser
print <<<HTML
<h3>$title</h3>
<p>$teaser  
[<a href="displayarticle.php?idx=$line[idx]"
    target="_blank">more</a>]</p>

HTML;

}  // End while

mysql_close($link);

?>
```

Figure 29-4 shows an example of the output from `teasers.php`.

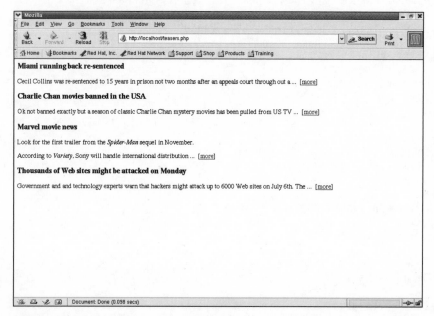

Figure 29-4   *Example of a teaser listing from* `teasers.php`

Enabling Search Functionality for Users

The last session showed an example of a simple search function, which was used in the article editing script. That same functionality can be used for users of the site as well. In addition to simple substring searches using MySQL's LIKE query clause, you can also implement powerful full-text searches.

The following two sections explain how to implement both types of searches for users.

Simple Substring Searches

Substring searches make for a quick, down-and-dirty means of finding text. The main benefit to a substring search is that it finds the text specified whether it is a single word or buried in the middle of a word. For example, if you use a substring search to look for try, you might find try, Gentry, and tryst.

However, substring searches are hampered by being case-sensitive; searching for try does not find Try.

Implementing a simple substring search is easy: You can add a simple form wherever you want the user to be able to search, and write a short script to return the articles in which the text was found.

The following HTML code should be included wherever you want a search form:

```
<form name="findform" action="findarticles.php" method="post">
    <b>Find article(s) containing this text:</b><br>
    <input type="text" name="findtext" size="90">
    <input type="submit" name="Find" value="Find">
</form>
```

You can then use the following script to display the results:

```
<?php

/*  findarticles.php
    Display articles that contain the text
    passed in POST var findtext
*/

include "common_pubsys.php";

// Open DB and init vars
$link = opendb();
$cats = getcats();
$auths = getauths();

// Start results page
print <<<HTML
<html>
<body>

HTML;
```

```php
// If no value passed to search on, gen error
if (!isset($_POST[findtext])) {

  $error = "Invalid search string!";

} else {

  // Get search text and perform search
  $findtext = $_POST[findtext];

  $query = "SELECT * FROM articles WHERE publish = \"1\" AND";
  $query = $query." title LIKE \"%$findtext%\"";
  $query = $query." OR article LIKE \"%$findtext%\"";
  $query = $query." ORDER BY pubdate DESC";
  $result = mysql_query($query,$link)
    or die("Query failed: $query");

  // If no results, say so via error
  if (mysql_num_rows($result) == 0) {
    $error = "<h2>No articles matching: \"$findtext\"</h2>";
  } else {
    print "<h2>Articles matching:  \"$findtext\"</h2>";
  }

  // Parse results
  while ($line = mysql_fetch_array($result, MYSQL_ASSOC)) {
    $temptime = strtotime($line[pubdate]);
    $pubdate = date("m-d-Y",$temptime);
    $pubtime = date("H:m",$temptime);
    $article = $line[article];
    $title = $line[title];
    $cattext = $line[cat];
    $authtext = $line[author];

    // Get author's email
    $query = "SELECT email FROM authors WHERE idx = ";
    $query = $query."\"$authtext\"";

    $authresult = mysql_query($query,$link)
      or die("Query failed: $query");

    $authdata = mysql_fetch_array($authresult, MYSQL_ASSOC);
    $email = $authdata[email];

// Print article
print <<<HTML
<h3>$title</h3>
<p><font size="-2"><b>Posted by:</b>
<a href="mailto:$email">$auths[$authtext]</a>
 <b>on</b> $pubdate <b>at</b> $pubtime</font><br>
```

```
$article</p>
<p><font size="-2"><b>Category:</b> $cats[$cattext]<br></font></p>
<hr width="10%" align="left">

HTML;

    } // End while

} // End if

// Output any errors
if (!empty($error)) {
  print "<h2>$error</h2>";
}

// Close page
print <<<HTML
</body>
</html>
HTML;

?>
```

Figure 29-5 shows an example of a search for "site."

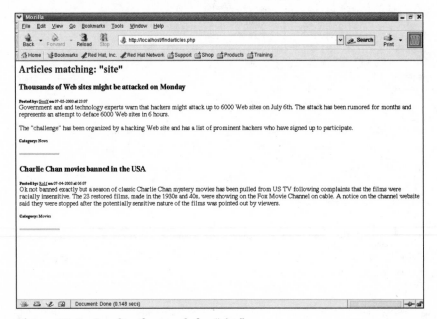

Figure 29-5   *Results of a search for "site"*

Full-Text Index Searches

As of Version 3.23.23, MySQL supports full-text indexing and searching. A full-text index is valuable for numerous reasons, especially the speed at which text can be searched and the results returned.

Before you can utilize a full-text search, you must create the index on the appropriate fields within the appropriate tables. In the case of the publishing system, a full-text index on the `title` and `article` fields of the `articles` table would be the most valuable.

Creating a FULLTEXT Index

To create a full-text index, use the FULLTEXT keyword in your table definition. The FULLTEXT keyword has the following syntax:

```
FULLTEXT (col1,col2,...)
```

For example, to create a full-text index on the `title` and `article` fields of the `articles` table, you would use the following command to create the table (and notice the index creation on the bold line):

```
CREATE TABLE `articles` (
  `idx` int(10) unsigned NOT NULL auto_increment,
  `pubdate` datetime NOT NULL default '0000-00-00 00:00:00',
  `cat` int(10) unsigned NOT NULL default '0',
  `author` int(10) unsigned NOT NULL default '0',
  `title` varchar(80) NOT NULL default '',
  `article` text NOT NULL,
  `publish` tinyint(1) unsigned NOT NULL default '0',
  FULLTEXT(title,article),
  PRIMARY KEY  (`idx`)
) TYPE=MyISAM;
```

To add a full-text index to an existing table, you can use the ALTER TABLE command. For example, to add the full-text index to the existing `articles` table, you would use the following:

```
ALTER TABLE articles ADD FULLTEXT(title,article);
```

Searching a FULLTEXT Index

To search a full-text index, use the WHERE MATCH clause with a SELECT statement. This clause has the following syntax:

```
SELECT ... WHERE MATCH (idx_col1,idx_col2...) AGAINST ('searchtext');
```

The columns specified after the MATCH keyword should correspond to the columns used to create the FULLTEXT index.

For example, to search the new full-text index for `months`, the following SELECT statement is used:

```
SELECT idx,title,article FROM articles WHERE
   MATCH (title,article) AGAINST ('months');
```

This query results in the following data set:

```
+-----+-------------------------------------------------------+
| idx | title                                                 |
+-----+-------------------------------------------------------+
|   7 | Miami running back re-sentenced                       |
|  13 | Thousands of Web sites might be attacked on Monday     |
+-----+-------------------------------------------------------+
2 rows in set (0.00 sec)
```

These articles are returned because `months` appears in the `article` column of both records.

MySQL uses the concept of words to conduct full-text searches. Words are identified by sequences of characters containing letters, digits, apostrophes, or underlines. Notice that this method of searching causes search words such as web **not to match** website. **To match all occurrences of** web, **you must use the wildcard character (*) in your search terms.**

Although the search just described is much faster than a regular WHERE LIKE search, the mechanism and results are much the same. However, you are just beginning to tap the power of full-text searching.

First, the search itself is case-insensitive — you could have searched for Months, MONTHS, or even MoNtHs and found the records you wanted.

Second, the search results are automatically scored by relevance. You can see this if you also return the MATCH in the results:

```
SELECT idx,MATCH (title,article) AGAINST ('months') FROM articles;
+-----+----------------------------------------+
| idx | MATCH (title,article) AGAINST ('months') |
+-----+----------------------------------------+
|   7 |                      0.63740956783295 |
|   8 |                                     0 |
|   9 |                                     0 |
|  10 |                                     0 |
|  11 |                                     0 |
|  12 |                                     0 |
|  13 |                      0.62855195999146 |
+-----+----------------------------------------+
7 rows in set (0.02 sec)
```

This enables the programmer to customize the results the user actually sees.

Third, although this search was a simple natural-language search, MySQL also supports boolean searching. To search in boolean mode, add the IN BOOLEAN MODE to the AGAINST arguments and specify the arguments using one of the modifiers listed in Table 29-1.

Table 29-1 *Boolean Search Modifiers*

Modifier	Meaning
+	Word *must* be present in results
-	Word *must not* be present in results
<	Decreases a word's contribution to the relevance score
>	Increases a word's contribution to the relevance score
~	Reverses the word's contribution to the relevance — that is, the presence of the word decreases the relevance instead of increasing it
*	Used as a wildcard — for example, month* increases the relevance when it encounters month, months, monthly, and so on
"	Used to enclose literal text

You can use parentheses to group words if required.

For example, to find an article that contains website but not Internet, you could use the following query:

```
SELECT idx,title FROM articles WHERE MATCH (title,article)
    AGAINST ('+website -internet' IN BOOLEAN MODE);
```

Modifying the Find Script for Full-Text Searching

To add full-text searching capability to the findarticles.php script discussed in the section "Simple Substring Search," earlier in this session, you would simply make the following change to the $query:

**10 Min.
To Go**

```
$query = "SELECT * FROM articles WHERE publish = \"1\"";
$query = $query." AND WHERE MATCH (title,article) ";
$query = $query." AGAINST ('$findtext' IN BOOLEAN MODE)";
$query = $query." ORDER BY pubdate DESC";
```

This change passes the text contained in $findtext to the BOOLEAN MODE full-text search. The user needs to know how to use the modifiers listed in Table 29-1. It would, therefore, be a good idea to offer help to the user — in the form of text by the search prompt or via a more extensive help file.

In addition, if you use a lot of full-text searches, you might modify the SELECT statement so that the relevance scores are also returned. You can then display the scores for the user.

More information on MySQL full-text searches can be found on the MySQL Web site (www.mysql.com/doc/en/Fulltext_Search.html).

Adding Authentication to Your Scripts

Thanks to PHP's `header()` function, you can easily add authentication to your scripts. The following code causes the browser to display its authentication dialog box:

```
header('WWW-Authenticate: Basic realm="My Realm"');
header('HTTP/1.0 401 Unauthorized');
```

A sample of the authentication dialog box is shown in Figure 29-6.

Figure 29-6   *The browser authentication dialog box*

If the user enters data into the dialog box and clicks OK, the data entered is stored in the PHP variables $_SERVER['PHP_AUTH_USER'] and $_SERVER['PHP_AUTH_PW']. The following script prompts the user and displays the data he or she entered (or displays configurable text if the user cancels):

```php
<?php
  // The realm to display
  $realm = "example.com";

  // The text to trigger auth dialog
  $authtext = "WWW-Authenticate: Basic realm=\"".$realm."\"";

  // Text to display if the user cancels
  $cancel_msg = "Please enter your login info.";

  // If no credentials have been set, display dialog
  if (!isset($_SERVER['PHP_AUTH_USER'])) {
    header($authtext);
    header('HTTP/1.0 401 Unauthorized');
    // If user cancels, print cancel message
    die($cancel_msg);
  } else {
```

```
        // Display authentication info
        $user = $_SERVER['PHP_AUTH_USER'];
        $password = $_SERVER['PHP_AUTH_PW'];
        echo "<p>Hello $user.</p>";
        echo "<p>You entered \"$password\" as your password.</p>";
    }
?>
```

Once the authentication information is entered, the browser caches it until the browser is closed. To force the user to re-authenticate, you can simply redisplay the authentication dialog box.

The password that is entered is not encrypted; it is stored in the PHP_AUTH_PW server variable as plain text. However, if you run the password through the MySQL password() function, you can match it against other passwords similarly encoded.

Using Authentication with PHP and MySQL

To test this method, create a simple database and run your authentication script against it. The database is created with the following MySQL code:

```
CREATE DATABASE testauth;

USE testauth;

GRANT SELECT ON testauth.* TO testuser IDENTIFIED BY "test";
FLUSH PRIVILEGES;

CREATE TABLE users (
  name varchar(40) not null,
  pwd varchar(40) not null
);

INSERT INTO users values ("Sampson",password("Delilah"));
```

The INSERT query creates an entry with the name Sampson and a password of Delilah (which is encoded by MySQL).

Now, modify your authentication script to work with the database:

```
<?php

    // The realm to display
    $realm = "example.com";
    // The text to trigger auth dialog
    $authtext = "WWW-Authenticate: Basic realm=\"".$realm."\"";
    // Text to display if the user cancels
    $cancel_msg = "Please enter your login info.";
    // Clear errors
    $error = FALSE;
```

```php
    // If no credentials have been set, display dialog
    if (!isset($_SERVER['PHP_AUTH_USER'])) {
      header($authtext);
      header('HTTP/1.0 401 Unauthorized');
      // If user cancels, print cancel message
      die($cancel_msg);
    } else {
      // Check authentication info
      $user = $_SERVER['PHP_AUTH_USER'];
      $password = $_SERVER['PHP_AUTH_PW'];

      // Open DB
      $link = mysql_connect("localhost", "testuser", "test")
        or die("Could not connect to MySQL");
      mysql_select_db("testauth")
        or die("Could not select testauth database");

      // Get user info
      $query = "SELECT * FROM users WHERE name = \"$user\"";
      $query = $query." AND pwd = password(\"$password\")";
      $result = mysql_query($query,$link)
        or die("Query failed: $query");

      // If user is not found, generate error
      if (mysql_num_rows($result) == 0) {
        $error = TRUE;
      }
      mysql_close($link);
    }

    if ($error) {
      die("Authentication failed.");
    }

    // Add appropriate code for authenticated users below
    print "Authenticated...";

?>
```

The script is very straightforward — if the user has not authenticated, the script displays the authentication dialog box. The information entered is then compared against the information stored in the database. If the information matches, the script continues; if not, a failure message is displayed and processing halts.

This script is meant to be included in other scripts — it uses die() functions to stop processing and closes the database after it is done reading it. You can use this script (with modifications for your database) by including it at the beginning of any script that needs authentication.

In the case of the scripts discussed in Session 28, this script can also be used to help constrain authors to editing only articles they originally posted. By adding the authentication script to the top of each editing script, you can ensure that each author logs into the system. Then, for each editing function, you can check the value of the $user variable against the author who is stored with each article. If the two match, the user can do whatever he or she likes to the article. If the two do not match, you can constrain the user to whatever degree you wish.

Scalability

If your site is visited frequently (several hundred hits an hour), this project does not scale well. PHP can be kept very busy dishing the same content (article headlines and so on) repeatedly. Despite the intelligent caching included in the PHP engine, the constant churning of code to drive content could bring the server to its knees.

In cases where heavy traffic is expected, you would be wise to construct scripts that build static HTML content from the database instead of always delivering dynamic content. A template would be necessary, with content markers for content instead of SSI calls. A master script would read and parse the template, calling content scripts when necessary. For example, the following code could be placed where the headlines are needed:

```
<!-- CONTENT: HEADLINES -->
```

The master script would simply output any line that didn't contain such a marker to a file. When a marker is encountered, the master script determines what subscript is necessary (in this case, the headline script) and runs the script to generate headlines in the output file. After the template is completely parsed and output to a production file, the new file replaces the old file on the live site.

You could run the master script as an automated process (via command-line PHP) or by an editor after adding several articles. The Web server would do what it is best at: delivering static content to the masses without the constant code churn overhead.

Done!

REVIEW

This session wrapped up the development of your publishing system by creating the user-interface into the system. Several scripts were created to publish the content in the system in a variety of formats. You learned how to implement two different methods of search functions for the user. Last, you learned how to provide authentication routines for your scripts.

The last session of this book also works with the publishing system to create an RSS feed of the content. (RSS can have several meanings; each is described in the next session.)

QUIZ YOURSELF

1. What are some disadvantages to using PHP to publish an entire Web page? (See "Methods of Publishing Dynamic Content.")

2. Why shouldn't you run all HTML files through the SSI processor? (See "Server-Side Includes.")

3. Why should you break out common functions into a library script? (See "Common Library.")

4. What is the benefit of teasers? (See "Teasers.")

5. What is the key benefit of a substring search? (See "Simple Substring Search.")

6. What is the main weakness of a substring search? (See "Simple Substring Search.")

7. How can you increase a word's relevance weight when using a full-text search? (See "Searching a FULLTEXT Index.")

8. How can PHP access the HTTP authentication information? (See "Adding Authentication to Your Scripts.")

Project: Building an RSS Feed

Session Checklist

✔ Understanding RSS feeds

✔ Creating an RSS feed script

✔ Running the feed generator

✔ Accessing additional RSS resources

**30 Min.
To Go**

I n the previous two sessions, you learned how to create a dynamic publishing system to publish dynamic content to your Web site. However, you can also use PHP to publish the same content globally through syndicated RSS feeds.

RSS feeds are the current rage in Web site content — many sites use this mechanism to syndicate their content. This session finishes the coverage of the publishing system by showing you how to utilize RSS feeds to syndicate your content.

What Are RSS Feeds?

Netscape introduced RSS in 1999 as a concept to syndicate content. At that time, RSS stood for *Rich Site Summary*. However, Netscape abandoned the concept in 2001 and UserLand Software began pioneering a similar technology as *Really Simple Syndication*. Still others refer to the RSS concept as *RDF Site Summary*.

In any case, RSS exists as a simple way to syndicate content.

UserLand Software maintains quite a bit of documentation on RSS at the Web site: http://backend.userland.com/rss.

Syndication is a means of distributing content with the intent of allowing others to publish it. Typically, syndication applies to newspaper columns, comics, and other works of art — and generally one derives a fee for each use.

In this case, syndication means an easy method for others to preview your content and optionally republish it. Sites such as slashdot.org, cnet.com, and others use RSS feeds to syndicate their content, as do many Weblog (blog) authors.

RSS Syntax

The syntax for RSS feeds varies considerably depending on the version of RSS that you adhere to. However, the feed is usually published as an XML file with a strict syntax. For example, a typical RSS feed file might resemble the following:

```
<?xml version="1.0"?>
<rss version="2.0">
<channel>
<title>title_of_site</title>
<description>description_of_site</description>
<link>http://link.to.site</link>

<item>
<title>title_of_article</title>
<description>short_desc_of_article  ...</description>
<pubDate>pubdate_in_ RFC 822_format</pubDate>
<link>link_to_article</link>
</item>

<item>
...
</item>

</channel>
</rss>
```

In XML format, the file's headers spell out its content and which version of RSS is being used. The beginning of the <channel> section provides details about the main site, while each <item> section provides details about a particular article. Each feed can have up to 15 <item>s and is generally arranged with the newest article first, the oldest article last. As articles are added to the feed, the older articles are moved off the feed.

Publishing the Feed

The XML file is made accessible via HTTP, and special applications can access the feeds and notify users when the feed is updated. For example, the open source project BottomFeeder can monitor several feeds and even seek out new feeds. Figure 30-1 shows an example of BottomFeeder in action.

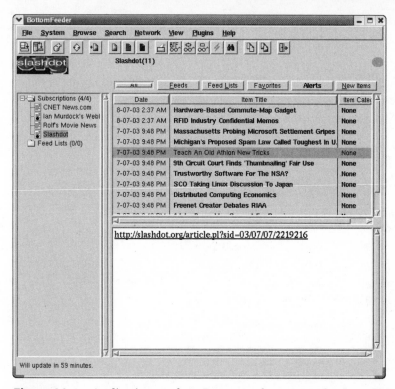

Figure 30-1 *Applications such as BottomFeeder can monitor several RSS feeds.*

You can download BottomFeeder from the BottomFeeder home page at `www.cincomsmalltalk.com/BottomFeeder/`. **Several other applications can monitor RSS feeds as well. Windows users should check out applications such as Trillian (`www.trillian.cc/trillian/index.html`) for monitoring RSS feeds. (The Pro version has a nifty news plug-in.)**

These tools monitor feeds by periodically accessing the RSS feed file and informing the user when the feed file changes. The individual `<item>` blocks are usually displayed for users, who can visit the site or see the complete article by clicking the listing.

Creating an RSS Feed for the Publishing System

**20 Min.
To Go**

Creating an RSS feed from a dynamic content database is actually fairly trivial. All that is required is a query to grab the most recent 15 articles, format them accordingly, and output them to an accessible file on the Web server.

The following script performs this task:

```php
<?php

/* rss-feed.php
   Generate an RSS feed from the publishing system.
*/

// Initialize settings
$rssfilename = "news/rss.xml";
$teaser_words = 20;

include "common_pubsys.php";

// Open DB and init lists/vars
$link = opendb();
$cats = getcats();
$auths = getauths();

// Open RSS file
$rssfile = fopen($rssfilename,"w");

// Build and publish the RSS header
$rsshead = <<<XML
<?xml version="1.0"?>
<rss version="2.0">
<channel>
<title>Sample Newsletter</title>
<description>Newsletter with articles on sports, news, and
movies.</description>
<link>http://www.example.com</link>


XML;
fwrite($rssfile,$rsshead);

// Get 15 most recent articles (published)
$query = "SELECT * FROM articles WHERE publish = \"1\"";
$query = $query." ORDER BY pubdate DESC LIMIT 0,15";
$result = mysql_query($query,$link)
  or die("Query failed: $query");

// Parse results
while ($line = mysql_fetch_array($result, MYSQL_ASSOC)) {
  $idx = $line[idx];
  $temptime = strtotime($line[pubdate]);
  $pubdate = date("r",$temptime);
```

```
    $article = strip_tags($line[article]);
    $title = strip_tags($line[title]);
    $cattext = $line[cat];
    $authtext = $line[author];

    // Generate teaser (1 to $teaser_words of article)
    $words = explode(" ",$article,$teaser_words);
    $teaser = "";
    for ($i = 0; $i < count($words) - 1; $i++) {
      $teaser = $teaser . $words[$i] . " ";
    }

// Build and publish the article (<item>)
$rssitem = <<<XML
<item>
<title>$title</title>
<description>$teaser ...</description>
<pubDate>$pubdate</pubDate>
<link>http://www.example.com/displayarticle.php?idx=$idx</link>
</item>


XML;
  fwrite($rssfile,$rssitem);

}  // End while

// Close open tags
fwrite($rssfile,"</channel>\n</rss>");

// Close file and DB
fclose($rssfile);
mysql_close($link);

?>
```

Figure 30-2 shows the feed being monitored by BottomFeeder.

Notice that the script creates a file named xml.rss in a news subdirectory. You need to provide appropriate write access to this directory for the script. If you run this script from Apache, you need to assign write access to the user under which the Apache server runs. If you run the script from the command line, you need to provide write access for the user who runs the script.

This script utilizes the here document format for assigning variables. This technique is valuable when you need to output complex or highly formatted text through a mechanism such as fwrite().

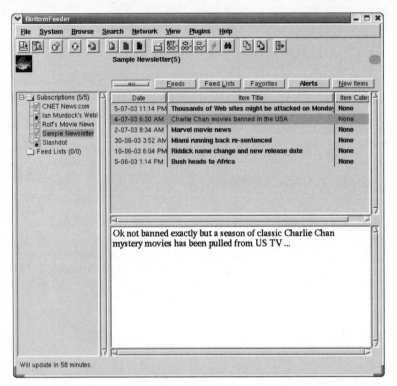

Figure 30-2   *Our RSS feed in BottomFeeder*

When to Run the RSS Generator

The easiest way to implement this script is by calling it from the article maintenance script whenever a new article is posted.

   The article maintenance script is discussed in detail in Session 28.

However, this use of the script does pose a few problems. For example, what happens when two authors publish articles almost simultaneously? A slim possibility exists that two instances of the RSS script may run simultaneously and the rss.xml file can be damaged in the collision.

A better way to implement this script is to run it on a regular basis from the command line via an automated process. For example, if you are running on Linux, you can place the script in your crontab as follows:

```
*/20 * * * *   nobody   /usr/local/php/bin/php /var/www/cgi-bin/rss-feed.php
```

This line causes the script to run every 20 minutes as the user nobody.

You can omit specifying the PHP engine in the command if you place the appropriate handler call at the top of the script:

```
#! /usr/local/php/bin/php
```

However, that limits the script's accessibility — it can no longer be run via the browser. Running the script manually through the engine enables you to keep the script accessible to be run from Apache if necessary.

Windows 2000 users can use the AT command to specify that the script should run periodically.

**10 Min.
To Go**

Additional RSS References

Although RSS has been around a while and several standards and specifications explain how to utilize it, you can also use many variations and options.

The main resource for RSS feeds is the UserLand Software Web site, which provides several specification listings, how-to tutorials, and more. Visit `http://backend.userland.com/rss` to get started.

After you have generated an RSS feed, it pays to validate it using an online tool such as the one at archive.org (`http://feeds.archive.org/validator/`). The validator helps you identify problems in your feed before they are discovered by users.

Finally, if your content is truly valuable, publicize it with a listing service. Danny Sullivan, an editor for SearchEngineWatch.com, has a great piece on getting your RSS feeds published. You can find his article at `http://searchenginewatch.com/sereport/article.php/2175281`.

Done!

REVIEW

This last session showed you how to widely publish content using PHP. You learned about the RSS protocol, the syntax of RSS files, and how easy generating a feed with PHP can be. You also learned the various ways to run the script that generates the feed.

This lesson wraps up coverage of Apache, MySQL, and PHP. Starting with installing the technologies, you learned how to get them to work together and examined a few useful projects showcasing how the technologies work together.

QUIZ YOURSELF

1. What is RSS? (See "What Are RSS Feeds?")
2. What is the value of syndication? (See "What Are RSS Feeds?")
3. How many <item> blocks can you have in an RSS feed? (See "RSS Syntax.")
4. What's the syntax of a here document assignment? (See "Creating an RSS Feed for the Publishing System.")
5. Why should you use a validation tool on your feeds? (See "Additional RSS References.")

## VI

Sunday Afternoon
Part Review

1. What is wrong with the following code?

```
$key = 225;
global $key;
```

2. Where is the Server-Side Includes Apache module stored?

3. What is the advantage of using PHP and MySQL to deploy content?

4. Should you follow standard, "good" database design when creating a dynamic content database?

5. What is the advantage of using a here document form of the assignment operator in PHP?

6. What is meant by "the script calls itself iteratively"?

7. How would you determine whether the following button was clicked on a form when the form data is passed to a PHP script as POST data?

```
<input type="submit" name="Guess" value="Guess">
```

8. What is the meaning of *state* when referring to a multipurpose PHP script?

9. What does the PHP variable $_SERVER['PHP_AUTH_USER'] reference?

10. What is a good PHP language construct to use when deciding what function(s) to perform based on a single state value?

11. Will a substring search on "%vior" find the word "Behavior?" Will a substring search for "Cat%" find "category"?

12. What are the two problems with the following code?

```
print <<<HTML
// Start the table and print header row
<table width="75%">
  <tr>
    <td>Sunday</td>
    <td>Monday</td>
    <td>Tuesday</td>
```

```
        <td>Wednesday</td>
        <td>Thursday</td>
        <td>Friday</td>
        <td>Saturday</td>
      </tr>
      HTML;
```

13. Why would you want to nest functions (definitions) within each other?

14. Why would you use the PHP `include_once()` function instead of the `include()` function?

15. What is the advantage of assigning date ranges to the content generated by dynamic content publishing scripts?

16. What do you have to add to INSERT and UPDATE queries when a table contains a FULLTEXT index?

17. How long do most Web browsers cache authentication information?

APPENDIX

A

Answers to Part Review Questions

Following are the answers to the Review questions at the end of each part of the book.

Friday Evening Review Answers

1. Hypertext Transport Protocol, or HTTP, is a protocol that was designed to deliver Web content.

2. Yes, and PHP is managed by the Apache Project.

3. On Windows, look in the directory `\Program Files\Apache Group\Apache2\logs` on the drive on which you installed Apache2. On Linux, look in the directory `/var/log/httpd` or the `logs` subdirectory of the directory in which you installed Apache2. If all else fails, look at the `ErrorLog` and `CustomLog` entries in the Apache configuration file (`httpd.conf`).

4. At the time of this writing, the MySQL AB site had the current production version, an alpha version of the next release, and one prior release. Windows users can download a version of each, with or without an installer. Linux users can download a Standard, Max, or Debug copy of each.

5. `mysql` and `test`

6. MySQL is a complex application that is typically relied on to provide bulletproof data storage and recovery. MySQL AB recommends that you use its compiled binary versions to ensure the stable operation of MySQL.

7. Port 80

8. It depends on your installation method — sometimes prerequisite users and groups are installed for you. However, it is advisable to create a MySQL user and group on Linux to run the server under.

9. It depends on how Apache was installed. On Windows, look in the `\Program Files\Apache Group\Apache2\bin` directory on the drive in which you installed Apache. Look for the file `Apache.exe`. On Linux, look for `httpd` or `apache` in directories such as `/usr/bin` or `/usr/local/bin`.

10. Apache uses MIME types to determine how to deliver various content.

11. On Linux and Windows, the `mysqladmin` script exists to handle command-line administration of MySQL.

12. On Windows, check the status of Apache using the Apache Service Monitor, accessible from the Start menu. On Linux, use the `ps` command to determine whether the server is running (`ps -A | grep "http"`).

13. Because the server installs without an administrative password, you should secure your server immediately after installation.

14. On Windows, use the Apache Service Monitor or the commands on the Start menu (Start ⇨ Programs ⇨ Apache HTTP Server ⇨ Control Apache Server). On Linux, use the `apachectl` script.

15. MySQL AB.

16. No. Most distributions of Linux ship with a version of PHP, but to date no version of Windows ships with PHP.

17. A multitude of platforms are supported by the Apache Project, including Linux, Windows, BeOS, Macintosh, Solaris, Unix, BSD, OS2, and more.

18. On Linux, add the following lines to the Apache configuration file (`httpd.conf`):

```
LoadModule php4_module modules/libphp4.so
AddType application/x-httpd-php .php .phtml
```

On Windows, add the following lines to the Apache configuration file (`httpd.conf`):

```
LoadModule php_module c:\<php-version>\sapi\php4apache2.dll
AddType application/x-httpd-php .php .phtml
```

Note that in both cases the path to the PHP module might be different.

Saturday Morning Review Answers

1. Web servers present a security risk because of the rich amount of content they can provide — typically through plug-ins and add-ons. Exploitable bugs also are occasionally found in them. Each additional protocol or open port presents another potential security risk.

2. On Windows, check the WinMySQLadmin icon in the tray on the system task bar — a green light means the server is running. (You can run WinMySQLadmin by double-clicking its icon in Windows Explorer.) On Linux, use the `ps` command to determine whether the server is running (`ps -A | grep "mysql"`).

3. As many columns as the table contains.

4. The Apache project's home page (`www.apache.org`), THAWTE (`www.thawte.com`), CERT (`www.cert.org`), and other third-party sites such as SecuritySpace (`www.securityspace.com`).

5. phpinfo();

6. The fact that it is widely used (so vulnerabilities are found quickly), updated regularly, and contributed to by a multitude of open-source programmers.

7. The following column would work:

   serial_num INT(7) UNSIGNED ZEROFILL AUTO_INCREMENT PRIMARY KEY

8. It is possible, if a vulnerability exists. Permission problems, misbehaving applications and scripts, and some plug-ins can all create such vulnerabilities.

9. Because several Apache security and access files (for example, .htaccess) begin with .ht.

10. One method is to place the following in the Apache configuration file (httpd.conf):

    ```
    <Directory directory_path>
    Order deny,allow
    Deny from all
    Allow from FQDN
    </Directory>
    ```

    Substitute the path to the directory for directory_path, and the server's fully qualified domain name (for example, example.com) for FQDN.

    A second method is to ensure that the directory (or the full server) has an AllowOverride ALL or AllowOverride LIMIT directive and to place the following lines inside an .htaccess file in the directory:

    ```
    Order deny,allow
    Deny from all
    Allow from FQDN
    ```

    Substitute the server's fully qualified domain name (for example, example.com) for FQDN.

11. SQL stands for *Structured Query Language* and is a standard language used to query databases. MySQL is SQL-compliant.

12. cgi-bin.

13. Add the following line to the end of the CREATE TABLE statement:

    PRIMARY KEY (column_names)

    Here *column_name* is the name of the column name(s) you want contained in the index.

14. A user needs SELECT privileges to access a database and select data.

15. You should use a CHAR data type when storing a single letter — specifically defined with CHAR(1). Other types require more storage; for example, a VARCHAR type would store two characters: one for the actual character and a second to define the length of the field.

16. The year 2001.

17. You would use the ALTER TABLE command with the following syntax:

    ALTER TABLE ADD [COLUMN] create_definition [FIRST | AFTER column_name]

18. No. Although the difference between MySQL and the SQL standard is shrinking, there are still notable differences (such as the capability to double-quote strings in MySQL queries).

19. When you supply values for *all* columns in a table, in the exact order that they appear in the table.

20. The order in which the columns appear in the table(s) being queried.

21. Yes. The wildcard % will match zero or more characters.

Saturday Afternoon Review Answers

1. This command shows you an appropriate CREATE TABLE statement to create the table specified.

2. The formatting of queries is a subjective preference, but the following format enables you to easily see the different elements of the query:

```
SELECT comp_id, comp_cpu, comp_speed
  FROM computers, mice
  WHERE mouse_comp = comp_id
    AND mouse_type != "PS2"
    AND comp_location = "B%";
```

3. The percentage sign (%) is a wildcard that can be used with a LIKE clause to mean zero or more characters.

4. The following command can be used to quickly output a database's structure and data:

```
mysqldump -p --add-drop-table --databases database_name >backup.sql
```

5. You can add as many as you like. However, each type that you add must be processed by the PHP engine before it is passed to the client browser — whether it actually contains any PHP code or not.

6. There are no values between the parentheses, so this call does not pass any arguments to the function. If the function requires arguments, this call generates an error.

7. Here is an example procedure:

    a. Visit the PHP site (www.php.net).

    b. Enter "swfsprite" in the Search For field at the top of the page.

    c. Select "function list" from the In The drop-down list.

    d. Press Enter or click the arrow to the right of the drop-down list.

8. The most effective way to use the MySQL monitor to troubleshoot MySQL is by using it to run sample queries. You can also use queries to output the contents of tables, table definitions, and more.

9. A user-defined function can have zero or more arguments defined.

10. Either of the two following methods returns the value of the equation x * y + 32:

```
return (x * y + 32);
```

    or

```
$temp = x * y + 32;
return ($temp);
```

The second method is generally preferred because it keeps the equation a bit more isolated and hence legible.

11. To pipe files to the MySQL monitor, you use standard redirection characters for your operating system, generally <. For example, to pipe the file `sample.sql` to the monitor, you would use the following:

```
mysql -p <sample.sql
```

12. The following function would work:

```
function start_html ($title, $bodyargs = "") {
  print "<html>\n<head>\n";
  print "\t<title>$title</title>\n";
  print "</head>\n";
  print "<body $bodyargs>\n";
}
```

13. The `func_num_args()` function returns the number of arguments passed to a function.

14. You can use all of the language's capabilities (such as integration with MySQL) from the command line.

15. The first time the function is called, it prints `$val + 21`. The second time the function is called, it prints `$val + 22`. The third time the function is called, it prints `$val + 23`, and so on. The `static` command sets a variable's value and maintains the variable through several calls to the function. Thus $num begins as 20 and has its value preserved, so it is 21 on the second call, 23 on the third, and so on.

16. The `else()` function executes a block of code if the expression in the matching `if()` is FALSE. The `elseif()` function also executes if the expression in the matching `if()` is FALSE, but enables you to specify an expression to evaluate that determines whether the block of code after the `elseif()` is executed.

17. The purist answer is "wherever you need it." However, it generally appears at the end of each `case()` section.

18. An inner join or equi-join returns data from two or more tables in which values of a column in one table match values of a column in another table.

19. The following function would work:

```
function getstate($abbr) {
  $states = array ("AL" => "ALABAMA ","AK" => "ALASKA ","AZ" =>
"ARIZONA ","AR" => "ARKANSAS ","CA" => "CALIFORNIA ","CO" =>
"COLORADO","CT" => "CONNECTICUT ","DE" => "DELAWARE ","DC" => "DISTRICT
OF COLUMBIA ","FL" => "FLORIDA ","GA" => "GEORGIA ","GU" => "GUAM
","HI" => "HAWAII ","ID" => "IDAHO ","IL" => "ILLINOIS ","IN" =>
"INDIANA ","IA" => "IOWA ","KS" => "KANSAS ","KY" => "KENTUCKY ","LA"
=> "LOUISIANA ","ME" => "MAINE ","MD" => "MARYLAND ","MA" =>
"MASSACHUSETTS ","MI" => "MICHIGAN ","MN" => "MINNESOTA ","MS" =>
"MISSISSIPPI ","MO" => "MISSOURI ","MT" => "MONTANA ","NE" => "NEBRASKA
","NV" => "NEVADA ","NH" => "NEW HAMPSHIRE ","NJ" => "NEW JERSEY","NM"
=> "NEW MEXICO ","NY" => "NEW YORK ","NC" => "NORTH CAROLINA ","ND" =>
"NORTH DAKOTA ","OH" => "OHIO ","OK" => "OKLAHOMA ","OR" => "OREGON
","PA" => "PENNSYLVANIA ","RI" => "RHODE ISLAND ","SC" => "SOUTH
```

```
CAROLINA ","SD" => "SOUTH DAKOTA ","TN" => "TENNESSEE ","TX" => "TEXAS
","UT" => "UTAH ","VT" => "VERMONT ","VA" => "VIRGINIA ","WA" =>
"WASHINGTON ","WV" => "WEST VIRGINIA ","WI" => "WISCONSIN ","WY" =>
"WYOMING");
    return ($states[$abbr]);
```

20. Once.

21. The break() function ends the current loop entirely, whereas the continue() function skips only the current iteration of the loop.

22. As much as you can put in.

23. No. Variables in PHP cannot start with a number.

24. The print() function outputs one string value, whereas the echo() function outputs a list of string values.

25. When you need to escape and/or reference a special character such as a tab (\t), a newline (\n), or a character that might be misunderstood, such as a quote (\").

26. This expression returns the modulus (remainder) of 12 divided by nine, or 3.

27. By joining them into one string. The concatenation operator (.) is a great tool for this purpose.

Saturday Evening Review Answers

1. PHP doesn't control access to its scripts; it processes only what it is told to process. Apache does have simultaneous user limits and could limit how many concurrent PHP scripts are run.

2. Not all operating systems support flock().

3. To change the position of the file data pointer — to read data from or write data to another position in the file.

4. Session data is stored in a file on the server — one file per open session. Each new session is given a unique PHP session number that is stored in a cookie if the user's browser supports cookies; otherwise, it is passed around between scripts via POST or GET.

5. The session_start() call is superfluous; registering a variable in a session automatically starts a session if one isn't already active.

6. By using the unset() function on the appropriate $_SESSION array element. More specifically:

```
unset ($_SESSION['password']);
```

7. To stop tracking session details — perhaps to reinitialize the session — or to free memory a session is using.

8. By encoding the session data with the session_encode() function and writing the resulting coded session data to a file.

9. To keep unscrupulous users from learning the version number of PHP you are running and exploiting its vulnerabilities.

10. The header data must precede any other output. In this case, the `print()` statement would invalidate the header.

11. The data is typically visible to the end user if you use GET (because it is appended to the URL).

12. One way is by using `print()` functions with embedded formatting codes:

```
print "<html>\n\t<body>\n\t\t<table>\n";
print "\t\t\t<tr><td>First Name</td><td>Last Name</td></tr>\n";
print "\t\t\t<tr><td>$fname</td><td>$lname</td></tr>\n";
print "\t\t</table>\n\t</body>\n</html>";
```

A second way is by using the here document print format:

```
print <<<HTML
<html>
  <body>
    <table>
      <tr><td>First Name</td><td>Last Name</td></tr>
      <tr><td>$fname</td><td>$lname</td></tr>
    </table>
  </body>
</html>
HTML;
```

13. So the data that they reference in HTML can be easily referenced in PHP and other scripting languages/tools.

14. It sets the lifetime of a session cookie to 600 seconds (10 minutes). You would use this setting if you wanted to ensure that sessions were tracked (via the session ID stored in a cookie) only for a certain amount of time.

15. By appending it to a URL in standard name/value GET format:

```
<a href="url?fname=$fname">Click here</a>
```

16. The GET method sends the data embedded in the URL; the POST method sends the data encoded in the HTTP header.

17. The data is stored in the superglobal `$_POST` array.

18. The name of the field becomes a key in the `$_POST` array. For example, consider the following field:

```
<input type="text" name="Address">
```

The value of this field is stored in the PHP array element `$_POST['Address']`.

19. When you need to specify the encoded type of the data. This is the case with multipart form data.

20. To ensure that they are correctly closed when you want them to be closed. Although PHP closes any open files and resources on reaching the end of a script, there are no guarantees if PHP encounters an error before it completes that task.

21. The file is open in binary format, its length is set to zero, and the file pointer is set to the beginning of the file.

22. Memory. Reading an entire file into a string occupies at least as much memory as the size of the file.

Sunday Morning Review Answers

1. PHP attempts to close them.

2. An IDE is an Integrated Development Editor. In addition to a capable code editor, such an editor provides a host of tools to manage a project.

3. Virtual hosting is a means to host several domains or Web sites on one physical machine.

4. You should have at least a short block at the beginning with the script's name and purpose, and you should document each program block.

5. Not really, unless the overhead associated with creating a function is more than simply duplicating the code it performs in your script.

6. Because the include() function suspends PHP processing for the included file. In other words, there are implicit ?> and <?php tags around the include() function. This makes it possible to also include HTML files just as easily.

7. You should format HTML just as you would if you weren't using PHP — that is, as legibly as possible.

8. The first step would be to duplicate the code in a comment for safekeeping. Then isolate the code and perform unique tests on it (with preset data and so on) to determine what is wrong. Last, if all else fails, break it apart line by line with ample print statements to determine exactly where the problem is.

9. You can open an error message file and output the errors and diagnostic information to the file.

10. It causes the PHP interpreter to interpret the code passed on the command line. Note that the PHP beginning and ending tags (<?php and ?>) are implicit and will cause an error if they are included on the command line.

11. The mysql_connect() function returns a MySQL link identifier that can be used to reference the connection in other PHP MySQL functions. The mysql_query() function returns a resource referencing the results of the query specified in the function call.

12. It stops the current PHP script and prints the last error encountered on the MySQL connection identified by the variable $link2.

13. The mysql_fetch_array() function always returns an array but can return an array with an associative index, a numeric index, or both.

14. To free memory used by a MySQL query result.

15. The purist answer is because single quotes adhere to the SQL standard. Another reason is that it makes constructing the query in PHP much easier because you typically use double quotes with strings while constructing the query in PHP.

16. When the setting is on, this causes special characters (quotes, backslash, nulls, and so on) to be automatically escaped in GET, POST, and cookie data.

17. Creating a pseudo-form enables you to create the design of a form before coding it into PHP. The result is better-designed forms — both functionally and cosmetically.

18. Grouping global variable definitions enables you to see at a glance which variables are used globally. All global declarations should appear at the beginning of the element to which they apply.

Sunday Afternoon Review Answers

1. The expected result — declaring a global variable and setting its value — does not happen. The global variable must be declared before its value is referenced or changed. Reversing the statements produces the desired and expected result.

2. In the "base" set of Apache modules.

3. You can deploy dynamic content — in various forms — based upon the current user session.

4. You should always follow good database design.

5. You can easily assign lengthy or highly formatted text to a variable. This is especially useful for lengthy queries such as the following:
```
$query = <<<QUERY
SELECT comp_id, comp_cpu, comp_speed
  FROM computer, mice \
  WHERE mouse_comp = comp_id
    AND mouse_type != "PS2"
    AND comp_location = "B%";
QUERY;
```

6. The script calls itself one or more times to perform other operations. In the examples within this book, the iterative calls are typically to perform the next operation in a series of operations.

7. The POST variable corresponding to the name of the field ($_POST['Guess']) is set to the value of the field ("Guess").

8. A script's *state* is defined as a value corresponding to its current function or particular conditions and values, set during the current iteration of the script.

9. The HTTP authentication "user" if it has been entered.

10. The SWITCH construct.

11. Yes and yes. In MySQL, substring searches are not case-sensitive and the wildcard (%) can substitute for zero or more characters.

12. The two problems are as follows:

    ■ The PHP comment appears inside the HTML output and is interpreted by the browser as literal text, not a comment. If you want comments inside HTML code, use the HTML comment tags (<!-- and -->).

    ■ The ending line of the here document print block (HTML;) does not begin in the first column; therefore, it is not recognized as the end of the here document.

13. To improve the organization of your script by combining dependant functions within each other.

14. Whenever there is a danger of a PHP script being included multiple times. For example, if you have a library that several included scripts use (by including it in their code), you could end up with multiple copies of the library loaded inside the parent script.

15. Limiting the amount of output. For example, if the newsletter database contains hundreds of articles, you would want to output only a handful (last few days, weeks, and so on) on a "what's new" page.

16. Nothing. MySQL maintains the FULLTEXT index internally — compiled from the columns the index contains.

17. Until the browser is exited or the information is flushed.

What's on the Companion Web Site

This appendix provides you with information about the contents of the book's companion Web site.

See the Web site for any last-minute information about the actual content on the Web site.

The URL for the book's companion Web site is www.wiley.com/compbooks/schafer.

Code Examples and related information

The Web site contains all the code and database examples used in the sessions of this book.

Code Snippets

Code snippets are provided in a `snippet.txt` text file for each session.

Complete Scripts

Complete scripts are provided in separate files, referenced by the script's name in the session in which it appears.

Example Databases

Example databases are provided in SQL files. These files can be loaded into MySQL by using the MySQL monitor and a command at the command line, such as the following:

```
mysql -p <filename.sql
```

Apache, MySQL, and PHP

Because of the frequency with which these programs are updated, they have not been included on the companion Web site. The first three sessions of this book tell you where to find current versions of each online.

Links, References, and More

The companion Web site also has links to other relevant content on the Web — where to find the latest copies of Apache, MySQL, and PHP, and useful utilities and information. You will also find any corrections to the text or code on the site.

Apache, MySQL, and PHP Weekend Crash Course Assessment Test

The companion Web site includes an assessment test with over 100 multiple-choice questions. You can use this test to assess how much you know about the technologies covered in this book. You are encouraged to take the test before and after reading this book — and then compare your results.

Index

Symbols

\<Directory\> tag, 64
\<DirectoryMatch\> tag, 64
\<Files\> tag, 64
\<FilesMatch\> tag, 64
\<IfDefine\> tag, 65, 66
\<IfModule\> tag, 65–66
\<Location\> tag, 64
\<LocationMatch\> tag, 64
\<mode\> parameter, 206
\<module file\> parameter, 152, 153
\<return_type\> parameter, 277
\<start_record\> parameter, 122
\<VirtualHost\> tag, 64
$action variable, 353
$Add variable, 353
$carry variable, 330
$files array, 268
$_FILES variable, 228
$findtext variable, 346
$PHP_SELF variable, 281
$_post, 224–225
$_POST variable, parsing, 225–226
$_SESSION array, 239, 240
$stalechk variable, 237
$submit_err variable, 337

A

a file open mode, 199
a+ file open mode, 199
AccessFileName directive, 62
access.log file, 54
action parameter, 222
Add/Update state, 348
  coding of, 352
AddIcon directive, 63
AddType directive, 63, 68
AddType lines, 28, 29
administration, with Apache, 47
Advanced Web Statistics (AWStats), 297–298
AFTER column_name parameter, 106
Alias directive, 63
ALL privilege, 92
Allow directive, 66–67
ALTER privilege, 92
ALTER TABLE command, 105–107
  adding columns with, 106
  changing column definitions with, 107
  changing indexes with, 107
  dropping columns with, 107
  positioning elements with, 106
analog, 296, 298
Apache
  access control, 380
  authentication, 73–75
  capabilities of, 7
  checking status of, 48–50
  configuration files on, 152, 153
  control script, 16
  documentation on, 9
  enabling to serve PHP pages, 26–30
  finding configuration options for, 59–60

Continued

Apache (continued)
  HTTP Server Web Site, 9
  individual file names for, 53
  installing
    for Linux, 13–18
    on Windows, 10–13
  instructions for building and installing, 14
  integrating PHP in, 26–30
  and Linux, 7, 13–18
  locating files on, 52–53
  log files, 54
  main configuration file for, 27
  modules directory, 152
  modules included with, 7, 27
  monitoring traffic on, 295
    with Analog, 296
    with AWStats, 297–298
    finding the right log analyzer for, 298–299
    with Webalizer, 297
  Open Source software for, 6
  platforms for, 6
  reasons for using, 5–7
  restarting, 28, 29
  server side includes (SSI) functionality, 384
    Web site for, 385
  Services Admin tool, 51–52
  Software Foundation, 7
  source archives for, 13–16
  source code for, unpacking of, 14
  starting and stopping, 50–52
  starting the server, 16
  status page, 54
  technical support for, 6
  test page, 48, 49
  testing installation of, 18–19
  verifying installation of, 15
  virtual hosting
    monitoring one IP address, 300
    monitoring several IP addresses, 299
    setting up hosts, 300
    of three domains, one IP address, 301–302
    of three domains, three IP addresses, 301
  Web site for, 7, 8, 9
    server-side includes, 385
Apache access control, 380
Apache authentication, securing directories with,
  73–75
Apache Red Hat Package Manager (RPM), 7. *See*
  also **Red Hat**

Apache Service Monitor, 29–30, 49
  starting and stopping Apache with, 50–51
  tray icon, 13
Apache Software Foundation
  Hypertext Preprocessor (PHP). *See* Hypertext
    Preprocessor (PHP)
  projects of, 7
***apachectl* script, 51, 52**
applications
  piggybacked, 48
  search, 53. *See also* search(es)
  telnet, 50
arguments
  call by reference, 190–191
  default, 189
  optional, 189–190
arithmetic operators
  combination assignment operators, 170–171
  integer values, 171
array data type, 167
arrays
  accessing values of, 168
  associate. *See* associative arrays
  removing duplicates from, 224
  two-dimensional, 228
  using $_Session, 239, 240
array_unique() function, 224
article editing scripts
  Add/Update state, 352–353
  Delete state, 353–354
  Edit state, 352
  entering a new article, 369
  Find state, 349–351
  finding an article, 369
  finished listing of, 359–368
  Start state, 349
  updating an existing article, 370
article editor
  adding an article, 348
  editing an article, 348–349
  states of, 348
    Add/Update state, 352–353
    Delete state, 353–354
    Edit state, 352
    Find state, 349–351
    Start state, 349
assignment operator, 170

associative arrays
and `getdate()` function, 304
and parsing return result sets, 281
returning rows in, 277–278
authentication
adding to scripts, 400–401
importance of, 403
dialog box, 400, 402
script modification, 401–402
using with PHP and MySQL, 401–403
authentication dialog box, 400, 402
`AuthName` **directive, 74**
author editing scripts, 375–379
Authorizaton Required page, 75
`AuthType` **directive, 74**
`AuthUserFile` **directive, 74–75**
`auto_increment` **attribute, 99**
auto-register globals, 226–227

B

b **file open mode, 199**
`BEFORE` `column_name` **parameter, 106**
`BETWEEN` **operator, 119**
`BIGINT` **column type, 102–103**
binaries, with Windows versions of MySQL,
81–82
binary archive, downloading, 26
Boolean data type, 167
Boolean search, 398–399
BottomFeeder
downloading, 407
RSS feed in, 410
braces, 177
brackets, for use with form handlers, 224
`break` **command, 182**
`break` **statement, 179**
button form element, 220
browser output of, 222
in code, 221
by reference variable assignment method, 163

C

`-c` **switch, 270**
calendar. *See also* **Dynamic calendar**
application functions, 324–325
appointment editing form, 324
coding of
`appt.php` (day view), 326–330
`calendar.php`, 325–326
with display-only functionality, 326
`editappt.php` (edit appointment), 330
script output, 337–339
database for, 322
day-view page, 323
functions of, 321
shortcomings of, 340
using pop-up windows in, 324
Web design of, 323–324
call by reference, 190–191
category editing scripts, 371–375
`CHAR` **column type, 100**
check box form element, 220
browser output of, 222
in code, 221
returning data with, 223
Choose Destination Location window, 38
`closedir()` **function, 207**
code debugging
determining problems in code, 263
and modular code, 257–263
remote, 266
code libraries, 252–253
files for, 252
referencing, 252
column data
date column types of, 103–104
numeric column types of, 102–103
text column types of, 100–102
column positioning parameters, 106
combination assignment operators, 170–171
command line
running scripts from, 269
switches for, 270
command-line PHP
executing code with, 154
function of, 153
shortcomings of, 154
command-line scripting language, using PHP as,
155–156
commenting code. *See also* **comments**
"Look Here!" comments, 253
placement of comments, 253
standard comment format, 254

comments
C programming-style, 253
defined, 161
guidelines for adding, 162
importance of, 218
inserting in code, 161–162
"Look Here!" comments, 253
placement of, 253
standard format of, 254
comparison operators, 171–172
Comprehensive Perl Archive Network, 293
concatenation operator, 171
conceptual data container, 84
conditional statements
and comparison operators, 172
function of, 175
types of, 176
configuration
of Apache, for server-side includes (SSI)
functionality, 384
Apache files for, 27
of MySQL, on Linux, 80–81
options for, 47
of PHP
in Linux, 152–153
in Windows, 151–152
configuration files
adding correct MIME type to, 29
for Apache, 27
location of, 27, 53
for MySQL, 81
opening, 28
saving, 28
`configure` **command, 14**
Content Publishing project
adding authentication to scripts, 400–401
article editing scripts. *See* article editing scripts
author editing scripts, 375–379
category editing scripts, 371–375
coding article editing scripts
Add/Update state, 352–353
Delete state, 353–354
Edit state, 352
Find state, 349–351
Start state, 349
database for
`articles` table, 343–344
`authors` table, 342
`categories` table, 343

editing tools for
article editor, 348–349. *See also* article editing
scripts
monolithic editor, 347
monolithic scripts, 344
Submit buttons, 345–346
enabling search functionality
with full-text index searches, 397–399
with substring searches, 394–396
methods of publishing dynamic content, 381
outputting a full page, 382–383
with server-side includes (SSI), 384–385
turning PHP on and off, 383–384
and the `printform()` function, 354–359
putting scripts together, 379–380
and RSS. *See* RSS feeds
sample scripts
for category listings, 390–391
for common library, 385–386
for full articles, 386–387
for headlines, 388–389
for teasers, 392–393
system for, 341–342
tools for, 342
using authentication, 401–403
content versioning system, 162
control value, 308
cookies, 237, 238
and HTTP headers, 239
count() function, 139–140
advantages of, 140
`CREATE DATABASE` **command, 97**
`CREATE` **privilege, 92–93**
`CREATE TABLE` **command, 98, 105**
`CREATE TEMPORARY TABLES` **privilege, 92**
Credentials dialog box, 75
`CustomLog` **directive, 63**

D

`-d` **switch, 270**
data. *See also* **data types**
non-ASCII, 48
parsed, 48
requests for, 48
data types
arrays. *See* arrays
changing, 168–169

converting, 169
supported by PHP, 167
testing, 169
database(s)
basic structure of, 83–85
for a calendar project, 322
conceptual data container, 84
construction of relational, 144
CREATE DATABASE command, 97
creating, 87–88, 401
on MySQL, 97–98
creating tables for. *See* MySQL, creating tables
design of, resources on, 144
DROP DATABASE command, 98
dropping, 98
dumping, 149
fields, 84, 85
MySQL. *See* MySQL database(s)
MySQL privileges. *See* MySQL privileges database
nonrepeating data table, 145
normalization of. *See* normalization
records (row), 84, 85
repeating data table, 145
selecting, 275
tables, 83–84, 85
creating, 87–88
displaying, 87, 88
visual representation of, 85
database design, resources on, 144
date() function, 185–186, 209, 215
and error control, 315
uses of, 304
DATE column type, 104
date handling, 304
DATETIME column type, 104
debugging. See code debugging
DECIMAL column type, 103
default argument, 189
default attribute, 99
DefaultType directive, 62
DELETE privilege, 92
DELETE query
syntax for, 124
transforming into SELECT query, 135
using WHERE clauses with, 124

delete state, 348
coding of, 353–354
deny directive, 66–67
DESCRIBE TABLE command, 115
describe <tablename> command, 91
DESCRIBE <tablename>; command, 108, 132
diagnostic output, 269
die() function, 290, 402
directive(s)
access, 66–67
AccessFileName, 62
AddIcon, 63
AddType, 63, 68
Alias, 63
Allow, 66–67
AuthName, 74
AuthType, 74
AuthUserFile, 74–75
common, 61–63
conditional, 65–66
CustomLog, 63
DefaultType, 62
delimiting, 64
Deny, 66–67
DocumentRoot, 30, 62
ErrorLog, 62
HostnameLookups, 62
in httpd.conf file, 60–61
Include, 63
KeepAlive, 62
Listen, 62
LoadModule, 62
LogFormat, 54, 63
LogLevel, 54, 63
PidFile, 61
Require, 74
scoping tags for, 64–65
ScriptAlias, 63
ServerAdmin, 62
ServerAlias, 300
ServerName, 62
ServerRoot, 61
splitting, 61
TypesConfig, 62
UseCanonicalName, 62
used by <Directory> section, 74–75
UserDir, 62

directories
  installing with Apache, 52–53
  making, 206–207
  reading contents of, 207–208
  removing, 207
`do while` **loop, 181**
document root, location of, 53
documentation, 254
`DocumentRoot` **directive, 30, 62**
`doquery()` **function, 280**
`DOUBLE` **column type, 103**
double data type, 167
`DROP DATABASE` **command, 98**
`DROP` **privilege, 92**
`DROP TABLE` **command, 108**
dynamic calendar. *See also* **calendar**
  calendar code
    `calendar.php`, 309–315
    explanation of, 315–316
    script output, 314–315
  components of, 305–308
  control value, 308
  data and state, 308
  functions of, 303
  pseudo-form for, 307
  pseudo-table for, 305–307

dynamic content, methods of publishing, 381
  outputting a full page, 382–383
  with server-side includes (SSI), 384–385
  turning PHP on and off, 383–384

E

`echo` **function, 216**
  versus `print` function, 164
  using escape characters with, 165–166
  using quotes with, 164–165
edit button, 345
edit state, 348
  coding of, 352
editing scripts
  article. *See* article editing scripts
  author, 375–379
  category, 371–375
`else` **statement**
  and `if` statements, 177–178
  syntax of, 177, 178
`elseif` **statement, 178**

Emacs, 250
`ENUM` **(enumerated) column type, 101**
equal signs, use of, 172
equi-joins, 141–142
error component, 228
error-handling function, 266–267
error trapping, 290
`ErrorLog` **directive, 62**
`error.log` **file, 54**
`error_log()` **function, 265–266**
`error_reporting()` **function, 264–265, 288**
errors
  avoiding, 288–289
  report of, 287–288, 290
  testing for, 290
  trapping of, 290
escape characters
  common, 165
  and quotes, 165, 166
  syntax of, 165
executables, 53
`expose_php` **setting, 214**
extension, with Apache, 47

F

`fclose()` **function, 200**
`feof()` **function, 202**
`fgets()` **function, 201, 202**
file(s)
  accessing with file pointer, 204–205
  closing in PHP, 200
  for code libraries, 252
  configuration of, 53
  deleting, 206
  document root, 53
  executables, 53
  importance of changing names of, 230
  information functions
    code for, 209–210
    code output, 211
    list of, 208–209
  locking. *See* file locking
  log, 53
  modules, 53
  opening in PHP
    in binary mode, 199
    modes for, 198–199
    in text mode, 199

reading from
    using `fgets()` function, 201, 202
    using `fread()` function, 201–202, 204
reading one character at a time, 205
uploading. *See* file uploads
writing to, 200–201
file browser, 24
file handler, creating, 229
file locking, 205–206, 235
    clearing stale locks, 237
    determining if a file is locked, 234–235
    using a lock file, 236
    using `flock()` function, 236
File Manager interface, 156
file operations, with PHP, 197–198
file pointer
    defined, 204
    positioning, 204–205
`FILE` **privilege, 92**
file uploads, 227
    `$_FILES` variable components for, 228
    basic form for, 229
    controlling amount of uploaded information, 228
    creating file handler for, 229–230
    and user ID, 230
`fileatime(<file>)` **function, 209**
`filectime(<file>)` **function, 209, 237**
`filemtime(<file>)` **function, 209**
`file_exists(<file>)` **function, 208**
files. *See* **file(s)**
`filesize()` **function, 204**
`filesize(<file>)` **function, 209**
`filetime()` **function, 209**
find application, 53
Find button, 345
Find state, 348
    coding of, 349–351
    display of, 351
    functionality of, 351
`FIRST` **parameter, 106**
`FLOAT` **column type, 103**
`flock()` **function, 205–206, 236**
    syntax for, 205
    valid modes for, 205
`flush privileges` **command, 93**
`fopen()` **function, 199**
`for` **loop**
    execution of, 181
    structure of, 181–182
    syntax for, 181

`foreach()` **function, 315**
`foreach()` **loop, 225, 226**
form handlers, 222–223
    and `$_post` variable, 224–225
    and auto-register globals, 226–227
    and file uploads, 227–230
    information from, 225
    output from sample data, 227
    use of brackets with, 224
`fread()` **function, 201–202, 204**
`fseek()` **function, 204, 205**
full-text searches, 397–400
`FULLTEXT` **index**
    creating, 397
    searching, 397–399
`function(s)`
    advantages of using, 252
    application, 324–325
    and arguments. *See* function arguments
    `array_unique()`, 224
    basics of, 185–186
    built-in, 186–187
    `closedir()`, 207
    `count()`, 139–140
    `date()`, 185–186, 209, 215
        and error control, 315
        uses of, 304
    `die()`, 290, 402
    `doquery()`, 280
    `echo`, 216
        versus `print` function, 164
        using escape characters with, 165–166
        using quotes with, 164–165
    error-handling, 266–267
    `error_log()`, 265–266
    `error_reporting()`, 264–265, 288
    evaluation precedence of, 186
    `fclose()`, 200
    `feof()`, 202
    `fgets()`, 201, 202
    file information, 208–210
    `fileatime(<file>)`, 209
    `filectime(<file>)`, 209, 237
    `File_exists(<file>)`, 208
    `filemtime(<file>)`, 209
    `filesize()`, 204
    `filesize(<file>)`, 209
    `filetime()`, 209

Continued

function(s) (continued)

flock(), 205–206, 236
    syntax for, 205
    valid modes for, 205
fopen(), 199
foreach(), 315
fread(), 201–202, 204
fseek(), 204, 205
fwrite(), 200, 409
get_data(), 336
getdate(), 304
getgraphics(), 263
getpost(), 346
gettype(), 169
get_vars(), 315, 329
global(), 329
guidelines for use of, 186
header(), 214–215, 400
include(), 217, 252, 253, 385
    for adding libraries, 269
    multiple uses of, 383
include_once(), 252, 383
is_boolean(), 169
is_dir(<path>), 209
is_double(), 169
is_executable(<*file*>), 209
is_file(<*file*>), 208
is_integer(), 169
is_readable(<*file*>), 209
is_string(), 169
is_uploaded_file, 230
is_writable(<*file*>), 209
mkdir(), 206–207
move_uploaded_file, 230
mysql_affected_rows(), 283
mysql_change_user(), 284
mysql_close(), 274–275
mysql_connect(), 273–274, 289, 291
mysql_create_db(), 284
mysql_data_seek(), 277, 278, 281
mysql_drop_db(), 284
mysql_errno(), 284
mysql_error(), 284, 290
mysql_fetch_array(), 277–278, 289
mysql_fetch_field(), 284
mysql_fetch_object(), 284
mysql_fetch_row(), 276
mysql_num_rows(), 277, 283
mysql_pconnect(), 284

mysql_ping(), 284
mysql_query(), 275–276
mysql_select_db(), 275
mysql_stat(), 284
nesting functions within, 186
opendir(), 207
parseresults(), 280
password(), 401
pg_free_result(), 283
PHP directory
    making directories, 206–207
    reading contents of directories, 207–208
    removing directories, 207
PHP file information
    code for, 209–210
    code output, 211
    list of, 208–209
phpinfo(), 224
print
    versus echo function, 164
    using escape characters with, 165–166
    using here document syntax with, 166
    using quotes with, 164–165
print(), 202, 215, 216
print_appt(), 336, 337
printform()
    calling, 352
    code for, 354–358
    for Content Publishing project, 354–359
printgraphics(), 263
print_list, 336
purpose of, 185
readdir(), 207
replacement of, 260
require(), 252
require_once, 252
rmdir(), 207
session_decode(), 241
session_destroy(), 240
session_encode(), 241
session_id(), 241
session_register, 239
session_start(), 239
session_unregister(), 240
set_date(), 316
set_error_handler(), 266–267
settype(), 169
static, 192
stripslashes(), 289

strip_tags(), 353
syntax for defining, 187–188
testing of, 291
trigger_error(), 267
unlink(), 206
Use, 260
user-defined, 187–192. *See also* user-defined
  functions
usleep(), 236
var_dump(), 268
variable scope, 191–192
  global scope, 192
  local scope, 192
write_appt(), 337
function arguments
  call by reference, 190–191
  default, 189
  optional, 189–190
fwrite() function, 200, 409

G

get_data() function, 336
getdate() function, 304
getgraphics() function, 263
getpost() function, 346
gettype() function, 169
get_vars() function, 315, 329
global() function, 329
global scope, 192
Gopher protocol, 47
GRANT command, 92–93
  and column privileges, 94
  operations performed by, 93
GRANT privilege, 92
graphical interface window, for MySQL, 42–43
grep command, 253
GROUP BY clause, 140
gzipped tarball, 13

H

hackers, protection against, 48
header(s)
  automatic HTML, 213–214
  content, 214–215
  Status, 215
  use of header() function, 214–215, 400
  WWW-Authenticate, 215

header() function, 214–215, 400
help option, 23
here document approach, 216
here document output, 166
here document print statement, 382
hidden form element, 220
  in code, 221
  returning data with, 223
hidden tags, 228
HostnameLookups directive, 62
.htaccess files, 71
  with securing directories, 72–73
HTML
  automatic headers, 213–214
  creating template files for, 253
  directory location, 30
  dynamic calendar. *See* dynamic calendar
  editing tools for, 383
  formatting conventions for, 217–218
  forms. *See* HTML forms
  other headers, 214–215
  outputting, 382–383
  outputting large blocks of
    with here document approach, 216
    with the include() function, 217
    with numerous print() functions, 215–216
    by turning PHP processing off, 216
  placing hidden tags in, 228
  removing tags in, 353
  static versus dynamic content, 403
  for substring searches, 394–396
HTML forms
  and file uploads, 227–230
  form actions, 222–223
  form handler, 222–223
  hidden fields, 224
  and PHP. *See* Hypertext Preprocessor (PHP), form
    data handling
  return of data, 223
  standard elements of, 219–222
.htpasswd file, creating, 73–74
HTTP. See HyperText Transfer Protocol (HTTP)
HTTP headers
  and command-line scripting applications, 155
  and cookie operations, 239
  and PHP interpreter, 155
HTTP Server Project, 7–8
HTTP servers, understanding, 47–48
httpd script, 52

httpd.conf ***file, 59–60***
    directives in, 60–63
    editing, 27
    for locating root directory, 30
    location of, 27
    updating on Windows, 28
Hypertext Preprocessor (PHP)
    accessing files with
        opening files, 198–199
        reading from a file, 201–204
        steps for, 198
        using file pointer, 204–205
        writing to a file, 200–201
    adding authentication to scripts, 400–401
    Apache module, 27, 28
    arrays. *See* arrays
    basic script syntax
        beginning and ending tags, 159–160
        command termination character, 160
        comments in, 161–162
        using quotes in, 164–165
        and white space, 160–161
    building code with, 249
        good habits for, 254–255
        guidelines for, 251
        importance of consistency in, 251–252
        text editors for, 250
        using functions for, 252
    built-in functions, 186–187
    by reference variable assignment method, 163
    calendar code, 309–315
    checking configuration of
        in Linux, 152–153
        in Windows, 151–152
    checking for latest version of, 24
    Classes Repository, 295
    closing files with, 200
    code building, finding errors in code, 263
    code libraries, 252–253
    command-line, 153–154, 269–270
    as a command-line scripting language, 155–156
    command line switches, 270
    commenting code, 253–254
    compiling for Linux, 23–24
    conditional statements
        and comparison operators, 172
        types of, 176
    constructing forms with, 305

creating dynamic content in. *See* dynamic
        calendar
data locking schemes, 236
    for clearing stale locks, 237
    with flock() function, 236
    with a lock file, 236
data types, 167–169
    changing, 168–169
date handling, 304
debugging code in. *See* code debugging
default configuration file, moving to correct
        location, 23
default options, 23
deleting files with, 206
deploying dynamic content with. *See* Content
        Publishing project
diagnostic output, 269
directory functions
    making directories, 206–207
    reading contents of directories, 207–208
    removing directories, 207
downloading for, 26
error code constants, 264
error control, 264–265
error handling, 266–267
evaluation precedence, 186
Extension and Application Repository (PEAR), 294
features of, 21–22
file documentation, 254
file information functions
    code for, 209–210
    code output, 211
    list of, 208–209
file operations with
    and data storage, 197
    guidelines for, 198
    and system security, 197
form data handling
    with auto-register globals, 226–227
    and file uploads, 227–230
    parsing $_post, 224–226
4.x executable, 154
functions. *See* function(s)
and here document output, 166
hiding, 214
HTML constructs
    automatic HTML header, 213–214
    formatting conventions, 217–218

other, HTML headers, 214–215
outputting large HTML blocks, 215–217
installation of
   on Linux, 24–26
   materials for, 22–24
   on Windows, 26
installing from a native package, 24
installing to another directory, 23
Integrated Development Environments (IDEs)
   for, 250
interacting with MySQL, 273–274
interpreter
   exiting, 154
   HTML header and, 155
   interactive mode, 154
   Script Interpreter, 156
libraries, 293–295
   Web sites for, 293, 294, 295
licensing fee for, 22
locating files with, 205–206
logging errors on, 266
and MIME, 68
module used for, 151–152
New York PHP, 295
object-oriented, 295
old hit counter example
   possible consequences of, 235
   the problem, 233–235
   solution to, 234
operators, 169
   arithmetic operators, 170–171
   assignment operator, 170
   comparison operators, 171–172
   concatenation operator, 171
   logical operators, 172
   precedence of, 173
outputting data with, 164–166
passing queries to MySQL server, 275
processor, 29
programming blocks, 175–176
programming loops, 180–182. *See also* loop(s)
   changing execution of, 182
   discontinuing, 182–183
pseudocoding calendars in, 305–308
pseudo-PHP, 308–309
reading files one character at a time, 205
scalability of, 403
sending errors to a file, 265–266
Session ID (SID), 241

sessions
   checking register status with, 240
   configuration options, 237–238
   destroying, 240
   encoding and saving session data, 241
   mechanics of, 237
   passing IDs between scripts, 240–241
   registering variables with, 239
   starting, 239
   unregistering variables with, 240
   use of, 237–241
single versus double quotes in, 289
source files for, 23, 28
superglobal variables in, 225, 228
switch command, 178–180
testing installation of, 30–31
turning on and off, 383
turning processing on and off, 160, 216
updating
   on Linux, 27–28
   on Windows, 28–30
using authentication with, 401–403
using escape characters on, 165–166
variable names
   conversion of, 163–164
   denotation of, 162
   functions of, 163
   use of quotes with, 163
Web site for, 22, 23
working with Apache, 26–30
HyperText Transfer Protocol (HTTP)
   and Multipurpose Internet Mail Extensions
      (MIME), 48
   and server-side scripting, 21
   Server Web site for, 9
   over TCP, 48
   understanding, 47–48

I

`-i` **switch, 270**
`IDE.PHP`**, 250**
`if` **statement**
   defined, 176
   and `else` statement, 177–178
   `elseif` option for, 178
   `FALSE` evaluation of, 177

Continued

if statement (continued)
     placing within a for statement, 182
     syntax of, 176
     TRUE evaluation of, 177
     valid expressions of, 176
image form element
     browser output of, 222
     in code, 221
include directive, 63
include() function, 217, 252, 253, 269, 385
     for adding libraries, 269
     multiple uses of, 383
include_once() function, 252, 383
indentations, importance of, 218
indexes
     changing in tables, 107
     creating on columns, 104–105
     primary key, 105
INDEX privilege, 92
informational commands, 108
init script, 52
inner joins (equi-joins), 141–142
InnoDB, 33
InnoDB storage engine, 80
InnoDB table format, 99
INSERT privilege, 92
INSERT query
     adding data with, 113–115
     alternative syntax for, 115
     omitting (column list) parameter from, 114
     with resulting errors, 115
installation
     of Apache
         for Linux, 13–18
         testing for, 18
         on Windows, 10–13
     of Hypertext Preprocessing (PHP)
         on Linux, 24–26
         from a native package, 24
         testing for, 30–31
         on Windows, 26
     of MySQL
         on Linux, 35–37
         testing for, 42–45
         on Windows, 37–42
INT (integer) column type, 102
integer data type, 167

integer values, 171
Integrated Development Environment (IDE), 250
IP address(es)
     configuring with multiple domains, 301–302
     monitoring one, 300
     monitoring several, 299
     sharing domains on, 299
is_boolean() function, 169
is_dir(<path>) function, 209
is_double() function, 169
is_executable(<file>) function, 209
is_file(<file>) function, 208
is_integer() function, 169
is_readable(<file>) function, 209
is_string() function, 169
is_uploaded_file function, 230
is_writable(<file>) function, 209

J

Java applet repositories, 293
joins, 140
     defined, 124
     equi-joins, 141–142
     outer join, 142–144

K

KeepAlive directive, 62
KPHPDevelop, 250

L

-l switch, 270
LAST parameter, 106
left join, 143, 144
libphp4.so module, 27
libraries
     Classes Repository, 295
     multiple appearances of, 383
     PHP Extension and Application Repository
         (PEAR), 294
     at PHPBuilder.com, 294
     sample scripts for, 385–386
     Web sites for, 293
license agreement, confirming acceptance of, 11

LIMIT clause
    <start_record> parameter, 122
    limiting results with, 121–122
    syntax for, 121
line breaks
    formatting queries with, 134
    importance of, 218
Linux
    <mode> parameter, 206
    and Apache, 7
    checking configuration of PHP on, 152–153
    configuration of MySQL on, 80–81
    and database names, 97
    directory contents on, 207–208
    distributions of, 9
    downloads for, 9
    Emacs, 250
    and Hypertext Preprocessor (PHP), 22
    installing Apache for
        from source, 13–16
        from packages, 16–18
    installing MySQL on, 35–37
    installing PHP on, 24–26
    main Apache HTML directory on, 30
    new line, 201
    PHP 4.*x* executable for, 154
    process status command, 49
    running MySQL server with, 86
    starting and stopping Apache server on, 51
    and telnet applications, 50
    testing installation of MySQL on, 43–44
    text editors for, 250
    tracking code development on, 162
    using MySQL monitor on, 86, 133
    using PHP as a command-line scripting language
        on, 155–156
    vim, 250
listen **directive, 62**
LoadModule **directive, 62**
LoadModule **lines, 27, 28–29**
local scope, 192
locate **application, 53**
lock file, 236
LOCK TABLES **privilege, 92**
lockstep loop, 235
log files, location of, 53
LogFormat **directive, 54, 63**

logical operators, 172
LogLevel **directive, 54, 63**
LONGTEXT **column type, 101**
loop(s)
    changing execution of, 182
    discontinuing, 182–183
    do while loop, 181
    and feof() function, 202
    for loop, 181–182
    function of, 175
    lockstep, 235
    while loop, 180

Ⓜ

magic_quotes_gpc **setting, 288–289**
make **command, 14, 23, 35**
    output of, 15
make install **command, 14, 23, 35**
    output of, 15
MEDIUMINT **column text, 102**
MEDIUMTEXT **column type, 101**
method parameter, 222
Microsoft C++ version 5.0, 9
MIME. *See Multipurpose Internet Mail Extensions (MIME)*
mkdir() **function, 206–207**
modes, for opening files in PHP, 198–199
MODIFY **parameter, 107**
modular code
    example of, 261–263
    techniques for writing
        use functions, 260
        using global variables, 260–261
modules
    directory for, 152
    loading, 152
    location of, 53
    in a Red Hat system, 152
    used for PHP, 22, 151–152
monitors. *See MySQL monitor*
monolithic editor, template for, 347
monolithic script
    basics of, 344–345
    flowchart of, 344
more **command, 23**
move_uploaded_file **function, 230**

Multipurpose Internet Mail Extensions
    (MIME), 48
    function of, 67, 153
    and PHP, 68
    types of, 67–68
`my.cnf` *file, 81*
`my.ini` *Setup tab, 82*
MyISAM table format, 99
`my-huge.cnf` *file, 81*
`my-large.cnf` *file, 81*
`my-medium.cnf` *file, 81*
`my-small.cnf` *file, 81*
MySQL
    accounting functions, 139–140
    ACID guarantee, 33
    altering tables
        adding columns, 106
        `ALTER TABLE` command, 105–107
        changing a table's name, 106
        changing column definitions, 107
        changing indexes, 107
        dropping columns, 107
        positioning columns, 106
    versus Apache, 37
    auto-incremented index (idx), 322
    avoiding errors in, 288–289
    basic information on, 33–34
    binary version of, 37
    boolean searching, 398–399
    calendar project in. *See* calendar
    changing root password for, 45
    Choose Destination Location window, 38–39
    choosing a database for, 87
    compiling for Linux, 35
    configuration of
        binaries for, 81–82
        file templates for, 80–81
        on Linux, 80–81
        with WinMySQL admin, 82
        on Windows, 81–82
    copyright information for, 38
    `count()` function, 139–140
    create statement, 342, 343
    creating a CNF file, 38
    creating an INI file, 38
    creating databases in, 97–98, 322, 401
    creating tables
        column attributes for, 99–100
        column data types, 100–104
        with column indexes, 104–105
        `CREATE TABLE` command, 98
    creation of, 79
    database normalization
        first normal form, 144–145
        second normal form, 145–146
        third normal form, 147
    database project. *See* calendar
    and databases, 83–85. *See also* MySQL
        database(s)
    debugging, 131
    delimiting string values in, 114
    deploying dynamic content with. *See* Content
        Publishing project
    determining affected rows with, 283
    displaying tables, 44
    downloads for, 35
    dropping databases with, 98
    dropping tables in, 108
    error-handling process, 289–291
    full-text searches, 398
        Web site for, 400
    functions of, 283–284
    graphical interface, 42
    history of, 33
    informational commands, 108
    installing
        archive of, 36
        choosing a method for, 34
        client packages, 37
        INSTALL-BINARY, 35
        Linux binary version of, 35–37
        on Linux from package, 36–37
        materials for, 34
        permissions, changing, 36
        README files, 35
        Red Hat system, 36
        server packages, 37
        symbolic mysql link for, 36
        types of installations, 40
        on Windows, 37–42
    integrating with PHP, 33
    mishandling of result sets, 289
    and misunderstanding of queries, 289
    monitor. *See* MySQL monitor

naming tables in, 98
versus Oracle, 33
versus PHP, 37
privilege control, 90–91. *See also* MySQL
    privileges database
and queries, 113
query functions in, 275–276
redisplaying graphical interface on, 42
returning to console prompt, 44
and RPM, 35
as a server. *See* MySQL server
setting password for, 86
setting root password for, 89–90
Server fields, 42
Setup Type window, 40
single versus double quotes in, 289
starting the monitor in, 43–44
stoplight icon, 42
and Structured Query Language, 79
tables supported by, 99
tarballs on, 35
testing installation of, 42–45
testing queries and functions in, 291
TIMESTAMP column in, 114
troubleshooting queries on, 134–136
turning off verbose error reporting in, 287–288
user compilation of, 34–35
using authentication with, 401–403
Web site for, 34
    RPMs on, 37
and Windows Explorer, 40
on Windows NT computer, 38
and WinMySQLAdmin, 40–42
working with, 278–283
MySQL AB
builds of each version of, 34
version 4.0, 80
Web site for, 113
MySQL database(s)
backing up, 147–148
dumping, 149
query interface, 281
querying, 275–276, 281–282
    by resetting the result set pointer, 277
    by returning the result set in an associative
      array, 277–278
    by returning the result set row by row, 276–277
restoring, 148

MySQL 4.0, 80
MySQL monitor
basics of, 132–133
commands of, 132
creating databases on, 87
for debugging MySQL, 131
exiting, 88
functions of, 131
on Linux, 133
logging sessions on, 133
notee command, 133
piping files to, 133–134
prompt for, 87
running, 132
tee command, 133
using, with Linux, 86
viewing database names on, 91
MySQL privileges database
column privileges, 94
and the GRANT command, 92–93
reloading permissions table on, 93
removing UPDATE privileges from, 94
and the REVOKE command, 94
setting and changing user privileges in, 91–94
updating privileges in, 94
user privileges in, 92
MySQL server, 33
connecting to, 273–274
disconnecting from, 274
running
    with Linux, 86
    with Windows, 85
testing connections to, 91
Mysqladmin **command, 90**
mysql_affected_rows() **function, 283**
MYSQL_ASSOC **value, 277, 278**
MYSQL_BOTH **value, 277**
mysql_change_user() **function, 284**
mysql_close() **function, 274–275**
mysql_connect() **function, 273–274, 289, 291**
mysql_create_db() **function, 284**
mysqld **binary, 81**
mysql_data_seek() **function, 277, 278, 281**
mysqld-max, **82**
mysqld-max-nt, **82**
mysqld-nt binary, **82**
mysqld-opt, **81**
mysql_drop_db() **function, 284**

mysqldump *program, 147*
mysql_errno() *function, 284*
mysql_error() *function, 284, 290*
mysql_fetch_array() *function, 277–278, 289*
mysql_fetch_field() *function, 284*
mysql_fetch_object() *function, 284*
mysql_fetch_row() *function, 276*
MYSQL_NUM *value, 277*
mysql_num_rows() *function, 277, 283*
mysql_pconnect() *function, 284*
mysql_ping() *function, 284*
mysql_query() *function, 275–276*
mysql_select_db() *function, 275*
mysql_stat() *function, 284*

N

-n *parameter, 52*
name *component, 228*
name *parameter, 222*
Nautilus, 24, 25
Network Domain field, setting name of, 12
newlines, 201, 203
    legibility purposes of, 316
nonmodular coding, 258–260
normalization
    first normal form, 144–145
    second normal form, 145–146
    third normal form, 147
not null *attribute, 100*
notee *command, 133*
null data type, 167
NuSphere phpED, 250

O

object data type, 167
old hit counter example
    the problem, 233–235
        solution for, 234
    the "so what if a simple counter fails?"
        argument, 235
Open With dialog box, 156
opendir() *function, 207*

operator(s)
    arithmetic, 170–171
    assignment, 170
    comparison, 171–172
    concatenation, 171
    logical, 172
    precedence of, 173
    used in WHERE clauses, 118
optional arguments, 189–190
ORDER BY *clause, sorting data with, 120–121*
outer joins, 142–144
    Left, 143
    Right, 144

P

packages
    advantages of, 16
    installing Apache from, 16–18
parameter(s)
    <mode>, 206
    <module file>, 152, 153
    <return type>, 277
    <start_record>, 122
    action, 222
    AFTER column name, 106
    BEFORE column name, 106
    column positioning, 106
    FIRST, 106
    LAST, 106
    method, 222
    MODIFY, 107
    name, 222
    omitting from INSERT query, 114
    Update, 352
parentheses, using to determine operator
        precedence, 173
parseresults() *function, 280*
password box form element, 220
    browser output of, 222
    in code, 220
    returning data with, 223
password() *function, 401*
passwords, setting for MySQL, 86, 89–90

Perl, downloads for, 297
Perl module, 293
`pg_free_result()` *function, 283*
PHP. See Hypertext Preprocessor (PHP)
PHP Apache module, 27, 28
PHP Extension and Application Repository
    (PEAR), 294
PHP 4.x executable, 154
PHP interpreter
   exiting, 154
   HTML header and, 155
   interactive mode, 154
PHP processor, 29
PHP Script Interpreter, setting as default
    interpreter, 156
PHPBuilder.com, 294
PHPEdit, 250
`php4apache2.dll`*, changing path of, 29*
`php4ts.dll` *file, 26*
`phpinfo()` *function, 31, 224*
`php.ini` *file*
   editing, 26
   moving to expected location, 23
`php.ini-dist file`*, 26*
`PidFile` *directive, 61*
plug-ins, 48
pop-up windows, 324
post method, 223
`primary key` *attribute, 100*
primary key indexes, 105
`print` *function*
   versus `echo` function, 164
   using escape characters with, 165–166
   using here document syntax with, 166
   using quotes with, 164–165
`print()` *function, 202, 215, 216*
   embedding HTML tags into, 215
`print` *statement, 180*
`print_appt()` *function, 336, 337*
`printform()` *function*
   calling, 352
   code for, 354–358
`printgraphics()` *function, 263*
`print_list()` *function, 336*
Privileges. See MySQL privileges database

process status (`ps`) *command, 16, 49*
programming blocks, 175–176
   defined, 175
   delimitation of, 175
programming loops. See loop(s)

queries
   `DELETE`, 124
   formatting with line breaks, 134
   `INSERT`. *See* `INSERT` query
   `SELECT`. *See* `SELECT` query
   simplifying, 135–136
   troubleshooting, 134–136
   `UPDATE`, 124.–125
query interface, 281–282
`QUIT;` *command, 132*
quotes
   escape characters, 165, 166
   single versus double, 164–165, 289

r file open mode, 198
r+ file open mode, 198
-r switch, 270
race condition, 235
radio button form element, 220
   browser output of, 222
   in code, 221
   returning data with, 223
`readdir()` *function, 207*
Red Hat, 7
   directory contents, 207–208
   locating Apache files on, 53
   modules directory on, 152
   and MySQL installation, 36–37
   RPM (Red Hat Package Manager) format, 16
   Update Agent, 16, 17, 18, 24
      for installation of PHP, 25
   version 7.3, 9–10
   version 8.0, 9, 24
Red Hat Linux, 50, 52
register globals, 227

regular expression, 65
require directive, 74
require() function, 252
require_once() function, 252
reset button form element, 220
  browser output of, 222
  in code, 221
  returning data with, 223
resources data type, 167
result sets
  mishandling of, 289
  parsing, 281
  returned from query, 282
  working with, 278–283
return() statement, 188
REVOKE command, 94
right outer join, 144
rmdir() function, 207
root directory, locating, 30
row pointer, resetting, 277
RPM (Red Hat Package Manager) format
  database files and, 37
  installing, 16–17, 37
  MySQL executables and, 37
RSS feeds
  in BottomFeeder, 410
  creating
    from a dynamic content database, 407
    script for, 408–409
  documentation on, 405
  function of, 405–406
  publishing, 406–407
  references for, 411
  running a generator for, 410–411
  syntax, 406
  validator for, 411

S

-s switch, 270
scoping tags, 64
script syntax. See Hypertext Preprocessor (PHP),
  basic script syntax
ScriptAlias directive, 63
scripts, securing access to, 76–77

search(es)
  for Apache file names, 53
  boolean, 398–399
  case-insenstive, 398
  full-text index, 397–399
    modifying the find script for, 399
  modifiers for, 399
  substring
    benefits of, 394
    code for, 394–396
implementing, 394
search feature, 53
search modifiers, 399
security
  of Apache sites, 71
  audit, 77
  of directories
    with <Directory>, 72
    with authentication control, 73
    with .htaccess, 72–73
  issues of, 69–70
  of MySQL privileges system, 90–91
  on PHP, 197, 214
  of scripts, 76–77
  Web sites with tips for, 77
security audit, 77
security issues, on the Web, 69–70
select list form element, 223
SELECT privilege, 92
SELECT query
  basics of, 116
  joins. See joins
  and LIMIT clause, 121–122
  and ORDER BY clause, 120–121
  selecting data from more than one table,
    122–124
  selecting data with, 116
  selecting specific data with, 117–119
  specifying columns with, 140–141
  transforming queries into, 135
  using with multiple tables, 140–144. See also
    joins
  and the WHERE clause. See WHERE clause
SELECT statement, 397
selection list form element, 220
  browser output of, 222
  in code, 221

Server Information window, 12

Server Name field, 12

server processes, number of, 50

server-side includes (SSI) functionality, 384–385

server-side scripting. See Hypertext
Preprocessor (PHP)

ServerAdmin directive, 62

ServerAlias directive, 300

ServerName directive, 62

ServerRoot directive, 61

servers. See MySQL server

Service Status window, 51

services, piggybacked, 48

Services Admin tool, 51–52

Session ID (SID), 241

session.auto_start configuration option, 238

session.cookie_domain, 238

session.cookie_lifetime configuration
option, 238

session.cookie_path configuration option, 238

session_decode() function, 241

session_destroy() function, 240

session_encode() function, 241

session_id() function, 241

session.name configuration option, 238

session_register() function, 239

sessions

checking register status with, 240

configuration options, 237–238

destroying, 240

encoding and saving session data, 241

mechanics of, 237

passing IDs between scripts, 240–241

registering variables with, 239

starting, 239

unregistering variables with, 240

using, 237–241

session.save_path configuration option, 238

session_start() function, 239

session_unregister() function, 240

session.use_cookies configuration option, 238

SET column type, 102

set_date() function, 316

set_error_handler() function, 266–267

settype() function, 169

Setup Complete window, 40

Setup Type window, 40

SHOW CREATE TABLE <table_name>; command,
108, 132

SHOW DATABASES; command, 108, 132

SHOW DATABASES privilege, 92

SHOW INDEX FROM <table_name>; command, 108

SHOW TABLE STATUS; command, 108

SHOW TABLE STATUS LIKE '<expression>';
command, 132

SHOW TABLES; command, 108, 132

size component, 228

source archives, 13–16

source code

downloading, 22

uncompressing, 23

source files, for Hypertext Preprocessor
(PHP), 23

SQL. See Structured Query Language (SQL)

SSL, 48

stale lock checking, 237

start state, 348

coding of, 349

static content, 403

static function, 192

string data type, 167

stripslashes() function, 289

strip_tags() function, 353

structured query language (SQL)

creation of, 79

delimiting string values in, 114

function of, 113

submit button, 345

submit button form element, 220

browser output of, 222

in code, 221

returning data with, 223

substring searches

benefits of, 394

code for, 394–396

implementing, 394

superglobal variables

$action, 353

$Add, 353

$carry, 330

$_FILES, 228, 230

Continued

superglobal variables (continued)
  $findtext, 346
  $PHP_SELF, 281
  $_post, 224–225
  $_POST, parsing of, 225–226
  $stalechk, 237
  $submit err, 337
  function of, 225
  returning from POST data, 346
switch **command**
  and break statement, 179
  print statement in, 180
  syntax for, 178–179
switch **statement, 176**
syndication, 406
syntax highlighting, 251

T

_t_ **file open mode, 199**
tables
  adding columns to, 106
  altering in MySQL. _See_ MySQL, altering tables
  changing column definitions in, 107
  changing indexes in, 107
  changing name of, 106
  column attributes for, 99–100
  column data types for
    date columns, 103–104
    numeric columns, 102–103
    text columns, 100–102
  creating in MySQL. _See_ MySQL, creating tables
  dropping in MySQL, 108
  positioning columns in, 106
  supported by MySQL, 99
  using SELECT query for, 140–144
tags, for PHP, 159–160
tape ARchive, 10
tarball
  gzipped, 13
  for Hypertext Preprocessor (PHP), 23
  for MySQL, 35
TCP
  port 80, 48
  port 81, 48

  port 85, 48
  port 443, 48
  port 8080, 48
tee **command, 133**
text area form element, 219
  browser output of, 222
  in code, 220
  returning data with, 223
text box form element, 219
  browser output of, 222
  in code, 220
  returning data with, 223
text editors
  for Linux, 250
  for PHP, 250
  for Windows, 250
TextPad, 250
TIME **column type, 104**
TIMESTAMP **column, checking correctness of, 114**
TIMESTAMP **column type, 104**
timestamps, 304
TINYINT **column type, 102**
TINYTEXT **column type, 101**
_tmp_name_ **component, 228**
traffic
  finding the right log analyzer for, 298–299
  monitoring tools, 295
    Analog, 296
    AWStats, 297–298
    Webalizer, 297
tray icons, Apache Service Monitor, 13
  green triangle in, 49
  opening monitor window with, 50–51
  red dot in, 49
_trigger_error()_ **function, 267**
Trillian, 407
type **component, 228**
TypesConfig **directive, 62**

U

UltraEdit, 250
unlink() **function, 206**
unsigned **attribute, 100**
update **parameter, 352**

UPDATE **privilege, 92**
UPDATE **query, and *WHERE* clauses, 125**
upload_max_filesize setting, 228
USE <database>*; command, 132*
UseCanonicalName **directive, 62**
user-defined functions
 and arguments, 189–191
 returning values from a function, 188–189
 syntax for defining, 187–188
user privileges, 92
UserDir **directive, 62**
UserLand Software Web site, 411
usleep() **function, 236**

var_dump() **function, 268**
VARCHAR **column type, 100–104**
variable names
 conversion of, 163–164
 denotation of, 162
 functions of, 163
 use of quotes with, 163
verbose error reporting, turning off, 287–288
vim, **250**
virtual hosting
 defined, 299
 monitoring one IP address, 300
 monitoring several IP addresses, 299
 setting up hosts, 300
 of three domains, one IP address, 301–302
 of three domains, three IP addresses, 301
VirtualHost **tag, 300**

W

w **file open mode, 199**
w+ **file open mode, 199**
Web content, evolution of feature-rich, 47–48
Web scripting, 249
 commenting and documenting code, 253–254
 good habits for, 254–255
 guidelines for, 251
 importance of consistency in, 251–252

 revisiting old code for, 252
 syntax highlighting, 251
 text editors for, 250
 using functions for, 252
Webalizer, 297, 298
WHERE **clause, 117**
 and BETWEEN operators, 119
 with DELETE queries, 124
 operators used in, 118
 searching substrings with, 119
 in UPDATE queries, 125
 use of parentheses in, 120
 using complex expressions with, 120
WHERE MATCH **clause, 397**
whereis **application, 53**
while() **condition, 236**
while **loop, 180**
white space, in script syntax, 160–161
Windows
 checking configuration of PHP in, 151–152
 configuration of MySQL on, 81–82
 and database names, 97
 downloading binary installer on, 10
 downloads for, 9
 File Manager interface, 156
 and Hypertext Preprocessor (PHP), 22
 installation of Hypertext Preprocessor (PHP)
  on, 26
 installing Apache on, 10–13
 installing MySQL on, 37–42
 locating Apache files on, 53
 main Apache HTML directory on, 30
 monitoring RSS feeds with, 407
 new line, 201
 Open With dialog box, 156
 PHP 4.*x* executable for, 154
 running MySQL server on, 85
 server versions of, 26
 testing installation of MySQL in, 42–43
 TextPad, 250
 tracking code development on, 162
 UltraEdit, 250
 updating *httpd.conf* file on, 28
 using PHP as a command-line scripting language
  on. 155–156

WinMySQLAdmin, 40–42, 82
    checking MySQL server status with, 85
    for editing configuration files, 82
    finding, 82
    main interface for, 41
    my.cnf file, 41
    my.ini Setup tab, 82
    opening graphical interface on, 42–43
    shortcut for, 40
    starting
        from the Start menu, 43
        username and password for, 41
        using ps with Linux, 43
WML, headers for, 214
World Wide Web, beginnings of, 47
write_appt() function, 337

xor operator, 172

YEAR column type, 104

Zend Studio, 250
zero fill, 102
zerofill attribute, 100